Why Stalin's Soldiers Fought

Why Stalin's Soldiers Fought

The Red Army's Military Effectiveness in World War II

ROGER R. REESE

 University Press of Kansas

Published by the University Press of Kansas (Lawrence, Kansas 66045),
which was organized by the Kansas Board of Regents and is operated and
funded by Emporia State University, Fort Hays State University, Kansas
State University, Pittsburg State University, the University of Kansas, and
Wichita State University

Photo credits: The photographs in chapters 5, 6, 9, and 12 are reprinted
with the permission of the Russian State Archive of Film and Photo
Documentation (RGAKFD). The photographs in chapters 3 and 4 are
reprinted with the permission of the Bakhmeteff Archives of Columbia
University, New York, NY.

Library of Congress Cataloging-in-Publication Data

Reese, Roger R.
  Why Stalin's soldiers fought : the Red Army's military effectiveness in
World War II / Roger R. Reese.
      p. cm. — (Modern war studies)
  Includes bibliographical references and index.
  ISBN 978-0-7006-1776-0 (cloth : alk. paper)
  1. Soviet Union. Raboche-Krestíianskaia Krasnaia Armiia—History—
World War, 1939–1945. 2. World War, 1939–1945—Social aspects—Soviet
Union. 3. Sociology, Military—Soviet Union—History. 4. Soldiers—
Soviet Union—Social conditions. I. Title.
  D764.R4168 2011
  940.54'1247—dc22   2010048286

British Library Cataloguing-in-Publication Data is available.

Printed in the United States of America

10 9 8 7 6 5 4 3 2 1

For my parents
RON AND CARLEEN

Contents

Preface

This study of the Red Army in WWII is based on the idea that the military effectiveness of the army rested on the performance of the individual soldier. It is essentially a study of people at war, and less so of military institutions, battles, strategy, and tactics. Therefore, it follows naturally that the study takes a thematic approach, especially because, as the subtitle indicates, this work is designed to gain perspective on the human condition of soldiering, not to trace an overall flow of events.

For more than two decades, a strong and continuing movement to understand civilian life and behavior in the Soviet Union through social history, pioneered by Sheila Fitzpatrick and Moshe Lewin, has yielded significant insight into the revolution, civil war, collectivization of agriculture, rapid industrialization under Stalin, and the terror. Other than forays by Mark Von Hagen and Catherine Merridale, the Soviet people's experience as soldiers has largely and unfortunately been neglected.[1] Inexplicably, the same workers, peasants, general urban population, and Communist Party functionaries who seem so important to social historians of the Stalin era become invisible when they put on the Red Army uniform and go to war. Yet an examination of the wartime experience of the average person is more critical than ever if we are to come to a meaningful understanding of how the Soviet state and military won the war.[2]

Before 1991, Western scholars cannot be seriously faulted for not exploring the experience of the ordinary Soviet soldier because of the dearth of primary materials and limited access to Soviet veterans.[3] The military archives were—and remain—closed to all but a few select individuals who are given only limited access. Available to scholars was the official history of the war, slanted to meet the ideological dictates and political needs of the party leadership, along with volume upon volume of hero literature that unrealistically portrayed soldiers as uniformly courageous, self-sacrificing martyrs for the cause of defending the Soviet homeland. The literature officially ignored and even suppressed the existence and activities of traitors, draft dodgers, shirkers, cowards, and malingerers. Supporting this theme was a plethora of heavily censored memoirs of senior officers produced during a thaw under Khrushchev in the early 1960s, which gave a fragmented, self-serving, top-down picture of the Red Army at war. Despite these obstacles, some historians, such as Seweryn Bialer, John Erickson, Albert Seaton, Richard Overy, David Glantz, and Jonathan House, have produced useful and even masterful works that tell the story of the war from the top, from the view of the generals.[4]

In the 1990s, access to military archives, primarily the Russian State Military Archives (RGVA), became possible (though not reliably so); the Central Archives of the Ministry of Defense (TsAMO) still seems to be off-limits to foreigners, but it is allowing the publication of vast document collections relevant to many aspects of the war. Especially helpful is the tremendous outpouring of reminiscences and memoirs by ordinary soldiers and junior officers now appearing in print in the Russian popular press and on the Internet. These personal accounts tend to put a nostalgic spin on the wartime experience, however. The best website at the moment is that of Oleg Sheremet, Valerii Potapov, and Artem Drabkin titled "I Remember" (*Ia pomniu*). This site (http://www.iremember .ru) has published scores of interviews and reminiscences by veterans. All are in Russian, but some are also available in English. Audio files of some interviews are also available on the site, along with wartime or current photos of the authors and sometimes copies of original letters, diaries, and military documents.

There are several print sources of special note, such as the three-volume work *Zhivaia pamiat'*, which consists mainly of short firsthand accounts by privates, sergeants, and junior officers, both male and female, divided by year. Another significant post-Soviet resource is a five-volume collection, organized by year (1941–1945), called *Poslednie pis'ma s fronta*, which, as the title indicates, are last letters from the front by soldiers who were later killed. This collection was assembled by soliciting letters from surviving family members, who in many cases sent along the last few letters they wrote to their men, so we in fact see an exchange of letters that reveals a tremendous amount about the soldiers' morale, conditions of military service, and their interpretation of the meaning of the war. Vladlen S. Izmozik, who wrote about correspondence from the 1920s, attests to the value of such letters: "Daily correspondence is especially interesting since it reflects the concerns and meditations of ordinary people. Of course, even such letters—these 'snapshots of time'—are extremely subjective. Indeed, popular moods at any given moment depend on many factors, including the relationships with and personalities of the persons to whom these letters are addressed. But collectively they give a glimpse of the concerns, thoughts and moods of the most diverse groups."[5]

One cannot build a thesis on war stories, and such is not intended here. However, the concerns, thoughts, and moods of Soviet soldiers, which illustrate their broader conception of the war, can help us understand why the soldiers fought as they did and how the war affected them. Incorporating their voices gives texture and a sense of reality to what would otherwise be an unfortunately and unnecessarily abstract discussion. The voice of participants fundamentally humanizes history—an important aim of this book. Only a handful of scholars (Susan Linz, Catherine Merridale, Elena Seniavskaia, Nina Tumarkin, Amir Weiner, and Elena Zubkova) have studied the effect the war had on soldiers, civilians, and the Communist Party.[6] Other than Merridale's, however, their work neither studies nor illustrates the personal experiences of the people during the war, which generated their wartime and postwar behavior. This work is distinctive because it incorporates the individual experiences of Soviet citizens in an analysis of some of the broader issues of the functioning of the Soviet military and society during the Second World War. An anonymous English baron supposedly remarked that when it comes to history, he would rather have an eyewitness than a logical argument. Here I hope to provide both.

Other sources available to historians in the West that lend themselves to social history methodology are the academic journals *Istochnik: Dokumenty russkoi istorii, Istoricheskii arkhiv, Voennye Arkhivy Rossii*, and *Voenno-istoricheskii arkhiv* and the popular history journal *Rodina*, all of which publish extremely useful archival documents. Occasionally *Voenno-istoricheskii zhurnal* publishes reminiscences or other firsthand accounts of the war. During Gorbachev's era of glasnost (1985–1991), the popular magazine *Sovetskii voin* also published short, frank accounts by veterans. For those who are able to make use of Russian archives, the political reports found in the RGVA and TsAMO collections are very useful, as are soldiers' letters archived at the Russian State Archive of Social and Political History (RGASPI).

Collections of government and military documents have been published, and others are being published, that help balance and serve as a check against personal memoirs. The most prominent are Vladimir Zolotarev's *Velikaia Otechestvennaia*, a multiple-volume collection published between 1993 and 1998. It contains documents on almost every aspect of the war from the major military administrations, such as the General Staff, the Commissariat of Defense, and the Main Political Administration (GlavPUR), and it has special editions on major battles, such as Kursk and Berlin. The Federal Security Bureau (FSB), one of the spun-off parts of the former NKVD/KGB, has issued several document collections from its files covering the areas of discipline and morale. These documents show the negative side of soldiers' behavior that seldom appears in memoirs and letters.

Two of the better diary-like treatments of the war (written in a style somewhat reminiscent of Isaac Babel's *1920 Diary*) are Konstantin Simonov's *Sto sutok voiny*, written in 1942 but not published until 1999, and Vasily Grossman's *A Writer at War: Vasily Grossman with the Red Army 1941–1945*, edited and translated by Antony Beevor and Luba Vinogradova.[7] An outstanding example of an emigrant memoir is Gabriel Temkin's *My Just War: The Memoir of a Jewish Red Army Soldier in World War II*. Although Temkin is a Polish Jew, his experience, if not his outlook, is generally in line with that of the ordinary frontline soldier—the *frontovik*.

From the firsthand experiences of Soviet citizen-soldiers, we can fill in many gaps left by official histories in terms of how military effectiveness was achieved and maintained. We can also correct misconceptions as they become evident, being careful, however, not to overgeneralize the individual experience. With this information, historians can now construct a more balanced and long-overdue portrayal and understanding of the personal experience of war in Russia. Not surprisingly, the word from the foxholes sometimes contradicts long-held official interpretations and explanations, as well as popular memory, of how the military operated. Probably the most important observation is Soviet citizens' perseverance during the hell of war, all the while holding ambivalent attitudes toward the Stalinist regime.

There remain problems in rendering a thoroughly balanced portrayal of the Soviet soldier, owing to the lack of sources on non-Russian minorities and especially non-Slavic minorities (e.g., Central Asians, Caucasian peoples). Peasants, though they were the most numerous of the rank and file, are vastly underrepresented due to literacy problems. Of course, there is also the problem of interpreting letters subject to censorship because there is often—but not always—an element of self-censorship to avoid problems with authority. This work uses the personal experiences of individual Soviet people to illustrate the mobilization of society, the various forms and degrees of voluntarism in Soviet society, and the diversity of motivations to serve and fight in the hope that this will expand our knowledge of popular participation in the war and enable us to interpret anew the meaning of the Great Patriotic War for Soviet history.

Reading soldiers' letters, diaries, and memoirs can lead one to glorify their deeds, sympathize with their sufferings, and justify their behavior, particularly because we hear from the better educated, more cultured, and more successful in the postwar period. We should keep in mind, however, that the majority of soldiers were from the peasantry and workshop floor, not the universities and institutes. The two generations of peasants and workers that fought in World War II had already seen and endured enough violence and suffering for a lifetime in the revolution, the civil war, and collectivization and famine. That they should easily commit wholesale mayhem in liberated Eastern Europe and conquered Germany ought not come as a surprise, especially because they were encouraged by the state's call to hate and its cries for vengeance. We seldom hear the stories of deserters, criminals, malcontents, and illiterates. So the tendency to elevate the esteem of our subjects must be resisted, not simply for the sake of historical objectivity but for the sake of letting the men, and the whole army, be human—warts and all. At great cost, these men and women saved their country and liberated Eastern Europe from fascist oppression—all accomplishments worthy of praise; however, in the process, they also committed atrocities and perpetrated the same type of mayhem as those they fought. This must not be overlooked, rationalized, or justified; it must be included in the historical record as part of the ugly reality of war.

Rather than map out the flow of this book, which is easily seen in the table of contents, I suggest that the conclusion be read first. This, I hope, will pique readers' interest and help them focus on the arguments I make to defend my ideas.

Acknowledgments

I would like to thank Roger Beaumont, Catherine Merridale, Reina Pennington, Melissa Stockdale, and Laurie Stoff for their time and effort in reading chapter drafts and for the invaluable insights they provided. I owe many thanks to Ruth Fields for her keen editorial eye, which helped clean up my grammar and clear up my exposition. I thank Jim Rosenheim and the Melbern G. Glasscock Center for Humanities Research of Texas A&M University for two grants that enabled me to travel to archives. My university, Texas A&M, deserves thanks and my appreciation for the grant awarded to me under the Program to Enhance Scholarly and Creative Activities and for a one-year faculty development leave, both of which enabled travel for research and time to write. I also thank the Department of History for giving me time away from the classroom to concentrate on this project. I am appreciative of the help provided by the staffs of the Hoover Institution Archives at Stanford University and the Bakhmeteff Archives of Columbia University in New York City. I appreciate Bruce Vandervoort, editor of the *Journal of Military History,* not only for publishing my article "Lessons of the Winter War: A Study in the Military Effectiveness of the Red Army, 1939–1940" (2008), which derived from this project, but also for allowing me to use much of that material in chapters 2 and 3. Similarly, thanks go to David Glantz, editor of the *Journal of Slavic Military Studies,* for publishing my article "Motivations to Serve: The Soviet Soldier in the Second World War" (2007) and for allowing me to use parts of it in the preface and chapters 1, 5, and 6. I especially acknowledge Maggie and Hugo for their love and affection during the writing of this book.

A Note on Transliteration and Names

This work follows the Library of Congress transliteration system, without diacritical marks to transliterate Russian personal names, place names, and other words. For reasons of familiarity and historical context, I used Russian spellings for names and places as they existed in the time period. In the course of my research, I used translated works with a wide variety of transliteration styles, all of which I converted to the Library of Congress system when making direct quotes in order to establish some consistency and not confuse the reader. In these cases, the transliteration system of the original author is kept intact when identifying the published work in the notes and bibliography. Exceptions to this general style are words and names that are likely well known to the reader rendered in other transliteration systems.

Terms and Abbreviations

AWOL	absent without leave
dekulakization	process in the 1930s by which millions of kulaks were dispossessed of their property and often forcibly relocated to special settlements in remote areas run by the NKVD
DNO	*Divizii Narodnyi Opolchenie*, citizens' volunteer divisions
Ezhovshchina	terror purge of 1937–1939 supervised by and named after the head of the NKVD, Nikolai Ezhov
FSB	Federal Security Bureau
GKB	*Gosudarstvennoi Komitet Bezopasnosti*, State Committee for Security
GKO	*Gosudarstvennyi Komitet Oborony*, State Committee for Defense
GlavPUR	*Glavnoe Politicheskoe Upravlenie*, Main Political Administration of the Red Army
GUGKB	*Glavnoe Upravlenie Gosudarstvennoi Komitet Bezopasnosti*, Main Administration of the State Committee for Security
GUKR	*Glavnoe Upravlenie Kontrrazvedki*, Main Administration for Counterintelligence
Gulag	*Glavnoe Upravlenie Lageriami*, State Administration of Camps (GULag)—the Soviet prison camp system
GUPP	*Glavnoe Upravlenie Politicheskoe Propagandy*, Main Administration for Political Propaganda
GVSRKKA	*Glavnyi Voennyi Sovet*, Main Military Council of the Workers' and Peasants' Red Army, an organ of the military high command subordinate to the NKO; usually rendered simply as GVS

KGB	*Komitet Gosudarstvennoi Bezopasnosti,* State Committee for Security
Komsomol	see VLKSM
Komsomolets	male member of the Komsomol
Komsomolka	female member of the Komsomol
Komsomoltsy	plural, includes both male and female members of the Komsomol
Komsorg	Komsomol organizer, the person in charge of Komsomol activities in a battalion-sized unit
KOVO	Kievskii Osobyi Voennyi Okrug, Kiev Special Military District
kulak	wealthy peasant, dispossessed during the collectivization of agriculture in the 1930s and often forcibly resettled in special Gulag camps
NCO	noncommissioned officer
NKGB	*Narodnyi komissariat gosudarstvennoi bezopasnosti,* People's Commissariat for State Security
NKO	*Narodnyi komissariat oborony,* People's Commissariat of Defense
NKVD	*Narodnyi komissariat vnutrennikh del,* People's Commissariat of Internal Affairs
OGPU	*Ob'edinennoe Gosudarstvennoe Politicheskoe Upravlenie,* General State Political Administration, precursor to the NKVD
OO	*Osobyi Otdeli,* Special Sections of the NKVD in the Red Army
partorg	party organizer, person in charge of Communist Party activity in a battalion-sized unit; not a member of GlavPUR
politruk	*Politicheskie rukovoditel',* company- and platoon-level political worker in the armed forces; a member of GlavPUR
POW	prisoner of war
PVO	*Protivovozdushnaia Oborona,* antiaircraft defense forces
RGASPI	Russian State Archive of Social and Political History
RGVA	Russian State Military Archives

RKKA	*Raboche-Krest'ianskaia Krasnaia Armiia,* Workers' and Peasants' Red Army; usually rendered Red Army
RSFSR	*Rossiiskaia Sovetskaia Federativnaia Sotsialisticheskaia Respublika,* Russian Soviet Federated Socialist Republic
Smersh	*Smert' Shpionam,* a renaming of the reorganized OO derived from the acronym for "death to spies"
SS	*Schutzstaffel;* Nazi unit in charge of policing occupied areas and the mass extermination of "undesirables"
Starshina	highest noncommissioned officer rank
TsAMO	Central Archives of the Ministry of Defense
VLKSM	*Vsesoiuznyi Leninskii Kommunisticheskii Soiuz Molodezhi,* All-Union Leninist Communist League Youth, a.k.a. the Komsomol
voenkomat	*Voennyi komissariat,* draft board
Vsevobuch	*Vseobshchee voennyi obuchenie,* Directorate of Universal Military Training
Waffen SS	combat arm of the SS, which fielded divisions that fought alongside the German army
zampolit	*Zamestitel' politicheskie rukovoditel',* deputy political instructor

Theater of Operations

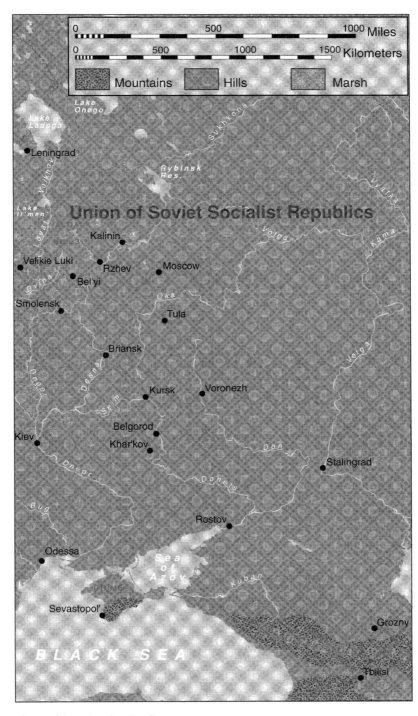

Theater of Operations (continued)

Part 1

MILITARY EFFECTIVENESS

1

Perspectives on Military Effectiveness

In this study I join the discussion of why the Red Army defeated the heretofore invincible German army. In so doing, I do not agree that it won through either might or skill or because lend-lease kept the Soviets in the war long enough for the Allies to divert German forces from the Eastern Front, although those elements all belong in the ultimate equation. Instead, I propose that the Red Army was victorious primarily because it proved to be a far more effective fighting force than the Germans had anticipated. Some have assumed that the Red Army was effective merely because it won. Such an analysis is simplistic. Effectiveness does not guarantee victory in battle or war, and neither does superior skill or numbers. I agree with Allan Millett and Williamson Murray that victory is not a criterion of effectiveness at all. For this study I apply a rather crude definition: military effectiveness is, at its core, the ability of an army to sustain battle. Measuring with this yardstick, I conclude that the Red Army was effective because it was able to keep fighting despite weak large- and small-unit leadership, inadequate training, slipshod planning, unreliable logistics, confusing command structures, meddlesome political interference, a disrupted economy, and, above all, massive casualties. The strength of the Red Army's effectiveness fluctuated during the course of the war. Its ability to keep forces in the field and fighting rose and fell relative to the severity of the aforementioned problems. That it did not disintegrate under the weight of its internal problems and German firepower was a monumental tribute to and proof of its military effectiveness. Credit for its success must be shared among the military, the Stalinist political system, the Communist Party, and Soviet society.

To reach an understanding of the Red Army's foxhole-level effectiveness, we must study the *frontovik* (the frontline Soviet soldier who experienced the dangers of enemy fire) and the small group of comrades with whom he lived and fought. The Soviet soldier has received far less scholarly attention than the German soldier opposite him, yet for a balanced understanding of the war on the Eastern Front, the roles of the peer group, formal discipline, and ideology are equally pertinent and valuable as the soldier's relation to the broad military institution, national political forces, and societal factors of life and war, which often had a direct effect on the soldier's attitude and behavior. The complexities of the mobilization of wartime Stalinist society—what it took the Soviet state to get people to fight and keep fighting under unimaginably hellish and deadly conditions—are here analyzed from the grass roots. In so doing, this work examines the various forms and degrees of voluntarism in Soviet society and the diversity of motivations to serve and fight (or to avoid serving and fighting). It establishes a basis for understanding popular participation in the war and enables new interpretations of the meaning of the Second World War for Soviet history. Furthermore, examining the military experiences of Soviet citizens sheds valuable light on the everyday lives of ordinary people during the trauma of total war. This study also looks beyond the Slavic male soldier to female soldiers and the national minorities to establish a sense of a multinational empire and professed gender-equal society at war.

Defining Military Effectiveness

Military effectiveness, or combat effectiveness, probably cannot be strictly defined. It revolves primarily around the willingness, and only secondarily around the ability, of a military unit, large or small, to impose its will on the enemy. As John Jessup noted in the 1980s, the Soviet armed forces pose a special challenge because of the political nature of their relation to the state. Jessup then refrained from anchoring his assessment of Soviet military effectiveness on a particular definition of effectiveness, for two reasons: "the lack of a fundamental definition of Soviet military effectiveness and the equally fundamental lack of accurate data upon which such an estimate might be made."[1] That was in the mid-1980s. Since then, many reliable archival data have been released in various media to enable a reasonable analysis, and from that derive meaningful measurements, if not an airtight definition, of military effectiveness for the Red Army.

The social sciences use the idea of effectiveness for predictive purposes, but, in this work, the predictive criteria of military effectiveness are adapted to serve as tools of historical evaluation. According to Sam Sarkesian's predictive formula, some of the criteria of military effectiveness are cohesion, staying power, quality of leadership, domestic value systems, will to fight, and ideological commitment, but not technical capability and skill proficiency.[2] Roger Beaumont and William P. Snyder add that military effectiveness can be measured on three different levels—macro-organizational, micro-organizational, and individual—pointing out that, "however difficult to define and measure, military effectiveness can only be obtained through control of an increasingly complex system of people, machines, organizational structures, and operational doctrines. Effectiveness, therefore, depends heavily on how well the overall system is integrated."[3] I accept this rationale but add that how soldiers feel about both their technical capability and their skill proficiency influences their effectiveness. Millett and Murray, taking a more historical approach, propose a definition analogous to all those above that divides military activity, and hence areas for measuring effectiveness, into four overlapping levels: political, strategic, operational, and tactical. They, and I, acknowledge the importance of sociological factors of unit cohesion, group solidarity, small-unit leadership, and comradeship (the primary group), as well as operational factors such as doctrine and tactical systems and their proper utilization on the battlefield. I also accept H. Wayne Moyer's analysis that the external social and political environments affect a military force's ability to maintain integrity and cohesion under stress. In particular, soldiers need to feel that the public they are fighting for supports the war's objective and their sacrifices. Soldiers also need to believe that success in battle will result in public recognition and reward. Appreciating all these viewpoints, I therefore include in this study the effect of the external social and political environments on the Red Army's various levels of military endeavor.[4]

John Lynn, in his study of the *Armée du Nord* of the French revolutionary army, exploits a wealth of social science–derived military effectiveness theory to develop one of his own that is also useful in analyzing the Red Army. His theory rests very heavily, and appropriately, on the motivation of the individual soldier and the elements that contribute to it. He "argues that the soldier's concept of his interest determines the type of motivation and control that will be most effective." In the case of the French army, "citizen-soldiers of the French Revolution identified their interests with those of the nation; consequently, obedience within the army rested primarily on the soldier's willing agreement rather than on force or material rewards."[5] Lynn observes that the French military leadership and the civilian political officials responsible for military affairs paid close attention to the soldiers' views. Those in authority sought out and accurately identified the soldiers' interests in order to create a motivational environment with appropriate leadership and discipline to take advantage of the soldiers' self-identified interests on the soldiers' terms. In the French revolutionary army, the state and the soldiers reached a mutually reinforcing relationship based on shared revolutionary ideals. It is this basic fact that limits Lynn's model for use with the Red Army of the Second World War. The Red Army was founded after the Russian Revolution and with great hope that its members too would identify with the nation as citizen-soldiers and that obedience could and would be motivated by willing agreement.[6] The revolutionary egalitarianism and optimism with which the Red Army was founded, however, faded rapidly during the course of the civil war, rebounded in peacetime, but gradually and steadily eroded under the Stalinist political system.

Between 1922 and 1930, the Soviet state and the Red Army shared fairly similar outlooks on their relationship and were mutually trusting and supportive. However, during Stalin's consolidation of power and his subsequent forced collectivization of the peasantry, as well as the rapid and chaotic industrialization and urbanization of society, the Stalinist state turned away from its benign attitude toward the army (and most other Soviet civil and political institutions) and assumed an unwarranted distrust of the military. Although many in the military were critical of some (or many) of Stalin's social and economic policies, there is no indication that this translated into a breakdown in the soldiers' loyalty or attachment to the Soviet Union or into a feeling that socialism or the Stalinist regime was somehow illegitimate, at least not on an institutional level. Yet the regime seems to have developed a sense of insecurity with regard to its relationship with the military and became less apt to use positive motivation and more willing to use coercion of the officer corps to maintain control over the armed forces.

This leads us to a brief discussion of Stephen Wesbrook's theory of compliance based on a power-involvement relationship with regard to military effectiveness and how it helps us understand the Red Army. Wesbrook identifies three types of power—coercive, remunerative, and normative—and three types of involvement—alienative, calculative, and moral. The military leadership's attempt to maintain control over the soldiers and keep them fighting takes the form of compliance relationships, which are combinations of one type of power and one type of involvement. Wesbrook's three congruent types of relations are coercive power–alienative involvement, remunerative power–calculative involvement, and normative power–moral involvement.[7] The most positive relationship is normative power–moral involvement, in which the leadership attempts to motivate the soldiery with symbolic rewards and appeals to the men's best instincts of service. The most negative relationship is coercive power–alienative involvement, in which the leadership relies on physical punishment and threats to maintain compliance. The remunerative power–calculative involvement relationship falls in the middle, with command elements using material rewards to motivate or punish at a relatively low level of intensity.

After the civil war (1918–1921), the Red Army began to operate based on the normative power–moral persuasion relationship, but this eroded in the late 1930s in the aftermath of fighting with the Japanese at the Battle of Khalkin-Gol, the invasion of Poland, and the Winter War with Finland, which exposed the many faults and flaws in the Red Army. In early 1940 army leaders explicitly called on the state to allow the chain of command to increase the level of coercive power to enforce discipline in the ranks.[8] As a result, unit commanders' powers of coercion increased dramatically in the new Disciplinary Regulations of 1940.

During the terror purge of the military (1937–1938), Stalin adopted an almost hostile attitude toward the armed forces, particularly the officer corps. Dual command, first used during the civil war, was reintroduced, with party-appointed commissars equal in authority to unit commanders. The state no longer related to the army on terms of revolutionary idealism. Coercion, rather than persuasion, began to dominate civil-military relations. The same coercive behavior then began to manifest itself in military relations. The Stalinist regime still attempted to use positive reinforcement, but, because it no longer trusted that the soldiers' concept of interest was supportive of the state, the regime became predisposed to resort to coercion to ensure compliance. Simultaneously, feeling that its ideology was falling on many a deaf ear, the state sought to mold loyalty and patriotism through traditional nationalism. Therefore, in contrast to Lynn's model and the majority of Western social science models, we have to assign a greater role to the Soviet state in attempting to bolster effectiveness than is normally seen in studies of democratic societies. This is required not because of some inherent tendency in authoritarian societies but simply because, in this case, the state inserted itself into the equation in a way that democratic governments have not.

It is odd that Lynn's model, for the most part, fails to analyze how civilian governments attempt to influence military effectiveness, even though his study of the *Armée du Nord* includes the political representatives of the National Convention at the front (Representatives on Mission) and shows the attempt to influence soldiers through newspapers. The Communist Party, through its regimental and battalion commissars and company *politruki* (political officers), attempted to play a major role in shaping Red Army soldiers' definition of patriotism and in bolstering the ideological underpinnings of their outlooks on the war, their service, and their need to sacrifice. In 1941 these efforts may have had significant effects on morale and recruiting among certain segments of the population. For this reason, I add the "super-macro-organizational" level to the study of military effectiveness of the Red Army, which encompasses those external social and political environments identified by Moyer and can be encompassed in Millett and Murray's political and strategic levels of effectiveness. In the case of the USSR during the Second World War, the super-macro-organizational level consisted specifically of the party and government organs responsible for military affairs, such as the People's Commissariat of Defense (NKO), the State Committee for Defense (GKO), the Main Military Council of the Red Army (GVSRKKA), and the Main Political Administration of the Red Army (GlavPUR), which answered to the Communist Party Central Committee.

Without claiming any particular originality, the framework constructed here for use in this investigation relies on a combination of the following major categories: interest, motivation, the military system, and the state system.[9] Under the category of interest, the major elements are the willingness of the Soviet citizenry to volunteer for service or answer the call when conscripted, the ability of the state to motivate the country to sustain the war through its influence over the domestic value systems and ideology, and the ability of the state and military high command to mold soldiers' attitudes to foster compliance. Motivation includes the willingness of Soviet soldiers to fight and endure hardship, particularly in the face of adversity, and the ability of the military to sustain large- and small-unit cohesion in the face of near catastrophic losses. The applicable elements of the military system are its ability to train soldiers and leaders to fight proficiently, maintain discipline, arm and equip the fighting forces with adequate weaponry, and devise appropriate tactics and doctrine for employing the forces in the field. Finally, the state system comprises the determination and ability of the state to force the military and the citizenry to comply with its war-making agenda when voluntary methods fail, and the ability of the state to sustain the armed forces with material and personnel.

This study of the Red Army and Soviet society at war analyzes effectiveness at various levels, inside and outside the military, and ultimately shows how these factors played out on the front lines. The investigation of the individual soldier at the micro-organizational level—that is, at the company level and below, and including the primary group—was conducted through oral histories, memoirs, reminiscences, diary entries, letters, and archival military and political reports. The macro-organizational level, which consists of the battalion and higher, up to the high command (*Stavka* and the General Staff) and the People's Commissariat of Defense, was studied through memoirs and archival military and political reports, after-action studies, and administrative documents. Beyond the macro-organizational level is the super-macro-organizational level, which encompasses the state's and society's contributions to military effectiveness. For example, I examine the state's use of propaganda and ideology to motivate the individual to serve and fight and to condition society to accept sacrifice, as well as the state's commitment to the war and its ability to materially sustain the armed forces. Materials for this level essentially come from the same sources as for the macro-organizational level.

Methodology, Major Issues, and Patriotism

The basic questions and issues addressed are as follows: What motivated Soviet citizens to fight for a political system that had victimized so many, and what kept them going despite initial catastrophes and enormous casualties? What role did patriotism, ideology, and propaganda play in people's willingness to serve—the bedrock of effectiveness? How did the regime attempt to manipulate morale? Are there useful comparisons to the German experience of a totalitarian population at war or to the American and British antifascist, democratic, capitalistic experience? For example, studies of German soldiers shortly after the war resulted in A. Shils and Morris Janowitz's conclusion that primary groups were a major factor in maintaining cohesion in the German army. Later, Omer Bartov claimed that draconian discipline was necessary to keep German soldiers going on the Eastern Front, and Stephen Fritz highlighted the role of Nazi ideology in the cohesion and motivation of the frontline soldier.[10] By comparing the experiences of soldiers of various belligerent countries, we can ask which of the Soviet responses to combat and frontline service might be universal to all people at war, and which were unique to the Soviet population and why. My hypothesis is that average Soviet citizens fought for the USSR for several basic reasons: loyalty to the idea of historic Russia; normal obedience to the state; the fact that the USSR had been invaded, making it a "just war"; the realization that life would not be any better under Nazi German rule; because the war represented a great societal and historical task for the first postrevolution generation; and out of self-interest, hoping to improve their place in society through wartime service. These reasons tended to overcome reservations and misgivings about, if not outright hostility to, the Stalinist state—at least temporarily. At the same time, I recognize that many citizens chose not to serve or fight, for a variety of reasons.

This analysis of the personal experiences of Soviet soldiers in the Second World War seeks to strike a corrective balance to the extreme views of the Soviet soldiery that have prevailed for so long. On the one hand, the Germans portrayed Soviet soldiers as a mob of soulless, indifferent, fatalistic automatons; on the other hand, the Soviet propaganda machine portrayed them as self-sacrificing, patriotic heroes. There were indeed men who went through the war resigned to their fate and those who acted courageously, but by and large, most soldiers' immediate goal was survival. In many cases, peer pressure played an important role in keeping men and women going. Feelings of patriotism, no doubt produced as a reaction to the invasion of their homeland, played a role in generating volunteers in the first few months after the German attack, but these feelings diminished in 1942. Overall, we see a complex negotiation between the state and its citizens, with negative reinforcement balanced against positive. Ultimately, the state succeeded, with difficulty, in keeping enough soldiers in the line, although desertion and draft evasion remained problems throughout the war.

The Historical Debate

One of the more contentious issues in Soviet history regarding relations between the state and society during World War II has been interpreting the behavior of soldiers in the first months of the war, when the Red Army went from defeat to defeat and millions ended up in German prisoner of war camps. In challenging Stalin's claim in a 1946 speech that "our victory signifies, first of all, that our Soviet *social* system was victorious, that the Soviet social system successfully passed the test of fire in the war and proved that it is fully viable,"[11] it has long been argued in the West that the huge number of Soviet soldiers captured in the first six months of the war represent a popular rejection of Stalinism.[12] In earlier works, I postulated that some responsibility for the poor performance of the Red Army in 1941 can be ascribed to lack of support for the regime by peasant soldiers disaffected due to collectivization and dekulakization, by workers disaffected by poor living and working conditions, and by others alienated by the terror purges. Yet, if we cast the question in terms of military effectiveness, we cannot fail to conclude that the surrender of millions of men represents a lack of effectiveness in its most basic form—many of those men may have lost their willingness to fight, assuming they had it in the first place.

Historian Robert Thurston would have us believe that these surrenders do not indicate a rejection of the Soviet social system, and the fact that these soldiers fought at all shows that they supported the regime. In contrast, it can be argued that if surrenders do not indicate a rejection of Stalinism, then by the same token, resistance to the Germans may not necessarily indicate support for the Soviet regime. Furthermore, the regime's wartime modifications of its governing style—a modest easing of literary censorship and the granting of more freedom of religious worship intended to garner popular support—indicate if not the failure of Stalinism then at least a conscious accommodation of the Soviet population along un-Stalinist and un-Bolshevik lines that ran counter to Stalin's preferred methods. The war lasted well beyond the disaster of 1941 and the defeats of 1942, but the essential questions from those months must be applied to the war as a whole. Why did Soviet citizens fight for an oppressive regime in the first place, and why did they keep fighting when the odds of survival, let alone victory, seemed so thin? Was this truly a test of the Soviet social system, or were other factors at work? Is there another dimension to the issue? Did soldiers have to be either for or against Stalinism, or could their assessment of the situation be more complex, more nuanced? I suggest that a variety of factors colored soldiers' decision making, which included political as well as social, economic, national, racial, and personal relationships.

This debate over who fought and why—to this point, limited to only two sides—contains a shortcoming: scholars assume that Soviet citizens in 1941 understood Stalinism in the same way as Western scholars did in the postwar era. Stalinism is defined as the social-political-economic system of the period 1928 to 1953, when Stalin dictatorially ruled a brutally coercive state dedicated to building socialism in the Soviet Union from the top down, using state institutions of power to suppress opposition, real or imagined, without counting the cost in lives or human suffering. By this definition, it is nearly inconceivable that many would have volunteered to fight and die for the Stalinist state. In comparison, at the outbreak of the First World War, the discredited and lowly regarded tsarist government, though hardly oppressive, attracted very few volunteers for its army.[13] It seems logical that, given the low esteem in which the Soviet people are thought to have held their government, they would have responded similarly; yet the opposite is true.

People certainly were aware of the repressive actions of the secret police, the abuses of power and privilege by party members and government officials, and the hardships of life brought on by the economic policies of the Communist Party; however, they did not generally ascribe them to some evil intent on the part of Stalin or see them as inherent to the economic and social systems. Instead, they saw them as abuses of the political system by unscrupulous people who were, in fact, sometimes punished for their misdeeds. For instance, both prewar chiefs of the OGPU/NKVD (secret police) under Stalin that were associated with the terror, Genrykh Iagoda and Nikolai Ezhov, were declared enemies of the people and executed. As Jeffrey Brooks has ably demonstrated, state control of the media greatly facilitated the cult of personality. This elevated Stalin above both the mundane and the serious faults of the government and party functionaries that people might have had contact with in their everyday lives. Simultaneously, the state-run media exalted Stalin as the great leader and visionary of all things good. He was the one in whom people could place their trust and hope.[14]

State control of information prevented people from knowing the full extent of the problems that Stalinist social and economic policies were causing in the country, such as the scale of the famine of 1932–1933, the violence associated with collectivization and repression of the kulaks ("wealthy" peasants), and the repression associated with the *Ezhovshchina* (terror purge). Furthermore, the state, through the media, sought to convince the population that these programs were necessary for the success and survival of the country and of socialism. Problems were explained away, and the regime escaped public blame for the social or economic troubles. Instead, the media publicized stories of achievement, particularly industrialization under the five-year plans and the elimination of rural capitalism through the collectivization of agriculture. At the same time, many people had positive experiences under Stalin. They attained higher education, held responsible jobs, and achieved amazing upward social mobility. Therefore, it should not come as a surprise that many people supported the regime when it faced a crisis of survival.

In contrast, there should be no doubt that many Soviet citizens were alienated by their treatment at the hands of the regime. A distinct minority were so disaffected that they became traitors, aided the Germans, or even fought against the USSR. The majority of people with well-founded doubts, skepticism, or anger against the regime, however, managed to subordinate those feelings to the idea that there was hope for change, or to the realization that a Nazi victory would not improve their lot. Many prudently kept quiet about their hopes for a Soviet defeat and went along with the crowd to avoid persecution. John Barber, in his study of Moscow's citizenry at the beginning of the war, persuasively argues that "the collective psychology displayed complex and sometimes conflicting characteristics. It certainly provided no guarantee of unwavering support for the government. On the contrary, it had the potential, under extreme pressure for producing a collapse of legitimacy, resistance to the authorities, failure of social control, breakdown of law and order, and even collaboration with the enemy."[15]

Thurston has a valid point that the majority of Soviet soldiers captured by the Germans in the first few months of the war were taken as a result of German tactics, not their own treason. During the war, 5.2 million soldiers were taken prisoner, most of them, approximately 3.8 million, in 1941. Yet there is ample evidence that some soldiers, particularly Ukrainians and Belorussians, did not fight as determinedly as they might have or chose not to attempt to avoid capture because of their dissatisfaction with the practices of the Soviet regime and their doubts that Soviet power would survive the war.[16]

Soviet Patriotism

The bedrock of military effectiveness is personnel, and an army gets its soldiers from civil society. In the modern era, feelings of patriotism greatly smooth the process of recruiting civilians into the military, so for this study, it is logical to begin with an analysis of Soviet patriotism. An investigation of what we mean by the term *patriotism* illustrates that the Soviet people took more than political motivations into consideration when deciding whether to serve or fight. When Soviet veterans are asked why they served or fought, they do not launch into a discussion of the merits or faults of Stalinist Russia. The most common answer is that they were motivated by simple patriotism—because their country had been invaded—yet our and their understanding of patriotism is not simple at all. According to historian Hubertus Jahn, who studied Russian patriotism in the First World War, "Like other forms of collective self-identification, patriotism is a complex and ambiguous phenomenon that exists along multiple axes." He notes, "It can be a deeply rooted personal conviction or a passing fashion." Furthermore, a person's understanding of his or her patriotism can change over time and take various forms in different contexts.[17] Rather than support for the state, one of those forms can be, according to Earl Hunter, criticism of the state and the prevailing authority.[18]

Historian Geoffrey Hosking argues that some Soviet citizens may have understood their patriotism very broadly as either ethnic Russian-based (*russkii*) nationalism or the more inclusive imperial Russian (*rossiiskii*) patriotism, both of which were co-opted and converted into a Soviet form (*sovetskii*) in which the homeland, or motherland (*rodina*), represented all the nationalities of the USSR.[19] In fact, Ilya Ehrenburg, one of the USSR's two most prominent war correspondents and propagandists during the war with Germany, promoted that connection in a 1942 article in which he wrote, "Soviet patriotism is a natural continuation of Russian [*rossiiskii*] patriotism."[20] Historian Serhy Yekelchyk shows that the regime sought to elicit a patriotic response from Ukrainians by promoting Ukrainian nationalism as well.[21] For some, what they labeled patriotism could have been less national and more local and personal; as Lisa Kirschenbaum says, "*Rodina*, home and family emerged as key constituents of Soviet patriotism."[22] The following analysis of the behavior of ordinary people and their explanations of why they chose to participate in the most dangerous activity available to them that involved a relationship with the state—joining the armed forces in wartime—reveals a variety of mentalities that can collectively be considered patriotic, which include indifferent, ambivalent, and pro- and anti-state attitudes.

Considering that people do not always act rationally, it is possible that for many citizens, patriotic sentiments are emotional and elemental and are not necessarily thoughtful or well informed. The testimony of ordinary citizens shows that claims of patriotism and acts against the fascist invaders did not necessarily equate to support for the Stalinist system. Rather, the majority of soldiers were conscripted into the armed forces and acquiesced because they feared the power of the state or were reacting to societal pressure; a small minority were motivated by antifascist ideology. Furthermore, once they were summoned to serve in the military, people did not passively turn control of their lives over to the state; rather, they continually assessed their interests and their motivations to serve and sacrifice.

Finally, according to Jahn: "Wars usually heighten self-awareness—they often sort out loyalties, harden convictions and polarizations. On such occasions, patriotism also comes to life because people have to decide where to locate the home where their hearts are."[23] In this vein, one Soviet soldier recalled: "At the front lines, especially after we were encircled, people talked very openly. There was nothing more to conceal. People said frankly, 'What are we fighting for?'"[24] Although the Soviet state put a tremendous amount of effort into trying to influence soldiers' answers to this question, ultimately, they had to sort it out for themselves and take responsibility for it.

Some important questions related to wartime patriotism are the following: Did support for preservation of the USSR mean support for the Stalinist system? Did answering the call for conscription constitute support for the regime, or was it merely falling into line out of fear of or obedience to authority? Were those who served following a sense of duty not directly akin to patriotism, or responding to family or peer pressure or just an internally generated reaction? Once at the front, did fighting indicate acceptance of the regime, its leadership, and its norms, or did it devolve into a matter of survival or of social acceptance by one's peers? Likewise, did opting not to desert indicate fear of the consequences, resignation to one's situation, or satisfaction that one was doing the right thing? Did deserting or otherwise becoming derelict in one's duty necessarily have anything to do with one's relation to the state, or was it personal and situational—a function of morale? Were deserters and shirkers cowards, ne'er-do-wells, or just individuals who were unable to overcome a very strong survival instinct, despite formal and informal pressures? These questions are addressed throughout this book, with examples drawn from the experiences of Soviet soldiers.

Another question that must be considered is what role, if any, Soviet citizens' prewar experiences played in their willingness to fight for the USSR. The social history of the late 1920s and 1930s, particularly that based on the early 1950s Harvard University Refugee Interview Project, and works by Sheila Fitzpatrick, Moshe Lewin, and Lynne Viola on the peasantry and workers suggest that there was some basis for considerable ill will toward the Stalinist regime. This was due to the coercive nature of Soviet society and the pervasive harshness of everyday life, which made lies of the promises of the revolution. Conversely, Thurston argues that Stalin's policies did not alienate the people from the state to any meaningful degree.[25] Another question we need to ask is how people viewed their relation to the state prior to the war, and what effect that had on their motivation to defend the state when the Germans invaded. Did people feel controlled, coerced, and marginalized, or did they feel like citizens with responsibility for themselves, their country, and the success or failure of the regime and the socialist experiment?

An examination of wartime patriotism necessarily raises the possibility that support for preservation of the USSR did not necessarily mean support for the faults of the Stalinist system. In the bigger picture of people at war and their manifestations and internalizations of patriotism, it is feasible for individuals to fight for a country whose leadership they do not like or whose policies negatively affect them personally. For example, the Nisei in the United States, dispossessed and disenfranchised, were recruited out of internment camps and formed the all-volunteer 442nd Regimental Combat Team, which became the most decorated unit of its size in the U.S. Army during World War II. The Tuskegee airmen, the men of the 761st Tank Battalion and the 777th Artillery Battalion, and all the other African American men and women who served in the U.S. armed forces were in no way endorsing Jim Crow society. In the same vein, are we to believe that British colonial troops fought to preserve colonialism? Hundreds of thousands of German workers, formerly members of the German Social Democratic Party or the German Communist Party, served in the German armed forces despite their anti-Nazi convictions. Therefore, individuals can fight for their country despite mental reservations about the government and the economic and social systems. In fact, people can fight for their country with the hope that their efforts will change the social and political order. For example, the concessions the Stalinist state made during the war—such as rehabilitating the Russian Orthodox Church, easing censorship, and tolerating a degree of individualism—indicate an accurate reading of the people's desire for change. People's spontaneous expression of why they fought, including published poetry, almost never mentions political themes.[26]

That Stalin's wartime moderation and appeal to patriotism ran counter to his basic nature is evident by his attempt to reverse it in the postwar years. The hypocrisy of the religious thaw is evident in the fact that even though the church was officially rehabilitated, party members who had church weddings or baptized their children were expelled or reprimanded.[27] This indicates that Stalin designed the concessions to garner popular support under emergency conditions. He intended for the party to remain loyal to the prewar Stalinist order and was careful to make no promises that the postwar years would bring further changes in social or economic policy.

David Brandenburger argues that the prewar rehabilitation of some of tsarist Russia's heroes to support the Stalinist state, particularly military and navy heroes such as Suvorov, Kutuzov, Nakhimov, and Aleksandr Nevskii, represents a Stalinist co-option of Russian history. For Brandenburger, this co-option represents a self-preservationist feature of the Stalinist state and not a failure.[28] Yet this can be seen as the state's failure to create a "new Soviet man" on the basis of revolutionary change. The new Soviet man was really not so new; he was a product of Russian history and genealogy. Furthermore, it is a reflection of a fear that, in anticipation of impending war with Germany, a call to defend the revolution and the socialist experiment on their merits would not touch on the interests of, nor be motivation enough for, the average citizen. In the end, patriotism anchored on Russian history proved to be a precursor to the main thrust of wartime propaganda from 1941 to late 1943.

Most likely the fundamental reason why Soviet citizens fought was that their country had been invaded. Hitler handed Stalin and the Soviet population a just war by invading and violating the 1939 Nazi-Soviet Nonaggression Pact. The Soviet propaganda apparatus predictably made much of the USSR's victimization to rally the people. For example, an article in *Krasnaia zvezda* read: "The Hitlerites wanted to conquer the whole world. . . . We entered the fight in order to defend our home, our land, and in this just war we have gained the love and recognition of all the nations of the world. Such is the force, such is the magic of genuine patriotism."[29] People could then justify fighting for their homes, villages, towns, and cities—the very soil of Belorussia, Ukraine, and Russia—against a foreign invader, without reference to the governing apparatus at all. Therefore, the Soviet regime had no need to justify the war because it had the right and duty to organize the defense of the country and to call its citizens to the colors.

It is impossible to gauge how many people actually thought about their relation to the state, but recent works of social history make it clear that many did. A study of the population of Magnitogorsk in the 1930s shows people there making conscious decisions about their behavior in response to state-defined parameters. Whether the people agreed with the state's programs and policies or not, their response to them had a substantial effect on how those policies and programs worked out.[30] This view is countered with the idea that although the state did set parameters, the people subject to the dictates of Soviet power exercised agency in approaching the Bolshevik program with independent ideas about how things ought to be, based on their own expectations of the revolution and their interpretations of Marxism-Leninism. Their behavior was goal directed, not merely reactive.[31]

Other social-historical work supports the idea that, despite communist propaganda, people were able to think independently and critically, and they internalized the state's ideals in their own way. They were critical of the state for not living up to its promises according to popular expectations.[32] Another line of thought supports the idea that people understood Stalinist parameters but responded to them with conscious self-interest while attempting to portray themselves as the kind of people the Bolsheviks required.[33] In sum, in the prewar years, Soviet citizens served the state and appeared to fall into line, but often in pursuit of their own agendas; many cases of volunteering for the army or reporting for conscription during the war can be interpreted similarly.

Anna Krylova suggests that the state was successful in generating among the post–October Revolution, prewar generation of Soviet youth, both male and female, a yearning for historical relevancy that a war with capitalism could provide.[34] During the 1930s, print and film media and literature promoted the inevitability of war with the "encircling" capitalist states. From 1936 onward, conflict was portrayed not only as inevitable but also as imminent, and it would be the historical task of the generation that had not created the revolution nor fought the civil war to fight the next one. In fact, in the decade before the German invasion, millions of youths, primarily Russian urban teenagers, participated in paramilitary training sponsored by the Society for Defense, Aviation, and Chemistry (Osoaviakhim). Krylova believes these young people consciously understood that they were preparing for close combat with the enemy. Yet, we must be aware that Krylova's focus is on culturally and politically aware, mostly urban Russian youth, which does not encompass all or even most of the teenage and young adult population. Fifty years afterward, Natalia Peshkova was asked if she had seen the war coming. She said, "You know, when you are seventeen you think more about romance than about politics."[35] It should not be surprising that many Soviet teenagers, like their counterparts in the West, then and now, ignored the major issues of the day in their preoccupation with personal matters.

Of those who turned their backs on the Soviet regime, we cannot be sure whether their actions reflected a rejection of Stalinism or were simply a manifestation of the desire for self-preservation.[36] All told, in the course of the war, more than 4 million men and women were charged with desertion, straggling from their units, draft evasion, or self-mutilation to get away from the fighting. Nearly 90,000 men and women were condemned as traitors. Thousands of others were arrested for counterrevolutionary agitation and anti-Soviet behavior.[37] Outright rejection of Stalinism was demonstrated by the hundreds of thousands of Soviet citizens who refused to be repatriated from Germany following the war. For many of them, however, the rejection was not intellectual but practical; they expected to be victimized upon their return to the USSR. Many such people expressed love for their homeland on the one hand, but fear or hatred of the Stalinist state on the other.[38]

Remembering the War

This work includes firsthand accounts of the experiences of war and the lessons that might be taken from them to assess interest, motivation, and other aspects of military effectiveness. It is therefore necessary to appreciate how people remember the war, how they have chosen to relate those memories, how the Soviet state tried to shape people's understanding and interpretation of the war, and who exactly is giving testimony. I investigate how Soviet citizens understood their patriotism and participation in the war in part through the unashamedly unscientific means of oral histories, which suffer from predictable pitfalls. The most important of these pitfalls is veterans' assimilation of the state's interpretation of the war, which was reinforced by restricting the public's ability to express contrary views. Over time, the state's version, designed to justify its conduct of the war and suppress or excuse its failings, took on a life of its own that became the touchstone for those who sought to tell their story.

Another shortcoming of the oral histories in this case is a pool skewed by the above-average level of education of the subjects, omitting the stories of the less intelligent or uneducated masses of soldiers. The people represented in the oral histories are by and large the educated, responsible element of society who generally led successful lives after the war, which is not necessarily representative of the army masses or veterans at large. Vast numbers of uneducated or undereducated, less intelligent, and morally suspect men served in the military but left no testimony to their experiences, their interpretation of the war, or their role in it. Therefore, we have to keep in mind that we are getting only a fragment of the soldiers' story. We learn of the others from observations in official reports about their morale and behavior, but more often about their misbehavior.

Furthermore, unlike James McPherson, in his study of the motivation of the American Civil War soldier, we have very few materials that were never intended to be made public or letters that were not subject to censorship.[39] Soviet soldiers were often, but not always, circumspect in their criticism of the army, the state, the Communist Party, and Stalin in their letters. Some interviewees, suspecting or knowing that their stories were destined for publication, may have self-servingly adapted their tales with a particular audience in mind and with an eye to history.[40]

Much of the oral history of Soviet veterans reflects an inherent nostalgia for the mythical good old days of the war years, when *russkii* and *rossiiskii* melded and everyone supposedly acted like one united family. Furthermore, as Katharine Hodgson has pointed out: "A collective, rather than individual standpoint produced an attitude towards the war in which the individual was aware of his role as part of the whole country's effort. Critical pressure to conform made it almost impossible for the individual to express reservations about his participation in the war."[41] Only the very recent revelation to the Russian people of the secret protocols of the Nazi-Soviet Nonaggression Pact has stirred some private questioning of the "just war" basis of their understanding. At the opposite end of the spectrum are the interviews of the Harvard University Refugee Interview Project, in which the story line has undertones of both genuine and artificial anticommunism. Most of the veterans interviewed for the project tended to portray themselves as victims of the Soviet state. Many had actually suffered under Stalinism, but others had not; nonetheless, they seem to have felt the need to give an anticommunist slant to their testimony.

It is also possible that individuals' postwar narratives are shaped by the lingering influence of wartime propaganda. Wartime propaganda was geared toward motivating people to fight for the state, identify their interests with its survival, and keep morale up. This set the groundwork for the official postwar interpretation that everyone had fought out of patriotism. It is especially hard to separate action from reaction, as some propaganda was created in response to people's genuine feelings about their wartime circumstances. As Kirschenbaum's work on wartime propaganda has shown, well into 1943, the state exhorted people to fight to defend the *Rodina-mat'*, which called on people to identify with their homes and families rather than with the state and to seek vengeance for the victims of Nazi aggression.[42] Elsewhere, as in the case of the siege of Leningrad, Kirschenbaum shows how the state attempted to shape and reshape people's interpretation of the meaning of the history of the war as it was being made, then after it was over, and through the change in regimes.[43]

A major thrust of propaganda was hate. In his May Day speech in 1942, Stalin, hoping to motivate soldiers to risk their lives in combat, said, "You cannot conquer the enemy without learning to hate him with all the power of your soul."[44] Tales of German atrocities, interviews with people who had suffered at the hands of the occupiers, poems, and short stories all inveighed the Soviet people to hate the Germans. Ilya Ehrenburg and Konstantin Simonov were perhaps the most prominent literary figures to promote the call for vengeance in print and broadcast media.[45] Of the twin themes of hate and vengeance, revenge crops up most often in postwar testimony; hate is expressed far less commonly, not because it was not extensive but perhaps because it is less pleasant to admit to or talk about. Those who openly claim to have hated the Germans, however, rarely cite propaganda as the reason; rather, they say it was personal experience and contact with victims of German persecution that elicited their hatred.

Valentin Shikanov told his mother in a letter written in May 1942 about liberating the area in front of Moscow and finding the villages uninhabitable: "where there had been homes and buildings of these remained only ashes and piles of smashed bricks, and nothing more."[46] He refers to the Germans as barbarians—consonant with the current propaganda. Even the spirit of vengeance, often expressed in oral histories, was nearly always generated by the loss of a loved one and did not require the state's prompting. For some, the state's message was the source of their feelings of hatred and a desire to avenge; for many others, official propaganda seems to have legitimized and channeled their natural and spontaneous emotions, which subsequently found their way into oral history.

An example of the hate-vengeance theme in personal letters is that of Georgii Eremin, a soldier with a safe job in the Kremlin who had only secondhand knowledge of the war. He wrote to his family in May 1942: "In me burns a big fire of hate and vengeance for the villainous enemy who kill civilians. I go to defend our motherland, to fight, weapon firmly clenched in hand. I go to avenge the suffering of our fathers, mothers, sisters, brothers, wives, and daughters. For this suffering, for this bloodshed I will avenge the death of my best friends."[47] Similarly, Mark Edele gives examples of how the state portrayed soldiers in posters to help condition their understanding of themselves and their role in the war. Like written propaganda, the posters visually depict soldiers defending the *Rodina-mat'*, women, and families but not the state, socialism, or the revolution.[48]

Nina Semenovna expressed her patriotic sentiment years after the war. She spoke not directly about the war but about her lifelong love for Russia, which helps explain patriotism and the idea of the motherland. She said: "My motherland, Russia, is the same for us all. But every one of us has a small corner of this vast motherland, our own motherland, where we were born, raised, went to school, and set off on life's path."[49] This is the motherland most soldiers easily identified with when they thought about defending Russia.

Only in the latter half of 1943, when it was clear that the war would not be lost, did the theme of propaganda shift to the role of Stalin and the party. The oral history record shows that either the people internalized the first "patriotic" message or it meshed with or reflected their natural inclinations; however, the second "Stalinist" message never found resonance in private postwar testimony. Brooks puts it succinctly: "the mix of narratives reflected participants' own pride in conducting the war and therefore a symbolic transfer of value from state, party, and leader to 'society' in their persons."[50]

During the war, newspaper reports were written mostly by military and civilian war correspondents, some of whom actually spent a good deal of time at the front experiencing the fighting and interviewing soldiers as they gathered material for their stories. With some degree of freedom to express themselves in their own words—but within the parameters set by the censors—and no longer confined to formulaic, prescribed phrases as in the prewar years, the more intellectual reporters sought to connect to the Soviet people on honest and realistic terms. Furthermore, after years of being forced to support the official lies of the Soviet regime, many writers, poets, and correspondents felt an incredibly strong need to tell the truth.[51] Therefore, the experience of some correspondents and their interaction with ordinary soldiers and civilians shaped their stories in such a way as to reflect what people genuinely felt and thought. Still, alongside these correspondents and writers with lofty moral goals there existed reporters who deliberately distorted events in the hope of generating hatred for the enemy and confidence in eventual victory by any means necessary. Of course, censorship did not cease; it became even tighter with regard to war news. Therefore, questions arise. How much did people's opinion mirror propaganda, and to what extent did propaganda reflect people's opinion? How far could the regime manipulate the press without losing credibility, and how did this affect reporters' memories of the war?

The major omission in wartime reporting—which comes as no surprise—was the lack of criticism of Stalin, the party, and the government for all the mistakes associated with the war's conduct. The press also refrained from publicizing any behavior by officers and men that would cast a negative light on the Red Army or the Soviet cause. No explanation was given to the forbidden question: why had the war started out so disastrously?

Other problems are shifts in interpretation related to political change: from the postwar Stalinist era to the Khrushchevian post-Stalin thaw to the Brezhnev re-Stalinization to Gorbachev's anti-Stalinist glasnost and finally to the post-Soviet era of near complete freedom of expression. Yet even in this contemporary phase, boundaries of expression exist in Russia based on social, political, and cultural expectations. These factors have to be considered in reading the oral histories of veterans. One obvious evolution in veterans' narratives is that only after the collapse of the USSR and the demise of the Communist Party did veterans admit to hiding or falsifying their socioeconomic backgrounds or their victimization as enemies of the people in order to serve. Consistent across eras is that, in general, veterans frame their memories as *sovetskii* patriotism to which the vast majority of them, especially Russians, cling. In the veterans' hearts and minds, they fought for the survival and ultimate glory of the whole Soviet Union.

The oral histories illustrate a marked reluctance to bring up mistakes made during the war and a pervasive lack of criticism of the state, party, and military. Nina Tumarkin, in her work on the cult of World War II in the Soviet Union, reinforces the idea that the Soviet state used the war to legitimize its rule, and she shows how the war generation bought into the idea that their sacrifice made them special and that subsequent generations ought to honor them forever.[52] Veterans, therefore, are invested in keeping the heroic image of the war unchanged. Social psychologist Elena Seniavskaia goes even further, identifying those who experienced fighting as the "front line-fighter generation" (*frontovoe pokolenie*). Their psychology of remembrance is shaped by the trauma of combat, making it somewhat different from those who did not serve at the front. She finds that *frontoviki* in particular are psychologically bound to the myths of the war, which not only justify their sacrifices but also validate various aspects of prewar Stalinism.[53] Twenty years of post-Soviet freedom of speech has had little effect on this outlook.

Oral histories and wartime letters both complement and contrast with each other. They are comparable in the depiction of everyday life during the war, particularly the hardship and comradeship and the pride in one's individual efforts. In contrast, consonant with the propaganda, letters often include ideas of revenge, but post-Soviet interviews rarely elicit comments along those lines. Consistently absent from oral and official histories of the war are many of the negatives of Soviet behavior, particularly the atrocities Red Army soldiers inflicted on German soldiers and civilians.[54] This is to be expected, as no belligerent has ever put forth a compendium of its official misdeeds or encouraged its soldiers to publicize their individual or collective acts of murder, rape, or mayhem. Furthermore, people who commit atrocities are naturally disinclined to admit them for both social and legal reasons. Instead of negative stories, one finds stories of Soviet soldiers performing acts of undeserved kindness to German POWs and civilians that quite obviously seek to prove the moral superiority of Soviet citizens and their cause.

An excellent example of the interplay among propaganda, personal experience, and memory and their implications for military effectiveness is Mansur G. Abdulin's memoir. Abdulin was a Tatar, the son of atheist working-class communist parents, and a miner and Komsomol member. He volunteered for the army in 1942. In many ways, Abdulin presents himself as the stereotypical Soviet soldier. Very early in his memoir he alludes to the concept of duty to the nation and the potential loss of one's life, which conflicts with the human desire to live. As he filed to the front line for the first time through a ravine filled with dead German and Soviet soldiers, knowing he could be facing imminent death, he thought, "If I had found myself, at this minute, a thousand kilometers away from the ravine, in the blossoming village of Brichmulla, I would again dash to the military registration bureau, and demand to be sent here." He did not want to die, but the weight of propaganda about the duty to serve played on his conscience. "One thought had tormented me back at the mine: what would I be saying when the war is over? That the rear also needed able men, especially in the mines, to work for the nation's defense? This is true. But you can't explain this to everyone; convince everyone. Even girls are summoned to the front."[55]

Feelings of hate and vengeance found their way into his memoir. For example, when his unit took Pitomnik airfield in the battle of Stalingrad in January 1943, it was covered with thousands of dying German soldiers in pitiful condition. His best friend had been killed just days earlier, and Abdulin thought, "I'm ashamed to think the way I do; I'm ashamed to feel this unwanted pity."[56] He steeled himself with the thought that he was required to avenge the loss of his friend.

Abdulin is one of very few people to admit to committing war crimes. His perpetration of the atrocity is intimately connected to the interplay between propaganda and the soldiers' reality of the barbarity of war. He remembers: "I was consumed by the idea that while alive, I would have my revenge on the Germans in advance: for I never expected to survive that slaughter. Once, on my initiative, we shot no less than 200 wounded Nazis in some vegetable store."[57] He does not say so directly, but this incident may have been in retribution for a German atrocity in a village that Abdulin's unit had previously liberated. There, all the inhabitants—old men, women, and children—had been lined up along the main street and shot to death. The Germans had also dumped some peasants' bodies into the village well, and the body of one of Abdulin's regiment's scouts was found mutilated nearby. Under these circumstances, Abdulin and his fellow soldiers did not need propaganda to incite murder, but the propaganda most likely helped them justify their actions and made them believe that they would be exonerated should charges of murder arise.

Abdulin's memoir also exhibits the sentiment spoken of by Tumarkin—that, despite the nation's collective effort in winning the war, members of the war generation believed their individual contributions to be significant. He felt that his and the country's fate were intertwined. When Abdulin was wounded and had to be evacuated, he recalls, "I became really terrified: 'How will things go on without me? Who will go on fighting, if I'm seriously wounded?'"[58]

When it comes to remembering the war, veterans almost always hearken back to the original story line from 1941–1943. They were patriots defending a self-defined *Rodina-mat'*. They were part of a morally justified worldwide crusade against fascism, and they fought a just war to liberate their country and to destroy at its source any potential resurrection of Nazi evil. Stalin and Stalinism rarely figure in their revealed memories, although many remain attached to the socialist ideals they grew up with. Those who have written their stories since December 1991 are dismayed by the collapse of the USSR. These feelings of patriotism, whatever their source, whether internally or externally generated, genuine or rationalized, helped secure the psychological-emotional foundation of the Red Army's military effectiveness during the Second World War.

2

The Winter War as Predictor of Military Effectiveness in the Great Patriotic War

The Soviet Union's war with Finland, commonly referred to as the Winter War, began on 30 November 1939 with an unprovoked attack by the USSR and ended on 12 March 1940 with a negotiated peace that vastly favored the Soviet Union. Finland was forced to grant the USSR valuable territory and the right to establish naval and air bases on its territory. Despite this apparently successful outcome, the Soviet Union's war against Finland is universally seen as a fiasco, for several reasons. First, Stalin failed to accomplish his secret goal of conquering the country and absorbing it into the USSR. Second, the losses inflicted on the Red Army were far out of proportion to the small size of the Finns' army and the casualties it suffered. New perspectives offered by time and access to fresh sources, both archival and memoir, suggest that despite falling short of its territorial goals and its initially dismal combat performance, the Red Army, however inefficient, was far more militarily effective than was appreciated then or now. Contemporaries such as news correspondent Alexander Werth and Soviet generals (as reflected in their memoirs) viewed the Winter War in overly pessimistic terms.[1] Later, historians John Erickson, David Glantz, and Albert Seaton (to name a few) followed that initial trend, missing clues of the Red Army's effectiveness in the Winter War and reporting only the lack of Soviet *proficiency* in that conflict.[2]

My opinion, which runs counter to the accepted wisdom, is that the Winter War in fact showed the Red Army to be effective. This conclusion is based on several criteria. First, the army overall as an institution, the forces in the theater of operations, and most individual soldiers never lost the desire to overcome the foe. Second, unit cohesion, though seriously challenged, remained intact, for the most part. Third, although morale sometimes waned and wavered, it never collapsed. Fourth, the soldiers' investment (interest) in the success of the mission never failed. Finally, discipline, though sometimes tenuous, did not give way. Essentially, the military's staying power proved robust. Civilian support of the war and soldiers' morale were shaken in the face of massive casualties, localized disasters, and visibly incompetent leadership, along with poor planning, chaotic organization, unexpectedly severe weather conditions, and a resilient, resourceful enemy. Nevertheless, the army held up long enough to give the high command and the government enough time to regroup and change strategy and goals.

That the Red Army persevered under these circumstances is all the more surprising given that, by all objective indices of its preparedness in the months leading up to the war and during the first six weeks of fighting, it might have been expected to collapse against a competent foe that could thwart its advance, defeat its attacks, and inflict the number of casualties the Finns did. Yet it did not collapse. The most salient question from the standpoint of "virtual history" and causal analysis is whether Hitler and his generals, had they appreciated the fiber of the Red Army, might have planned their war against the USSR differently—not as a blitzkrieg but as a longer, more extended, and more incremental series of campaigns lasting at least into the winter and perhaps for years. They may have been deterred altogether. Instead, the lessons of Soviet military effectiveness went unnoticed, and the Winter War proved to be a rehearsal for the Great Patriotic War. The same problems presented themselves again, with the same results: initial failure, reassessment, regrouping, recovery, and finally victory.

Background and Overview of the War

For several months preceding the invasion, the Soviet Union had engaged in negotiations with Finland about transferring Finnish territory to the USSR to build air and naval bases, granting the Soviet navy Finland's Hanko naval base, and ceding territory north of Leningrad for "security" purposes. Stalin also insisted that Finland sign a mutual assistance treaty that would give the Soviet military the right to enter Finnish territory to assist in its defense similar to those that would be forced on the Baltic States in 1940. The Finns proclaimed staunch neutrality and refused all Soviet demands.

The Soviet motivation may have been twofold: first, Stalin had mounted a campaign to restore the pre–World War I boundaries of the Russian empire, beginning in Poland and then expanding to Finland, the Baltic States, and Bessarabia; second, Stalin genuinely feared an attack by Nazi Germany, but he suspected, quite incorrectly, that Finland would ally with the Germans and provide a springboard for an attack on Leningrad. That he actually intended to absorb Finland in toto is reflected in the invasion plans, which called for the complete conquest and occupation of the country. Stalin had also created a puppet government in exile consisting of communist Finns, which would be installed after the victory. In the end, war with Finland resulted from failures in both diplomatic and military intelligence. Until attacked by the USSR, the Finns had no desire or intention to join the Axis or allow Germany to use its territory to attack the Soviet Union. After the war, Finland reluctantly allied with Germany, but out of fear of further Soviet aggression and a desire to regain its lost territory.

The Soviet People's Commissariat of Defense (NKO), headed by Stalin's longtime crony Marshal Kliment Voroshilov, and the staff of the Leningrad Military District, under the command of General Kirill Meretskov, began planning the invasion in September 1939. They envisioned the forces of the Leningrad Military District, which had been augmented by twenty divisions composed primarily of conscripts and reservists, quickly crushing whatever resistance the Finns might offer.[3] The depth of their fantasy was reflected by plans positing total defeat of the Finnish military and occupation of the country in only twelve days. All the more damning is Meretskov's claim in his memoirs that in late winter 1939, while touring the border, his staff car became stuck in the deep snow and he concluded that, "should hostilities break out in the winter it would be very difficult to conduct military operations in this region."[4] He claims he initially objected to the short timetable, but he proposed no alternative plan. However, chief of the General Staff General Boris Shaposhnikov did submit a plan, rejected by Stalin, calling for a campaign of several months' duration.[5]

Meretskov and his planners divided the war zone into four main areas along Finland's eastern and southern borders and assigned each to an army. One army was to attack on the Karelian Isthmus, another to the northeast side of Lake Ladoga, and the other two along the length of the eastern Finnish-Soviet border. Voroshilov and his advisers on the NKO staff approved of Meretskov's plan on 16 November and issued the operational directive to carry it out. The commanders involved had less than two weeks to prepare.[6]

Because of the intense and belligerent nature of the ongoing diplomatic negotiations, there was no question that, in the event of war, the Finns would not be taken by surprise. At least six weeks before the attack, the staff of the Leningrad Military District knew that the Finnish army was preparing to fight. Finland had completed its mobilization in October, calling reservists up to the age of forty to report for duty. The Finns had augmented their forces on their southern border and evacuated civilians from areas of likely fighting. Even the cities of Helsinki and Viipuri had sent most of their inhabitants to safety in anticipation of air attacks.[7]

When the war began, much went awry. Instead of the anticipated weak and ineffectual resistance, 7th Army ran into the Mannerheim Line on the Karelian Isthmus, a system of fortified strongpoints of well-camouflaged reinforced concrete bunkers and trench networks along the lines of the French Maginot Line. Soviet forces trying to break this line suffered casualties on a scale reminiscent of the First World War, and they did not succeed until late February 1940. By the time of the armistice, 7th Army had just barely reached Viipuri—a distance of about fifty miles from the Soviet border. Although 8th Army did not face such formidable defenses, it advanced only a few miles and never got around the north shore of Lake Ladoga. Likewise, 9th and 14th Armies paid a steep price in blood for minimal gains against much smaller Finnish forces in northern and eastern Finland. In the end, as an astonished world looked on, no Russian army accomplished its designated goal.

On 9 December, Stalin shook up command of the war. He relieved the Leningrad Military District headquarters from command of operations, sent Meretskov to command 7th Army, and then created the *Stavka* of the high command to oversee operations. The *Stavka* comprised Stalin, Voroshilov, General Shaposhnikov, and head of the navy

Admiral Kuznetsov.[8] These men directed the war from Moscow. Pursuing the same strategy, the new leaders only duplicated the results of their predecessors, shedding much blood for little gain. Finally, on 7 January 1940, after replacing and reassigning many high-ranking officers, Stalin put Marshal Semen Timoshenko in charge of forces on the southern Finnish border (7th and 13th Armies), under the supervision of the *Stavka*.

Stalin called for a new approach to the war, with far less ambitious goals. Timoshenko devised a strategy that took advantage of the strengths of the Red Army. Rather than attacking in all areas, he concentrated on the Karelian Isthmus, with the goal of breaking the Mannerheim Line and seizing Viipuri using massed artillery and tanks to support infantry attacks. The *Stavka* subsequently strengthened the forces at Timoshenko's disposal by an additional twenty-one rifle divisions, twenty artillery regiments, four battalions of super-heavy artillery, six tank brigades, and fifteen air regiments.[9] Timoshenko created a war of attrition rather than one of maneuver, a strategy endorsed by Stalin and implicitly accepting large numbers of casualties. This strategy ultimately succeeded. In February 1940 the Red Army, in what historian John Erickson terms "its second war with Finland,"[10] broke the Mannerheim Line and advanced on Viipuri, forcing the Finns to the peace table, where Stalin achieved his revised war aims.

All told, the Red Army is estimated to have lost 131,476 combat dead and permanently missing in action, 264,908 wounded and injured from combat action, 132,213 frostbite casualties, 5,486 captured, and another 12,000 missing who were later accounted for (546,083 total) out of the more than 900,000 men involved in the war. This equates to approximately 60 percent casualties.[11] The Red Air Force estimated its losses at nearly 3,000 aircraft and 40 percent of the aircrews. By comparison, the Finnish army, navy, and air force, with a combined total of 337,000 men and women, suffered 20 percent casualties. Losses included 22,430 killed and missing, 43,357 wounded, and 847 soldiers captured by the Soviets. In addition 1,029 Finnish civilians were killed by Soviet bombing.[12] The Winter War lasted 105 days, producing an average daily casualty count of 5,034 Soviet servicemen—1,252 dead, 2,523 wounded or injured, and 1,259 frostbitten. As for materiel, the Red Army averaged a loss of six aircraft and twenty-three armored vehicles per day. In comparison, the battle of

Stalingrad—one of the war's bloodiest, lasting from 17 July to 18 November 1942, when the Red Army completed the counteroffensive to encircle the city—produced a daily casualty count of 3,280 Soviet soldiers.[13]

The course of events in 1939–1940 raises several questions with respect to the Red Army's ability to maintain momentum and cohesion when surprised by the scale and tenacity of enemy defenses and by especially severe weather conditions. How, in the face of widespread disorganization, mission failure, and stunningly high casualties, did morale, motivation, unit integrity, and discipline—the bedrocks of military effectiveness—remain strong enough for the Soviets to prevail? Clearly, the Red Army faced grave problems with morale and discipline during the Winter War, difficulties that underlie the framing of any hypothesis about its ultimate success. The major cause of low morale and indiscipline was high casualties from both combat and weather. Although Soviet soldiers did retreat, desert, surrender, shirk, and inflict wounds on themselves to avoid combat, none of these factors escalated to the point that they threatened to destroy the overall effectiveness of the Soviet forces.[14]

The real test came once the Red Army was involved in combat and the men had to decide whether to persevere, risking their lives and safety. These decisions were more difficult than one might expect because at the beginning of the war, before many units had gone into combat, most men had been led to assume that the war would be short and victory would be easy. The official line imparted by the commissars of the Leningrad Military District was that "victory over the enemy shall be achieved with little blood."[15] Many soldiers took this to heart. For example, after conducting a reconnaissance forward of the Soviet lines, one soldier remembered: "We were returning to our camp. But the first thing we saw was not our forward detachments, and not the line of infantry, but a field kitchen and a cook, stuffing snow into his pot. Someone from our group told the cook that it had been a bad idea to come so far out, that the Finns were close. 'What Finns? I'll get them with my scoop.' Such [an] attitude was characteristic for the majority, until we were soundly bathed in our own blood."[16] It is highly likely that this overconfidence contributed to the initial disasters.

During the first three weeks of the war in Karelia, several Finnish regiments all but destroyed 7th Army's 75th, 139th, and 155th Rifle Divisions, inflicting more than 10,000 casualties well before these units even reached the Finns' solid fixed defenses.[17] The 155th Rifle Division, for example, suffered a loss rate of 93 men per day killed, wounded, or missing in the first two weeks of the war.[18] Simultaneously, farther north, 9th Army's 163rd and 44th Infantry Divisions were both decimated in their attempts to cut Finland in half, between them losing more than 2,000 prisoners, 53 tanks, and 114 artillery pieces. Ninth Army's battle order had predicted only five days of fighting, culminating in total victory.[19] In the far north, 14th Army's two divisions advanced deep into Finland unopposed. When Finnish forces did arrive, they forced the Red Army units back for miles. Once they stopped retreating, these forces dug in and remained immobile for the rest of the war.

Elsewhere, on Finland's southeastern border, the Finns encircled numerous Soviet divisions and carved them into smaller pockets of resistance called *mottis*. By the first week of January 1940 it was clear that Meretskov's initial plan had failed and that he, Stalin, and the Red Army high command had massively underrated their enemy and overestimated the abilities of their own forces. Nevertheless, despite tens of thousands of men killed, wounded, and captured and vast losses of materiel, Soviet forces somehow remained on the field of battle and continued to fight, although, with a few exceptions, more fiercely than well.

The Early Trials of the War

The first serious display of how motivation, morale, cohesion, discipline, investment in the war, and staying power would hold up came during the disasters of December 1939. To the Red Army's credit, all these elements held up, though at times tenuously. There were no mass surrenders, only small numbers of men were captured, and few refused to fight. There were, however, some panicky headlong retreats of whole battalions and regiments and some breakdowns in authority, which is almost to be expected of poorly trained, poorly led, and unblooded conscripts. There were also occasions when officers had to plead, cajole, or threaten to get their men to advance under enemy fire.[20]

Despite the adversity, few men surrendered or were captured. It is unlikely that they persevered out of fear of the consequences if they did not. Although the Soviet state—and the tsarist state in the First World War, for that matter—considered it a crime to surrender, but not to be captured, this was probably not a deterrent, for several reasons. Article 193 of the 1926 criminal code of the Russian Soviet Federated Socialist Republic, "Voluntary Abandonment of the Battlefield," listed surrender to the enemy not caused by combat action as a crime punishable by death, but most men in a position to surrender were in situations (*mottis*) caused by combat action.[21] It is also questionable how seriously the average soldier took this proscription and how thoroughly the men had been instructed on it, given the rather haphazard nature of their training. If the 5,486 men captured by the Finns had really believed they would be prosecuted for their capture upon repatriation, it stands to reason that more than 74 would have requested asylum in Finland. In fact, after the war, 4,704 were secretly prosecuted and either executed or sent to Gulag camps.[22] It was also a crime, punishable by execution, to desert the front in time of war, and it seems that many more men took that route to avoid combat.[23] So it is not clear that these threats served as a deterrent to the majority of Red Army men.

The dearth of surrenders was especially remarkable, for several reasons. First, weather conditions were frightfully cold, and surrender meant warm shelter and hot food. Second, the Russians had no fear of being murdered or mistreated by the Finns if they gave up. Third, there was little if any hatred of the Finns, which might drive men to fight to the death. Fourth, there were many opportunities and situations in which surrender seemed quite reasonable and would apparently qualify as legally legitimate grounds for surrender, such as the battles of the *mottis*. Finally, if a soldier were disaffected with the Stalinist state's social and economic policies, liberal and modern Finland would look very inviting indeed. Yet few Red Army soldiers pursued that alternative.

Lieutenant Ivan Iudin, a survivor of an encircled detachment of the 139th Rifle Division, recalled levelheaded and rational command of the *motti* his artillery battalion found itself in. The rifle regiment his battalion supported met determined Finnish attacks with resolve and counterattacked with spirited shouts of *Ura!* Fighting frequently terminated in hand-to-hand combat, once with his battery firing grapeshot over open sights and artillerymen being killed at their guns. No one panicked or suggested surrender.[24]

Other examples of the Red Army's stalwart defense against all odds were recounted by Finns, who reported that one company-sized *motti* of the 18th Rifle Division suffered the death or wounding of 83 of its 85 soldiers, but the last two unwounded men still refused to surrender. Another annihilated *motti* consisting of the encircled 34th Light Tank Brigade and assorted artillery and infantry battalions yielded 2,050 dead Russian soldiers but only 58 prisoners. Among the dead were 30 female soldiers who had served as clerks and nurses, some of whom died with weapons in hand. No women were among the captured.[25] Soldiers in surrounded units generally believed they would be rescued or could hold out until victory eventually released them from encirclement. They were sure the USSR would win the war and did not question the vitality of the Soviet regime. There were also a handful of small-unit actions outside of *mottis* in which officers and men who found themselves surrounded inexplicably committed suicide rather than be taken prisoner. For reasons unknown, some downed Soviet airmen also fought to the death or killed themselves to avoid capture.[26]

Challenges to Morale

Consideration of the mind-set and conditions under which Soviet soldiers fought in the Winter War offers perspective on the motivation and discipline that held the army together despite the forces that threatened to rend it apart. Most soldiers were shocked when they realized how unprepared they were for the type of fighting they were engaged in; they were further dismayed at the high losses suffered for little or no territorial gain. Dmitrii Krutskikh, an engineer platoon leader, had meager combat training—two years in a military-political school to become a commissar. He recalled that only he and seven other men in his unit came through the war unscathed, and he blamed improper training and the need to learn under fire. "Learning in combat means losing people. It must be said—our experience was earned through a lot of blood. In my unit, I practically had to replace everybody."[27] Lieutenant Aleksei Shilin had a similar story. In December, his infantry regiment attacked over and over for days. "Our losses were enormous," he said, "but there was no gain." In February, however, "it was a new war," but by then, "many of my friends were already dead."[28] The experience of Lieutenant Vasilii Davidenko was similar to Krutskikh's: "What else can I tell you? In the beginning we had very high losses, because we were not prepared. We were not prepared for the war."[29]

Despite the losses, none of these young lieutenants or their superiors considered the war hopeless or thought the invasion ought to be halted. Some, like Lieutenant Nikolai Ponomarenko, an artillery forward observer, were able to rationalize the high casualties. The Finns inflicted large numbers of losses on the Soviet infantry not because of their highly accurate mortar fire, according to Ponomarenko, but because of the laziness of the Soviet soldiers. Instead of digging foxholes in the hard ground, the infantry built one-meter-high, aboveground shelters of logs and earth. When a bombardment started, the "infantry would dive into those shelters and stick in them like herrings in a jar." Once, Ponomarenko observed a mortar round score a direct hit on one of these shelters, destroying it and killing all twenty men inside: "To be short, it was one big lump of human flesh. So the infantry of the 90th Rifle Division could blame themselves for such high losses."[30] More accurately, the officers were to blame for not ordering the men to prepare proper defensive positions.

Many just accepted the losses stoically. Lieutenant Semen Brovin of the 190th Rifle Regiment wrote to a friend that he was one of only three or four surviving officers in his battalion. "The chances of staying alive here, in my view, are poor," he observed, but "victory will be ours." He wrote that his unit had captured a Finnish officer who concurred with Brovin's outlook: "We know that you will win, but with heavy losses."[31]

Lieutenant Lukinov's regiment endured constant battle for twenty-two days. He recalled: "We turned into some half-beasts: frostbitten, dirty, lice infested, unshaven, in clothes burned from the fires, unable to say a single phrase without obscene cursing."[32] Although his battery lost five of its nine officers and many more privates and noncommissioned officers (NCOs), the regiment held together, maintaining its cohesion and the will to fight. Lukinov described the bleak march of the 306th Rifle Regiment back to Leningrad. It had entered the war at full strength, with three battalions of 700 men each, but on the way back it lacked the infantry to form a single battalion. "Companies were commanded by sergeants. We marched here in several columns, so huge was the regiment. Now the entire regiment formed a single column, and we artillerymen, walking in the end of the column, could see and hear the band playing marching tunes in the lead of the column."[33]

Like Lukinov's unit, Nikolai Shishkin's artillery regiment received no reinforcements during the war. He did not dwell on the casualties but suggested that "the command underestimated the enemy." He assigned no blame to the soldiers, who had, after all, accomplished their mission. "The defense of the Finns was competent, with concrete defensive walls, and automatic machine guns, and of course, if you advanced to this defense without reconnaissance, without preparation, and without reliably neutralizing weapons emplacements—this happened more than once—then losses would be great and unjustified."[34] Recognizing that their superiors were just as unprepared for the reality of war as they were often depressed the men's morale. By and large, however, because of the state's successful depiction of the war as just and the fatalistic recognition of the link between war and death, most soldiers, and especially the officers, accepted the tragic losses as inevitable and justified.

Red Army personnel policies proved to be challenges to cohesion and contributed to high casualties. Because of the enormous losses and the need to keep troop strength up, the army threw in thousands of untrained or undertrained replacements who, once at the front, had to be taught such basic tasks as shooting a rifle and throwing a hand grenade. Late in the war, one corps received in excess of 5,000 replacements that had not been taught how to handle rifles.[35] Many replacements were in their thirties and forties. They were reservists who had not seen military service for a decade or more, and they were physically unfit and reluctant to undertake strenuous efforts or risk their lives. Throwing these untrained and physically and psychologically unprepared men into the fray reduced unit morale and cohesion and increased casualties, rather than easing them.

Gregory Ugriumov was a reserve officer called up in the summer of 1939. His example illustrates the organizational and tactical practices that yielded high casualties, meager results, and low morale, but it simultaneously shows units' ability to maintain their effectiveness despite such problems. His battalion, lacking artillery and with only a few machine guns in support, had orders to attack a Finnish village early in the evening by charging across a frozen lake. As they ran across the ice, someone yelled, "For our fatherland! For Stalin!" When they were less than a hundred meters from the houses, the Finns opened fire, massacring them in the open. After lying in the snow for an indeterminate amount of time, shooting indiscriminately, men began to fall back without orders. Ugriumov and the surviving officers joined them. Subsequently, the battalion commander gathered them together and ordered them to attack once more: "And let's not lie in the snow dreaming of warm beds. The village must be taken!" He instructed company commanders to shoot anyone who fell back or turned around. Ugriumov, with only thirty-eight of his original complement of more than a hundred men, was skeptical that this second attack would succeed. "One didn't have to be a psychologist to know that the new attack, in which the soldiers would have to climb over the bodies of their killed and wounded comrades, would fail."[36] The attack did fail, at the cost of more dead and wounded soldiers. A subsequent assault also failed, leaving the battalion too depleted to attempt a fourth attack, as desired by the division commander.[37]

The diary entries of Lieutenant A. I. Matveev, a mortar platoon leader, show how unpredictable combat losses could be for a single unit. While attempting to break the Mannerheim Line in the February offensive, a battalion of his 49th Rifle Regiment suffered only two casualties while taking a Finnish strongpoint; however, a battalion on the right flank simultaneously suffered 144 casualties and the next day an additional 134. Three days later, both battalions attacked and suffered 50 percent losses. In another three days, the regiment again went forward against the Finns and suffered the death of one company commander and the wounding of another. Three-quarters of all platoon leaders were killed or wounded. After ten days of fighting, two rifle companies were down to only one officer each, and a machine gun company had only three.[38] Yet the regiment continued to fight, pushing the Finns back and holding its place in the line.

In contrast to the fatalistic resolve shown by Ugriumov's and Matveev's battalions, the commander of the 142nd Rifle Division reported numerous problems with men going to ground and staying down during attacks. "I remember the attack I led personally at Kiviniemi. As soon as we got under machine-gun fire, the men hit the deck and much energy was spent getting them to fulfill the task set by the army commander."[39] Because of the inexperience and ineptitude of many low-ranking leaders, senior officers often went forward to rally the troops. As a result, high-ranking officers, including regiment and even division commanders, suffered heavy casualties.[40]

The wretched weather also caused casualties, weakened morale, and tested the troops' commitment to the war. According to available data, the temperature rose above freezing only ten times during the entire campaign.[41] All told, the Red Army recorded more than 132,000 men lost to service from freezing to death or being frostbitten to such a degree that they had to be evacuated to field hospitals, where many lost toes, fingers, or ears. In one three-day period, for example, the encircled 18th Rifle Division suffered the loss of 532 men: 82 were killed in action, 150 were wounded, and 300 were lost to severe frostbite.[42] Private Nikolai Guzhva held the opinion that "not many died from fire, more died from freezing."[43] Lieutenant Lukinov recalled that one time his artillery battery had to spend the night under the open sky in freezing weather. Because their dugouts were filled with wounded, the healthy had to sit outside, huddled around fires. "It's bad to sleep while sitting in the frost by a fire. You get burned on the front, but the back freezes. When dozing off you lean forward and your clothes catch fire. Damn war."[44]

Morale was sometimes seriously challenged not only because of casualties and the weather but also because of inadequate logistical support. Lev Mekhlis, head of the Main Political Administration of the Red Army, expended a good deal of effort to remedy interrelated supply and transport shortages while temporarily serving as a member of 9th Army's military council. The army ran critically short of trucks due to a prewar shortage, combat action, and the effects of the cold.[45] The shortage of trucks hampered the delivery of food, fuel, and ammunition, as well as the evacuation of casualties. Horse-drawn transport was also in short supply because the cold killed and disabled horses, and snow hindered their mobility.

Everyday difficulties in the brief fight with Finland also challenged morale. Meager daily rations of a dry-tack biscuit and a piece of horsemeat sustained the men. If they were lucky, they occasionally got canned meat. Frontline troops went the whole war without bathing, and lice plagued the men. More serious was that the logistical services seemed to have forgotten to provide fresh water, so the men had to improvise to keep hydrated. One soldier reported, "There was no water at our positions. There was only a small brook in no-man's land where both sides drew water." When his unit's political officers found out they were sharing the brook with the enemy, they made the soldiers shoot the Finns when they gathered water. The Finns naturally followed suit, thus depriving both sides of the use of the stream. Afterward, the soldiers "melted and boiled snow but there must have been something wrong with the snow water—we suffered stomach pains and diarrhea."[46]

Lukinov recalled that his artillery battalion was fairly well fed. Horse-drawn field kitchens made daily trips from the rear to the front to feed the men hot chow: "The cooks hastened to give out the food and leave the way they came from under mortar fire. They were not allowed back with any food remaining. They said that one cook had been shot on the spot because he emptied the tank of his kitchen into the snow in order to get away from the front line as soon as possible." Some days the field kitchens did not make it to the front, so the men resorted to melting "tasteless snow for tea, warmed the frozen ice-covered bread in the smoke of a fire, and boiled wheat concentrate in mess tins."[47]

Leadership and Discipline

Leadership and discipline are integral components of effectiveness, and both proved to be uneven during the Winter War. Capable leadership seems to have been the exception rather than the rule. Some officers were able to inspire their men and make them feel that they were in capable hands. More visible, however, were officers who proved to be incompetent or uncaring. The most serious problem was the youth, lack of training, and inexperience of battalion-level officers. The vast majority of platoon and company commanders were nineteen to twenty-three years of age, graduates of abbreviated training courses of around eighteen months' duration.[48] Many others were junior lieutenants, men promoted from the ranks and given anywhere from three to six months of officer training.

Poor leadership was, for the most part, an institutional problem. Decades after the war, a lieutenant remembered, "Those days it was considered that a commander should only be in front of his troops, shouting: 'Forward! Hurrah!' and so on."[49] This style of leadership contributed to high losses among officers; some 29,000 became casualties. To make matters worse, Finnish snipers had orders to make Soviet officers their primary targets.[50] About the weak leadership and the lack of military expertise at higher levels, Commissar Semionov of the 50th Rifle Corps reported, "Regiments and divisions were sometimes given to incompetent, inexperienced and poorly trained people who failed at the slightest difficulty in battle."[51]

Sound leadership was made doubly difficult by the late formation of units on the eve of the war. At the onset of the invasion on 30 November, the Leningrad Military District had not finished forming its forces or filling out existing regiments and divisions. For several weeks the district underwent a chaotic shuffling and reshuffling of men and equipment as tens of thousands of reservists reported for duty.[52] As the Red Army personnel office assigned and then reassigned officers in the weeks and days before the march into Finland, most leaders were virtual strangers to their men. Their late arrival and unfamiliarity with their new units weakened command, control, and cohesion in the initial weeks of combat. Many divisions had been formed and relocated to Leningrad only six weeks to three months before the war began, and they fell far short of achieving a reasonable level of cohesion. The situation of units forming, re-forming, shuffling, reshuffling, and absorbing large numbers of new or untrained men on the eve of combat would oft be repeated in the Great Patriotic War, with similar results.

Incompetence and poor leadership skills could lead to trouble between superiors and subordinates. Rumors circulated throughout the army of soldiers killing their officers in battle. Lieutenant Krutskikh claimed to have been on friendly terms with his subordinates. He recalled: "The soldiers took care of me. Everything was in the open. Any rowdiness by an officer would end up by his death in the first combat. I have no doubt about that." By "rowdiness" he means the abuse of soldiers, which was not the norm but was by no means uncommon.[53]

If soldiers thought they were in the hands of leaders who would get them killed, discipline was in danger of being undermined. As a result of the hardship, inexperienced leadership, and scale of death, discipline problems began to surface. The most obvious manifestations of eroding discipline were desertion from the front lines and self-inflicted wounds.

General Aleksandr Zaporozhets of the 13th Army military council characterized the deserters primarily as peasants, some of whom fled all the way back to their villages. Others fled only to the rear areas, often in small groups, where they hid in the woods or dugouts, sneaking meals from field kitchens and then disappearing into their lairs. Besides desertion, 13th Army also experienced numerous cases of self-inflicted wounds. For example, at the end of one day in combat, the 143rd Rifle Regiment incurred 105 cases of self-inflicted wounds, mostly bullet wounds to the left hand or its fingers or to the fleshy part of the leg.[54] One Kalmyk soldier thought that his fellow Central Asian soldiers were particularly active in wounding themselves to avoid fighting.[55]

Ninth Army did not have a problem with desertion until January 1940. In the wake of the routs of the 163rd and 44th Divisions, groups of soldiers and NCOs began deserting their posts at the front. The 9th Army commander responded by establishing roving patrols behind the lines to apprehend wayward soldiers and military tribunals to try them. Ninth Army's military council decided there was no need to employ mass repression to handle the problem, but it pressured commanders to take their units in hand.[56]

Within the Red Army's organizational structure, its political officers—commissars and *politruki*—were responsible for morale and discipline, yet these officers apparently did little political indoctrination along the lines of Marxism-Leninism as they strove to motivate soldiers during the Winter War. As a consequence, commanders blamed many problems of a political nature on the *politruki*'s failure to properly indoctrinate soldiers. General Vladimir Grendal', commander of 13th Army, thought the political instruction of his soldiers left much to be desired. After the war he said, "reports from the special units [secret police] revealed a mass of riff-raff, and some cases of a counter-revolutionary nature. We must not close our eyes to this, because it did happen. Twenty-two years of Soviet power have not yet knocked sense into them."[57] Perhaps the root of the problem was that only the forces of the Leningrad Military District that had originally been scheduled to attack Finland were subjected to intense anti-Finnish propaganda before the war. The replacement troops and new formations sent to the front, such as 13th Army, which came largely from Ukraine, were not indoctrinated prior to shipping out to Finland.[58]

Soldier Georgi Prusakov stated, "I do not remember any propaganda materials, there were no leaflets nor loudspeaker speeches. The *politruk* did have some work with the Komsomol members, but you could not do much in those conditions. Anyway, we were all Komsomol members."[59] Prusakov's last statement implies that Komsomol members did not need to be subjected to political indoctrination because it would have been like preaching to the choir. Another soldier said that in his regiment "[commissars] conversed well with the soldiers, often making small talk about life, asking who was writing from home, how we were fed, and they never crammed agit-prop 'party of Lenin-Stalin' stuff into us."[60] They did, however, propagate the slogans "For the Motherland!" and "For Stalin!" Some soldiers, clearly aware of the general line of propaganda, reiterated it in their letters home. Some referred, for example, to the Finns as "white bandits" in the service of foreign imperialists. Others internalized and clung to the idea that they were on a liberating mission to free the Finnish people from capitalist exploitation, just as they had recently freed the Poles and Ukrainians in western Ukraine and Belorussia.[61]

Despite the propaganda, not every soldier accepted the party line on the war, and this exacerbated discipline problems. When his unit arrived at the front in January 1940, one private in a signal company protested that the war with Finland was not right and he could not engage in operations against the Finnish army. He was turned over to a military tribunal, declared guilty of violating his commander's orders, and shot.[62] The staff of this soldier's division subsequently admonished its subordinate elements to raise the quality of their political work among the men. Sergeant Ivan Chetyrbok knew that not everyone in his division wanted to fight. He recalled that the state's rationale was accepted by most but not all of the men. In his platoon, a Belorussian soldier threw down his machine gun and said, "A Finnish farmer has 30 hectares of land, while I have 100 times less. What for am I fighting him?"[63]

The more adroit and cautious soldiers kept their criticisms of the regime to themselves until they were captured. Private Nikifor Gubarevich told his Finnish captors about the hard life on collective farms and the unfair treatment meted out by the Soviet government. A veteran of the September invasion of Poland, he noted that Polish farmers lived better than Russians. Another captive, a deputy *politruk*, wrote to the Finnish minister of justice and asked to stay in Finland on the grounds that the USSR was "a land of false 'democracy and freedoms' without bread."[64] He deplored the poor treatment of workers and peasants and the destruction of religion under the dictatorship of Stalin. Some diaries taken off dead Red Army soldiers and officers echoed these sentiments.[65]

Nikolai Shishkin did not remember any rationale being given for the war. He did recall, however, that the commissar and his people would drop by to visit the men in the front lines from time to time. "As regards to our battery, . . . we never assembled the personnel of the battery for three months of the war for the commissar to talk with us. There wasn't the opportunity—we all by our own guns carried out the orders of the infantry battalion."[66] For Shishkin, it seems that elemental obedience was at work: it was enough that his country asked him to serve, so he did, trusting that there was good reason for it.

Discipline and morale were further challenged by news from the home front. Despite state control over the media and the initial patriotic response by many in Soviet society, after only a month of fighting, indications surfaced that some were beginning to have doubts. The German ambassador in Moscow, von Schulenberg, reported to Berlin in January 1940 that the war was becoming unpopular. The Soviet population did not have reliable news about the course of the war or conditions at the front, yet the fighting had already lasted longer than the regime had led them to expect, causing speculation that things were not going well. The large number of wounded and frostbitten soldiers flooding hospitals in Leningrad and Moscow was evidence of the high human cost of the campaign.[67] The stories told by these casualties confirmed people's worst fears. One soldier said to a crowd: "In the first days of our forces' attack (Petrozavodsk direction) there were numerous losses, as a result of wrecking on the part of the command. The commander of one regiment gave an order to attack and he himself fled." He then described how his regiment had been surrounded and destroyed in a dense forest. He lamented that many soldiers had frostbitten feet and had to be evacuated because "only in the last few days have soldiers got warm footwear."[68]

The reality of the heavy losses began to make some people doubt that the war was worth the price being paid. Some areas were particularly hard hit, such as Vologda province, which had 2,366 young men killed or missing and thousands more wounded and frostbitten out of 43,403 men mobilized for the war.[69] The unexpectedly severe losses must have made people weigh the necessity of the war. Such concerns had been reaching the soldiers through letters from their families since the war began.[70]

The reaction of the civilian population of Soviet Karelia, bordering Finland, was particularly noteworthy because that area constituted the attacking forces' immediate rear. These people had mixed feelings about the war, in contrast to young workers and students in the cities of the USSR. NKVD reports indicate that despite the state's propaganda campaign, collective farmers, families whose members had been repressed in the purges, those with family in Finland, and even some workers exhibited antiwar and anti-Soviet sentiments. Before the outbreak of hostilities, some had expressed skepticism at Molotov's speech to the Fifth Session of the Congress of Soviets, which had clearly been a precursor to war. Many could not believe that a country with only 3 million inhabitants would deliberately provoke the USSR, with its 170 million. Others expressed doubt about the Red Army's capacity to win and the hope that if the Soviet Union lost, the Finns would incorporate them into Finland.[71]

As the war dragged on, people also began to fear that prices would go up. The economy was already suffering shortages, and only a few years had passed since the end of food rationing. These concerns were also expressed in letters the soldiers received from their families.[72] In this vein, a Leningrad worker commented, "the Bolsheviks send soldiers to fight in Finland and starve people. The soldiers should kill the Bolsheviks rather than the Finns."[73]

Discipline Problems away from the Front

In January 1940, when it became clear to Stalin and Voroshilov that the forces of the Leningrad Military District alone would not be able to beat the Finns, the NKO began transferring units from other military districts. Rumors of the horrific bloodletting spread throughout the army and triggered negative responses, such as one soldier's gloomy observation that "we're going to certain death. They'll kill us all. If the newspapers said that for every Finn you need ten Russkies, they'd be right. They are swatting us like flies."[74] In the Kiev Special Military District's 13th Rifle Corps, when a rumor spread that some of the divisions would soon be sent to Finland, a wave of soldiers went AWOL, and there was excessive drinking among soldiers and officers and the singing of antiwar songs.[75] The 97th Rifle Division experienced an especially large number of desertions while en route to Finland. Another unit in Ukraine reported several self-inflicted wounds by soldiers hoping to avoid service in Finland.[76]

One of the more extreme cases of indiscipline occurred in the 62nd Rifle Division, from which 292 men deserted in two days' time while getting ready to move to the front. Another 240 men of the unit were listed as AWOL, including a dozen who fled from their train during a stop at a station.[77] One soldier told his buddies, "If they send me to the front I'll sneak off into the bushes. I won't fight, but I will shoot people like our unit commander Gordienko."[78] Such dissident sentiments, though troubling, were in the minority. In the end, most men maintained their self-discipline, stayed with their units, and obeyed orders to go to war, albeit apparently without enthusiasm.

With great dismay, 13th Army reported the arrival of the 4th and 8th Rifle Divisions from Belorussia in February 1940. The 8th Rifle Division was in disarray and barely under the control of its officers. While moving by rail from its base to Leningrad and then from Leningrad to the front, 400 men deserted or attempted to. The division's 151st Rifle Regiment lost 190 men, and the 310th Rifle Regiment lost 150 men. The officers themselves were undisciplined as well. For example, Junior Lieutenant Zhdanovich, commander of 9th Company, showed up drunk. Command of the company would have been handed over to the assistant platoon commander, Shan'ko, but he had run off, as had many of the men. The company was left with no officers. When they arrived in the war zone, 9th Company had only 50 men, and 8th Company had only 42. Each had started with nearly 100 men.[79] Those men who did arrive exhibited anti-Soviet opinions and regularly broke discipline. The division commissars did nothing about it. One report declared that Commissar Burilin appeared "inert." The officers of the division failed to accomplish numerous elementary and essential tasks, such as issuing *valenki* (felt boots) or issuing *valenki* without instructing soldiers how to wrap their foot bindings before putting on their boots, which resulted in numerous foot injuries on the march to the front. The military council of the front recommended that the division commander, General

Fursin, and Commissar Burilin be relieved of their duties. The military council of 13th Army concurred with Burilin's removal. Furthermore, Lieutenants Zhdanovich and Shan'ko were both to face a military tribunal for demoralizing their companies. Sparing the details, the report declared that the 4th Rifle Division had arrived at the front in the same condition as the 8th Rifle Division.[80] In the case of these two divisions, it seems that poor leadership, disorganization, and lack of confidence in their preparation for battle were the key problems, rather than any particular political attitude about the war.

Motivation and Morale

Why did most Red Army men persevere and fight hard in support of the regime's goals? First, the Soviet regime, though the obvious aggressor in the Winter War in the eyes of much of the world, was able to justify the conflict to the Soviet people, portraying it as a just war in defense of the socialist homeland against a hostile capitalist enemy. In the weeks prior to the attack on Finland, the USSR's state-controlled media repeated the themes that the USSR was merely seeking to push the border back to protect Leningrad and that the Finns were being unreasonable and uncooperative. General Meretskov, in his mobilization order to the soldiers of the Leningrad Military District, decreed that the war was against the "capitalist exploiters" of the Finnish government who had victimized the ordinary Finn. Raising the possibility of lifting the yoke of capitalism from the Finnish people, he concluded with the standard imprecations: "For the security of the northwest border of the USSR and the brave city of Leningrad! For our beloved homeland *rodina*! For the great Stalin! Forward, sons of the Soviet people, soldiers of the Red Army, to completely destroy the enemy!"[81] This message evidently found resonance among many Soviet citizens and soldiers. Perhaps most important, in propagandistic terms, the media worked to convince the Soviet people, especially soldiers, of the lie that the Finns had started the war, supposedly drawing first blood in an unprovoked artillery attack.[82] Because Russian soldiers and society at large had no access to the foreign press for alternative perspectives, the regime's "just war" claims cemented the acquiescence of most of the nation to the conduct of the war.

The imprint was long and deep. Sixty years later, Viktor Iskrov clearly recalled the rationale laid out in Meretskov's order to the troops, then repeated in *Pravda*, and asserted that he and his fellow officers and men had had faith that those claims were valid. He remembered the *politruki* of his regiment telling the soldiers about negotiations with the Finns in October and the subsequent appearance of such stories in the newspapers. "Our government proposed Finns moving the border, as the border was just 32 kilometers from Leningrad," he said. "To compensate, we were proposing [to give] Finns areas in the north, at the eastern borders of Finland, the territory was four times larger than the one that we asked for from the Finns." Iskrov recalled that the negotiations lasted for six weeks or so but came to nothing. "Then, I think also on November 26, a few shots were fired from the Finnish side in Mainila area. As a result, two men were killed, four wounded." The Soviet government protested and then attacked on 30 November. "If you do not want to do it in a peaceful way, we will move our borders by force. This is the way I understood the whole thing then."[83] So it was the Finns' fault. They rejected the peaceful way and, in Iskrov's mind and in the memories of many other veterans, the USSR had no choice but to wage a preventive "defensive" war.

The German invasion of the USSR in 1941 would spark mass voluntarism among young people, but not so the Soviet attack on Finland. Still, because the people perceived the conflict as a just war, at least in the short run, the state had little difficulty in mobilizing a crucial segment of society—urban youth—and chose not to mobilize the public at large. The Communist Party's propaganda machine did not seek to ignite public activism or generate a volunteer movement. Instead, the state sought to generate volunteers in a controlled, low-key manner; once they met their quotas, recruiters turned away would-be volunteers.[84] Although thousands volunteered during the Winter War, they were approached by the state, specifically through the Komsomol, and asked to join. They did not represent any sort of mass outpouring of support for the war or the state. Anatolii Muzhikov, a student in Leningrad, said that among his peers, volunteering for the war "was the thing to do at the time."[85]

The army and party together used local Komsomol, Osoaviakhim, and youth sports organizations to seek out young men, especially skiers and proficient marksmen, to form ski battalions of 100 to 150 men for the duration of the war.[86] When he was approached, Georgi Prusakov, a Komsomolets working in a factory, agreed to volunteer. His institute's Komsomol Committee spearheaded recruitment for the 100th Volunteer Ski Battalion, made up of workers and college students. "The committee's secretary was a girl called Tsilia Donde," he recalled, "and she told me that volunteer ski battalions were formed for fighting the White Finns. . . . She asked me if I would like to participate. I immediately agreed."[87] Unlike in the Great Patriotic War, when the state made much of the volunteer units created in 1941, in 1939 the government did not publicize the formation of the Leningrad volunteer battalions.

Nikolai Shishkin had a similar experience while a freshman at Sverdlovsk Polytechnic. "Within two months after I started my studies and at the same time of the start of the Finnish War, they announced a voluntary call for students for war service. Perhaps I could not have gone to the army, but we were all patriotic. Almost my entire class decided to volunteer for the defense of the Motherland."[88] Rather than forming ski battalions, the students from his class were sent with volunteers from neighboring universities to transit camps, where they were parceled out to serve in regular army units.

Besides patriotism or a desire to defend the USSR, the younger generation's deference to the government served the purpose of the regime. A veteran who was part of a follow-on unit not subjected to political instruction about the need for the war beforehand, and apparently ignorant of prewar press reports, wrote: "One of the peculiarities of this war was the fact that we fought because we were ordered. This was different from the following Patriotic War, when we hated the enemy that attacked our native land. Here they simply told us: 'Forward march!'—without even an explanation of where we were going. We simply did our soldier's duty during the Finnish war, and understood the sense and the necessity of the fight later."[89]

The army also used various positive inducements to maintain obedience and raise morale. It bestowed 50,000 awards for merit and courage during the Winter War; 400 of them (an average of almost four per day) were the most prestigious title, Hero of the Soviet Union. In the hope of motivating widespread emulation, the army publicized the heroism of its soldiers to all the forces at the front through unit and army newspapers and bulletins. The army also awarded several units the prestigious Order of the Red Banner.[90] A more concrete but mundane incentive took the form of a daily vodka ration, a gesture that took some soldiers by surprise because drinking had officially been discouraged in peacetime. Lieutenant Lukinov reminisced about the daily 100 grams, saying, "It warmed and cheered us during frosts, and it made us not care in combat."[91] With so much vodka floating around, it was not surprising that some officers and men managed to get more than their share and occasionally overindulged.[92]

For those whose motivation failed them, the army responded with negative consequences. Rather than addressing the growing problem of unauthorized retreats, shirking, and desertion through better leadership, training, and supply, the army resorted to draconian measures, most notably capital punishment, hoping to intimidate soldiers into compliance. Executions of unsuccessful senior commanders foreshadowed those to come during the Great Patriotic War. Shortly after the start of the war, several battalions of Finns annihilated the 163rd Rifle Division and mauled and routed the 44th Motorized Rifle Division along the Raate road, where the two divisions had been assigned to cut Finland in half at its narrowest point. Mekhlis, a member of 9th Army's military council, then under the command of General Vasilii Chuikov, investigated the disaster. With the approval of Chuikov, Mekhlis ordered the arrest of General Vinogradov, the commander of the 44th Rifle Division; his chief of staff Volkov; and his commissar Pakhomenko. Arrested for the debacle involving the 163rd Rifle Division were Colonel Sharov, commander of the 662nd Rifle Regiment, and his commissar Podkhomutov, along with Captain Chaikovskii, commander of the 3rd NKVD Regiment, and his commissar Cherevko. Based on the findings of military tribunals, all were subsequently executed in two separate proceedings as subordinates looked on.[93] The deaths of the commander and staff of the 163rd Rifle Division at the hands of the Finns probably spared them a similar fate. The message to the rest of the army's leaders was unmistakable: die fighting or before a firing squad, but do not panic and abandon your command under fire.

Other punitive measures short of death included relief of commanders and termination of careers. On the tenth day of the war, 9 December 1939, General Vsevolod Iakovlev, 7th Army commander, was reassigned in disgrace to administrative duties in the Leningrad Military District after apparently missing an opportunity to break through unprepared Finnish defenses. General Meretskov was demoted from command of the district to succeed him, but things did not improve immediately. People's Commissar of Defense Voroshilov suggested to Stalin that Meretskov be court-martialed and that the entire staff of 7th Army be removed. He also proposed "a radical purge of corps, divisional and regimental commanders. [We] need to replace these cowards and laggards (there are also swine) with loyal and efficient people."[94] Luckily for Meretskov, Stalin ignored Voroshilov's advice and ordered the *Stavka* to draw up plans for a new offensive.

Two weeks later, General Vladimir Kurdiumov was relieved of command of 8th Army and replaced by General Khabarov. Khabarov lasted only a few weeks before being dismissed on 12 January and replaced by General Grigori Shtern. Besides these two army commanders, the *Stavka* and subordinate headquarters found it necessary to relieve of their commands or dismiss from their responsibilities three army chiefs of staff; three corps commanders and their chiefs of staff; five division commanders, several division chiefs of staff, and several division artillery chiefs and their chiefs of staff; and numerous regimental commanders.[95] In the aftermath of the 44th Division disaster, for example, 9th Army lost its commander, its chief of staff, and one corps commander to punitive reassignment or demotion.[96] After the executions of Vinogradov and his subordinates and the removals of Iakovlev, Kurdiumov, and Khabarov, the command atmosphere from the *Stavka* down to the front lines became very tense. Senior officers began to threaten their subordinates with dire consequences if orders were not fulfilled.

At the end of January 1940, as hundreds of deserters and stragglers roamed the Soviet rear areas, the NKO and NKVD decided to impose order from above. They ordered the formation of twenty-seven blocking detachments of roughly a hundred men each to patrol the rear areas, mainly behind 7th and 8th Armies, to round up soldiers who were away from their units without permission. Simultaneously, the *Stavka* sent out orders to shoot deserters and men AWOL from their units. In the first week or so of January, even before creation of the blocking detachments, 8th Army had already shot eleven deserters.[97] General Zaporozhets, commander of 13th Army, said: "When the NKVD task squads appeared, they helped us restore order in the rear. Until then the situation in the rear was deplorable."[98] His 13th Army also began shooting deserters in January.

Draconian measures had actually started "from below" in December 1939; only later were they adopted by higher headquarters. Division and regiment commanders did not wait for the *Stavka* to tell them to take severe measures to keep the men in line. The 315th Rifle Regiment, for example, executed five men in the first four weeks of the war—not out of hand, but after proceedings before duly convened tribunals. One soldier was shot for "accidentally" shooting and killing one man and wounding another while "cleaning his rifle." Another was executed for refusing to fire his weapon at the enemy even after being directly ordered to do so by his company commander. Three other soldiers were shot for intentionally wounding themselves.[99]

On 16 December, General Ponedelin assumed command of the 139th Rifle Division after the disgraced General Beliaev was dismissed. Ponedelin's first act as commander was to create penal (*shtrafnyi*) companies of cowards and men who had panicked under fire.[100] When General Kurdiumov found out about it, he rebuked Ponedelin; however, when Kurdiumov was removed a few weeks later, his replacement, General Shtern, endorsed Ponedelin's repressive measures. It is unknown how serious the desertion or shirking problem was, as the number of men detained by these detachments and their fates were not recorded. In the end, we have no way of knowing whether such "firm" measures contributed to the army's effectiveness, because shortly thereafter the Red Army poured in massive reinforcements of men and materiel and changed its strategy and tactics.

The Big Picture of the Soviet "Defeat" in Finland

In addition to military and domestic issues, diplomatic problems loomed larger and larger for the USSR the longer the conflict lasted. Anti-Soviet sentiment became more vocal abroad, coupled with rising international sympathy for the Finns. Fueled by international indignation and acrimony over the invasion, the League of Nations expelled the USSR on 14 December 1939. Overtly motivated by anti-Soviet sentiment, foreign aid for Finland increased steadily as the war dragged on. Shipments of arms, supplies, and volunteers from Europe and the United States arrived weekly in 1940.[101] Thus, besides the military difficulties, it is likely that negative foreign and domestic factors had a considerable influence on Stalin's decision to reduce his war aims and press for an early end to the war.

Stalin held on to his minimum acceptable goals but wisely abandoned his maximum goals, the pursuit of which would have prolonged the war and ensured the lasting enmity of Britain and the United States. Had he chosen to keep going, however, it is more than likely that the Red Army would have gotten a second wind and conquered Finland, absent foreign intervention. Stalin forced his generals to stick with it until they could deliver victory, and the generals in turn kept the troops closely engaged with the Finns while revising their strategy and assembling more forces. Even Stalin, for all his ruthlessness and cynicism, recognized that there were limits to the use of heavy-handed methods. The key methods used by Soviet authorities to keep the men fighting were appeals to patriotism and duty, based on portrayals of the war as just and necessary, and brutal but selective punishment of noncompliance, desertion, and cowardice.

As noted earlier, the fact that army leaders and the vast majority of individual soldiers never lost the desire to impose their will on the enemy was what maintained the Red Army during the Winter War. Even when surrounded and facing annihilation, when capitulation appeared warranted and perseverance seemed to offer only senseless death, Soviet troops almost never surrendered. Overall, the military's staying power proved robust; soldiers kept fighting, and regiments remained cohesive. Most important, the army did not fall apart or take flight en masse. Morale ebbed at times, but it did not break in the face of massive casualties, adverse weather conditions, supply failures, and poor leadership and training. The *Stavka*, together with the political leadership, was able to abandon its failed original plan and devise a new, successful war-fighting strategy and set new war aims, which succeeded in the end.

Part 2

SURRENDER OR CAPTURE:

A NEW APPRECIATION

3
New Perspectives on the Great Encirclements of 1941

This chapter addresses the apparent failure in the Red Army's effectiveness as reflected in the Wehrmacht's capture of roughly 3 million Soviet soldiers in the initial campaigns of 1941. Those events, in terms of the scale of prisoners taken, are unprecedented in the history of warfare. They are examined in the context of the historical debate over whether those captures were due to German military expertise, which would indicate Soviet *inefficiency*, or due to anti-Stalinist political motivations by those who laid down their arms, which would be a measure of military *ineffectiveness*.

Identifying the causes and motives that led to the surrenders is vital for any analysis of this cataclysm, because surrender connotes a voluntary act in which combatants reject further resistance, even though it may be possible, and lose the will to fight. In that sense, surrender offers an index of military ineffectiveness. From ancient times, it was often accepted that compelling circumstances could make surrender an honorable act. For example, when lack of ammunition, food, or water or ineffective or absent leadership robbed the men of the means to resist successfully, continued fighting would result in useless deaths. Under many of the laws and customs of war, choosing to fight on in a hopeless situation, or after a formal call to surrender to the besieged,was seen as martyrdom or fanaticism rather than duty. During the twentieth century (and, arguably, since the early modern period or the Renaissance), soldiers throughout the world, as well as many observers, came to view surrender as generally unworthy. With the rise of nationalism and increasingly virulent ideologies, surrender came to be considered cowardly, treasonous, or immoral.

A question not previously examined is what should be made of the fact that so few men surrendered or were captured in the Winter War in contrast to the vast number who became captives during the Great Patriotic

War, especially its opening phase. If motivation is taken as the critical factor, one could interpret the Finnish case to mean that soldiers consciously supported the Stalinist state; or, one might view the huge number of captives taken by the Germans in 1941 to mean that soldiers rejected Stalinism. During the Winter War, out of approximately 700,000 Soviet combat and combat-support troops involved, fewer than 5,500 Red Army men (0.7 percent) ended up in captivity. By comparison, during the war with Nazi Germany, approximately 3 million out of fewer than 8 million soldiers in the battle area became captives between June and December 1941 (37.5 percent).[1] The numbers, however, are not the point. Obviously, the Germans' use of armored formations intent on encircling vast numbers of Soviet soldiers led to more opportunities to take prisoners than did the mostly linear infantry war in forested Finland. The point is to analyze the behavior of Soviet soldiers faced with the prospect of capture in encirclements.

In the grand paradox noted in chapter 1, people sometimes fight for regimes they do not support, or they may choose not to fight for regimes they do support. Therefore, soldiers' inner feelings about the regime cannot be precisely metered, certainly not to the extent needed to determine whether they are the primary factor in the decision to either fight or surrender. This is not to dismiss the influence of soldiers' feelings about the state but to suggest that they are only one element in a complexity of factors that must be considered. These factors include social integration, individual and group psychology, tactics and doctrine, and the immediate circumstances on the battlefield. This chapter suggests that there are multiple reasons why troops were captured at a higher rate by the Germans in 1941 than by the Finns in 1939–1940. They include antiregime sentiment, German tactical doctrine and its skillful implementation, flawed Soviet doctrine, poor Soviet military leadership, civilian political interference, and chaotic battlefield conditions that often left soldiers leaderless, disorganized, and inadequately armed.

A Reconsideration of the Great Encirclements

In analyzing this phase of the war in the east, it is crucial to understand at the outset that the great encirclements of Soviet units were part of the

German invaders' tactical design. The initial phase of the German attack on the USSR, code-named Operation Barbarossa, was intended to destroy major elements of the Red Army deployed in the Baltic States, Belorussia, and Ukraine before moving to capture Leningrad and Moscow. The Wehrmacht high command planned a series of double envelopments in Belorussia and Ukraine designed to capture Soviet soldiers by the hundreds of thousands. The first of those major encirclements occurred only eight days into the campaign at the expense of the Western Front commanded by General of the Army Dmitrii Pavlov. German Army Group Center sent Panzer Group 3 racing from the Soviet border more than 200 miles eastward to the Berezina River, penetrating or shattering improvised Soviet defenses along the way as the Germans headed to invest the Belorussian city of Minsk from the north. At the same time, the corresponding pincer of Panzer Group 2 closed in on Minsk from the south, obliterating the Soviet 4th Army in its path.

In between these two armored thrusts, three German armies, composed primarily of infantry divisions, compressed Red Army units into a large pocket just to the west of Minsk. When Pavlov recognized the threat of impending encirclement and realized his inability to prevent it, he ordered his armies to withdraw to the east. Breakdowns in communication, however, prevented many units from receiving those orders. The lack of fuel for their vehicles and the relentless pressure by German forces thwarted the escape of most of the 400,000-plus soldiers of the 3rd, 10th, and 13th Soviet Armies of the Western Front.[2]

After only two more weeks, the Western Front virtually disintegrated in the face of the German onslaught as Army Group Center pushed on toward Smolensk. In a response akin to that of the 44th Rifle Division disaster in the Winter War, Stalin personally ordered the arrest and trial of those he deemed responsible for the calamity. Pavlov was relieved of his command on 29 June and ordered to report to Moscow; an investigation ensued. The investigators, including the widely disliked chief of GlavPUR, Lev Mekhlis, concluded that the following men were culpable: General Pavlov, his chief of staff Major General V. Klimovskii, his chief of signals Major General A. Grigor'ev, 4th Army commander Major General A. Korobkov, 41st Rifle Corps commander Major General I. Kosobutskii, 60th Mountain Rifle Division commander Major General M. Selikhov and his commissar I. Kurochkii, and 30th Rifle Division commander Major General S. Galaktionov and his commissar I. Eliseev. On 16 July, on behalf of the State Committee for Defense (GKO), Stalin formally accused Pavlov and members of his staff of panicking and losing control of their forces.[3] After a short trial, the Military Collegium of the USSR Supreme Court convicted Pavlov, Grigor'ev, Klimovskii, Korobkov, and Galaktionov of cowardice, and all five were executed by firing squad. The court sentenced Kosobutskii and Selikhov to ten years in prison. The two commissars, Kurochkii and Eliseev, were reassigned.[4] On 27 July a copy of the report detailing Pavlov's and the others' failures, and the consequences, was provided to unit commanders or commissars to read to their men.[5]

An interesting aspect of the handling and manipulation of Pavlov's case was the way Stalin used it to change his relationship with the armed forces. The first report on Pavlov's case, prepared by the NKVD, couched everything in a political framework reminiscent of the purges. Pavlov's links to men repressed in the purges were highlighted, as was his activity in Spain, where he had the opportunity to contact Trotskyites and other enemy elements.[6] Stalin quashed this line of investigation and redirected it toward Pavlov's military performance in the field, professional behavior, and courage. It was in these areas that Stalin—unjustly—claimed Pavlov had failed. This freed officers from the fear of guilt by association with enemies of the people and the no-win situation of trying to defend themselves against fictitious charges of political unreliability. It also was an important first step in restoring confidence in the officer corps' political reliability in the eyes of the soldiery. During the difficult months of retreat in 1941, soldiers often voiced concern that their officers were traitors and that the purges had not gotten rid of all the enemies of the people. Now officers would be held accountable for their performance in the field, which they had some control over, and the NKVD would not automatically generate charges of treason in cases of military failure.

It appeared that Stalin not only sought scapegoats for the shortcomings that might be attributed to the regime but also wanted to make a grim example of his senior officers to counter any defeatist attitudes or behaviors. Whether his officers were truly defeatist is unknown; however, it is evident that at every turn they counseled retreat—in most cases, wisely. These constant appeals—often made with a good deal of emotion—seem to have worn on Stalin's nerves. Subsequently, in his capacity as head of the *Stavka*, Stalin published Order No. 270 on 16 August 1941, warning officers of severe penalties if their failures could be construed as cowardice. In this order, Stalin gave examples of the heroic efforts of several surrounded units that had fought their way out of encirclement against huge odds and purportedly inflicted heavy casualties on the Germans in the process. In one example, Pavlov's deputy commander, General-Lieutenant Boldin, organized the remnants of various destroyed divisions that then fought their way through the German rear for forty-five days until they reached Red Army lines. In another instance, 1,778 survivors of 8th Mechanized Corps and the 406th Rifle Regiment managed to reach Soviet lines more than 650 kilometers away.

The main point of the order, however implicit, was that other generals had failed to follow in the courageous path of these exemplars. *Stavka* accused General-Lieutenant Kachalov, commander of 28th Army, General-Lieutenant Ponedelin, commander of 12th Army, and Major General Kirillov, commander of 13th Rifle Corps, of failing to mount escape attempts. When Stalin heard reports that most of the troops under these commanders had been captured without offering serious resistance, he judged that the three cowardly generals had voluntarily gone over to the enemy, even though Kachalov had actually been killed in action. In a similar vein, Stalin accused Kirillov of fleeing the field of battle before his capture. From this episode came the harsh penalties of Order No. 270, which included the arrest of the families of officers or commissars who deserted the battlefield or allowed themselves to be captured. Furthermore, division commanders were ordered to immediately relieve any officers who were not up to their tasks, shoot them on the spot, if necessary, and replace them with capable junior officers or the best of the enlisted ranks.[7]

Assaying this phase of the war in the east is not much easier now than it was for Stalin and his lieutenants. A great many observers in the USSR and throughout the world saw the Red Army's collapse as highly likely. Even the foes of the Third Reich were willing to give the Wehrmacht and its allies full due for a stunning martial success. Effective planning, leadership, training, and equipment, put to use in blitzkrieg tactics, had overwhelmed the unevenly prepared and poorly led Soviet defense. At the same time, it was not clear exactly why the Red Army, despite obvious signs that war was imminent and after taking serious steps to bolster the western defenses, proved unable to react efficiently.

Arguably, the Soviets' most significant disadvantage was that the Germans had the initiative. The Soviet high command was left to guess where and when the enemy would strike and what the objectives might be. It often proved impossible to mass sufficient forces at the right place and at the right time to intercept and defeat the Axis assault. At the outset, the Luftwaffe (German air force) interdicted Soviet aerial reconnaissance efforts, denying the Soviet high command a clear picture of the Germans' movements before they made contact with the Red Army. German bombing raids destroyed telephone lines and radios and often killed commanders and their staffs. Soviet units often ran out of fuel and ammunition because of extended maneuvering and fighting. Logistical elements often failed to keep up due to poor planning, disrupted communications, or the destruction of transport—or all three. Even when combat units reached their intended destinations in a timely fashion, they often arrived in piecemeal formations, sometimes without artillery or lacking armor, with little or no ammunition, and out of contact with higher headquarters. That allowed the Germans to overwhelm Red Army units in short order with their local superiority in armor, artillery, and tactical airpower.

Following its victory at Minsk, the Wehrmacht's Army Group Center sent its forces onward toward Moscow, with Smolensk as the intermediate objective. Once again, Panzer Group 3 swung to the north of the Minsk-Moscow highway and swept around behind Smolensk; meanwhile, Panzer Group 2 attacked from the south, joining 2nd Army's infantry to conduct significant encircling operations at Roslavl, Krichev, and Gomel' that netted 116,000 prisoners. The two panzer groups and their supporting infantry armies finally closed the ring around Soviet General Rokossovskii's 16th and 20th Armies on 23 July, although the city proper had fallen on 16 July. The Red Army made truly heroic efforts to relieve the entrapped armies, including a successful but short-lived offensive at El'nia. This convinced the Wehrmacht to delay its drive on Moscow and instead secure Ukraine by destroying the Southwest Front and seizing Kiev.[8] The resultant loss of roughly a quarter million soldiers and their equipment also obviously depleted the Western Front's resources.

The widely publicized German triumph at Smolensk, and the Soviets' subsequent ferocious relief attempts, led to the greatest of all the Wehrmacht's catastrophic encirclements of Russian forces in the September 1941 battle for Kiev. It was obvious to the high command that Kiev would soon become a target, so it declared the city and its environs a fortified area and began to bolster its fixed defenses and personnel.[9] As Army Group Center maintained its eastward momentum, Army Group South struck southeast, and by the first week of August it was poised to strike across the Dnepr southeast of Kiev. With that goal in mind, Army Group South launched a frontal assault on Kiev in July but failed to make headway against formidable fixed defenses and gave up the attempt. Nevertheless, as the German Seventeenth Army swung south of the city, it encircled and destroyed twenty Soviet divisions near Uman. Now Kiev was a westward-pointing salient between Army Group Center to the north and Army Group South to the south in another grand exposure of sizable Russian forces to a double envelopment.

The *Stavka* recognized the danger of the situation and strove to shore up the flanks of the bulge, but to no avail. Hitler, against the wishes of some of his generals, postponed the attack on Moscow and directed Panzer Group 2 and Second Army straight south to get behind Kiev, while Army Group South's Seventeenth Army and Panzer Group 1 forced the Dnepr at Kremenchug and headed north to link up with Panzer Group 2. As early as mid-August, General Georgi Zhukov, chief of the General Staff, had seen the danger, and he advised Stalin in early September to abandon Kiev and pull out of the salient. Stalin forthwith dismissed Zhukov.

After a two-week battle, it became clear to Marshal Semen Budennyi, commander of the Southwest Front near Kiev, that his forces could not stop the German pincer movement from the south and that General Eremenko, commander of the Central Front, could not stop the thrust from the north. Budennyi asked Stalin to authorize the abandonment of Kiev to save his armies. A furious Stalin reacted by firing his longtime crony and replacing him with Marshal Semen Timoshenko, victor of the Winter War. Order No. 270 failed to deter Soviet commanders in the field from asking to retreat when necessary, and they did not fear fatal repercussions from questioning Stalin's orders.

Without sufficient forces, especially armor, Timoshenko fared no better than Budennyi. The trap around Kiev closed on 14 September when the vanguards of Panzer Groups 1 and 2 linked up, having trapped five Soviet armies. Only at 11:30 PM on 17 September, in a vaguely worded message, did Stalin authorize a withdrawal from Kiev east across the Dnepr, with orders to destroy the bridges and military installations.[10] This order was distinctly unhelpful, considering that the bulk of forces in the encirclement were already east of the Dnepr. The city fell within twenty-four hours.

The commander of the surrounded Red Army forces, General Mikhail Kirponos, was killed during the attempt to break out. Thousands of officers and men, including many senior generals, managed to escape the encirclement, but there was no coordinated attempt to withdraw on a large scale. Coherent command and control did not exist within the pocket, and the five armies had never been commanded as a unified whole by Kirponos, Budennyi, or Timoshenko. When the situation deteriorated and the word to flee was given, chaos ensued. Units randomly and vainly sought holes in the unyielding German line. Finding none, it became every man for himself. The exact number of soldiers captured is unclear; the Wehrmacht claimed 677,000 captives taken, and the Soviets claimed that 526,500 were lost.[11] Whatever the actual number, in Moscow and throughout the world, the Kiev debacle was viewed as a crack of doom in the east.

The collapse of the Stalinist regime was thought to be imminent, especially as the situation worsened. More large-scale encirclements took place in October. On 6 October, in south Russia, as the Germans drove east toward Rostov, Panzer Group 1 and Eleventh Army surrounded and captured about 100,000 soldiers from the Red Army's 9th and 18th Armies. The next day, as Hitler ordered the advance on Moscow to resume, four Soviet armies on the Western Front, the 16th, 19th, 20th, and 24th, were encircled near Viaz'ma, partly due to Stalin's refusal to grant his commanders operational freedom to withdraw when faced with envelopment. The following day, 8 October, as part of the same operation, German forces surrounded three more Soviet armies, the 3rd, 13th, and 50th, in the vicinity of Briansk. There was a slight shift in the tactical balance at this point, however, as the 3rd and 50th Armies maintained their cohesion and punched through a weak point in the German lines. The 13th Army also fought its way out, but through a much more heavily de-

POWs captured in the Kiev encirclement, September 1941.

fended sector of the front.[12] All told, well over 600,000 Soviet soldiers were surrounded, but, during the next few weeks, tens of thousands of them managed to escape the trap or become partisans in the forests and swamps.[13]

When the German army tried to emulate the grand encirclements of 1941 during its summer 1942 offensive into Ukraine, the task proved beyond its capacity. The Germans once again sent fast-moving panzer forces crashing into Soviet lines, then turned them to surround and capture the disrupted units; however, Stalin was now prepared to let Red Army commanders withdraw before it was too late. As a result, the scale of Wehrmacht triumphs shrank dramatically. For example, when some units of the 9th and 38th Armies were surrounded near Millerovo, Ukraine, in July, as were part of the 12th and 18th Armies north of Rostov, only about 54,000 prisoners were taken.[14] Apparently, a simple change in attitude at the top of the Soviet military hierarchy substantially improved the Red Army's battlefield performance. Yet this does not explain the behavior of the trapped units in 1941, especially why attempts to break out from the largest encirclements so often failed, why so many men were captured, and why so few escaped. It is certainly no simple matter to interpret how much of that collapse was due to tactical deficiency, to a contagion of fear and panic, or to a form of political expression.

The Encirclement Issue: Differences between the Winter and Great Patriotic Wars

To the extent that the massive collapses of 1941 can be seen as a sign of military ineffectiveness, an analysis of the Winter War becomes essential. Yet that causal link has never been traced, nor has anyone suggested that the tenacity of the *mottis* reflected a commitment to Soviet power. Can we assume that the experience of encirclement in the Winter War had at least some effect on the behavior of encircled units in the Great Patriotic War? It is, of course, very difficult to determine why specific units or individuals chose not to break out, why they lost so much equipment and suffered such heavy casualties when they did try, and how and why leadership broke down in the major encirclements, causing panic to set in. We also have to ask what lessons the Red Army took from the experience of encirclement in the Winter War and what role this played in 1941. Finally, we have to look to the highest levels of the armed forces to see how encirclement doctrine and the *Stavka* may have influenced the flow of events.

Comparing the Winter War and the Great Patriotic War experiences requires an examination of Red Army doctrine regarding encirclement, which turns out to have been a blend of formal definitions and informal practices. Most pertinently, neither the temporary field regulations of 1936 nor those of 1939 dedicated a single paragraph to handling encirclements. They mentioned encircling the enemy on offensive operations, but that is all.

In 1939 unit commanders understood that if their units were surrounded, their immediate task was to break out of the encirclement and rejoin friendly forces to the rear. As General Boris Shaposhnikov of the General Staff noted at a postwar conference on the lessons of the Winter War, this maneuver was regularly practiced in many pre–Winter War war games. "All our training problems devoted much time to fighting in encirclement and breaking out of encirclement," he said. "This was the favorite subject of our games. This was done in all military schools, it was played everywhere, one encircled, the other broke out." He complained, however, that those skills disappeared when the war began. "Troops were encircled but there was no breaking out of encirclement," he lamented.[15] General Kurdiumov refuted Shaposhnikov by insisting that it was "a big minus in our manuals that, while we have paid attention to defenses and the guarding of flanks and junctions, we have not taught the troops how to act properly in encirclement."[16] General Meretskov later added that the problem was unit commanders' passivity: once surrounded, they just hunkered down and waited for someone to save them. He assessed the deficiency as a lack of initiative, not a lack of training.[17] In summary, despite the absence of a well-defined Red Army policy on how to respond to encirclement by a foe before the war with Finland, it was clear that the Red Army viewed encirclement not as a blunder or a crime but as a normative contingency in the conduct of wartime operations.

In April 1940 a clear sense of how Stalin felt about encirclements and how he expected the army to act in the future seemed to emerge during a joint session of the army and the Central Committee of the Communist Party (henceforth referred to as the April Conference). Furthermore, precedents were set regarding the consequences for failing to break out of encirclements during the Winter War. One session of the April Conference included an intense discussion of envelopment, which cited two examples of gross failure. The first was the twin disasters of the 163rd and 44th Rifle Divisions of 9th Army located at Finland's midsection during late December 1939 through early January 1940 (mentioned in chapter 2), and the second was the plight of the 18th Rifle Division and 34th Light Tank Brigade of 8th Army caught in a pocket north of Lake Ladoga.

In the first phase of 9th Army's attempt to cut Finland in two, the 163rd Rifle Division attacked west and then turned south to capture the town of Suomussalmi and its important road junction. The 44th Rifle Division drove west along the Raate road toward the same objective, striving to link up with the 163rd. First, the Finns, in a series of battalion-sized assaults, attacked the 163rd while it was strung out on the road, tearing it to pieces; then they did the same to the 44th. The Finns successfully destroyed the division command, two of the 163rd's rifle regiments, and accompanying artillery and support troops, while taking several thousand prisoners. The last two Soviet regiments to be attacked were closest to the border—the 662nd Rifle Regiment and the 3rd NKVD Regiment. Investigators determined that while they were under attack, with encirclement imminent, the 662nd Regiment's commander, Sharov, and the commissar, Podkhomutov, abandoned the regiment and fled with a handful of soldiers.[18] In their absence, regimental chief of staff Captain Rodin took over conduct of the defense and later led the regiment in a successful fighting breakout. For their cowardly flight, Sharov and Podkhomutov were executed, but not summarily. Rather, they were arrested on 30 December 1939 and accused of cowardice and panic. A formal investigation was conducted, testimony from witnesses was taken, and a military tribunal delivered the verdict. (Such would be the procedure for Pavlov and others in 1941.) They were executed in front of their men on 12 January 1940.

In the case of the 44th Rifle Division, the Finns encircled and divided the road-bound division into several *mottis* during intense fighting, all the while inflicting heavy casualties. Forbidding an immediate breakout, the *Stavka* ordered 9th Army commander General Dukhanov to send a relief expedition. Dukhanov was told that he would be held personally responsible for the success of the mission and that "neither one heavy weapon nor a single machine gun would be left in the hands of the enemy."[19] Dukhanov lacked sufficient forces to mount an effective relief effort, but to show the *Stavka* that he was trying, he threw ski battalions into battle as they became available. Nothing but casualties resulted. After nearly a week of fighting, the division managed to fight its way out, but with only 1,000 men remaining in each regiment. Beyond the severe loss of materiel, including all the division's artillery, tanks, and wheeled transport and hundreds of machine guns, 40 percent of the men who made it out had abandoned their rifles.[20] The division was destroyed.

The loss of equipment was so heavy because of Finnish tactics, difficult terrain, and poor decision making on the part of 9th Army leadership. Because the division was surrounded, it could not be resupplied with fuel; thus, the tanks and motor vehicles ran out of gas, which meant the loss of artillery towed by these vehicles. At the same time, horse-drawn artillery was lost because the horses were killed in combat, froze to death, or starved for lack of fodder. The 44th Rifle Division was surrounded by the thick forest, heavy snow, and hillocks, so when the Finns blocked the road, any heavy equipment that might have been muscled out by human effort had to be abandoned. Because 9th Army had delayed the order to break out, the scattered artillery and tanks were useless to the encircled forces and could not be brought to bear in the breakout effort. It was unfair of the *Stavka* to blame the division command for the extensive loss of equipment, and the order to bring it all out, issued from a warm office in Moscow, was unreasonable and unrealistic.

Even though the 44th Rifle Division's commander, Vinogradov, managed to extricate his division's remnants from the encirclement under incredibly adverse conditions, he, his chief of staff Volkovym, and his commissar Pakhomenko faced the same fate as the leaders of the 163rd. All were arrested, and, following an investigation, a military tribunal convicted them of negligence and overall failure of leadership and ordered their execution. Simultaneously, General Dashichev, the commander of 47th Corps, which commanded the two divisions, was reduced to the rank of colonel and relieved of his command. General Dukhanov, 9th Army commander, was also relieved of his command but not demoted.

The case of the encircled 18th Rifle Division and 34th Light Tank Brigade differed somewhat. The two units, acting in tandem, became encircled in January 1940. The Finns immediately cut them into thirteen separate *mottis* of varying sizes. As in the case of the 44th Rifle Division a few weeks earlier, the *Stavka* withheld permission to break out. General

Shaposhnikov, chiding 8th Army for overestimating the Finns' strength, insisted that only one hard "fist" was required to punch through the enemy.[21] He urged 8th Army to avoid "the disgrace experienced by the 44th Rifle Division." In the end, it turned out that the *Stavka* had underestimated the Finns' strength. Although the Finns were not strong enough to destroy the rifle division and tank brigade all at once, they eventually concentrated their forces long enough to annihilate the smaller *mottis* and most of the 34th Light Tank Brigade.

The 18th Rifle Division ended up holding out for a month before attempting to break out. During that time, the Finns took the high ground and key terrain without a fight. General Kurdiumov noted at the April Conference: "Anarchy reigned in the [encircled] garrison. The commanders of the 18th Rifle Division and the 34th Light Tank Brigade actually gave up trying and only sent panicked telegrams to all and sundry." At the critical moment when the detachments broke out of the encirclement on the night of 28–29 February, the two commanders delegated command to their chiefs of staff.[22] General S. I. Kondrat'ev, commander of the 34th Light Tank Brigade, escaped the encirclement but soon thereafter lost his life to a firing squad for negligence and cowardice.[23] Not until July did an army tribunal convict the commander of the 18th Rifle Division, Grigorii F. Kondrashov, of treasonous and negligent handling of his unit.

Waiting so long to break out made doing so all the more difficult because the men suffered extreme hunger and were greatly weakened by the lack of food. At the time of the breakout, the main *motti* of the 18th Rifle Division was down to 1,237 men, of whom about 900 were wounded or frostbitten.[24] A month before the breakout, a sergeant of the 34th Light Tank Brigade wrote in his diary: "Today we received one biscuit weighing 15 grams and watery pea soup. Before dinner I felt weak. My legs trembled and I could barely see. When I went to the kitchen, my legs gave way and I felt that I could hardly stand on my feet. We keep alive as before, on horsemeat, but now it is dangerous to eat much, and food without salt is like grass. Several comrades are suffering stomach ailments."[25] Physical weakness and clouded minds tremendously undermined the men's fighting capacity and reduced their chances of success.

The anarchy Kurdiumov referred to seems to have been rampant among the commanders rather than the soldiers. At the April Conference, Commissar Vashugin reported that Kondrat'ev, commander of the 34th Light Tank Brigade, had suggested they break out without waiting for the 18th Rifle Division to prepare and abandon all heavy equipment. As the Finnish encirclement tightened, the leadership of the 18th Rifle Division panicked. Despite their initial intent to hold out, a few days later they asked 8th Army headquarters for permission to break out. While waiting for that assent, officers in the various *mottis* sent pathetic radio messages to 8th Army, like that of Chief of the Special Section (NKVD) Moskovskii and his deputy, Solovev: "We are done for, please issue our March pay to our families, send our greetings, etc." Another from an unnamed signal officer said, "The day is against us, we are perishing, greetings to all."[26] The most notable aspect of all these cases is that even when the leaders thought they were facing certain death, they did not consider surrender.

Overall, the tenor of the April Conference was that unit commanders who became encircled were somehow deficient, as were their superiors who failed to extricate them in good order and in a timely fashion—definitely a shift from the prewar outlook. The informal lessons the Red Army hierarchy took from the Winter War regarding encirclements were as follows: commanders were not to panic or lose control over their forces; units were expected to break out, but only with permission; when breaking out, units were expected to bring their equipment with them; although relief efforts would be mounted, encircled forces should not count on them getting through; and punishment awaited those who lost their heads. Subsequent to the April Conference, the Red Army produced training guidelines and established the emphasis of training for the summer of 1940, based on the experience of the Winter War. This training consisted of attack and defense of fortified areas, night training, and use of armor and cavalry on the flanks. Dealing with encirclements, however, was conspicuously absent.[27]

Between the 1940 April Conference and June 1941, additional thought was given to the issue of encirclement in a future, more mobile form of warfare. In October 1940 A. I. Starunin, in an article in *Voennaia mysl'*, the military's leading theoretical journal, argued that in mechanized warfare, mobility is crucial. Surrounded forces, therefore, ought to initially accept encirclement and consolidate an all-around defense of vital road and river crossings to deny the enemy the means to efficiently conduct further offensive operations. By drawing the opponent's forces into an attempt to seize key transportation nodes, the encircled forces would buy time for relief to arrive.[28] Starunin's idea, however, never became doctrine, and it is unknown how many officers read it, agreed with it, or later translated it into action. However, the General Staff read and approved of it, inasmuch as *Voennaia mysl'* was published under its authority.

Had the high command recognized the potential usefulness of encircled forces in slowing down mechanized forces through determined defense, the mass captures of Soviet soldiers in 1941 and 1942 would have been less likely. Although the Wehrmacht's grand envelopments from July to October 1941 surrounded hundreds of thousands of Red Army troops that were seemingly capable of creating fighting pockets, only two such pockets—Brest and Mogilev—matched the resistance of those formed in the Winter War.

The three major battles of encirclement in the Great Patriotic War noted earlier—the battles for Minsk, Smolensk, and Kiev in 1941—might have changed the course of the war if the Soviet leadership, both military and political, had been willing to take the risk of employing this tactic on a large scale.[29] In late 1941, however, the generals and Stalin had apparently lost their nerve when commanding large numbers of men. They became accustomed to ordering encircled units, large or small, to break out without considering whether key terrain was at stake. Thus, when it came to the truly vital urban locales of Minsk, Smolensk, and Kiev, the *Stavka* could not change its habit of withdrawing to a "more defensible" position. With the exceptions of Brest and Mogilev, the *Stavka* ordered every unit encircled in summer 1941 to break out.

Reassessing the Disasters at Minsk, Smolensk, and Kiev

The encirclements of the Winter War provide perspective on the debacles of the late summer and autumn of 1941. Obviously, the scale of the encirclements made command and control more difficult in 1941. Units were under sustained artillery and aerial bombardment and strafing in an unanticipated crescendo of violence. This compounded stress, fear, and confusion at all levels, within the pockets and outside them. The destruction of much of the Red Air Force made the situation more difficult physically and psychologically. Some things, however, had changed that might have mitigated these German advantages. Because so many Red Army units, both large and small, were being surrounded, the stigma of being encircled quickly faded. The Soviet high command now reacted far more quickly in giving commanders permission to break out—sometimes within hours of a unit being surrounded—and in organizing powerful relief forces. These changes greatly facilitated breakouts, as encircled units sometimes found weak spots in the German lines before they could be reinforced. In addition, the *Stavka* stopped requiring units to bring out all their heavy equipment and concentrated on getting the units out as cohesively as possible.

Some of the lessons the high command assimilated in the months between March 1940 and June 1941, but which were not enshrined in doctrinal change or the Timoshenko reforms of 1940, are evident in the encirclements of the 87th and 124th Rifle Divisions in June 1941.[30] From 22 to 24 June 1941, two regiments of the 87th Rifle Division and the entire 124th Rifle Division were cut off in separate encirclements by German forces. When apprised of the situation on 23 June, the commander of 5th Army, Major General Mikhail Potapov, who was experiencing encirclement for the first time, radioed Southwest Front headquarters for instructions. Southwest Front referred the matter to the very top—the *Stavka* in Moscow. On 24 June Southwest Front passed down the *Stavka*'s orders verbatim: "Leave your equipment, bury it, and with small arms fight your way through the woods to Kovel'."[31] In the attempt to comply, the 283rd Rifle Regiment of the 87th Rifle Division was destroyed, with only 200 soldiers reaching friendly lines. The other regiment tried but failed to break out and held on for several more days with ever-dwindling stocks of food and ammunition. It was never heard from again.

Meanwhile, the 124th Rifle Division had suffered heavy losses from German ground and air attacks, including the serious wounding of its commander and the death of the division commissar. It had also lost communications with corps headquarters, so it probably never got the order from 5th Army. The survivors decided to break out anyway on the night of the twenty-fourth, but the attempt failed. The division remained encircled, and fighting at close quarters continued. A relief effort by 8th Mechanized Corps failed, and eventually the 124th Rifle Division succumbed to the Germans.[32]

Perhaps because of the Winter War experience, the commanders of 5th Army and Southwest Front hesitated to take action, deferring to Moscow. The *Stavka*, however, reacted immediately to the situation, authorizing breakouts and freeing commanders from the burden of evacuating heavy equipment. The officers of these two divisions maintained control and cohesion, even to the point of their units' annihilation. Despite the loss of communications and eventually any hope of relief, these two divisions did not simply surrender, and their leaders did not give up. It is unknown how many soldiers survived as prisoners of the Germans.

These examples foreshadowed the debacles at Minsk, Smolensk, and Kiev. In considering the latter cases, it should be recognized that even though hundreds of thousands of men were captured, it cannot be assumed that there were mass surrenders. Due in large part to the fog of war and the subsequent loss of documentation, there is no evidence that whole divisions or armies either spontaneously or by order laid down their arms in these great encirclements. The roots of these three disasters can be traced to the Soviet command structure. Reflecting the preference of most European armies at the time, the basic problem lay in Soviet doctrine, which ordained an active rather than a static defense, fighting and maneuvering in the open field, and avoiding close combat in cities. Ultimately, as noted earlier, the problem extended to the very top in Moscow, where Stalin refused to let commanders fall back to avoid encirclement. This produced a predictable reflex—breaking out from encirclement as a matter of course. This mentality of breaking out rather than holding out denied the Red Army the opportunity to stop the blitzkrieg. If encircled forces had held key terrain, rail and road networks, and bridges, they could have tied up significant numbers of German forces, delaying their advance while they worked to reduce the encircled forces. In the meantime, the Soviets would have denied the Wehrmacht the use of vital transportation and communications hubs, admittedly at the risk of large numbers of men.

In 1941 Minsk was a city of tremendous strategic importance. As capital of the Belorussian republic and headquarters of the Belorussian Communist Party, it had a prewar population of 300,000 and scores of factories. Most important, its location as the westernmost city on the highway to Moscow (the one used by Napoleon in 1812) made it the key to Smolensk—the gateway to Moscow. Minsk is situated on the Svislach River, at the intersection of the highway and rail lines linking the city to Baranovichi and Brest to the southwest and with Smolensk to the northeast. A highway running northwest to Vil'nius and a railway to Gomel' to the southeast also pass through it. Thus, in the eyes of the German war planners, the capture of Minsk was essential for their drive on Moscow. They needed the highways, the railroads, the bridges, and the airfield to facilitate and sustain their momentum eastward. The Germans had seized all these by the fifth day of the war, despite the efforts of three Soviet armies, the 3rd, 10th, and 13th, composed of fifteen divisions, including two armored divisions and a tank brigade, assigned to defend the city.

On 1 July all three Soviet armies were trapped in an area shaped like a parallelogram with a frontage of approximately 150 miles, bounded on all sides by highways, each under the control of German forces. As Operation Barbarossa began, the Germans swung around these armies to capture Minsk on 26 June. The Soviets had positioned themselves in front of Minsk, hoping to intercept a head-on attack.[33] Instead, once the Germans held Minsk behind the Soviet field forces, more than twenty German divisions pressed on the collected armies, driving them together. The Germans were aided by the Soviets' first major strategic error—not defending the city of Minsk proper. In keeping with Red Army doctrine, which called for a fight in the field, not a battle for the city, the road and rail bridges around Minsk had not been mined, nor had the power plant been prepared for demolition.

The second critical mistake came when the three Soviet army commanders asked for permission to break out, in keeping with informal doctrine but contrary to Starunin's vision. The Western Front commander, General Pavlov, and Moscow complied. Each army acted to break out separately, compounding the mistake. One army attempted to break out across the Minsk-Vil'nius highway, another in the opposite direction across the Minsk-Baranovichi highway toward Baranovichi, and the third to the west. Three separate jabs, rather than one solid punch, ensured that the Soviet soldiers would be outnumbered and outgunned wherever they turned. No unit breaking out had the objective of the vital city of Minsk. Although General Eremenko mounted a relief effort from the east, on the far side of Minsk, none of the breakout attempts was directed to meet it. General Pavlov had approved all these measures, but he failed to name an officer within the ring to command the encircled forces. He simply did not consider the possibility of treating the assembled armies as one maneuverable unit that could do more than escape, but neither did anyone else.

As a consequence, the Nazis successfully parried the Red Army's attempts at relief and escape. The Germans mercilessly pounded the surrounded Red Army soldiers with continuous artillery bombardments unlike anything seen during the Winter War. At the same time, the Luftwaffe disrupted command and control within the pocket by bombing and strafing anything that looked like a headquarters. German aircraft pounced on troops as they massed for breakout attempts.

The Soviets' second mistake—the failure to mount an effective defense within the encirclement—contributed to the third. It is not that the defense failed; rather, there was never any real intention to defend the pocket. Pavlov's orders were to break out, and, as the three army commanders concentrated their efforts to that end, they steadily lost control as unit cohesion at all levels crumbled. This produced a chaotic mass of small units and individuals, 400,000 of whom ultimately became prisoners of war.

The fourth mistake was the *Stavka's* failure to identify Minsk as key terrain. One can only speculate, but reasonably so, that if Minsk had not been lost in the first place, or if it had been retaken by the encircled armies and then held, even for only two or three weeks, it would have seriously delayed the German advance on Smolensk. The effort would have bought crucial time for a more organized defense of the distant approaches to Moscow. In hindsight, we can see that the attempt to escape encirclement was futile, especially considering the way it was implemented, and the sacrifice of those men was in vain. If, however, those men had been lost holding Minsk, perhaps their sacrifice would have been justified. As it was, it was only a tragic loss and a great psychological coup for the Germans, and it helped weaken the Soviets in subsequent battles during the drive on Moscow. It also gave a cachet of invincibility to the blitzkrieg mystique, which would endure for another two years.

From Minsk, German Army Group Center moved eastward on

Smolensk. It was now even more vital for the Soviets to hold Smolensk than it had been to hold Minsk. Smolensk was that much closer to Moscow, and it was the last significant urban area in the Wehrmacht's path. Located on the Minsk-Moscow highway at the Dnepr River, Smolensk was only about half the size of Minsk in prewar population (157,000), but it had a growing industrial base and commanded important road and rail networks and river crossings. It was a vital communications hub and a choke point of Dnepr and Desna river traffic, besides being provincial party headquarters.

Here, the Red Army repeated the mistakes of the Minsk operation as though it had learned nothing. Two armies, the 16th and 20th, were caught to the north of the city in a salient with limited contact with Soviet forces to the east, as the Germans rushed into Smolensk from the south. Initially, several divisions of 16th Army contested the Germans' seizure of the city. Fighting house to house, block by block, and street by street, in a manner foreshadowing the urban warfare that would characterize the battle for Stalingrad, General Lukin allowed his men to retreat to the north side of the Dnepr River and blow the bridges.[34] On 17 July the *Stavka* ordered Lukin to organize an all-around defense of the north bank of the city, as if to hold it. Unfortunately, neither Lukin nor General Konev, commander of 20th Army, saw holding the city as his primary mission and chose not to anchor the defense of the encirclement within city limits. Instead, while being inadequately sustained by airdropped supplies, they focused on the relief effort aimed at getting them out of the pocket.

Stalin put General Zhukov in charge of a massive counterattack, which was designed primarily to stop the Germans and secondarily to relieve the 16th and 20th Armies. Zhukov was not ordered to recapture Smolensk. For a brief period, 31 July to 3 August, the relieving forces punched a hole in the German ring. Rather than pour reinforcements in to hold the northern part of the city, which would have denied the Germans use of the Dnepr River, the railroads, and the highways, Generals Lukin and Konev followed normal expectations in this situation. They pushed troops out of the pocket to avoid capture and abandoned the city.

Few of the principals in the Soviet high command, from Stalin on down, appreciated the strategic importance of cities and their linked infrastructure to the success of the German blitzkrieg. Evidently, those who had read Starunin wisely kept their mouths shut. No prewar military strategist or theorist, including Starunin, had proposed integrating the defense of cities with the active defense. All sought decisive battles in open terrain. Not until late November 1941 did the *Stavka* accept the value of combat in cities. In a directive issued on 24 November to the commanders of fronts and armies, it pointed out the advantages of defending population points and encouraged them to work towns and cities into their defense plans.[35] But even this fell short of advocating the defense of surrounded cities. No one can say how long a defense of Smolensk would have lasted if it had been attempted; however, one can safely assume that, in the face of many counterattacks, especially those west of Smolensk, German operations would have been exceedingly more difficult had the Wehrmacht not secured Smolensk to its rear.

The significance of capturing key transportation networks to the success of German offensive operations is highlighted in the analysis of German historian Klaus Schüler. In his study of the transportation and supply aspects of Operation Barbarossa, he notes that in July 1941, before the war was even a month old, transportation difficulties had led to supply shortages in all sectors of the Eastern Front and were especially serious in the northern and central sectors. There the forces had already moved past the supply boundaries of the Dvina and Dnepr rivers projected in the original planning. Regarding the shortages, he articulates the obvious: when the demand for supply exceeds the supply system's ability to provide resources to the front, there will be an inevitable "slackening of offensive power," allowing the enemy to increasingly stiffen its resistance.[36]

The problems experienced to this point by Army Group Center were caused by shortages of trucks and trains. If the Red Army had denied the Germans use of the Minsk-Smolensk railroad and highway for several weeks or months, it is possible that subsequent offensive operations toward Moscow or Ukraine would have been delayed a similar length of time or longer, if the bridges were destroyed in the process. "In the course of the offensive," Schüler notes, "operational developments had increasingly become directly and totally dependent on the transportation situation, which had deteriorated drastically."[37] Inability of the transport services to supply the front caused German operations to slow in October and completely cease in November. If the battles of Minsk,

Smolensk, and later Kiev had turned into protracted sieges, the German offensive may very well have ground to a halt weeks earlier than it did.

The next catastrophe for the Red Army was not long in coming. In good part because of the intensity of the Soviet attacks in the Smolensk operation, Hitler temporarily changed the focus of the main German thrust away from Moscow and toward Ukraine. There, he hoped to finally destroy the bulk of the remaining Red Army field force and secure Ukraine's rich natural resources for the Nazi war effort. This made Kiev and the Soviet forces defending central Ukraine prime targets.

Anticipating the attack, the Red Army had constructed an extensive defensive line along the east bank of the Irpen River to the west of Kiev. Elements of German Panzer Group 1, along with Seventeenth Army, which just days earlier had encircled and captured some 80,000 men at Uman, first bumped into this line on 10 July and were soundly repulsed by four Soviet rifle divisions and five rifle brigades. They attacked again on 20 July and were again bloodily repelled. A third major assault on 8 August supported by panzers and *Stuka* dive-bombers also failed. These setbacks led the Germans to mount a flanking movement to the north of Kiev, hoping to work their way behind the city. Despite these defensive successes, the Soviet commanders in the area—which included General Mikhail Kirponos, Marshal Budennyi, Zhukov, and Communist Party first secretary of Ukraine and front commissar Nikita Khrushchev—asked Stalin for permission to fall back when they saw the danger of envelopment. Their concerns were well founded. The Germans planned a much larger envelopment, with Panzer Group 2 driving south from Smolensk to get nearly 100 miles behind Kiev. This would put it in position to link up with Panzer Group 1, which was driving north after swinging wide to the southwest of Kiev.

Despite the success of Kirponos's forces in holding the Germans back on the west side of Kiev, no one in the army suggested imitating these successes by forming an all-around defense to hold the vital city—the USSR's third largest, with 850,000 inhabitants. Kiev, located at the confluence of the Desna and Dnepr rivers, was a strategic anchor to the right flank of the Soviet war effort south of the Pripet Marshes. Like Minsk and Smolensk, the city was a major road and rail node, as well as an important communications center. It also had a developed airport. More so than the other two cities, it had a significant industrial base. It was the capital of Ukraine and headquarters of the Ukrainian Communist Party. Also, as headquarters of the prewar Kiev Military District, the city had many important military installations. Holding it for only two weeks—which was not an unreasonable scenario, considering the German Sixth Army, with half as many men, would hold out in encircled Stalingrad for nearly three months—would have significantly delayed and obstructed the Germans' advance southwest into Ukraine and their drive on Rostov and into the Caucasus.

Historically, Stalin has been blamed for the losses incurred at the Kiev encirclement, but, ironically, he initially insisted that the Red Army hold Kiev at all costs. In hindsight, that may have been a better course of action, but Stalin lost his nerve at the last moment and reluctantly, and with obvious irritation, allowed himself to be swayed by his generals' persistent pleas to retreat.[38] The doctrine of maneuver warfare so dominated the thinking of the Soviet high command that they could not grasp the benefits of holding on to a strategic but surrounded city.

The Germans closed their pincers on the Soviet 5th, 21st, 26th, 37th, and 40th Armies of the Southwest Front on 14 September, but, this time, there was a designated commander of the forces in the pocket—General Kirponos. Rather than rally this huge force to defend Kiev and tie down German forces while the high command organized a counteroffensive, the *Stavka* pressed Stalin, on Kirponos's behalf, to authorize a breakout, which he did late on the night of 17 September. While fighting on the defensive, the trapped armies had assumed that they would shortly be ordered to break out; thus, no thought had been given to a lasting and coordinated defense. Under tremendous pressure from the tanks, infantry, and artillery of German Panzer Groups 1 and 2 and Sixth and Seventeenth Armies, along with constant aerial bombardment, Kirponos failed to unify the subordinate armies under his command. When he gave the order to break out, an already turbulent situation turned chaotic. No coordinated large-scale breakout attempt materialized because Kirponos never tried to organize one.

Kirponos and his chief of staff were killed on 20 September while trying to escape the pocket with the remnants of a battered infantry division. His death had no effect on activities within the pocket, because he had never exercised any real control over the various armies. Within the pocket, communication between commanders of individual armies and their subordinate units was tenuous at best. In the ensuing chaos, army commanders soon became less concerned with their armies and more concerned with getting themselves out of the pocket. In any case, they lost control over their armies when the Germans began slicing into the Soviet lines. All told, it is estimated that only 15,000 men made it out by the time most of the fighting was over on 24 September. A handful of Wehrmacht units stayed behind to mop up until 4 October, but the majority of German forces moved east and south to continue the conquest of Ukraine—units that would have been tied down if Kiev had been defended.

Based on these three major battles of encirclement and their associated breakout attempts, we can conclude that vast numbers of soldiers were lost due to doctrinal and command failures, not troop-level military ineffectiveness. Most critically, forces became encircled because the *Stavka* failed to allow forces in the field to maneuver to avoid being cut off. Surrounded forces were destroyed because they were not ordered to dig in and hold on, and huge numbers of soldiers were captured because leadership and organization disintegrated. This left soldiers to choose between fatalistic resistance, with no clear purpose, and saving themselves through flight or surrender. Some parallels with the Winter War are visible. When small units took up an all-around defense, they were often annihilated, but very few surrendered. The following chapter shows that it was the act of breaking out from large, disorganized encirclements, not soldiers' political outlooks, that most often led to catastrophic losses.

4
The Small-Unit and Individual Experiences of Encirclement

Stepping back from large-scale operations, we now look from the soldiers' perspective to gain a more complete understanding of how and why so many men went into captivity. Personal narratives convey some sense of the chaos and trauma of breaking out of encirclement and illustrate the life-and-death choices soldiers had to make. When units lost contact with their headquarters, in keeping with informal doctrine, commanders of divisions, regiments, or even battalions generally tried on their own to punch holes in the German lines, usually unsuccessfully. The psychological impact on the soldiers was devastating when divisions and regiments began to disintegrate—often with the death of the commander. Stephen D. Wesbrook defines disintegration thus: "Military disintegration is a condition of organizational paralysis characterized by the total and often sudden collapse of the willingness of the average soldier to resist or to attack the enemy. A military organization can suffer defeat without suffering disintegration so long as the average soldier continues to fight, however unsuccessfully, under the control of the military organization."[1] When the chain of command loses control over the unit and the fighting, and combat degenerates into a matter of individual survival, then a unit has disintegrated and become ineffective.

Disintegration was not unknown to the Red Army high command. Identical situations had occurred in the Imperial Russian Army during the First World War. When a unit's officers were all killed, wounded, or otherwise taken out of action—a not uncommon occurrence—soldiers rarely took the initiative to create a new chain of command and continue the mission. Almost universally, peasant Russian soldiers reverted to the social survival patterns they had brought with them from the village, which focused on risk-averse decision making for the preservation of the collective.[2] This did not always result in capture, but it did represent ineffectiveness as the men lost the will to overcome the enemy and sought only self-preservation. The prime example of inefficiency, leading to ineffectiveness, during World War I was the capture of several hundred thousand prisoners in the twin battles of Tannenberg and the Masurian Lakes in August–September 1914. Likewise, in 1941, when commanders and their staffs either lost or gave up organizational control of their units, disintegration ensued, and men were guided by their survival instincts. Divisions deteriorated into thousands of leaderless soldiers who no longer sought to attack objectives or defend positions but sought only to save their own skins.

The Experience of Encirclement at the Foxhole Level

Lieutenant Anatolii Khoniak described the situation in the Kiev encirclement in three words: *panic, chaos,* and *anarchy*.[3] These terms aptly describe any disintegrated unit and characterized most unsuccessful breakout attempts. Decimated battalions sometimes made it through, but most often only smaller groups of several dozen men or fewer managed to evade capture. The odds of reaching safety were against them, however, as friendly lines were continually shifting eastward and could be up to 100 miles away, sometimes across the open, treeless steppe.[4] The following accounts illustrate the psychological states of soldiers under great stress as their units and overall military organization disintegrated, and they challenge the idea that political motivations were paramount when soldiers faced surrender or capture.

Israel Peltzman was an infantryman in a hastily organized and poorly trained *opolchenie* unit (a citizens' volunteer force; more on this in chapter 5). After being surrounded on the Karelian Front in the early weeks of the war, his regiment tried but failed to break out. The regimental commander abandoned all hope of breaking out or of being relieved and ordered the men to sneak out in small groups. Peltzman and his group easily slipped through the first line of encircling forces but soon ran into trouble. As they were running across a road in the enemy rear area, he tripped and fell into a ditch. At the same moment, a German armored car opened fire on them with a machine gun and killed everyone still standing. "I was lucky," Peltzman recalled. "I only survived because I fell into that ditch." He was wounded above the left eye but still managed to crawl to the safety of Soviet lines. His unit suffered nearly 100 percent casualties from death, wounding, and capture, but none from surrender.[5]

Nina Erdman, a medic in an infantry regiment, experienced the chaos and breakout from the Smolensk encirclement. She recalled, "We were surrounded. It was terrifying—weapons lying around, no one knew where to go, panic! How awful! We were not traveling lightly, because we had the wounded with us. We are going out to the field: in which direction to move? Everything around us is burning. The leaders are running about. Where to go—he doesn't know. We couldn't find our way out for a long time."[6]

Vasily Grossman, writer and war correspondent for the Red Army newspaper *Krasnaia zvezda*, encountered many soldiers who had escaped from the Kiev disaster: "Everyone who has escaped back can't stop telling stories about being encircled, and all the stories are terrifying."[7] Grossman recorded the story of a fellow correspondent who escaped from encirclement in the 1941 campaign for Rostov. He was retreating with a group of soldiers under heavy fire from machine guns and mortars. As a reporter, he was an employee of GlavPUR, so he appointed himself group leader with the title "commissar." The men willingly followed him. "At the Markovskii farmstead, we squatted in a trench, under a terrible fire, and then slipped through the encirclement. We lay down in [a field of] wheat. Germans appeared. A red-haired one shouted: '*Rus, uk vekh!*' We fired bursts from our sub-machine guns and knocked four Germans off their horses. We broke through, shooting with a sub-machine gun and a machine gun."[8] Sixteen of the men survived.

This group's experience was typical, in the sense that once they were outside the immediate area of the encirclement, they walked east at night across fields, avoiding roads and villages. Occasional German patrols fired at them in the dark when they were detected by the noise they made. Sometimes they carried their wounded with them; other times they risked entering a village to leave casualties with sympathetic peasants. Inevitably, if they got far enough east without being caught, fugitive Red Army men faced a river crossing right under the noses of the Germans. Some men felt it was worth any risk to escape the Germans,

POWs' first meal in captivity.

but after going hungry for several days, many lost the will to fight or flee and let themselves be captured.

In his memoirs, Marshal Konstantin Rokossovskii described how thousands of men who had escaped the Minsk encirclement filtered into his lines weeks later. Most had broken out in medium-sized groups but then divided into smaller and smaller groups to avoid being detected as they headed east. Most finally reached Soviet lines individually or in groups of just a few men. Many had abandoned their weapons by the time they reached safety. Rokossovskii rearmed them and assigned them to units under his command.[9]

Medic Natalia Peshkova, her friend Nina Erdman (who had escaped encirclement once before), and a few others from their unit found themselves surrounded in the renewed German advance on Moscow in October. We "were in encirclement and ambled somewhere taking direction from the sun, without a slightest idea of where our troops were and where the Germans were. There was no food." After weeks of evading Germans and digging up frozen potatoes for sustenance, they finally slipped through the German lines near Tula. They were immediately sent to a filtration camp, where the NKVD sought to ascertain whether they were deserters, escapees, or in the employ of the Germans.[10]

Even when well organized, small-unit escape attempts encountered difficulties. In October 1941 the 16th Border Guard Regiment, already depleted by previous combat and acting as rear guard to 19th Army, found itself encircled as the army retreated. The commander wasted no time in organizing a breakout to the east. Concentrating the fire of his artillery, mortars, and machine guns on one sector, he pushed his men forward. The wounded followed in the unit's eight surviving trucks. After three hours of fighting, leading elements broke through the German defenses, but then the Germans laid down a torrent of mortar and machine gun fire on the breach in their lines. The Soviet commander failed to counter by shifting his artillery fire to the flanks. At that point, the men of the regiment broke into smaller groups and continued to fight their way through to a designated meeting point. Command and control broke down, six of the eight trucks loaded with wounded were destroyed, and, in the end, only 244 men survived the ordeal, 60 of them wounded.[11] Such was the cost of a "successful" breakout.

The experience of soldiers facing the choice of death, capture, or surrender—not necessarily related to encirclement—sheds some light on how those choices were shaped by circumstances and personal outlook. Vasilii Kotov, a tank gunner in 1941, presents the following situation: "Look, a unit like ours is left by itself for several days. The officers are scared to sneeze without a special order. There is neither an order to withdraw nor a food supply. And besides, they are running out of ammunition. Silly gossip circulates through the unit. The unit becomes demoralized. And at that very moment the Germans are approaching in armored cars. Bitte-dritte, welcome to surrender!"[12] In this example of capture, the situation did not lend itself to successful or meaningful resistance. The battalion's leadership was paralyzed by the breakdown of communications with higher headquarters. They were out in the open, with no defensive works, as the Germans' armored vehicles quickly moved right on top of them. The men were tired, hungry, and nearly out of ammunition. They had no heavy weapons to counter armored vehicles.

It is easy to read the officers' reluctance to take decisive action as referred blame for Stalin's purges and the psychological state of the officer corps, which some have claimed deprived leaders in the field of a spirit of initiative. Yet there is neither documentary nor anecdotal evidence of officers claiming that they refrained from taking action because of the fear of arrest. It seems more likely that these men simply lacked adequate training to take the initiative, and the breakdown in communications denied them a clear idea of the tactical situation. It is reasonable to assume that they hesitated to make decisions out of fear of being killed by the enemy or disrupting the plans of higher headquarters. In this case, the Soviet officers appear to have had very little time to react, so the element of surprise worked against them.

The case of Alexei Gorchakov, commissioned a cavalry lieutenant in June 1941, provides an example of surrender. His cavalry regiment had been badly mauled in the border battles in June and July, to the point of disintegration. His cavalry troop, which had taken in a large number of soldiers separated from their units, was acting as a rear guard when an unknown major general drove up and ordered Gorchakov to lead his men in an attack on advancing German tanks. Gorchakov protested: "Comrade General, we have only one light machine gun for the whole troop. What can that do against tanks?" The general shot back: "Don't try to reason! Go at the tanks with bayonets and grenades!" Gorchakov turned the column around, and the general drove off to the rear, leaving the motley assemblage of men scared and angry. Sizing up the situation, Gorchakov concluded that advancing against the approaching panzers would be both suicidal and unsuccessful. Consequently, he led the men into the forest, out of sight of the Germans, where he tried to organize a defensive position. About twenty men, stragglers from other units, remained mounted on their horses with their rifles casually pointed in Gorchakov's direction and prodded one of their members to address the lieutenant. "Comrade Commander, we have decided to go over to the Germans," he said. "The Soviet power won't hold out and we don't want to sacrifice ourselves in vain." Sensing the threat to his life, Gorchakov told them that because they were not in his unit he had no authority over them, and they could do as they wished. The men immediately turned their mounts and rode off in the direction of the Germans. Gorchakov and the remaining men decided not to stay and fight; they continued east and eventually rejoined their regiment.[13]

Clearly, the men who went over to the Germans did so because they lacked the will to fight. They rejected further resistance due to ideological motivations or because they saw no point in fighting on for a lost cause. Although Gorchakov did not surrender, he was not inclined to engage in combat that might result in the fruitless loss of life, nor would he allow his men to be captured. This vignette supports the idea that some people decided not to support Soviet power if it seemed likely to collapse. Yet their reluctance to do everything in their power, to the point of self-sacrifice, to ensure the regime's survival does not necessarily prove that they wholly rejected it.

Vasily Grossman recorded a more pointedly politically motivated example of surrender. In October 1941 a rifle regiment commander told him, "One of our squads surrendered to the enemy, under the slogan 'Down with Soviet government.'"[14] A participant in the Harvard University Refugee Interview Project rejected fighting on for the Soviet government, admitting that he and several others in his unit intentionally went into captivity after being encircled in 1941. They refused to try to break out and waited for the Germans to take them prisoner.[15]

Another example is that of Alexei Maslov. His entire regiment was captured in summer 1942 when it bumped into a column of recently captured Soviet POWs as it was marching to the front. Maslov's regiment was simply surrounded, disarmed, and melded into the herd of prisoners by their German guards without a shot being fired. He said: "Thinking about the moment of my capture, I have come to the conclusion that everything happened more prosaically and less precariously than on other sectors of the front and for other prisoners. Everything happened somewhat quietly, without extraneous noise, without excesses." He later asked himself whether he and his comrades could have fought and escaped and concluded that they could have, but "with great difficulty." When asked why they did not try, he responded, "We had no desire to."[16] The only clue Maslov offered to his comrades' lack of desire to fight was that morale was very low. Here, the Germans had the element of surprise and were upon Maslov's unit before the men could even think of offering cohesive resistance. In any event, Maslov seems to have concluded that offering resistance would have resulted in heavy Soviet casualties with little chance of success. It just was not worth it.

Another experience of encirclement and capture was that of Private Georgii Khol'nyi. In the battle for Smolensk in 1941, his battalion lost contact with its parent regiment, so the commander called a council of war among the leaders and headquarters staff to decide on a course of action. The commander proposed that the unit dissolve and that the men sneak through German lines in small groups of three or four. Khol'nyi spoke up, even though he "was only a private," and suggested they form a partisan unit. He brought up the example of 1812 and reminded them that with the coming winter, the Germans would be vulnerable, just like the French had been, because winter "was our weather." His commander rejected the idea of becoming partisans and ordered that the battalion disband and the men make their way east. Aware of the consequences for desertion and fleeing combat, Khol'nyi wanted a note from his commander saying that he had been ordered to leave the unit, hoping to avoid trouble with the NKVD when he returned to Soviet lines. Khol'nyi headed east with a trio of comrades, armed with just one rifle. For days they walked from village to village, exchanging pieces of their Red Army uniforms for peasant garb. In the end, on the outskirts of a peasant hamlet, German soldiers surrounded them with submachine guns leveled and asked to see their papers. Having none, they were taken prisoner.[17]

In this case, the battalion commander was the key actor in the tactical dynamic. He did not want to fight to the death or attempt a breakout, which may have been the most rational decision under the circumstances. Khol'nyi does not tell us the battalion's situation regarding armaments, food, communications, and the strength of the enemy. Whatever the case, this commander's decision was diametrically opposed to those of regiment and battalion commanders in the Winter War, who chose death over the rational choice of surrendering or fleeing, every man for himself.

Whereas Private Khol'nyi was implicitly critical of his commander for not fighting, Lieutenant A. Nevskii was explicitly critical of his battalion commander for just the opposite reason. When his battalion was encircled as part of the Liuban operation in spring 1942 and had the chance to exfiltrate through German lines, as Khol'nyi's battalion did, the battalion commander defied his subordinates' counsel and chose to try to fight his way out. The result was the annihilation of the battalion. Only three men survived to reach friendly lines—none were known captured.[18] Nevskii's commander followed the pattern of commanders in the Winter War, but the results were no better for the men or for the Red Army.

The Bigger Picture

The published photographs and newsreels of dispirited hordes of Soviet prisoners of war should not be misinterpreted as being the result of single events. Those men were not captured all together or all at once in the manner of the German mass surrender of 90,000 men at Stalingrad in February 1943 and a quarter million at Tunis, the British surrender of 70,000 men to the Japanese at Singapore in February 1942, or the American surrenders at Bataan and Corregidor in April–May 1942, which gave the Japanese 11,000 POWs. In these cases, commanders ordered capitulation to spare the lives of the remaining soldiers, absent any hope of victory or relief. When one reads of the huge numbers of prisoners taken in the major encirclements of 1941, it is easy to imagine that similar situations unfolded and that tens or hundreds of thousands of Soviet soldiers were captured together. But the reality noted in the aforementioned examples, in German war diaries, and in the photographic evidence is quite the opposite. Most soldiers were captured in small batches in a multitude of separate instances across a vast landscape as combat ebbed and flowed. Evidence is lacking of any large Red Army unit or group of units laying down their arms on the orders of their officers.

All told, of the approximately 3.2 million Soviet soldiers taken captive in 1941, 1.972 million, or almost two-thirds of them, were rounded up by the Germans in the battles of encirclement at Uman, Minsk, Roslavl', Krichev, Gomel', Smolensk, Kiev, Viaz'ma, and Briansk. Likewise, the remaining 1.2 million who were captured in smaller encirclements did not emulate the behavior of encircled units in the Winter War—in most cases because they were not expected or ordered to. The number of men caught in these encirclements was so large that the *Stavka* became fixated on getting them out to fight again another day. Yet the scale of the encirclements worked against successful escape. Because of command and control problems, the greater the number of men and units in a pocket, the lower the chances of successfully breaking out (more on this later). The very act of trying to escape encirclement increased the chance of being captured as the chain of command disintegrated and soldiers were left to their own devices. Much of the evidence at the small-unit and individual level suggests that most of these men were trapped and did not formally surrender.

Prison camp for Soviet soldiers captured in the advance on Stalingrad, 1942.

There continued to be encirclements in 1942, but they were fewer and smaller. In south Russia, during the German drive to the Don River and beyond to the Caucasus, the pattern of encirclement followed that of the summer and autumn of 1941. In these cases, however, the pockets were smaller because Soviet commanders usually had more freedom to maneuver than they had in 1941 and could better avoid being surrounded.

A rather unexpected encirclement took place in the north when the Volkhov Front launched the Liuban operation, a winter offensive to break the German stranglehold on Leningrad. The attack moved forward slowly for several weeks until the Germans countered by cutting off the lead elements of the Soviet 2nd Shock Army. They besieged it for nearly six months and finally overran it at the end of June. Unlike most of the 1941 encirclements, the 2nd Shock Army had a clear chain of command to control operations, yet this seemed to make no difference in the end. The breakout attempt resembled the 1941 encirclement at Smolensk, where an escape corridor was temporarily opened and thousands got out. The thousands who did not were subsequently killed or captured in the attempt to escape individually or in small groups.

It was during the Liuban operation that General A. A. Vlasov was captured, and soon thereafter he began to actively support the German cause, culminating in the formation of the Russian Liberation Army. One explanation for his treason was that he resented the failure of the Soviet high command to devote sufficient resources to free his besieged army, which he interpreted as deliberate abandonment. The problem

A lone Soviet soldier from Central Asia, captured in the summer of 1942.

was that the high command, uncharacteristically, had waited too long to authorize a breakout. By the time the 2nd Shock Army was ordered to escape, it was out of fuel, and the horses had all died from lack of fodder. The men had already been reduced to consuming the dead horses and had not eaten for days at the time of the breakout attempt. Ammunition stocks had dwindled to insignificance, and medical supplies had long been exhausted. All told, the Red Army lost nearly 140,000 men killed, missing, and wounded and 10,000 captured in this operation.[19]

Toward a Series of Explanations

Historians and military professionals have tended to credit the Germans with superior doctrine and execution and have faulted the Soviets for theirs. In short, the Soviet high command did as much to put the Red Army soldier at risk of capture as did the Germans. In the broadest terms, two simple facts contributed to the major strategic imbalance that yielded such one-sided results: the Wehrmacht took the overwhelming initiative as the Germans advanced during the summer and early autumn of 1941, forcing the Soviets to fall back in disarray, and Stalin and

Soviet pilot being questioned by an SS soldier.

the *Stavka* played into the Germans' hands with their delays and refusal to allow their forces to maneuver to avoid encirclement. Other problems included the *Stavka*'s delay in allowing the largest pockets (at Minsk, Smolensk, and Kiev) to break out, combined with the flawed execution of breakouts by encircled formations large and small. Another defect in Soviet doctrine was that units of all sizes were blindly ordered to break out, making no allowance for nuance or exceptional situations when it may have been strategically possible for large formations to hold key terrain and endure a sustained siege. As we have seen, units in the largest encirclements failed to break out intact, and it was the act of breaking out that destroyed their ability to resist and caused their demise. The collapsing pockets were characterized by a mad scramble of broken divisions, support troops, and staffs trying to escape under fire. In the process, soldiers were left leaderless, without prepared defenses, and vulnerable as they wandered eastward.

The paradox of why larger encircled Soviet forces usually failed to break out, whereas smaller ones often succeeded, begins with the idea that it is sometimes easier to capture half a million or more men whose units have been destroyed and their leaders killed than it is to capture small, well-led, cohesive units. Generally speaking, in military operations—and as seen in the Winter War—it is often easier for an isolated regiment or battalion to form a pocket of resistance or break out than it is for a division, corps, or larger unit to do so. A solitary beleaguered commander does not need to coordinate his activities with others or wait for orders. The isolated regiment or battalion commander can see the terrain that will shape his choices and movements, and he can meet personally with his subordinates without having to rely on radio or telephone communications. In contrast, for major units, such as 10,000-man divisions or 100,000- to 600,000-man armies and collections of armies, to act effectively, they must coordinate their activities through a complex chain of command over great distances. Both communication failures and geography can make it difficult or impossible for large units to coordinate their efforts, take the initiative, or act independently of the chain of command. The terrain to be defended or broken through is usually extensive, making internal communication more difficult. In addition, communication is often disrupted by enemy activity. So in this regard, we can accept that poor Soviet generalship and doctrine, compounded by the scale of forces involved, communication difficulties, the fog of war, and German tactics (they did not carve large encirclements into smaller *mottis*), led to a massive haul of prisoners. These encirclements made cohesive defense very difficult—especially for Red Army generals who had little training for defense—and they made individual surrender or capture seem unavoidable or inevitable.

It should be noted, however, that some small units chose to fight to the end, and there were some successful large-scale breakouts from encirclement. Herein lies the basic dilemma: why were these the exception rather than the rule? Cohesion seems to be the common denominator in successful large- and small-scale breakouts both in Finland in 1939–1940 and in the first half year of fighting on the Eastern Front. In the Great Patriotic War's numerous successful breakouts of army-sized forces, the commander was firmly in control, had freedom to act, and acted quickly; that is, higher authorities did not bridle him to a specific course of action. In such cases, the odds favored the Soviet side. In every case of the successful escape of envelopment during the Winter War, cohesion was facilitated by the small numbers involved. Regiment and battalion commanders had closer relations with their subordinate officers than did corps or army commanders. Where cohesion crumbled, the fault could most often be traced directly to a personal failure by the commander, or to his death. Therefore, it appears that the magnitude of operations was inversely proportional to the likelihood of encircled units making their way out.

Scale played a role in the amount of violence the enemy could bring to bear against encircled forces. With their initial advantage in the air and in artillery, tanks, and assault guns, the Germans could concentrate a tremendous amount of firepower against encircled Soviet units and the forces trying to relieve them. In contrast, the Finns were almost always heavily outnumbered on the ground, even when they surrounded Soviet forces. They also had few tanks and insufficient numbers of up-to-date artillery pieces and ammunition. Likewise, the Finnish air force was rather small and had no *Stuka*-like dive-bombers to terrorize Red Army soldiers; it never had air superiority. Therefore, it is reasonable to expect that units surrounded by German forces in the early battles in Belorussia and Ukraine would suffer heavier casualties and more severe disruption of command and control than did those during the Winter War.

The scale of the battlefield also played a role in shaping tactical dynamics. The war in Finland was fairly static and covered a well-defined area in the Karelian Isthmus between Lake Ladoga and the Gulf of Bothnia. There was no latitude for grand maneuvers, and movement forward, backward, or laterally was measured in meters or a few kilometers at a time. Without rapid or long-distance maneuvering, units seldom got separated from their headquarters, and, if they did, it was not for long. The main exceptions were the two worst disasters of the Winter War—the destruction of the 163rd and 44th Rifle Divisions when they were strung out along roads. By contrast, in the 1941 battles in Ukraine, wide-ranging maneuvers were the norm, and the Red Army was usually under air attack, which caused extended breaks in contact. Units frequently went into battle in piecemeal fashion without an appreciation of the larger picture, which hindered coordinated action and degraded their ability to go to one another's aid.

There was also a social element that influenced who was or was not captured that greatly complicates our understanding of the surrenders.

The demographic composition of the Red Army changed during the two years prior to the German invasion. Because of the massive and rapid expansion of the military, the rural component increased far more rapidly than did the urban, to the point that many considered the Red Army "re-peasantized." Simultaneously, it experienced an unprecedented influx of non-Slavic minorities from Central Asia numbering in the hundreds of thousands. Conscripts from the newly acquired western Ukraine, western Belorussia, Bessarabia, northern Bukovina, and the Baltic States—young men who had not been reared and educated as Soviets—further diversified the population of the army. Most significant in this tumultuous process was that the percentage of "ideal" soldiers, as defined by the regime—Russians, factory workers, students of higher education, and Komsomol or Communist Party members—was reduced. The German invasion ripped open many unhealed fissures in the Soviet body politic. On 17 July 1941, barely a month into the war, the NKVD informed the high command that there had been mass desertions and betrayals of the motherland by conscripts from the aforementioned newly acquired areas, and it urged military councils at the front to examine the political reliability of such people under their commands.[20]

The Soviet government had lowered the draft age in 1939 from twenty-one to nineteen, bringing into the ranks mostly peasants. Students and workers in essential industries usually received deferments or full exemptions, and students who were conscripted served a much shorter time in the ranks than did the less-educated peasants. As a result, peasants, who may have held a grudge against the regime for collectivization and the 1932–1933 famine, and national minorities, primarily Central Asians, men from the Caucasus, and those whose native lands were not immediately threatened by the Germans, were less likely to share the Russians' conception of and attachment to the motherland (*rodina*). As an aggregate, these disparate and potentially disaffected subsets of Soviet society predominated in the ranks. The officer corps was also substantially peasant. It appears that most Red Army soldiers taken into captivity in 1941 and 1942 were conscripted peasants and non-Russian minorities—the very elements most likely to be alienated by recent trends in Stalinist governance—and they were much less inclined to feel compelled to die for the Soviet homeland.

Another difference between the Winter War and the Great Patriotic

War was the psychological impact of reverses in battle. Despite the tactical failures in the first months of the Winter War, on a strategic level, the men were always confident that the USSR would win in the end. Even before battle, the soldiers were sure of victory in some form, and this feeling did not diminish, even during the worst moments. These thoughts made throwing in the towel on a personal level seem dishonorable. When fighting the Germans and their allies, however, not only victory but also the survival of the state was in doubt. Until the great victory at Kursk in July 1943, the troops had frequent cause to ask themselves whether it was worth fighting if the USSR was ultimately doomed. In keeping with John Bushnell's observation that obedience among Russian soldiers during the Revolution of 1905 rose and fell with their perception of the strength and legitimacy of the government, the same might well be asked of the soldiers' motivation to fight in 1941 and 1942, if not well into 1943.[21] Still, referring back to the question of political attachment to the Stalinist state, soldiers who viewed the war as a lost cause and who refused to fight in hopeless situations were not necessarily anti-Stalinist. Supporters of Stalin who benefited personally from Soviet power could and often did conclude that a lost cause was, after all, a lost cause.

Another psychological problem was that, instead of stimulating confidence, the successful escape of encirclement could breed fear of repetition. A report to Stalin in August 1941 noted: "Those who fear encirclement the most are staffs and commanders who have formerly been encircled in western Belorussia. Staffs, therefore, always jump aside and lose supervision and communications with their forces, and commanders, without exception, do the same like V. I. Kuznetsov and Golubev, who all the time look behind them."[22] Both those generals had lost the majority of their men in the Minsk encirclement. For the next several months they exhibited a sort of "encirclement psychosis," always preparing to retreat to avoid being surrounded.

Another related difference between the Winter War and the Great Patriotic War, also associated with differences in scale, was that the type of soldiers caught in encirclements was more varied. In the Winter War, it was overwhelmingly combat troops that were encircled, but in the Great Patriotic War, tens of thousands of noncombatant soldiers were caught in the encirclements. These were largely administrative, medical, and logistical personnel who operated in the rear of the frontline soldiers. Because the Germans drove deep into the rear areas to complete the encircling operations, support troops were caught in the noose along with combat troops. These people were completely unprepared to fight. They had few small arms and no heavy weapons whatsoever, and they were not trained or organized to fight as tactical units. In breakout attempts, they were more a liability than an asset to the fighting troops. Additionally, many construction battalions, composed mainly of non-Slavic minorities, were caught in the fighting. Being unarmed, for the most part, they were likewise unable to engage in combat but added to the soaring number of prisoners taken.

When analyzing the causes of military success or failure, it is necessary to evaluate a unit's preparedness for its experience. The Red Army, confronting the might of the Wehrmacht and its Axis allies, faced some serious problems—most of them of its own making—that would contribute to the disasters of the encirclements. In the year before the outbreak of war, the Red Army was in the midst of a great expansion. Units facing the Germans in Poland or units that would soon be at the front were in the process of being reinforced by 50 percent or more. The infusion of so many new soldiers created tremendous turmoil. Divisions were broken up, and each of their three regiments would then be reinforced to become whole new divisions. In the process, officers were assigned, then reassigned, and reassigned once again (a process condemned after the Winter War, obviously to no effect). A colonel or general could command two or even three divisions in the space of eighteen months, creating and re-creating staffs with little or no hope of getting to know the majority of his subordinates. The influx of personnel and the instability of officer assignments greatly impeded training and cohesion, which would be all-important when bullets began to fly. Some units received thousands of untrained conscripts on the eve of battle, many of whom did not speak Russian. Such reinforcements likely degraded rather than enhanced a unit's cohesion and readiness for battle.

Two examples from the U.S. Army's experience in the Second World War add comparative perspectives. First was the experience of the 168th Infantry Regiment of the 34th Infantry Division, which first saw action against the Wehrmacht in North Africa in February 1943. It experienced outcomes eerily similar to those of many Soviet units in the summer of 1941. Prior to entering combat, the 34th Infantry Division, a National

Guard unit that had been activated in 1941, had undergone numerous shifts in manning and many changes in officer personnel that greatly disrupted its cohesion. It received 450 new and virtually untrained recruits the week before it went into combat. As a result, like most Soviet units, this division was unprepared to meet the Wehrmacht on equal terms. Its training had been neither thorough nor appropriate for facing the Germans' combined arms attack. In its initial engagement during the battle of Kasserine Pass, the inexperienced 168th Infantry Regiment was surrounded, cut off from the rest of the division and with no way to call for artillery fire or air support. Resupply was impossible, and the regiment soon ran low on ammunition and water. Finally, the commander ordered the men to head for American lines in small groups in a nighttime breakout. The result was the death or capture of approximately 1,400 of 2,200 men. All that was left of the regiment was one depleted battalion.[23] Unlike the Soviet experience, however, the men taken prisoner were considered neither traitors nor unpatriotic.

The other example is the 106th Infantry Division in the battle of the Bulge in December 1944 and January 1945. This new and untested division, put into the line for the first time in the winter of 1944, was better trained for war than the 34th Infantry Division, but it was just as green. When the German surprise attack hit the 106th Infantry Division in December, the commanding general underestimated the seriousness of the assault and did not permit his subordinate regiment commanders to maneuver to more favorable positions. When two regiments lost contact with the division staff, the regimental commanders did not take the initiative to maneuver on their own. As a result, the 422nd and 423rd Infantry Regiments became encircled. Surrounded for two days, the regiments engaged in close combat and suffered heavy casualties in officers and men. Soldiers from destroyed or broken units roamed about the pocket, looking for leadership and orders. Running out of food and ammunition, with the hope of imminent relief or air supply fading, the two commanders surrendered their regiments on the fourth day of fighting to avoid what they considered the useless loss of life. Subordinate officers objected, suggesting that it was possible to hold out longer or at least attempt to break out. The colonels commanding the regiments, however, insisted that surrender was the only practical alternative to annihilation.[24]

Up to the point of capitulation, most of the men had fought valiantly; some battalions had been overrun while holding their positions, and at least one company chose annihilation rather than retreat or surrender. Hundreds of men disobeyed the order to surrender and escaped the encirclement to continue the fight. A group of about 100 men from various destroyed battalions emulated Red Army partisans and formed a guerrilla band that operated in the German rear, ambushing convoys and small patrols, until the Allied counteroffensive reached them.[25] The actions of the 106th Infantry Division commander and the commanders of the 422nd and 423rd Infantry Regiments, with their collective loss of between 8,000 and 9,000 prisoners, have gone down in history as the worst performance of the U.S. Army in the European campaign. Recriminations followed the disaster, and, although no one ever faced court-martial, these events are colored with the stain of shame in popular memory. Accusations of cowardice on the part of the colonels occasionally crop up in discussions of this incident, but no one's patriotism is questioned.

Both these examples from the American experience of war with Germany lead us to some obvious and universal truths of war: Military units of poorly trained, inadequately led, and inexperienced soldiers are apt to suffer heavy losses, defeat, and capture when confronted by better led and organized units. Without appropriate training and effective leadership, morale and courage play a subordinate role in military performance, and political reliability and loyalty play almost no role at all. That is, politically reliable and loyal soldiers who are badly trained and ill led will fail just as surely as those who are politically suspect and of indifferent loyalty under the same circumstances.

Part 3

MOBILIZING SOCIETY

5
The Great Patriotic War: The Mobilization of Society for Armed Service

The success of the Stalinist regime in mobilizing Soviet society for military service through institutional, voluntary, and coercive means ultimately stands as the foundation of the Soviet army's war-winning military effectiveness. Keeping the Red Army in the field required first expanding peacetime forces to a wartime footing and then continually replacing losses. Within the larger context of how the Soviet state mobilized nearly 30 million men and women for uniformed service after the outbreak of hostilities and millions others for defense work,[1] we explore the question of why Soviet citizens fought for what is commonly acknowledged to have been a brutally repressive regime. This is a paradox that has long haunted Soviet historiography.

As stated in chapter 1, the postwar consensus of Western scholars is that many did not fight at first, and the millions of Soviet soldiers captured in the first six months of the war indicate a popular rejection of the politics and policies of Stalinism.[2] Their analysis, however, stops there. They fail to explain why so many people volunteered to serve well before they learned of Nazi atrocities and the maltreatment of the average citizen, which some historians posit as the motivation for subsequent resistance to the German invasion. In contrast, Soviet historiography trumpets the millions of Soviet citizens who volunteered to serve or reported for conscription as evidence of widespread popular support for the regime. But this ignores the warm reception given to the Germans by people in the Baltic States and Ukraine as far east as Kiev well into September, the difficulty in mobilizing peasants and non-Russians, desertion, and draft evasion.[3]

I argue that there were seven basic reasons why people served in the Red Army, and these can be divided into two categories of motivation—intrinsic and extrinsic.[4] The intrinsic category includes self-interest, hatred for the Germans generated by personal experience, an appreciation of the benefits of Stalinism, and an innate love of country. This love of country could be based on a historic conception of Russia or a belief in the socialist experiment, both of which enabled people to claim patriotic motivations without necessarily endorsing the Stalinist state. Extrinsic motivations to serve were promoted by the state or generated by society. They include fear of the consequences of evading conscription if caught, hate promoted by official propaganda, and social pressure to conform. People could be influenced by several of these factors simultaneously. Furthermore, citizens' decisions to serve were affected by family issues and political ideology, which could be both intrinsic and extrinsic. At the same time, some people rejected service in the Soviet armed forces for a variety of reasons. Although it is impossible to definitively determine why people served or not, or to resolve this issue decisively, we can illustrate the range of complex human motivations and external factors that influenced popular responses to the issue of serving in the Soviet armed forces during World War II and how the state sought to take advantage of them to create an effective war machine.[5]

The Volunteers

During the course of the war, approximately 4 million people served as volunteers in *opolchenie* divisions; in *istrebitel'nyi*, workers', and communist battalions; and in the regular Red Army.[6] Although Soviet historiography professes that, at the start of the German invasion, the Soviet people rose up in a surge of patriotism and love for Stalin to defend the USSR, the primary materials now available offer numerous challenges to this version and show the need for substantial qualification. Rather than the all-inclusive "Soviet people," it was Russians who overwhelmingly volunteered. Among Russians, urbanites proved far more willing to volunteer than peasants, and, among urbanites, blue-collar workers were more likely to step forward than white-collar workers, as were young party and Komsomol members and unmarried people in their teens and twenties with higher education. These people represent the idealistic youth of the post–October Revolution generation, and historian Anna Krylova suggests that the state successfully fostered a yearning for historical relevancy among this group that a war against capitalism could provide.[7] During the 1930s both the media (print and film) and literature promoted the inevitability of war with the "encircling" capitalist states. From 1936 onward, conflict was portrayed not only as inevitable but also as imminent and destined to end in Soviet victory. It would be the historical task of the generation that had not created the revolution or fought the civil war to fight this war.

Aleksandr Bodnar' is one Soviet youth who took the regime's prewar conditioning to heart before the German invasion. He graduated from high school in 1940 and entered a military school for officer candidates later that same year.

> I have to say that in the years when I was studying in school, everything was geared towards preparing the population's morale for the inevitable war with fascist Germany. So I saw myself as a man in the future war. Besides that, my uncle was a military man, and in '39 he told me, "Sasha, you will finish high school. I advise you to go to college. We cannot avoid the war, so it's much better to be a commander in war—you can do more because you will be better educated." These words played a part in the making of my decision.[8]

In the decade before the German invasion, the state prepared millions of youths, primarily urban Russian teenagers, for future war through paramilitary training sponsored by Osoaviakhim. Krylova believes these young people consciously understood that they were preparing for close combat with the enemy, and perhaps the training generated a yearning to do so. This helps explain the initial rush of young Russian urban students and workers to the military in the summer of 1941. The issue of what part of the state's message they accepted or rejected, however, is very much under debate. Although many responded the way the state desired, it does not necessarily mean that they were inspired by the state.[9] Furthermore, Soviet youths did not live in a vacuum. The older generation provided alternative views that often challenged official propaganda and the party line.[10]

It is worth noting that eighteen- to twenty-three-year-old males, born between 1922 and 1927, accounted for the most wartime volunteers not only in the USSR but also in the United States and in Canada. The same generation provided the greatest number of conscripts in all the belligerent states as well.[11] One can interpret this as a simple matter of demographics. All the belligerents concentrated their recruiting on this age cohort.

Motivation to Serve

An analysis of motivating factors is complex and necessarily prone to speculation. Soviet historiography claims that patriotism was the primary motivating factor among the broad masses, yet people's love of country is an internally generated feeling as well as a social and community issue, and it is subject to official manipulation. The state had an obvious interest in framing the call to arms as an emotional appeal to people's idea of the USSR as their motherland, and it had the advantage of controlling the media to achieve this end. In such appeals, the regime portrayed the homeland as the ancient *rodina*, not the revolutionary or Stalinist state, yet some people did associate the *rodina* with contemporary times. Aleksei Shalashkov, for example, appealed to his local district military commission, asking that he and his three brothers be allowed to join the army to defend the "Soviet *rodina*."[12]

When historian Catherine Merridale conducted interviews with veterans in the 1990s, love of country emerged as a topic of discussion. After one group session, a woman came to her privately and said: "We did not fight for Stalin. We fought for our families, for our city [Leningrad]."[13] For her, mother Russia was—and remained—local and did not encompass the totality of the Soviet population or geography. Merridale also discovered that veterans tended to use the word *patriotism* to cover a multitude of positive attributes they attached to their personal definition of *rodina*.[14] The upshot is that the more local attachments and identification figure into people's motivation to serve, the less confident we can be in labeling it patriotism; *le patrie,* after all, is the essential element in patriotism. Soviet propagandists of the day seemed to be cognizant of this and sought to merge the local element with the national.

In July 1941 forty-seven-year-old Nikolai Kiriaev expressed a combination of Russian and Soviet interpretations of the homeland when he told the district military commission of Kursk province:

Two times in my life I have fought for the motherland. The first time was in the imperialist war with Germany, the second in the civil war. Now for a third time I will fight with all my strength. I have no military obligation and the state of my health is no secret, but when they talk about defending the rodina I am not able to sit with my arms folded. I know the business of war and will use it to crush the fascist vermin enemy.[15]

Arsenii Rodkin had a different perspective on patriotism. When war broke out, he chose not to volunteer. When conscripted in 1942, Rodkin expressed mixed feelings about reporting for duty:

In all honesty, I did not want to go to war and fight, and if I had a choice I would not, I would not do any favors for the Soviets. Surprised? Do you think everyone was screaming "Hurrah-Hurrah!" at the time? In 1941, my uncle was arrested. At school I learned that he had died somewhere up north. I was all upset about the whole situation. I was thinking of deserting the school, however, later I decided that Kremlin bastards come and go, but the Motherland stays forever.

Being from Samara, on the Volga, the thought that the Germans had reached the river grieved Rodkin. "What the heck!? We needed to kick their asses. That is to say, I was defending my country not the Soviets," he reported.[16]

In the First World War, the tsar and then the Provisional Government governed Russia; in the civil war, it was Lenin and the aspiring Bolshevik state. Now Stalin was in power, but, luckily for him, Kiriaev, Rodkin, and millions of others identified the motherland as something separate from and superior to politics.

The role of ideology is perhaps most difficult to isolate as a motivating factor for wartime service, because few people address it directly or clearly identify their thinking as ideological. Still, some people imply ideological commitment in their decision making. Nina Solovei, for example, associated patriotism for the *rodina* with love for the broad idea of the socialist state. As a young Komsomol member, she felt compelled to resist the fascists, who "proposed to destroy the world's first socialist state and our pride and hope."[17] Menache Borochin, a sailor in the naval infantry, said: "Under Stalin we were believers, not in God, but in socialism, the Soviet Union, and Stalin. Local authorities were the bad guys. We believed in Stalin, we fought for this."[18] Here, he intertwines faith in socialist ideology with the state that embodied it and that Stalin personified as its leader. The state occasionally worked into its broad propaganda effort the idea that the fascists' goal was the destruction of socialism.

One dying soldier wrote to his son from a field hospital, saying that after the war, he was confident his son would "live in a free, prosperous country—in a country of socialism."[19] He goes on to say that the sacrifice of blood in the war will earn his son the right to a happy life. Both ideas suggest that the soldier, at the time of his writing, did not believe the USSR was as free, prosperous, or thoroughly socialist as it ought to have been, or that life had been as happy as it should have been. Nevertheless, it was worth fighting for, if doing so would create a truly socialist country in which the promises of the revolution would be fulfilled.

Another element of ideological motivation was antifascism, which had long been a staple of Soviet propaganda up to the 1939 Nazi-Soviet Nonaggression Pact. It was quickly revived after the invasion. In May 1942, as soon as he was old enough, Nikolai Zheleznov and his workplace comrades volunteered for the army. He said, "At that time there was no one who did not want to go into the army, then they yearned to go into the army! They yearned, not because civilian life was bad, [which it was] but because they wanted to put an end to fascism!"[20] Zheleznov claims to have been particularly motivated to fight by the stories of refugees who had escaped German occupation. Thus his hatred of fascism can be seen as both ideological and practical, based on what fascism represented politically and on what the fascists had done to his country. We cannot, however, equate antifascism with pro-Stalinism.

So far, completely absent in the discussion of popular motivation has been religion and the role of the Russian Orthodox Church. Soviet historians deliberately omitted from the historical record the work of Orthodox priests who called on their parishioners and youth in general to volunteer to defend the fatherland. Metropolitan Aleksii of Leningrad was the first to make a public appeal. On the evening of 22 June 1941 he called not only on the believers in Leningrad but also on all Russian men to defend their fatherland. One Russian historian claims that, as a result, thousands of Russian believers volunteered for the front.[21] Metropolitan Sergii, in Moscow, also published a letter on 22 June "To Pastors and Parishioners of the Orthodox Church of Christ." It included this passage:

> This is not the first time that the Russian people have endured suffering. And on this occasion, with God's help, they will grind the hostile forces of fascism into dust. . . . Our native land is being defended by the force of arms, by the common heroism of its people, and by a general willingness to serve our country in this difficult trial. The Church of Christ confers its blessing on all Orthodox believers in their defense of the holy borders of our Motherland.[22]

These appeals may have persuaded believers who were prone to anti-communism to set aside their differences with the state and fight for "holy Russia."

People's feelings about Stalin and what he represented were somewhat related to ideology. Without a doubt, many volunteers associated Stalin with the nation in a favorable way. The growing cult of personality surrounding Stalin in the prewar years influenced many young people when the war came.[23] Daniil Zlatkin remembered that his buddies all volunteered to serve on 3 July 1941 after hearing Stalin's speech calling people to rally to the defense of their country.[24] Molotov's speech in June, immediately after the German attack, had left them unimpressed, but they found Stalin's appeal compelling. Some soldiers even had Stalin's image tattooed on their chests to show their support for him.

In contrast, others blamed Stalin for Russia's problems but were able to separate their feelings about him from their feelings about the nation and the state, and they understood that the *rodina* was not the equivalent of Stalin or the Communist Party and its failings or evils. Antonina Dubkova was one such person. She claimed to have hated Stalin from the moment she heard of Kirov's murder in 1935, and she attributed that murder and the deaths of other high party officials to Stalin. On 22 June

1941, having heard Molotov's radio broadcast calling Soviet citizens to fight "for our country, for the motherland, for Stalin," Antonina and some friends went to the local military commissariat to enlist. She remembered, "I told the boys when I heard this broadcast that said 'for our country, for the motherland, for Stalin' that the motherland is all right, but why should I fight for Stalin? He's a man—let him fight for himself!"[25]

To avoid blame for the war's disastrous start, Stalin selectively removed himself from the center of public attention. He carefully reduced his public profile, especially in times of crisis, from August through October 1941 and from May through November 1942. In addition to dissociating himself from military reversals, he let others take credit for successes. He made few public appearances, and his picture seldom graced the pages of *Pravda*.[26] Stalin's image was conspicuously absent from propaganda posters during the war. As head of the Communist Party, Stalin needed the party's profile to rise and fall with him. Konstantin Simonov, novelist and correspondent for the Red Army's daily *Krasnaia zvezda*, summed up the first six months of the war for the Red Army soldier in December 1941. His article admitted the losses but reaffirmed certain victory. He honored the heroism of the soldiers and acknowledged the faith of the people, all without mentioning the Communist Party or Stalin.[27] Downplaying the role of Stalin and the party helped accentuate the appeal of serving the *rodina*.

The state went to great lengths to whip up hate as a motivating factor. In his May Day speech in 1942, Stalin told the Soviet people, "You cannot conquer the enemy without learning to hate him with all the power of your soul."[28] The state-run media used reports of German atrocities, interviews with people who had suffered at the Germans' hands, and poems and short stories to inveigh the Soviet people to hate. Of the twin themes of hate and vengeance, revenge cropped up most often during the war and in postwar testimony; hate, far less so, perhaps because it was unpleasant for veterans to admit to or talk about. For those immediately affected by the fighting, official propaganda legitimized and channeled their natural and spontaneous emotions to achieve the state's ends.

The state also used propaganda to foster hate and a desire to avenge among those who were far removed from the war. For example, Georgii Eremin, a soldier with a safe job in the Kremlin, wrote to his family in

May 1942: "In me burns a big fire of hate and vengeance for the villainous enemy who kill the peaceful population. I go to defend our motherland, to fight, weapon firmly clenched in hand. I go to avenge the suffering of our fathers, mothers, sisters, brothers, wives, and daughters." Yet to that point, the Germans had harmed no one in his family.[29]

The interplay of propaganda and real experience is less clear. For example, Liudmila Popova claimed to be motivated to fight by a desire for vengeance. Her father, a reserve officer called into active service in 1941, had been killed at the front. "From the moment I found out he had been killed," she said, "I was determined to go into the military and avenge his death."[30] Until then, however, she had not considered fighting for her country.

Others, such as S. M. Ermashova, had a suspiciously delayed reaction. Ermashova was targeted for service by her district party committee, which was responsible for recruiting eighty Komsomolkas for Red Army antiaircraft service. She reportedly said to the recruiter: "I apply to enlist in the ranks of the RKKA because I want to defend our *rodina* with weapon in hand. I want to sweep aside the impudent fascists who killed my mother and brother Lieutenant Ermashov, who died 28 November 1941." This was exactly what the state wanted to hear, and the official who recruited Ermashova made sure to include it in his report.[31] It rings somewhat hollow, though, because she enlisted in April 1942, five months after her brother's death, and only when she was personally asked to do so in the context of her membership in the Komsomol. Up to that time, she had passively worked at her job while the Germans continued to advance.

Social pressures played a role in prompting some people to volunteer not just to serve but to serve at the front. Many who had friends or relatives, especially siblings, in the service felt they were being left out of what was likely the biggest event of their lifetimes. At the Uralmash factory in the Urals, the three Koshevnikov brothers, aged thirty-two, twenty-eight, and eighteen, all volunteered to join the army soon after the invasion. Among other things, they may have been motivated to honor their other two brothers already on active duty.[32]

Vladimir Shliakhterman's decision to volunteer illustrates a form of social pressure: "In August 1942, when the Germans were tearing at Stalingrad, I got the notion that I needed to go fight in order to be able to comfortably answer the question, 'What did you do during the war?'"[33]

Likewise, Nina Solntseva spent her free time looking after wounded men in a local hospital. Her interaction with the men convinced her to become a medic and go to the front "to help injured men on the field of battle."[34] She was motivated by a feeling of social responsibility toward her fellow citizens, not the state. Georgii Kidin, in a wartime letter, articulated personal and social motivations that were shared by many: "We know that our wives, children, fathers, our mothers, everyone, who by chance found themselves in the hands of the invaders are waiting for us."[35] Simultaneously, a potential negative social ramification of avoiding service was ostracism by one's social circle.

The Soviet State, Volunteers, and Recruitment

At the outbreak of war, the huge number of volunteers caught the regime off guard, and it was not prepared to handle them. There had been no public outpouring of support in 1939 for the conflict at Khalkhin-Gol with Japan, which had been fought to help the Soviets' Mongolian allies; for the invasion of Poland, in which the USSR had been the aggressor; or for the war with Finland, in which there was some question about who was responsible. None of these foes had posed a deadly threat to the USSR. The conflict with Nazi Germany was a far different case. The threat was real, the stakes were high, and the Soviet cause was just. These factors, combined with the prewar conditioning of youths, generated a grassroots movement of tens of thousands of young people who mobbed local commissariats, wanting to join the army.

The state had further encouraged young people with the message that any war would be short, victorious, and fought on the enemy's territory.[36] Consequently, when Soviet citizens heard that Germany had invaded, many thought the war would be as short and successful as other recent conflicts.[37] One can easily imagine young people's eagerness to participate in what they assumed would be a few exciting months of victorious campaigning before getting back to their ordinary lives. Those who were too young for service in 1941 thought they would miss out on the war altogether. It was inconceivable that the fighting would last more than a couple of months.

Reacting quickly, the regime took steps to capitalize on the volun-

Workers enlisting in the Red Army, July 1941.

teerism of the young urban population, which it considered politically reliable. The Soviet state was more comfortable arming this group than the peasantry, given the emergency conditions and the few formal military and political controls. In the areas nearest the front—Ukraine, Belorussia, the Baltic States, and Karelia—Stalin ordered the NKVD on 23 June to organize, on a voluntary basis, *istrebitel'nyi* (shock) battalions of 100 to 500 people. These people were recruited primarily from the trusted categories of party and Komsomol members, as well as the "soviet active" at factories or institutions of higher education. First and foremost, their mission was to secure the rear areas by combating domestic enemies such as deserters, panicmongers, rumormongers, spies, and "diversionists." The state also expected them to put down uprisings by anti-Soviet elements in the local population and to be on the lookout for enemy parachute detachments. They were armed with only small arms and hand grenades because that was all the authorities could scrounge up at the time.[38]

In July, fearing for the security of the capital, Stalin added Moscow to the list of areas to form *istrebitel'nyi* battalions. The city's shock battalions, 35 in all, were recruited from the same loyal cohort but were larger than the others. Each, led by a local NKVD bureaucrat, numbered 500 volunteers, including 15 secret policemen. Unlike detachments elsewhere, they were supplied with heavy machine guns.[39] In short order, 12,581 Muscovites stepped forward to join these detachments. By 30 July, a total of 1,500 *istrebitel'nyi* battalions had formed.[40]

In a direct appeal to Russian (*rossiiskii*) patriotism, the party and army called on the heritage of the Great Patriotic War against Napoleon when it initiated the voluntary formation of *opolchenie otriady*. These detachments, consisting of a few hundred ill-equipped but enthusiastic mainly Russian urbanites, were distinguished from *istrebitel'nyi* battalions by the lack of NKVD involvement.[41] Their mission, like that of the *istrebitel'nyi* battalions, was to secure the rear areas. However, when the military situation at the front deteriorated, the army threw both *istrebitel'nyi* and *opolchenie* units into the fray. Fighting the Germans with little or no training routinely led to their annihilation.

In contrast to its lauding of the working class, Soviet historiography remains silent on the subject of peasant voluntarism. With regard to the draft, we do know that the mobilization of Russian peasants had its difficulties. In July through August 1941, in the mostly rural province of Orel in western Russia, 110,000 men were summoned for conscription, but by the end of the reporting period, 65,000 remained unaccounted for.[42] Given their reluctance to report for duty when drafted, it is highly unlikely that significant numbers of peasants, young or old, volunteered to serve. The Soviet historical record is replete with examples of urban volunteers, but it does not mention peasant volunteers. One peasant woman told her Harvard University interviewer that there were two kinds of peasants: those willing to sacrifice the motherland to get rid of Stalin, and those who wanted to get rid of Stalin, but not at the expense of the motherland.[43] A 1941 report by Soviet agents in German-held territory stated, "In some localities the women and non-mobilized men even stated that they wished only for the end of the war; they did not care who won and who was in power, provided they were left alone."[44]

Historian S. A. Smith has examined the idea that Russia lost World War I because the peasants, who constituted the primary manpower pool for the tsar's army, did not feel like citizens. The idea of citizenship is also relevant as a motivating factor in World War II and could account for peasants' reluctance to volunteer in 1941. If Soviet peasants—recent victims of forced collectivization, famine, an internal passport system aimed at keeping them on collective farms, and a drastic decline in quality of life—did not feel like full citizens, it stands to reason that they would have less of a stake in the regime's survival. Ironically, after the war, their sense of citizenship and nationalism may have been strengthened by their wartime sacrifices.[45]

Farther from the front, the regime began to form *opolchenie* divisions (DNOs) at the end of June. The party, army, and local governments pooled their resources to raise these volunteer units, much as they had done to raise the volunteer ski battalions for the Winter War. Recruitment focused on major urban areas, especially Moscow and Leningrad. Information on their founding reveals that middle-age *apparatchiki* (officeholders in the party bureaucracy) were quite willing to cajole young party and Komsomol members to join the DNOs but avoided donning uniforms themselves. Furthermore, the depth of voluntarism among urban populations had its limits; neither Leningrad nor Moscow met the admittedly ambitious manpower quotas for the *opolchenie* units, even though they sometimes resorted to social coercion and manipulation to man what were supposed to be volunteer formations. Boris Sokolov, a thirty-year-old engineer in a factory, recorded in his memoirs: "I went to war, one might say, voluntarily, that is neither resisting nor refusing, as many did, though clearly knowing better. In this my law-abiding character influenced me, as did my lack of knowledge of life outside my comfortable circle, and quite simply, my propensity not to think."[46]

The demographics of the volunteers were precisely what one would expect—the overwhelming majority, almost by definition, were Russian, urban, working class, and young. There were, however, numerous exceptions. Older men, many in their thirties and forties, also joined. Some men in their fifties, veterans of the First World War and the civil war, were accepted for service. Even the exceptional veteran of the Russo-Japanese War managed to find his place in the ranks. Exceptions notwithstanding, the general profile of the *opolchenie* was that of the ideal Soviet citizen-soldier. The majority were working class, followed by white-collar service people and intelligentsia, students in higher education, and finally peasants from villages in the vicinity of the major cities. The 18th DNO from Moscow, for example, comprised 57 percent

Training opolchentsy, *July 1941.*

working class, 24 percent white-collar workers, and 19 percent peasants. Another of the city's divisions boasted 85 percent workers. About half of Moscow's volunteers were party or Komsomol members, and three-quarters were Russian.[47]

Soviet historiography has always portrayed the motivation of *opolchentsy* as support for the Soviet state and social system, yet a closer look challenges that claim. The young Anatolii Muzhikov volunteered to join one of Leningrad's eleven *opolchenie* divisions, inspired by the simple idea that he would be defending the city—his home—a sentiment echoed by thousands of other Leningraders.[48] If we consider that joining the *opolchenie* represented a rejection of service in the Red Army, then local loyalties and the social factor of being able to serve with one's school- or workmates were of equal or more importance than national or ideological factors in *opolchentsy*'s decision to serve. The regime cleverly took credit for such volunteerism, labeling it patriotism. By promoting local defense, the state avoided testing people's loyalty to and feelings about the Stalinist state. In recruiting for the *opolchenie* and *istrebitel'nyi* units, the authorities placed great emphasis on the idea that the volunteers would be defending their local cities, towns, or areas and would not go off to fight for the nation in the Red Army far from home.

Among *opolchentsy* there was likely the hope that the enemy would never even get to their cities; thus, membership in the *opolchenie* could keep them out of the Red Army and, if the front stabilized some distance away, out of combat. For instance, when the Moscow and Leningrad *opolchenie* units began recruiting, the front was still hundreds of miles away. Some men, hoping to avoid fighting, joined the *opolchenie* after recruiters misleadingly told them that they would be given safe jobs away from the front.[49] An artillery captain assigned to train Moscow *opolchentsy* in October as the Germans approached the capital recorded: "The first division I got consisted purely of intellectuals who could not fight and considered themselves doomed to perish. The mood was clearly defeatist."[50]

The idea of staying close to home had quite an effect on prospective volunteers, as reflected in the recruitment breakdown for Kursk province in August 1941. Nearly 105,000 people volunteered for the *opolchenie* and 10,650 for *istrebitel'nyi* battalions, but only 5,700 opted for service in the Red Army.[51] The contrast between the desire to stay close to home and the willingness to go off to fight for the USSR could not be more starkly drawn.

Moscow provides another example of the effect of local patriotism in recruiting. Muscovite pride and heritage matched that of the Leningraders; many Muscovites volunteered as groups or with a close friend or two. Recruitment was carried out on a district basis, as was unit assignment, meaning that people would serve with others from their neighborhood. More than 1,000 students and faculty of Moscow State University volunteered for the *opolchenie* on the first day.[52] Knowing that they would serve with fellow Muscovites probably facilitated the extensive voluntarism exhibited by the city's population. This allowed for the interplay of local and national patriotism, as well as social acceptance and peer pressure.

Altogether, the city of Moscow and its environs sent 1 million men and women to the armed forces. In the end, Moscow produced seventeen rifle divisions. Twelve had originated as *opolchenie* divisions, all of which were unexpectedly converted to regular Red Army divisions by mid-1942 without the consent of the soldiers.[53] During the battle for Moscow, after the army had successfully defended the city and went over to the offensive, the regime converted Moscow's 154 *istrebitel'nyi* and volunteer march battalions (replacements for casualties) into regular Red Army units.[54] Thus, many men and women who had probably not intended to ended up serving in the Red Army anyway.

Despite the evident success of mobilizing volunteers, not everyone in Leningrad or the capital felt enthusiastic about the war or the idea of serving in any capacity. One worker in Moscow was heard to say: "I don't want to be cannon fodder. I won't serve in the army and I won't join the reserves."[55] Numerous party members and Komsomolets in the capital doubted an eventual Soviet victory and took pains to hide their membership and avoid military service. Furthermore, some resisted peer pressure to volunteer for the *opolchenie*. Nineteen-year-old Iuri Averbakh was exempt from the draft as a result of his enrollment in Bauman Higher Technical Institute. He rebuffed peer pressure and refused to volunteer. Instead, he found work at a tank repair facility that guaranteed he would never be sent to the front. Viktor Merzhanov, a professionally trained musician freshly graduated from a conservatory, declined (along with three of his friends) to volunteer for the *opolchenie* at a meeting of the conservatory's faculty and student body. He put his colleagues off, saying he would join after traveling to Tambov to say good-bye to his family. In Tambov he joined an aviation academy's military band and later transferred to a military band in Central Asia, even farther from the fighting. Merzhanov thus served in the military but avoided the front altogether.[56]

Later, as the German army approached Moscow in October 1941, and hard on the heels of the "Moscow panic" during which most of the government evacuated the city, the authorities once again called on residents to rally to the colors. On 16 October the call went out to form twenty-five "Communist Battalions." Each of the twenty-five districts of Moscow was asked to raise a 400-person detachment of party and Komsomol members for immediate dispatch to the front to defend the city. In a matter of a week, 7,963 men and women volunteered, and on 30 October, along with several of the local *istrebitel'nyi* battalions that had been formed in July, they were committed to the front lines as the 3rd Communist Division.[57] One young man refused to be evacuated with his university and volunteered to join the Bauman District Communist Battalion. Years later, he revealed the thinking behind his decision: "For us, young students educated on patriotic slogans, who had recognized the inevitability of the war coming soon, the decision to voluntarily enroll was natural and logical and not an impulsive feeling of the moment. The decision to volunteer to go to the front was regarded as normal, as a common occurrence."[58]

Voluntarism flourished in less prominent urban areas as well. Attendees were asked to enlist at several mass meetings after Stalin's 3 July speech at the Middle Urals Metals Factory, which was attended by nearly 15,000 workers. As in Kursk, Leningrad, and Moscow provinces, the desire to serve with one's friends and coworkers was evident in the factories in the Urals. Immediately, 1,048 men volunteered. The majority (655) wanted to join the newly forming *opolchenie* division, and the other 393 volunteered to join the Red Army.[59] Cities in the industrial provinces of the interior also raised *opolchenie* divisions: Kuibyshev provided 90,000 *opolchentsy*, Saratov 40,000, and Stalingrad 50,000.[60]

The Belorussian Communist Party, in order to meet its quota of raising 78 *istrebitel'nyi* battalions and *opolchenie* detachments by 15 July, reached out to both collective farm peasants and factory workers.[61] It succeeded in organizing 121 small battalions and detachments. With a total of 4,151 men and 329 women volunteering, the average size of a group was only 37 people. The overwhelming number of volunteers came from one province—Vitebsk—which raised 3,528 volunteers.[62]

As for Ukraine, Nikita Khrushchev, the Ukrainian Party's first secretary, promised to raise, arm, and equip 657 *istrebitel'nyi* battalions. In fact, he succeeded in raising 651 "battalions" with 118,000 members. With an average membership of less than 200, they were more like company-sized units. By 1 October, however, Ukraine was down to only 143 *istrebitel'nyi* battalions with 26,000 members. The others had been annihilated in battle or disbanded, and their members were either conscripted into the Red Army or evacuated with their factories to the east.[63]

Besides *istrebitel'nyi* battalions, Khrushchev thought it would be possible to raise 375,000 volunteers from Kiev, Khar'kov, Odessa, Dnepropetrovsk, and the cities of Stalinskoi and Voroshilovgrad provinces for *opolchenie* divisions. As of 5 July 1941, however, Khrushchev lamented to Stalin that he had no weapons with which to arm these divisions.[64] He made no mention of recruiting collective farmers or other peasants. In the short term, the city of Kiev, the largest in Ukraine, managed to raise only 32,800 volunteers—two-thirds of them communists and Komsomolets—for *opolchenie* units.[65] Once the German advance got closer in August, the reality of the threat spurred another 140,000 Kievans to volunteer for local defense. All told, the Soviets claimed that Ukraine's twelve provinces produced 1.3 million men and women for the *opolchenie* and other volunteer units.[66]

Although they usually fared better than *istrebitel'nyi* battalions, *opolchenie* divisions sometimes suffered heavy casualties in their initial baptism of fire owing to incomplete training. Too much has been made of the militarization of Soviet society in the 1930s, with its universal military obligation for males, supposedly mandatory preconscription training, and paramilitary instruction offered by the Osoaviakhim. The reality is that vast numbers of Soviet youth received no training whatsoever. Nikolai Kudrin, a founding member of Leningrad's 2nd DNO, reported that 70 percent of the volunteers in July 1941 had no experience with firearms and had never fired a shot.[67] Vladimir Dolmatov, a Moscow teenager who found himself in the *opolchenie* in October 1941, recounted: "I was in the eighth grade. One day our entire school was assembled at Potylikha, in the yard of a middle school. They gave us hunting rifles, one for every five men, small caliber rifles—also five men for each one, and also gave us five sabers. That was it! No uniforms—everyone wore whatever they came in with, and went to fight." They marched straight from the school into combat with the enemy. German tanks encircled his unit, and Dolmatov was ordered to slip through the lines to report the situation to higher headquarters. "Basically, no one came back from that *opolchenie*! They all perished!" he remembered.[68] He was only seventeen years old at the time and too young to be drafted. This experience did not dampen his desire to serve, however, and several months later, still underage and against his parents' wishes, he finagled a deal with a commissar to get himself conscripted into the regular army—a decision he would later regret.

The Voronezh *opolchenie* had a short and inglorious life. The regiment was formed in August and, with little training, no uniforms, and few weapons, was sent to participate in the defense of Kiev. In transit, the regiment was bombed by German aircraft, which killed forty-seven men. The rest of the regiment scattered. Some looted a nearby warehouse and then headed home on foot with their booty, but others pressed on. The intrepid souls who went forward were eventually intercepted by a German armored column that was closing the ring of the Kiev encirclement. Rather than machine-gunning them to death, the Germans told the ragtag bunch to turn around and go home, which they did.[69]

The Red Army recognized that voluntarism and the current parameters of conscription could not fulfill its manpower needs over the long haul. So, in October 1941, the regime passed a new military service law to supplement the decree of 23 June 1941, which had enabled the conscription of all males born in the years 1905 through 1918.[70] The new law stipulated that all males aged sixteen to fifty were liable for military duty, either in the ranks or in military industry. This *levee en masse* made it possible for the military to take just about any man it wanted, as needed. Indeed, spirited, idealistic voluntarism was a short-lived phenomenon. It had begun to taper off by December 1941, when the realization set in that the war would not be short, and victory was in doubt.

Not only did voluntarism wane, but in the dark days of the German advance to the outskirts of the capital, Moscow teemed with people who were looking out for themselves and shirking their duty. A report by the commandant of Moscow, Major General Sinilov, to Beriia, head of the State Committee for Security (GKB), which covered the period 20 October 1941 to 30 April 1942, revealed that the GKB had detained 183,519 people, mostly men, for specific military crimes and infringements. This included 21,346 men caught evading military service. By the end of April, the GKB had taken into custody 98,018 soldiers and others with military obligations and assigned them, with GKB or police escorts, to military transit points or march companies to go to the front. Of these miscreants, the authorities executed eight who had appeared for conscription but subsequently failed to report for duty, and nine others who chose not to show up for conscription at all. An additional 1,130 men were sentenced to time in Gulag camps for draft evasion.[71]

Voluntarism continued to ebb in 1942, but it never ceased over the course of the war. The nature of voluntarism, however, did change over time. First, the stimulus for young adults to sign up to defend their cities was absent in 1942. Leningrad and Moscow had been successfully defended; the cities of Belorussia and Ukraine had already fallen. Second, the army altered its approach to the recruitment of volunteers. Beginning in 1942, the army began to raise new divisions locally along the lines of the *opolchenie*, but they were no longer called *opolchenie* because they were not intended for local defense. Instead, the army labeled them *volunteer* divisions or brigades, which were explicitly Red Army units that would deploy to the front.

Volunteer units were typically organized deep within the USSR, in the Urals and Siberia. For example, in 1942 the Urals produced 100,000 volunteers and Siberia produced 207,000.[72] Why the regime chose to rely on volunteers to man these divisions is unclear. In general, voluntarism gave the people agency, a feeling of empowerment rather than one of being controlled and subservient. Such was the case with the 6th Stalinist Rifle Corps of the Siberian Volunteers, comprising one rifle division and four rifle brigades. Formations such as this generated enormous pride in the cities that produced them. Before the war, local patriotism had been seen as potentially dangerous to the Stalinist regime, so resorting to voluntarism may have been a practical measure forced on it. Because the centralized record keeping of the Commissariat of Defense was in disarray due to the government's movement out of Moscow in October 1941, its ability to call men up was hindered. In contrast, the U.S. armed forces abolished voluntary enlistment in 1942 to create a more predictable flow of recruits into the various branches of service.

This tactic of going to the people succeeded in attracting a different cohort of volunteers. For example, in the spring and summer of 1942, the army raised two infantry divisions and a "Stalin Brigade" in the Altai *krai*. The men volunteering for these divisions were usually older than the young idealists who had flocked to the colors in the summer of 1941. One of the typical volunteers for the 150th Volunteer Rifle Division raised in the Altai *krai* was Aleksandr Shvets. In his early thirties, Shvets was a party member and a former teacher on a collective farm named "Death to Capitalism." His father, a village blacksmith, an old Bolshevik, and a veteran of the First World War, had been killed in 1926 "defending the gains of the revolution in the village."[73] With credentials like these, one would have expected Shvets to volunteer in June 1941, rather than almost a year later when the army came knocking on his door.

The Stalin Brigade was able to recruit slightly fewer than 5,000 men into its ranks—20 percent of them either communists or Komsomolets. Just over half had some prior military training or were reservists. The majority were younger than thirty-five and Russian by nationality.[74] In the end, the volunteers for these two divisions and the Stalin Brigade were but a drop in the bucket of the manpower mobilized in the Altai *krai* in the first eighteen months of the war. By the end of October 1942, the regime had mobilized 398,000 into the active army and several thousand more into construction battalions and labor columns.[75]

In 1943 the provinces of Sverdlovsk, Perm, and Cheliabinsk joined together, at Stalin's request, to raise the Urals Volunteer Tank Corps. The party and organs of local government involved in raising the corps professed a commitment to the principle of voluntarism. They stipulated a goal of at least 70 percent party and Komsomol volunteers and hoped to limit to 30 percent nonparty men with military obligations. The responsible agencies overwhelmingly focused their recruiting on factory workers aged twenty-three to forty.[76] As with the units raised in the Altai, the majority of volunteers were in their mid-twenties or older, and many had served in the Red Army as young men. One man, P. K. Remizov, a thirty-one-year-old worker with several years of military experience during his youth, petitioned the provincial party boss to intercede on his behalf to enable him to join the volunteer tank corps. He had attempted to join the army three times previously, but his factory director and local party boss had forbidden him to go. From the tone of his letter, it is clear he felt he was missing out on something very important. His sentiments were echoed by many others who sent letters petitioning to be admitted to the corps, professing patriotism and the desire to do more for the war effort than their undeniably important factory work.[77]

Overall, the authorities' appeal proved quite effective. One city party committee reported that 10,222 men volunteered for the corps at a rally. After interviews and physicals, however, only 533 were accepted. Reports from other party committees mirrored a similar acceptance ratio of 5 to 10 percent of applicants. It is possible that many of these men expected to be rejected and volunteered just to win social approval for their attempt to join. When complete, the corps consisted of 51.5 percent Communist Party and Komsomol members and 73.5 percent workers, attesting once again to workers' and urbanites' proclivity to volunteer and the peasantry's corresponding reluctance to do so.[78]

The fact that the army tended to rely on recruitment to get volunteers and the examples of Shvets and Remizov combine to illustrate several noteworthy points. First, by 1942, the draft cohort of 1941 had been used up or was otherwise engaged in essential industry or occupations that kept them out of the military. Second, although a large number of men in their mid-twenties to mid-thirties were willing to serve, many were unwilling to take the initiative and volunteer. Only when the army came to their locales, calling on local patriotism and generating peer pressure, did these men come forward. Recruitment in 1943 was particularly important because of the enormous number of casualties that had to be replaced. To make up for the shortfall, the army went deep into the interior looking for volunteers and planned to call up men from the 1922–1925 birth cohorts, who had earlier secured deferments. In desperation, the army would even consider conscripting seventeen-year-olds (born in 1926) if this failed to produce the numbers necessary.[79]

Unexpected Volunteers

Willing participation in the war by people who had unmistakably been victimized by Stalinism occurred on a fairly large scale. This seems illogical and counterintuitive, especially given the results of the Harvard University Refugee Interview Project (the basis for much of the postwar scholarship on the USSR). For the most part, project participants had negative experiences with Soviet power and consequently avoided or fled military service. Therefore, willing service by the victimized was an alien concept for Western historians. Voluntarism by victims of Stalinism also caught the Soviet regime by surprise. It was seldom welcomed by the boards of local military commissariats because of worries about potential political unreliability. We can more easily accept the vindictive reaction of Iratovna, whose husband had been arrested in 1938 and was serving a ten-year sentence in the camps for political crimes. When she heard of the Nazi invasion, she told some communists, "Previously I wept, now you will weep."[80]

In contrast, Boris N. Leont'ev joined the army at age nineteen, soon after the invasion. He became an artillery officer despite the fact that his father had been arrested on false charges in 1937. After ten days in NKVD custody, his father came home "thoroughly ill" and soon died. Leont'ev's mother subsequently found it hard to get work to support the family, and they spent the next four years in poverty.[81] Iulii F. Khruslov lied about his age to join the army in 1943, and his older brother was already serving. This seems rather odd, given that their father, a civil war veteran and longtime party member, had been arrested in December 1937 and shot a few months later. Their mother was then dismissed from her job, convicted of being a "member of the family of a traitor to the Motherland," and sentenced to five years in the camps.[82] Despite being expelled from the party for "connections with Trotskyites and liberals" in 1937 and then being arrested and released a year later, thirty-eight-year-old Nikolai Makarov joined a Leningrad *opolchenie* division in July 1941.[83]

Such individuals would have been justified in not supporting the regime, given the treatment of their loved ones by the secret police and often their own loss of rights and status; however, they and many other people who had suffered at the hands of the Stalinist regime willingly participated in the war. I argue that some victims of the regime chose to serve out of a sense of self-interest, which many of them labeled "patriotic" only after the fact. In the case of victims of the purges, the self-interest would lie in regaining the legitimacy of citizenship in the eyes of the state and society. Military service, particularly in the nineteenth and twentieth centuries, emerged as an important indicator of citizenship. Military service involves a reciprocal relationship between the individual and the state: citizens are obligated to defend the state, and, in return, the state is required to recognize the individual's right to receive all the benefits of citizenship and inclusion in the national community. So, for the outcast, the great reward of service was acceptance into the national community and acknowledgment of citizenship.

Historian Orlando Figes, in his study of the victims of Stalin's repressions, observes: "Looking back on their teenage years, many of these 'strange orphans' recall that there was a moment—a moment they had all hoped for—when the stigma of repression was at last lifted and they were recognized as 'Soviet citizens.'" It is his opinion that nearly all children of enemies of the people felt the desire for social acceptance, and "there were few who turned their backs on the Soviet system or became opposed to it."[84] Figes focuses on the children's joining of the Young Pioneers or Komsomol as a milestone in acceptance; however, military service was probably a more profound experience. It not only represented official acceptance by the state but also obligated the state to recognize, after the war, that these volunteers shared in the rights of all citizens and the privileges of veterans.

Mikhail Nikolaev, orphaned by the execution of his parents as enemies of the people, volunteered for the Red Army in 1943 at age fourteen (his documents incorrectly listed him as seventeen years old), not out of patriotism or to restore his place in society but out of desperation. He had been forced into industrial labor at age twelve, putting in twelve-hour days and sleeping in his work clothes on the factory floor. He and his fellow orphans were not paid. To escape the hunger and misery of the factory, he illegally abandoned it and joined the army.[85]

The military had discriminated against family members of repressed individuals since the purges. In the summer of 1938 the Main Military Council (GVS) decreed that all men with a military obligation whose parents or other family members had been repressed in one way or another during the recent cleansing of the party and society would still be drafted; however, they would serve in special detachments—usually unarmed construction battalions—away from the border areas and major cities. This made hundreds of thousands of previously exempt sons of kulaks eligible for the draft. The decree also stipulated that men whose nationalities were deemed suspect (Poles, Germans, Finns, Bulgars, Turks, Estonians, Latvians, Karelians, and Greeks) would be conscripted and assigned to special detachments.[86] In April 1942, to replace the dreadful losses of the winter counteroffensive and to prepare for the Red Army's upcoming spring offensive, the decree was altered to allow sons of repressed parents to bear arms at the front.

Iurii Koriakin was drafted in October 1941 and quickly rose to the rank of sergeant, but, because his father had been arrested in the purges, personnel officers twice rejected him for service at the front. The third time around, he decided to lie to make himself politically acceptable to agents of the state. He remembered thinking: "What should I say? I'll say that my father's in evacuation. Who will sort it out?"[87] It worked, and in February 1942 he finally got to the front. The war provided Koriakin and millions of others the opportunity to rewrite their official biographies and erase connections to enemies of the people, giving them clean slates to begin their postwar lives.[88]

Did social and criminal outcasts know that they would be rehabilitated or fully accepted into Soviet society as a result of their service? On the one hand, the state was explicit about rehabilitating criminals if they served in penal (*shtrafnyi*) battalions, and it granted former kulaks and their families internal passports that enabled them to leave the special settlements to which they had been exiled.[89] On the other hand, there is no evidence that the state made any blanket promises to the families of people tainted by arrest or those related to enemies of the people. Yet it seems that people had the expectation, justified or not, that if they served in regular or frontline units, the state and society would owe them acceptance and restoration of their citizenship rights. After all, the various Soviet constitutions invoked military service as the right and duty of full citizens.[90] Social and criminal outcasts could have interpreted the fact that they were allowed to serve as meaning that the state recognized them as citizens with full rights.

It has been argued that the expectation of inclusion in the national community as full citizens through service in the armed forces was widely promoted and internalized in Russia during the First World War and continued into the Soviet period immediately after the civil war.[91] The idea that victims of terror could regain acceptance through service may very well have rested on these earlier precedents. Alexander Pil'syn, a penal company commander, recalled that many army officers serving out criminal sentences imposed before the war began to volunteer for frontline service in penal battalions in late 1944 and early 1945, knowing that the war would soon end. According to Pil'syn, many did so both to avoid the stigma of having sat out the war and to reenter civil society as *frontoviki*.[92]

Another category of unexpected volunteers consisted of those actively being persecuted by the regime during the war. By volunteering, they stood to gain immediate release from the camps or internal exile and eventual rehabilitation. Some—how many is unknown—of the million men released from the camps to the army volunteered for combat, not just some safe rear-echelon job. For example, Vasilii V. Korotkov, an army lieutenant, had been arrested in 1937 as an enemy of the people and sentenced to ten years' internal exile without contact with his family. When the war with Germany began, he petitioned to be sent to the front but did not get his wish until March 1942, when he was assigned as a private to a mortar battery. His fellow soldiers held nothing against him; in fact, when the battery commander was killed, they convinced the regiment commander to make Korotkov their commander.[93]

Petr I. Iskratov, winner of two St. George Crosses in the First World War and a self-proclaimed participant in the storming of the Winter Palace in October 1917, had been arrested as an enemy of the people in August 1937 and received a sentence of eight years' internal exile. He was serving it in a small city in Siberia when his case was reviewed in 1943 and he was released. He did not have to serve in the military because of the state of his health, but he insisted on joining the army and going to the front, where he was killed.[94] Iskratov may have gone to the front out of patriotism or to restore his reputation and civil rights, which did not come automatically with release from the camps.

Two other unexpected volunteers were twin brothers Teodor and Robert Klein, whose family suffered unjust persecution before and during the war. Because of their German ancestry, in August 1941, they and all "Russian-Germans" were forcibly relocated to Kazan. Soon thereafter, able-bodied males were taken for forced labor in Siberian concentration camps. Teodor recalled that experience as the most horrific of his life. At the same time, their father was in a labor camp, having been arrested in 1937 for holding secret religious worship services as a Protestant pastor. In 1942 the Red Army began to recruit Russian-Germans with technical specialties. A Russian friend of the Kleins vouched for them, and the brothers volunteered for active service despite their unfair persecution and the fact that their father had died in the camps that year. Teodor survived the war as a truck driver in an artillery battery, and Robert became a Hero of the Soviet Union as a military intelligence scout. Both were restored to full citizenship after the war, but when telling his story to his children and grandchildren over the next forty years, Teodor stressed his love for Russia—his homeland.[95] In contrast, thousands of other Russian-Germans elected to serve the Germans both as noncombatant *Hilfswillinge* auxiliaries and as combatants.[96]

Some victims of Stalinism continued to support the regime, blaming their misfortunes on bad people such as Ezhov or Beriia or simply assuming that a mistake had been made in their case. They did not interpret the "misbehavior" of NKVD agents as typical of the Stalinist system; they saw it as aberrant. Certainly, the Stalinist regime benefited greatly from people's inability to accurately assess Stalin's and the state's responsibility for the suffering they were subjected to. When it came to the purges, many people believed the state's claim that these internal enemies were Trotskyites, fascists, and foreign spies who needed to be rooted out. Whatever their reasons, in the end, hundreds of thousands, if not millions, of people who had suffered at the hands of the Soviet state fought to save it. In so doing, they regained some degree of acceptance by the regime that had earlier rejected them. Patriotism and hope for the future could go a long way in people's minds, enabling them to rationalize their victimization and willingly serve the Stalinist state.

6

Mobilizing the Nonvolunteers

The Conscripts

During the war, the majority of men and women who ended up serving as soldiers and junior officers did not volunteer for military service. Even before the German invasion, virtually all of the approximately 4.5 million Soviet soldiers and sailors on active duty on 22 June 1941 were there as a result of ordinary conscription. The draft of the 1922–1923 birth cohort—the first to be called up after the German invasion—provided 2,221,967 soldiers in the first eighteen months of the war.[1] But, like volunteering to serve one's country, answering the call to the colors does not unequivocally equate to support for the political system. Conversely, waiting to be called up rather than volunteering is not necessarily a sign of nonsupport of or hostility to the regime. Many men knew that they would inevitably be drafted and were in no hurry to be parted from their families and their safe, ordinary lives.

The Soviet state did not take it for granted that all who were called would report for duty. Therefore, besides the positive motivation of patriotic appeals, the Soviet state sought to enforce compliance through the fear of harsh consequences for draft evasion and for aiding and abetting draft evaders. Thus, when assessing people's response to conscription, the coercive power of the state must be considered. In extreme cases, the penalties for draft evasion included execution or assignment to disciplinary battalions. Few would be sentenced to the Gulag to sit out the war. To discourage families of draft evaders from helping their loved ones avoid service, they too were subject to arrest, imprisonment, or internal exile. Local police, the NKVD, the government, and party and Komsomol officials all sought to enforce conscription and pressure the population to conform through periodic hunts for draft evaders using roadblocks, random street checks, and door-to-door searches of apartment buildings.

The authorities constantly reminded the population of the penalties for assisting draft dodgers and deserters, which resulted in a steady stream of denunciations of such people, including by family members.

More than 250,000 military-age men unsuccessfully attempted to evade conscription. For example, on 16 November 1941, when the German army was on Moscow's doorstep and only ten days after Stalin's speech in Red Square, Moscow security forces conducted a massive verification of documents. They inspected men's papers on the city's main roads and in squares, the subway, markets, queues at shops, and so forth. This single day's work yielded the arrest of 206 men evading conscription.[2]

During the course of 1943, the security organs rounded up 65,259 men who had evaded the draft in areas liberated by the Red Army that year.[3] Later, in April, May, and June 1944, the NKVD detained nearly 23,000 draft evaders in newly liberated areas.[4] Throughout the rest of the USSR, in just the month of May 1944, the NKVD apprehended 26,300 draft dodgers. With few exceptions, the state quickly pressed these men into service in the ranks of the infantry. Officially, 500,000 men are listed as having successfully but illegally avoided service.[5]

Historian Amnon Sella helps us understand the willingness to serve— but not to volunteer—when he postulates that obedience to the point of self-sacrifice is possible in two types of people. "Soldier-philosophers" believe in the values represented by their side in a war; "soldier-victims" are prepared to die because they do not know how to avoid it.[6] Understanding the full import of this distinction, however, is rather complex. After all, to one degree or another, most people accept the values of their society and the legitimacy of the state; however, this does not lead the majority of the population to volunteer for military service in peacetime or in war. Usually, men of the appropriate age wait for the government to summon them individually before joining the armed forces. We can label these people unenthusiastic or even reluctant soldier-philosophers. In contrast, those who successfully avoid service and avoid victim status may strongly believe in their society's values, but they selfishly place their own well-being above that of the state and society. True soldier-victims are fairly unsophisticated people with little sense of personal power.

Fedor Bachurin related his conscription experience in a style that indicates he was a soldier-victim: "On December 14, 1941 they took me into the army. They were taking birth years '23 and '24 year at the time.

We went on foot from an assembly point to Balashev. There, they put us on a train and shipped us to the Far East."[7] His tone is very passive, almost sheeplike in its imagery.

Another broad category of soldier can be postulated beyond Sella's two: the soldier who is obedient, for whatever reason, but not to the point of self-sacrifice. These people are not easily identified. One might think that those who surrender, straggle, or desert automatically fall into this category, but it is not so clear-cut. A soldier-philosopher may surrender if he or she considers the immediate situation hopeless and realizes that a personal sacrifice would be in vain.

A fourth idea must also be considered: that soldiers in the heat of battle do not fight for their country or for ideas at all; rather, they fight for their comrades and their personal reputations and to maintain their standing within a primary group of peers.[8] As the previous analysis of mass mobilization shows, citizens join the armed forces for the same reason. Still, Sella's premise is useful, and, when it is applied with some qualifications, it provides a framework to more thoroughly appreciate Soviet citizens' service.

Mikhail Kuznetsov's entry into the army exemplifies the external forces acting on fairly passive, unmotivated people who were ultimately willing to serve but would not take the initiative to do so. Kuznetsov told his interviewer:

> When the war began, I was working in a factory in Khimky and I had a reserve order, so they didn't take me. In the spring, the order came for all men born between certain years to voluntarily come to the recruiting center. I arrived and I had an advance order. There they demanded my passport. I had had my passport taken at the factory and in return they had given me a certificate with a red star. The officer says: "I cannot take you." I left and I say to the guys I came with: "Everybody, they're not taking me." Lesha Orekhov says: "Oh f—k it! In half an hour, dressed in my coat and hat, stop back by and tell them that everyone has left the factory, and so you want to go into the army!" So I did.[9]

Kuznetsov clearly succumbed to peer influence and did not claim patriotic motivations in hindsight.

Others felt a desire to volunteer at first but changed their minds after their initial enthusiasm was curbed by reality. Lev Kolodenko and his friends wanted to volunteer in 1941 but were too young. As the months went by, hundreds of wounded and invalid soldiers passed through their town, a sight they found rather sobering. After talking to some of these veterans and hearing about the horrors of war, no one was in a hurry to enlist. Said Kolodenko, "We waited to be conscripted."[10]

Valentin G. Kukhtin, a proud Don Cossack whose father had been dekulakized and died in prison in 1933, entered the army in an almost accidental fashion. In 1942, at age seventeen, he had no intention of enlisting and going to war, but neither had he rejected the Soviet state. On the contrary, he hoped to benefit from it. He had been accepted to Moscow State University (which had been relocated to the east) for the next fall's class and thus had secured a deferment from conscription. In the meantime, he was living at home with his mother on a collective farm when, as it turned out, the war came to him. The German summer offensive of 1942 reached the eastern Donbas, forcing Kukhtin to decide where his loyalties lay. He told his mother, "If I stay at home, the Germans surely will force me to dig trenches against the Red Army. I shouldn't stay here. It would be better for me to dig trenches against the Germans for the Red Army."[11] So, in dramatic fashion, he hopped on a horse just as the Germans were advancing on the farm, galloped eastward, and ran into a handful of fleeing Red Army soldiers. Using his knowledge of the area, he led them to safety, and the lieutenant in charge of the group spontaneously drafted him into the platoon. It is not clear what Kukhtin's original intentions were. He might have intended to avoid service to the Germans or volunteer for defense work (manual labor) for the Red Army until classes started in the fall. In fact, his fifteen-year-old brother had been dragooned into digging trenches for the army not far away. It is, however, safe to say that if the Germans had not reached the Donbas, Kukhtin would not have ended up in the army.

It stands to reason that far more conscripts than volunteers suffered from Stalinism in the prewar years. Tens of millions of peasants experienced forced collectivization and dekulakization, which lasted into 1939. The same peasants suffered through the famine of 1932–1933. Millions of urban families were victims of political persecution before, during, and after the Great Terror, or *Ezhovshchina*, yet the vast majority reported

Peasant conscripts leaving their village to report for duty, September 1941.

for duty when called. Pavel Rogozin is a typical example of the urban victim of the *Ezhovshchina* who eventually found himself in the Red Army. Two generations of his extended family had been killed in the terror; only he and two aunts had survived. He likened the NKVD to the Gestapo. Yet, when drafted in 1943, Rogozin kept silent about his family's repression and served faithfully, if reluctantly.[12]

The case of Nikolai Blizniuk illustrates the more expected reaction of people cast out from the good graces of Soviet society. They weighed their options and chose to reject the state that had rejected them. Blizniuk was a peasant who hoped to realize his dream of becoming a pilot. In 1938, as he was walking to the railway station to catch the train to enroll in an aviation technical institute, a relative caught up with him and brought him home so his mother could break the news to him that his father had been arrested and taken away. That put an end to Blizniuk's dream of becoming a pilot. He did, however, manage to attend a civilian polytechnic institute. On graduation in 1940, the local military commissariat summoned him and slated him to attend an officers' military school. Now disenchanted with the Soviet regime, Blizniuk chose to use his father's arrest to avoid military service. He boldly stated to the commissioners that as the son of an enemy of the people, he was not suitable for military service. The commissariat, however, announced that because his father had been released and rehabilitated, he was suitable in their eyes. Blizniuk countered that a recent state decree exempted the most recent class of higher education graduates from military service, but this earned him only a six-week delay. The vindictive draft board secured an exception in his case and sent him off to the army as a private.[13]

Mikhail Kalashnikov, the famous weapons designer, was one who answered the call for conscription and did not associate his victimization with the Stalinist state. He remembered: "I never drew any connection between the tragedy that had struck our family and the person of Stalin. I thought the fault lay with little local bureaucrats. In my view, they were the ones really guilty for the deportation of our family to Siberia and my brother's exile to the Gulag. As for Stalin, he was beyond suspicion as far as I was concerned."[14]

A final example is one conscripted victim of repression who found a way to rationalize the problems of the USSR. This man was in the front lines when a Russian soldier who had been captured by the Germans sneaked back across Soviet lines. The Germans had sent him to try to get other soldiers to desert. This soldier told his fellow Russians that they would be better off if they went over to the Germans.

> I said to him, "Look, you think that things are better under the Germans. Well then go back to them if you want to, but I will not go with you. We are Soviet people, and we are fighting the Germans." And mind you, I am a man who had spent five years in a Soviet prison. Why did I say this? I felt that the road to socialism was not an easy one. We workers could have everything that we wanted, but we were encircled by the capitalist world and the capitalists would not let us have these things. So first we must fight them, and in the future we will have everything.[15]

Even though he had been victimized by the regime and had not volunteered, this man had reported for service holding on to the idea that someday a prosperous socialist state would emerge.

Whether a Soviet soldier was a soldier-philosopher or soldier-victim is nearly impossible to determine, except in individual cases in which soldiers articulate their thinking on why they served. For example,

Mikhail Chistiakov wrote to his wife in June 1942, "In order to stay alive we need to defend the independence of our motherland, all the common wealth of the government of the Soviet Union, and not spare our lives."[16] Yet he goes on to speak of fighting as necessary to safeguard the future of his family, which confuses the issue. Is he philosophic about society's values or his own family? Other soldiers were also philosophic about the war, but labeling them in Sella's terms is difficult, as the following two examples show. Boris Viaznikovtsev wrote to a friend: "Well now, apparently the world's cauldron is again beginning to boil with human blood. Again millions of people are shedding blood, one is doomed to famine, privation, the complete decay of farms, and to find the whole world not alive, but vegetating. Again tens of millions of people are supplied with guns and probably not one does not think about returning alive." He noted that the next day his unit would be shipping out to participate in a big offensive "to the west, where there is much blood and fire."[17] It is as though he was stoically waiting his turn to become a victim. Ivan Kopiistov wrote to his wife in May 1942 and described being bombed and strafed by German aircraft. He said, fatalistically, "there are no wars without sacrifice, there are sacrifices of comrades."[18]

Logically, we would expect those people who had benefited from Soviet power, such as army officers and party members, to support the regime and show an active loyalty to the Soviet cause by volunteering for active service; however, some did not. Bashir G. Amirov, an army lieutenant, dejectedly wrote home on 27 June 1941 that he had been looking forward to being discharged; now, he lamented, he would have to wait until after the war.[19] Thousands of former officers who were desperately needed in 1941 chose not to volunteer to return to active duty; instead, they waited to see if they would be summoned. Vasilii E. Burychev, a peasant with only a primary school education, achieved remarkable social mobility due to Soviet socialism, yet he was not motivated to volunteer. From his humble village origins he had risen to become an army officer and later secured a civilian position working in a district party finance section. This suggests that he supported the regime and its values, yet he and many others ignored numerous appeals for former officers to return to the colors, sitting tight at home until summoned in 1942.[20]

An example of the nonvolunteers—that is, the majority of soldiers and junior officers—is Evgenii Moniushko. His experience, as related in his memoirs, completely refutes the hypothesis that his generation welcomed the chance to prove itself worthy of the revolutionary generation by going to war for the USSR. Despite being the son of old Bolsheviks and a Komsomol member, Moniushko did not volunteer at the outbreak of war at age seventeen, or when he turned eighteen in July 1942, or when his brother was conscripted in November 1942. He waited until he was summoned in February 1943. As a conscript, he was assigned to attend a field artillery school for officers and was commissioned a junior lieutenant on graduation. He did not get to the front until 1944 and made no effort to get there sooner.

In contrast to others' wartime memoirs, Moniushko never says he wanted revenge, even though he had plenty of reason to feel that way. He survived the first terrible winter of the siege of Leningrad, where he saw many people, strangers and friends alike, die at the hands of the Germans. He does not claim he wanted to fight alongside his brother, even though he was old enough to join the army with him at the time. He does not incorporate any elements of wartime propaganda whatsoever into his narrative. He never mentions a yearning to get to the front while in training. He fails to mention motivation at all or the idea of patriotism, yet at the time he wrote his memoirs, he was clearly a *Soviet* patriot and makes snide, critical comments about the post-1991 Russian governments and defends Stalin's postwar policies in Hungary. Moniushko's pride in the Red Army and in his service is evident throughout his memoir.[21] His experience is representative of many soldier-philosophers—willing but not eager to serve, glad to receive the formal and informal social benefits of having served, and happy he survived.

A rather intriguing case of both unexpected volunteerism and nonvolunteerism is that of Toivo Kattonen. Though Finnish by nationality, when Finland was established as a nation in 1918, Kattonen's village ended up on the Soviet side of the border. His family first suffered under Stalinism in 1930 when the state collectivized the farms of his village. Next, in 1936, all the Finns were forcibly relocated from a zone thirty kilometers from the border. Kattonen's distress is reflected in this statement: "We do not know whose idea it was, who was guilty of this." His family ended up in Vologda, but Toivo moved to Leningrad in 1937. Soon thereafter he joined the Komsomol. He volunteered to fight against Finland in the Winter War in 1939 and was the only Finn in his otherwise all-Russian ski battalion. He remembers being treated very well by his comrades, yet "everyone was amazed that I was fighting the war on the Red Army side."[22] Kattonen had three brothers. One was drafted during the Winter War and was killed while spying for the Soviet army. The other two neither volunteered nor were drafted. Like all the other student and worker volunteers, Kattonen was discharged after the war. He never explains why he fought against his kinsmen or for the USSR, but he had ample reason not to fight: he was Finnish by origin, and the Soviet state had stolen his family's property through collectivization and uprooted them from their home.

In 1941 when the Germans invaded, Kattonen, already a trained soldier with combat experience, was just the kind of man the Red Army needed, but he did not volunteer this time. Instead, he was drafted into a labor battalion in 1942, where he served out the war. One of his brothers was drafted and killed at the front. His last brother died as a civilian in the siege of Leningrad. He makes no claim that he volunteered for the front, even though vengeance could have served as a motive. Some psychological or emotional turn that he could not or would not express must have happened between 1940 and 1941 to turn Kattonen into a nonvolunteer.

The vast majority of nonvolunteers were conscript soldiers, but many other people found themselves in the army through an extraordinary, little publicized process called *front mobilization*. Front mobilization was the term used to describe the act of military units shanghaiing men on the spot, which probably brought more soldier-victims into the army than any other method of recruitment. Men were not sent to reserve regiments for training but were clothed, armed, and trained on the job by the unit. Eventually their names were added to regimental rolls, and then the NKO would be informed. It was not unusual for such soldiers to be killed before they officially became members of the Red Army.

Front mobilization was instituted at the beginning of the war and lasted until the fighting passed beyond Soviet territory in 1944. The earlier example of Valentin G. Kukhtin represents a case of front mobilization. In 1942 the high command criticized this practice, citing the high casualties it produced for such meager results, and it declared that only military councils at the army level were authorized to conduct such mobilizations. This criticism had no effect; in fact, the practice became even more widespread in 1943 as the Red Army worked its way west, liberating towns and villages teeming with young men. In late 1943 the NKO reasserted its order of 1942 and further required that men mobilized at the front be sent to reserve regiments for training and later assignment to frontline units. The various fronts were given quotas of men to mobilize from the liberated areas and were told to inform the NKO if they exceeded those quotas. The fronts were reassured that they could keep the men they mobilized—within their quotas.[23]

A Russian rifle platoon commander gave the following account of an attack involving men who had been hastily mobilized, without authorization, during the battles in Belorussia in December 1943:

A human chain in civilian dress passed by along the communications trench. "Slavs, who are you and where are you from?" I asked.

"We're from Orlovshchina, reinforcements."

"What kind of reinforcements in civilian clothes and without rifles?"

"They told us we'd get them in battle."[24]

After a five-minute artillery barrage, the replacements joined the attack. Despite the battalion commander's threat to shoot anyone who held back, the attack faltered. Heavy casualties among the untrained replacements validated the concerns of the high command.

Natalia Peshkova alluded to front mobilization in 1942, describing the aftermath of a battle she was in. One of the battalions of her regiment had a contingent of 280 graduates of a military college at the start of fighting, which was reduced to only 16 men when the fighting was over. "Our recruits after the battle were the boys of sixteen and older from the nearby villages. They knew nothing and were scared of everything. These were our fresh forces."[25]

Normally, the state conscripted boys sixteen and seventeen years of age for work in factories, but in 1944, due to a serious manpower shortage, the personnel section of the Commissariat of Defense proposed putting them into the ranks. It suggested calling on sixteen-year-olds to form volunteer youth brigades—something akin to the German Waffen SS division "Hitler Jugend." The proposal was rejected on the grounds that at that age, teenagers were just not up to the demands of war.[26] The report did not speculate how many boys might have been inclined to sign up.

Other nonvolunteers, many of whom may have considered themselves soldier-victims, were impressed into the army from the Gulag. The army actively sought manpower from the NKVD's prison camps early in the war. By the end of December 1941, 420,000 men from labor camps, special settlements, or internal exile had been sent to serve in the armed forces. In 1942 and 1943 an additional 157,000 Gulag inmates were turned over to the army. By the end of the war, the state had released or pressed into military service approximately 975,000 ordinary criminals, political prisoners, and former kulaks and thousands of the 436,600 officers and men who had been arrested and sentenced to the Gulag since the beginning of the war.[27]

Criminals from the camps, commonly referred to as *zeks,* typically had little or no social conscience or patriotic feeling. In 1943 Evgenii Mazo's division received reinforcements of zeks who had been released early to "atone for their guilt in blood, now that the *rodina* was in danger." The zeks looked down on the soldiers. With a rather warped sense of self-worth, they considered themselves to be citizens but regarded the soldiers as slaves. While in transit on trains, they deserted or caused trouble at train stations, so the army began to halt troop trains outside of towns and cities until they could pass through without stopping. If a train had to stop, the officer in charge wired ahead for extra police to guard the trains and the station.[28] The mobilization of so many Gulag prisoners meant the NKVD needed fewer camp guards, so 117,000 guards were eventually transferred to the Red Army too.[29]

In the spring of 1942 Fedor Gorb was serving a sentence in a Gulag labor camp, working in an oil field along with hundreds of other prisoners. He was told his sentence had been commuted and that they all were free men—free to be mobilized into the army. In the ensuing months, though, the men continued to be treated as prisoners. They were kept in their camp and still worked in the oil field. In November the army took them by train under guard to reserve regiments. There, they received no training before being assigned to a rifle division. They were treated as pariahs in their new division and were subjected to strict discipline. The Special Sections kept a close watch on them.[30]

Resistance to Mobilization: National and Ethnic Minorities

In contrast to the Soviet state's success in mobilizing urban Russian youths, who identified most closely with the ideals of the revolution, socialism, and the *rodina*, the state had the most difficulty mobilizing those from the opposite end of the social-ethnic spectrum—the rural, non-Russian minorities whose race, culture, historical experience, and local identification lay largely outside *rossiiskii* and *russkii* patriotism. Sweeping generalizations about minorities' reluctance to serve are ill advised. However, we can say that, in general, their reluctance stemmed less from ideological or racial bases and more from practical short- or long-term issues, but not predictably or consistently. Because their social and economic lives were located primarily outside the Russian-oriented mainstream, national and ethnic minorities had almost no intrinsic motivation to volunteer and little basis for self-interested service. Furthermore, extrinsic motivations were weak. There was little or no social pressure to conform to the dictates of the Soviet state and no hate for the German victimization of Russians. Besides feeling little or no attachment to the Soviet state, the men of Central Asia and the Caucasus doubted the Soviet government's ability to enforce conscription, and they were willing to test it.

In the Caucasus, the Chechens, Ingush, Kabardins, Karachais, Balkars, Ossetians, and Georgians still resented the reconquest and reabsorption of their lands into the Soviet Union in the 1920s. Their anger still smoldered from the regime's attempt to collectivize agriculture in the 1930s. Partly because of topography and clan social structures, these groups had been more successful in thwarting the Sovietization of their societies than any group in the Slavic areas. A full-scale rebellion against the collectivization of agriculture broke out in 1932, which ended in the death of more than 300 Chechens. Afterward, the peoples of the North Caucasus continued to passively resist collectivization and committed occasional acts of violence into 1941 in Chechnya and Dagestan.[31] Many of the peoples of the Caucasus were Muslim and were more than put off by the antireligious campaigns launched against them. These campaigns resulted in the destruction of mosques, the death of mullahs, the unveiling of women, and the erosion of traditional forms of male dominance.

With such simmering resentment against Russian cultural hegemony and Soviet economic and social policies, mobilization of the peoples of the Caucasus would prove to be very difficult.

At the outbreak of war with Germany, few northern Caucasians rallied to the Soviet cause. For example, the initial voluntary mobilization in Dagestan in June and July 1941 netted 1,692 people; of these, 1,298 were Russians, and only 332 were natives of various Dagestan ethnicities. By the end of 1942 a total of only 3,066 men and women had voluntarily entered the Red Army from Dagestan, most of them Russians.[32] An additional 3,763 people (including 1,491 women) eventually volunteered for the *opolchenie*.[33]

When the Soviet government made a push to conscript men from the Caucasus in late autumn 1941, open rebellion broke out, leading to bombing and strafing by the Red Air Force to suppress it. In the spring of 1942 the attempt to conscript Chechens was clearly a failure. Thousands of young men fled to the mountains. The state had the names of some 14,000 men liable for duty but managed to conscript only 4,395. Of those, 2,365 deserted before being transferred out of the Caucasus. During the course of the war, the state managed to get only 17,500 Chechens and Ingush into uniform, and, at one point, nearly that many (13,000) were listed as deserters and draft evaders. More than 20 percent of Kabardins (5,506 of 25,000) deserted. In September 1942 the lone Chechen-Ingush cavalry regiment and cavalry division were finally sent to the front. The head of the Chechen-Ingush Provincial Committee of the Communist Party reported that there were still 45,000 Chechens and Ingush of military age who had yet to be drafted. Fearing resistance, he recommended to Moscow that future national formations be formed on a voluntary basis.[34] Instead, Stalin decided to round up the remaining Chechens and Ingush in 1943 and exile them to Siberia.

The authorities in Dagestan also experienced resistance to the draft. By early November 1941 the military council of the Caucasus Front called on the city defense committee of Makhachkala to assist the 44th Army in forming blocking detachments to combat desertion. The fighting against deserters turned into a war behind the front—with members of blocking detachments awarded medals for bravery under fire.[35] By the middle of April 1942 blocking detachments had detained and arrested 1,535 deserters, were hunting 312 more, and had arrested 2,261 draft evaders.[36] Dagestan authorities ceased their attempts to conscript men in 1943 and instead continued mobilization on a voluntary basis. The republic was assigned a goal of 4,850 recruits but could produce only 4,135 natives of Dagestan by the end of the year.[37]

All told, between June 1941 and June 1944, 62,751 men of the North Caucasus deserted or successfully evaded the draft.[38] In the case of the North Caucasus, we can say that the prewar experience of Soviet power negatively affected the people's willingness to support the war and risk their lives for the continuation of the Stalinist system. Not even German occupation of their territories led them to take up arms in defense. When one resident of the North Caucasus was asked, "What did you think of the invasion of Russia by the Germans?" the Azeri responded, "I said thank God. The Germans have come to liberate us. I was so happy I could not sleep, wondering when the Germans would come."[39] Only after the Nazis' initially soft occupation policies turned harsh did appreciable opposition to them materialize.[40] But that opposition to the German occupation can in no way be characterized as pro-Soviet.

Mobilization in the Crimea, home to the Tatars, further illustrates the difficulty in recruiting non-Slavic populations. Of 153,000 eligible collective farmers, mostly Tatars, the state successfully mobilized only 43,000 (28 percent) in the first months of the war before the peninsula was overrun. All told, the organs of the party and government managed to recruit 160,000 people for four *opolchenie* divisions and numerous *istrebitel'nyi* battalions, relying heavily on Russians, Communist Party members, Komsomolets, students, and factory workers from the main urban areas.[41] In the aftermath of the Crimea's liberation from German occupation, the Soviet state took its revenge on the Tatars, accusing them as a whole of disloyalty. To justify the mass deportation of Tatars to Uzbekistan in 1944, the GKO claimed that, "during the Patriotic War many Crimean Tatars betrayed the Motherland, deserting Red Army units that defended the Crimea and siding with the enemy, joining volunteer army units formed by the Germans to fight against the Red Army."[42] The report went on to accuse the Tatars of being particularly savage in their reprisals against Soviet partisans—mostly Russians—while acting as members of German punitive detachments during the German troops' occupation of the Crimea.

Turkmenistan gave a better showing than the Caucasus, but not by

much. The population of this vastly agrarian, Muslim republic replicated the pattern of minimal volunteerism and service. There was no
significant rush to volunteer as there had been in the Russian republic.
In the first days after the start of the war, only about 3,000 men in all of
Turkmenistan volunteered for military service. During the war, fewer
than 14,000 residents of Turkmenistan volunteered for the armed forces,
many of whom were Russian. Another 125,000 men were conscripted.[43]

The Turkmenistan Communist Party was not particularly impressive
in leading the way. In the first six months of the war, when passions were
at their highest, only 3,013 communists volunteered to serve. In all of
1942, just 4,639 party members joined voluntarily, and only half that
many in 1943. All told, just over 11,000 party and Komsomol members
volunteered, while 19,960 Komsomolets and 7,268 communists waited
to be drafted.[44]

Turkmenistan did not form any *opolchenie* or *istrebitel'nyi* units, but
it did man two nationality-based cavalry divisions and two national rifle
brigades, one of which never went to war. In each of these units, the
manpower consisted of approximately one-third communists or Komsomol members. There was no clamor on the part of the men or the republic's leadership to get these forces to the front. None of the Turkmen
units saw action until late in 1942.[45]

The situation in Kazakhstan was similar to that in Turkmenistan.
During 1941 and 1942 the Red Army formed nine rifle divisions and two
rifle brigades in Kazakhstan. Documentary accounts, however, make no
claims that they were manned either in whole or in part with volunteers.
As in the Crimea, recruitment through conscription was overwhelmingly concentrated in the cities and included many Russians, Ukrainians,
and Jews. Numbers of party and Komsomol members were especially
low. One of the first divisions to be formed, the 391st Rifle Division,
claimed only 7.6 percent Komsomolets and 5.7 percent communists at
its founding in September 1941.[46]

The state did not direct the Kazakh republic to form *opolchenie* units,
and the local authorities took no initiative to do so. Nor did they form
any nationality-based units. One can only speculate that the nearly 1
million deaths and the total upheaval of Kazakh rural life during collectivization made the regime shy away from what could have been an

embarrassing show of nonsupport by Kazakh peasants. In general, authorities in the Kazakh Communist Party and the Central Asia Military District, as well as the North Caucasus Military District, found it difficult to man and supply the mandated nationality-based units. They were ordered to raise twenty cavalry divisions and fifteen separate rifle brigades, amounting to no more than 250,000 men. As it turned out, conscription and the enrollment of Slavs were essential to fill them out.[47]

The Bashkir republic also had a mixed record regarding patriotic mobilization. There was an embarrassing lack of enthusiasm for volunteering, and the entire republic produced only about 3,000 volunteers in the first two days after the German invasion. Intensive work over the next few days yielded pitiful results. The republic's authorities blamed local party officials for working slowly and without enthusiasm.[48] In subsequent months, efforts by the party and Komsomol resulted in the recruitment of some 75,362 people into various *opolchenie* units. The republic conscripted another 231,993 by the end of 1941, with Ufa, the capital, contributing the largest single contingent.[49]

By mid-1944 the Bashkir republic claimed to have contributed 559,671 men and women to the Red Army on a volunteer and conscription basis. The problem is that the numbers of Bashkirs and Tatars are unknown; documentary evidence suggests that this number includes many Russians. Some were Russians who had resided in Bashkir before the war and were working in recently created industries; others were Russians and Ukrainians who had been evacuated from the western regions of the USSR in the face of the German advance. For example, a local Russian commanded the *opolchenie* regiment formed in Sterlitamaksk province; his chief of staff was also Russian. In the top leadership, only the commissar was a Bashkir.[50] In an attempt to create nationality-based units, the republic recruited enough Bashkirs and Tatars to man only two very small cavalry divisions.

Other minorities showed an equal reticence to perform wartime service. The Tadzhik republic managed to produce about 10,000 men for the Red Army during the war—not all of them Tadzhiks—and fewer than 1,000 volunteered. Out of those 10,000 men, the army formed three very small cavalry divisions and an artillery battalion.[51] Similar to the peoples of the Caucasus, many Central Asians still saw themselves as conquered peoples. The legacy of forced integration was not that distant; the Red Army and NKVD had crushed the Basmachi tribes into submission as recently as the mid-1920s. In September 1941 the NKVD reported that the Basmachi were openly resisting the draft in both Tadzhikistan and Uzbekistan.[52] The Udmurtia autonomous republic produced two artillery battalions, a rifle division, and an aviation regiment, strictly through conscription. The state did not even bother to call for volunteers or appeal to the party active.[53] GlavPUR's suggestion to the Uzbek Central Committee to use the political education theme, "The Russian people is the older brother of the Uzbek people," unwisely reinforced the idea of Russian domination and failed to stimulate recruiting.[54]

Ukrainian and Belorussian Slavs could also be reluctant to report for conscription. One Ukrainian peasant, whose family had been dekulakized in the 1930s, remembered being called to Kholovka to report for conscription. He and some friends went, but when they learned how close the Germans were, they returned to their village. He said, "We didn't go into the *voenkomat*. Because we waited for the Germans as we waited for God, as the liberation."[55] Another peasant, a Belorussian youth, recalled, "When the war started and they started to take people into the army I didn't go. So some regional committee or other in Gomel' came after us in the night, but we fled in the night, and after three days the Germans came."[56] He then went home and resumed farming. Both these men and their friends and families seem to have been indifferent to the fate of the *rodina* and glad to be out from under both Russian and Soviet rule.

As alluded to earlier, the People's Commissariat of Defense began forming nationality-based units in the fall of 1941. This was a reversal of the army's prewar policy, which had been to disband nationality-based territorial units in the late 1930s. At that time, national minorities began to be integrated into regular army units when they reported for duty. One thought on the revival of national units was that it would help spur voluntarism among the obviously reluctant males of the various ethnicities.

The first unit to be formed under this change was a Latvian division. The Latvian army had been absorbed into the Red Army and reduced to two divisions in 1940, after the Soviet occupation and annexation of Latvia. These two divisions were destroyed in action in the summer of 1941. A new Latvian division, officially titled the 16th Latvian Rifle Division, was formed to replace the destroyed divisions. The intent was to man it by recruiting the many Latvians who had fled or been evacuated in the face of the German invasion. As it turned out, about 70 percent of its eventual complement of 10,374 actually did volunteer, but only 32 percent of the enlisted men were ethnic Latvians. Of the rest—29 percent Russians, 34 percent Jews, and members of thirty other nationalities—most had resided in Latvia at the start of the war and, for propaganda purposes, were referred to as Latvians. The majority were workers and white-collar personnel. Only a paltry 9 percent were peasants. There were 171 female soldiers, too. About 20 percent of the division's officers and men were Komsomolets or communists. The division began forming in December 1941, but it did not enter combat until February 1943 and sustained enormous casualties—47 percent losses due to death, wounding, frostbite, and those who went missing. After two weeks of fighting it was withdrawn to the rear, without having accomplished its mission.[57]

The Estonian Communist Party made no attempt to rely on volunteers. Estonians and others who lived in the formerly independent Estonia, including soldiers and officers of the Estonian army, were conscripted into two divisions. The membership fluctuated between 80 and 90 percent ethnic Estonians, except among the leadership, which was about 60 percent Estonian. Russians constituted the majority of non-Estonians. These two divisions did not see action until 1943. A Lithuanian division was also formed, but Lithuanians accounted for only one-third of the manpower.[58]

During and after the war, the Soviet state made much of the participation of national minorities. We can assume, however, that this publicity—intended as proof of minority loyalty—was meant to divert attention from the overall poor support of the war by said minorities, although it should be balanced against the reality that some members of every nationality served loyally, even heroically.[59] The forced resettlement of the Chechens, Volga Germans, and Crimean Tatars was hushed up, and the fiction of the Soviet brotherhood of all nationalities was written into the history of the war. The populations of the non-Russian republics and autonomous regions were much smaller than that of the Russian republic, of course; however, the most striking features of these numbers were the woeful lack of volunteers and the extent of draft evasion. Volunteers were lacking not only in the general population but also among party members, who should have supported the war effort wholeheartedly. Youthful Komsomol members, supposedly of the idealistic generation most prepared to fight for the Soviet homeland, also proved reluctant to join, in contrast to their Russian counterparts.

Part 4

MOTIVATION AND MORALE

7
The Fear Factor

The experience of the Great Patriotic War was remarkably similar to that of the Winter War, but on a larger scale. The tests of motivation and morale would be greater because the losses, the gravity of defeats, and the failures of leadership were greater. Ideology, patriotism, and basic loyalty to the state would be put to a more severe test under far more intense battle conditions. The most marked difference was that in the Great Patriotic War, Stalin and the Soviet state were faced with the challenge of motivating the *frontoviki* to fight over the long term and, for nearly two years, in the context of uncertain victory for a cause about which many held deep-seated reservations.

For decades, two camps of historical wisdom have assumed that it was either the Red Army's harsh, fear-based discipline or patriotism that kept the men in the line and made the army effective. Little if any research has been done on the individual and the small unit to either substantiate or challenge these assumptions. This chapter analyzes how the Soviet state and the Red Army strove to enhance effectiveness by controlling and manipulating the soldier through fear of punishment. I do not use the Soviet experience to make universal observations about motivation or morale; instead, I illustrate the particular circumstances experienced by the Red Army collectively and by the Soviet soldier individually that helped define the role of punitive measures in the Red Army's eventual success in World War II.

There is no doubt that people who are intrinsically motivated to serve and fight and who can maintain their morale and motivation regardless of their social or physical environment will always represent a minority of any population. Thus, it is fundamental to military effectiveness that the state and the army be able to motivate and elicit compliance from its population and its servicemen extrinsically. It is a given that motivation and morale can be bolstered or weakened by both internal and external factors. Scholar Stephen D. Wesbrook identifies essentially three types of power that can be used to bring about compliance: coercive, remunerative, and normative. He argues: "Coercive power rests in the actual or threatened application of physical sanctions; remunerative power rests on the control of material resources and rewards; normative power is based on the allocation and manipulation of symbolic rewards and deprivations."[1] In essence, this is the classic "carrot and stick" approach to organizational management and leadership, which is found sprinkled throughout management and organization theory. Whether the carrot, the stick, or a combination thereof is used depends in large part on how soldiers are behaving at the moment and on the leadership ability of the commanders.

The experience of the Red Army shows what one would expect—that the more talented the officers and the more compliant the soldiers, the more likely leaders were to take a positive approach. When the officers were less capable, the soldiers would often be less compliant, and the leaders typically responded by employing sterner forms of coercion. This usually led to a pathological cycle of dissent and disobedience.

From the vantage point of military folk wisdom, compliance seems more likely when a unit is highly cohesive and when soldiers relate well with NCOs and officers, as well as with one another. Other crucial variables appear to be the soldiers' skill, their grasp of the mission, and their acceptance of hard necessities and linked risks, along with a sense of being supported by society at large, with evidence of the people's trust in their military institution. At best, amid an ideal mix of these factors, officers command with moral authority, without having to resort to implied or actual coercion. At the lowest level of compliance relationships, both the threat and the reality of coercion appear to be nearly constant when soldiers do not accept or even comprehend their cause or their mission. This leads to minimal cohesion, distrust of the military establishment or the regime, and alienation from society. As one might expect, during the Great Patriotic War, the compliance relationships in the Soviet armed forces varied from unit to unit and situation to situation, usually falling somewhere between the ideal and worst cases. Compliance was, as it is in the armed forces in general, reflected in a particular unit's morale and motivation.

The Bolsheviks founded the Red Army intending to base it on the ideal type of compliance relationship; however, the army came close to switching to the worst-case relationship during the Great Patriotic War, when many officers often relied exclusively on coercive power. Stalin, hard-pressed by the string of major Nazi victories in the late summer and autumn of 1941 and again in the spring of 1942, veered sharply in the direction of coercion by issuing Order No. 270 in August 1941 and Order No. 227 in July 1942. As early as 17 July 1941, he had signed an order authorizing the Special Sections to shoot noncompliant men on the spot.[2] Although the Red Army never abandoned efforts to motivate soldiers with positive approaches, coercion remained the most visible tool for the duration of the war. The following analysis considers how these ideas of morale and motivation affected compliance, how the military and Soviet state sought to manipulate them, and how successful they were.

Historical Representations of Motivation

Before we can begin to create a new understanding of the Soviet soldier—as a person subject to emotional and intellectual shifts in the understanding of his duty and his role as a soldier, and his willingness to fulfill them—we have to overcome decades of misinterpretations of who he was. Throughout the Cold War, the impressions of German officers and soldiers rendered in novels, memoirs, and monographs unfortunately became the principal corpus of Western historiography and were given validity because they were written by men who had fought the Red Army. They are, however, very misleading if not outright erroneous or deliberately falsified.

The experience of Waffen SS Lieutenant General Max Simon's forces repulsing a massed Red Army attack across open ground in August 1941 is typical of German depictions: "At 600 meters we opened fire and whole sections of the first wave just vanished leaving here and there an odd survivor still walking stolidly forward. It was uncanny, unbelievable, inhuman."[3] In this instance, General Simon's units destroyed three waves of attackers before a fourth wave—jumping over, stumbling into, and walking around the bodies left from the first three attacks—came at them. He said this fourth wave and subsequent assaults came "without hesitation." In his opinion, only an inhuman army could perform such a feat.

A German enlisted man's account of another attack in 1941, which he characterized as desperate and hopeless, gives a similar impression. He wrote: "Whether they come in with tanks or whether the infantry comes in without support; whether their Cossacks charge in on horses or whether they come rolling forward in motor lorries, the end is always the same. They are driven back with such losses that one wonders how they can find the courage and the men to keep coming on." This attack took place over terrain covered with the decomposing bodies of Soviet soldiers that had lain there for weeks. The stench was overpowering. This caused the German soldier to ask rhetorically: "Do they have no feeling of fear?" He could detect no hesitation on the part of the Soviets and concluded, "The Bolshevik soldiers are a strange mixture of fanaticism and oriental despair."[4]

German general Kurt Dittmar, a well-known wartime radio commentator with a reputation for relative objectivity in Western Allied military circles, was asked after the war his opinion of the general characteristics of the Russian soldier. He answered, "I would put first, what might be called the soulless indifference of the troops—it was something more than fatalism."[5] General Günther Blumentritt's opinion was that warring against "the Red Army of 1941–1945 was far harder than the Tsar's Army, for they were fighting fanatically for an idea."[6] In numerous German writings on World War II, traits such as fanaticism and "oriental" despair are cited as separating Soviet soldiers from the rational, Western, German soldiers in a negative way. To the Germans, who managed ethical and logical flip-flops routinely and artfully, the Russians were not really courageous; they were fanatics whose moral sense had been numbed by communist ideology and brutal discipline. They were perhaps to be feared, but not respected. Unfortunately, even more than sixty years after the war, historians repeat stereotypical descriptions of the Soviet soldier, such as his "indifference to human life, whether his own or others."[7]

The fundamental problem with these assessments is that those making them had no personal knowledge of Soviet soldiers, and in a special irony, they kept alive aspects of Nazi racial ideology. Neither contemporary observers nor subsequent historians knew what was going on in the hearts and minds of *frontoviki*. And contrary to the popular perception, interviews, letters, diary entries, and memoirs of the average Soviet soldier, as well as reports by political officers and the secret police, reveal that they were no more fatalistic, indifferent, cruel, courageous, or brainwashed than their Nazi enemies; arguably, they were less so. The following accounts, gathered from veteran Soviet soldiers who participated in infantry attacks against the Germans, paint quite a different picture from the German-generated Western stereotype. They also challenge the official Soviet version that depicts every soldier as a courageous and heroic patriot.

In addressing the question, "What was the most terrifying thing?" Semion Aria answered: "An attack—that's the hardest test. You know that you might get hit, but you have to keep moving toward it—that's horrible! It was difficult to get up, and the feeling that most probably you wouldn't come back, that was also hard. Mortar shelling was terrifying and [so was] machine gun fire. Tracer fire, when it starts from above, and you only see the luminescent line lower, lower, falling toward you, now it will reach your level and cut you in half."[8]

Most Soviet veterans' descriptions of wartime and battle experiences reveal an essential humanity similar to American and British soldiers' depictions. Russians experienced the same full range of emotions as their German adversaries. For example, decades after the war, Daniil Zlatkin described his initiation to combat, which occurred after several minutes of instruction on how to use a machine gun. He came under fire as soon as they neared the front lines and was wounded almost immediately.

> I'm not a coward, on the contrary, I was a daredevil, but there I felt death—I crouched, my hands and legs shook, I couldn't get up, I felt that everything was shooting at me, but why wasn't I getting hit?! At that time some captain yelled: "Scum, forward, for the Motherland! For Stalin!" And stuck the revolver to the back of my head. I yelled "Forward!" But who's behind me?! Nobody. . . . Me and him—the two of us. And where were all our people? They were lying around. It wasn't a battle, it was simply slaughter: we were lying on the bare ground, not seeing the enemy, but the enemy saw us and didn't let anyone at all get up. I fell on the ground again, then raised my hand,

yelled to somebody, and I had no idea who I was screaming to: "Forward! For the Motherland! For Stalin!"[9]

Neither fearless nor a coward, Gennadii Shutz recalled his baptism of fire: "At the Serebriannie Prudii station we were bombed for the first time. I jumped head first into the closest bushes and sat there shaking with fear until the planes left."[10] Ivan Shelepov recounted his first battle with no reference to his motivation or idealism: "I thought that there will be a cry 'Forward!' we would shout 'Hurrah!' and attack. Everything was quite different though. Our company commander told us quietly 'Let's go, guys!' and climbed on to the parapet. I did the same. I followed him purely automatically, not realizing what I was doing."[11]

Although wartime and postwar Soviet propaganda was fond of the terms *fearless* and *valiant* when describing Soviet soldiers in combat, few men denied being afraid. Semen Aria remembered that everyone was afraid to die: "Death was around us every day, every hour, and on all sides. You could sit quietly, drink tea, and a stray shell would fall on you. It was impossible to get used to that. It doesn't mean that we constantly were all jittery, that everyone sat, walked expecting death any minute. Death simply came or it didn't." Like Shutz, Aria trembled with fear during air raids. "People lost their minds from fear. The feeling was as if every bomb was falling straight at your head. It was horrible!" Bombs howled as they fell "like hail" from what seemed like 200 or 300 aircraft. It was sheer hell. "I remember, there was one Nekrasov—he almost went mad. When the air raid was over he couldn't be found anywhere." When they eventually found him cowering in a trench, his comrades called to him, but he refused to come out. "And what terror was in his eyes," remembered Aria.[12]

Ivan Kobets had a slightly different take on fear, which he thought was routinely overcome by experience. "Over time, when you get used to it, you'd understand—this shell is just gonna go by and this one is dangerous."[13] But when soldiers were away from the front for any length of time, the fear returned when they came back. Naturally, Soviet soldiers felt the same fear any normal human being would, and it took some measure of motivation to overcome it and go forward.

A broader understanding of the Soviet soldiers' humanity, relative to fear in wartime, is given by Konstantin Simonov: "War is not utter peril or the wait for death and the idea of same. If this were so, then not a single person could endure the gravity of it, even for a month." Instead, "war is the sum total of mortality, danger, and the constant possibility of being killed and the chances for all peculiarities and details of daily living, which are always present in one's life."[14] He points out the obvious fact that soldiers, even in the front lines, have a host of duties and responsibilities related not only to the fighting but also to daily living that occupy their minds, so they cannot simply dwell on their safety. These other preoccupations blunt soldiers' fears so they are able to maintain themselves without becoming fearless.

Many interviews of *frontoviki* substantiate this assertion. A wide variety of experiences peripheral to combat distracted the men's thoughts from the fear of death. When asked what was the hardest thing in war, Nikolai Dupak replied: "The hardest thing was when we had to march 100 kilometers in one night. Trot—gallop—trot—gallop. Endless commands: 'Don't spare the horses! Don't spare the horses!' because by morning we had to be in another place. Time! Time! People fell asleep and dropped from horses. And horses collapsed with a ruptured heart."[15]

Mikhail Badigin shared the experience of millions of soldiers—constantly moving and digging in and moving again: "During the night you redeploy and dig the gun in. No time to sleep. It is not insomnia—there is just no time to sleep. In the morning there is an artillery preparation, you move on together with the infantry. The next you are digging again. Three or four days exhaust you to such an extent that you become indifferent, you are not even happy to be alive anymore."[16]

Fatigue, lack of sleep, hunger, cold, homesickness, relations with comrades and superiors, and worries about home and family—and the personal efforts to address these concerns—distracted soldiers from the immediacy of death at the front and the fear associated with it. These divergent forces led Elena Seniavskaia to hypothesize that "in war two basic hypostaces of life exist: danger—the battle, the extreme situation—and everyday living. In this regard one overcomes the other and danger becomes a part of life, but petty social details are inseparable from the functioning of a person in the environment of continual danger."[17] In sum, soldiering, even in wartime, is more than just combat. It encompasses myriad activities that require the soldiers' attention and, like fear, just as surely affect their motivation and morale. In this respect, Soviet soldiers were no exception.

Role of the Army and the State in Motivation and Compliance

In his study of courage, based on his observations as a frontline doctor in the First World War, Lord Moran writes: "Courage is a moral quality; it is not a chance gift of nature like an aptitude for games. It is a cold choice between two alternatives, the fixed resolve not to quit; an act of renunciation, which must be made not once but many times by the power of the will. Courage is will power."[18] Moran believes this willpower is internally generated and is sustained or degraded by how the individual reacts to the stress of combat. No doubt there is much truth to this; however, it would be wrong to neglect external factors that can impinge on the soldier's willpower. The belief that courage for the fight and the willpower to go on could be influenced from without drove the United States, Germany, and the Soviet Union to employ a variety of approaches to manipulate and sustain the motivation of their soldiers.

Coming from the opposite end of the spectrum, a short but to-the-point study of American veterans of the Abraham Lincoln Battalion of Spanish Civil War fame suggests that courage is bolstered primarily by external factors. When asked, "What would you say are the most important things that help a man overcome fear in battle?" these men offered a straightforward view of human emotions in stressful situations. In descending order, from most to least important, they listed belief in war aims, competent and caring leadership, confidence in one's military training, sufficient materiel, accurate information about the military situation, esprit de corps, understanding fear and making conscious efforts to control it, hatred of the enemy, and being distracted and keeping busy to avoid boredom. They were also concerned about not letting their friends down.[19] This analysis assumes that all soldiers have the basic capacity to engage in combat in the first place, an assumption Lord Moran does not share. These tenets and the preceding paragraphs highlight the value of studying military effectiveness from the perspective of individual soldiers, including their perception of their place in the world and their appreciation of the immediate circumstances, in order to understand the behavior of the Red Army as a whole.

Recognizing that their men were human and not inherently fatalistic, the Soviet state and military high command used a variety of approaches to influence the motivation of the Red Army soldier. Scholar William L. Hauser postulates: "There are four factors which appear to persuade or compel men to fight: *submission, fear, loyalty,* and *pride.* Each comes from a number of sources, and each is interdependent to some degree with the others."[20] In the Soviet army, as in virtually all modern armies, submission was enforced with discipline and fear with punishment; loyalty was encouraged with rewards, nationalist propaganda, and social cohesion (the primary group); and pride was bolstered by tradition and moral appeal. In addition, each of these four factors was reinforced by ideology and institutional identification as the Red Army (like all armies) promoted submission to its organizational goals, rules of behavior, and obedience to superiors under formal military discipline. This discipline was characterized by obedience to the daily tasks of soldiering within the military organization, such as maintaining barracks or living quarters, cleaning and caring for weapons and equipment, standing guard, attending formation and parading, training, and so forth. All were designed to accustom the soldier to obeying orders and to habituate him to military culture.

Fear, as a coercive tool to deter or punish noncompliance, was institutionalized in a code of military justice, which, at its extreme, included the execution of soldiers for disobedience. The harshest punishments were reserved for failures in combat effectiveness. The following excerpt from an interview of Aleksandr Bodnar' illustrates the effect of discipline-based submission on combat behavior and the balancing of Soviet soldiers' fear of the Germans and fear of punishment by the Red Army. Bodnar' was ordered to take the battalion's last three tanks and lead an attack on the Germans in a village, then await the arrival of Soviet infantry. After a day of fighting Bodnar' was down to two tanks, when he was ordered to return to friendly lines because the infantry could not break through to him. In the process, his tank was hit, Bodnar' was wounded, and one of his crewmen was killed. The last remaining tank left them behind. Bodnar', the gunner, and the driver abandoned their tank and began to think of how to escape. Then Bodnar' noticed the tank had stopped burning.

> I lie there and say, "Why aren't you burning, why aren't you burning?"
> After all, if it doesn't burn I'm facing the penal battalion, because I
> had the right to leave the tank under two circumstances: the first, if it

caught fire and the second, if its armaments were out of commission. But now the gun was fine and the tank stopped burning. It turns out that the tank itself wasn't burning but vapors within were. And the vapors burned out and the oil burned out on the bottom as well and the tank stopped burning. I lie there, thinking about the responsibility for an abandoned tank, what will become of me.[21]

Fear of the consequences of abandoning a working tank was greater than the urge for immediate survival. Bodnar' sent the driver back to get the tank and then pick him up. The driver succeeded in starting the tank, but unfortunately, he panicked and drove off, leaving Bodnar' and the gunner on the battlefield.

At the outset, the battalion commander had been ordered to attack, but because he had only three tanks, he assigned the task to Lieutenant Bodnar'—not wanting Bodnar' to be killed, but perhaps hoping the tanks would be destroyed so the battalion would be withdrawn for rest and refitting. After his tank was hit, Bodnar' wanted it to burn so he and his crew could escape to safety. When it did not burn, he risked the life of his driver to retrieve it so they would not be shot for abandoning equipment. The driver, however, chose to save his own life and abandoned his officer and fellow soldier, perhaps gambling that they would die in the field and be unable to take revenge on him. This vignette shows the complex thoughts and emotions exhibited in combat at different levels of the military hierarchy. Bodnar's strong desire to live comes through very clearly, but he and his men were caught between the threat of punishment by their army and death at the hands of the enemy, to a degree not experienced by their counterparts in the Allied armies. Whatever the means of enforcement, conditioning troops to submit to military rules of behavior and to obey orders is the basis of maintaining discipline in any army. It is in the degree of the threats used that the Soviet military stood apart from most other armed forces in World War II.

Coercion and Its Effectiveness

The harsh discipline of the Soviet army in the Second World War, like that of the Imperial Russian armed forces in history, has become legendary. Although many historians and memoirists have deemed it a key ingredient in the final outcome of the war in the east, the actual dimensions of that putative effectiveness in keeping troops in the fighting line have not been closely examined. Careful scrutiny of the draconian discipline of the Red Army reveals that much mythmaking has transpired and calls into question the efficacy of coercion to motivate.

Stalin set the tone for negative reinforcement by introducing a coercive element in his very first wartime speech. In his 3 July radio address, he threatened those who would obstruct the war effort with these words: "We must wage a ruthless fight against all disorganizers of the rear, deserters, panic-mongers, rumor-mongers, we must exterminate spies, diversionists. . . . All who by their panic-mongering and cowardice hinder the work of defense, no matter who they are, must be immediately haled before a military tribunal."[22] Just the day before, unknown to the public, the General Staff had stipulated that men caught away from their units without proper documents were now liable to be taken before military tribunals and tried under wartime regulations.[23] It did not, however, make a blanket call for executions.

Stalin was responsible for the most well-known foundations of negative motivation, Order No. 270, read to the men in August 1941. It called for harsh punishment of deserters and for the arrest of their family members. In peacetime, the Commissariat of Defense had to sanction the execution of a soldier for any crime, and this carried over to the start of the Great Patriotic War. Within five days of the German attack, however, the Supreme Soviet authorized front-level military councils to impose the death sentence on cowards, deserters, and traitors on the recommendation of military tribunals. Two weeks after that, this authority was passed down to the military councils of armies and corps.[24]

Despite these changes in the authority to execute soldiers, it took Order No. 270 to unleash a torrent of bloody executions. Josef Finkelshtein, a soldier in Leningrad at the time, witnessed an execution that took place on 1 October 1941. His unit was assembled in a vacant plant near his polytechnic college to watch the execution. "This was done as a lesson for us," he noted. "There were three deserters, all tank crewmembers from our company. 'Shoot the traitors of the motherland,' commanded the senior officer. Blood flew from their faces and all of them fell. Two still moved. An NKVD man walked up and shot these two in the head with his pistol."[25] Such executions were not uncommon, especially in 1941 and 1942.

In the panic-filled days of late summer 1941, the use of violence against soldiers got so out of hand that Stalin intervened, probably at the urging of *Stavka,* since he was not known for softening his repressive measures. Order No. 391, distributed to colonels and higher-ranked officers on 4 October 1941, criticized commanders for too often resorting to abuse, physical assault, and "repression" (summary execution) to cover their own panic and confusion on the battlefield. "Repression," it said, "is an extreme measure, allowable only in circumstances of direct disobedience and open resistance in conditions of battle, or in cases of attempting to undermine the orders of their commanders." He insisted that morale could and should be maintained by a proper combination of persuasion and compulsion. He asserted that much of the repression was unjustified, and many shootings had been illegal; further, resorting to arbitrary behavior and the use of personal physical violence was evidence of a lack of will and lack of ability on the part of commanders and commissars. Stalin, or whoever was really behind Order No. 391, correctly surmised that such harsh and capricious punishment contributed to a decline in troop discipline and morale and could push wavering soldiers over to the side of the enemy.[26]

Stalin undoubtedly initiated Order No. 227, which was issued in July 1942. This "not one step backwards" order threatened death and disgrace to those who surrendered or retreated without good cause. This order did not come out of the blue and was in no way inconsistent with prior disciplinary policies. Stalin was very interested in the soldiers' perception of Order No. 227 and had the NKVD investigate how it affected the soldiers' attitudes. Overall, reactions were mixed. Some felt it should have come earlier; others criticized it. Others who were fighting where the lines were fairly static—in the north or northwest—just ignored it, assuming it was directed at the units retreating in south Russia.

Private Mansur Abdulin remembered that Order No. 227 instilled fear in him and his fellow soldiers. "The order provided a strong psychological incentive for the men. As did the knowledge that there were special holding detachments in the rear, authorized to shoot anyone who actually did drop back."[27] The latter widely held assumption was untrue, but the authorities made no attempt to dispel this misconception.

Order No. 270, and the executions associated with it, had not stopped retreats and desertions, and many were skeptical that Order No. 227 would change anything either. One soldier astutely noted to his comrades that this was just one of many orders against retreating, and the previous ones had made no difference.[28] Some saw it as a sign of desperation on the part of the regime. Private Filiukov, on the Stalingrad Front, was arrested for observing out loud that a higher law, the law of survival, trumped Order No. 227. He was accused of saying: "Orders are orders, but when German aviation begins to bomb, then one goes backward and flees. We know this *prikaz.*"[29] Private Dubovik told his fellow soldiers: "The organization of blocking detachments—this is the second front. From the front we will be shot by the Germans, from the rear by blocking detachments."[30]

Officers, too, had their doubts. Lieutenant Shevchenko, an infantry company commander, thought Order No. 227 was a bad idea that would only help the Germans. "Soviet soldiers with rifles cannot resist Germans with submachine guns and mortars, but cannot fall back because of blocking detachments. There is only one way out—hands up," he said.[31] Military doctor Ol'shanetskii said: "This order of the *Stavka*, is the last cry of despair, when we no longer have the strength to hold out against the Germans. All measures similar to this have come to nothing."[32]

Order No. 227 instructed the army to create combat penal battalions (*shtrafbaty*) and blocking detachments behind the front lines. In fact, the use of blocking detachments had been authorized in principle since 27 June 1941, only five days after the start of the war. On that day Marshal Timoshenko and General Zhukov signed Directive No. 35523, establishing conditions and procedures for their use. The first blocking detachments were implemented on 5 September 1941, when *Stavka* authorized their use at the request of the commander of the Briansk Front.[33] One week later, *Stavka* ordered the forces of the Southwest Direction to create blocking detachments for every division under its authority. It spelled out their duties—namely, to detain and return to combat any soldiers who fled the field of battle in panic, as well as any soldier away from his unit without authorization. In practice, these detachments primarily manned roadblocks close behind the front lines with squad-sized details. There they detained fleeing soldiers and turned them over to courts-martial, shooting them outright only if they resisted arrest or tried to escape. In fact, depending on the personalities of the members, blocking detachments sometimes did not detain soldiers but merely warned them to get back to their units before they got into trouble.[34] The main function of blocking detachments, then, was not to intimidate soldiers into staying in the lines or to machine-gun retreating troops wholesale but to keep shirkers and stragglers from fleeing too far from the front and return them to their units. Blocking detachments were never given carte blanche to execute soldiers.[35]

Blocking detachments had only small arms—rifles and pistols—and therefore were not considered tactical units. In fact, if the front lines broke during an attack, rather than gunning down fleeing soldiers, as myth would have it, blocking detachments usually fled in advance of the retreat. As the war dragged on, army commanders began to disband blocking detachments on their own initiative, preferring to let officers control their own men. Eventually, Stalin found out about this and issued an order in October 1944 stating, "In connection with the change in the general situation at the front it is necessary to disband blocking detachments, which have fallen into disuse." He insisted that all divisions disband their blocking detachments by 15 November and reassign the men to frontline units.[36]

Fourth Tank Army, as it fell back toward Stalingrad in August 1942, was one of those units unmistakably targeted by Order No. 227. Complying with the order, 4th Tank Army formed three blocking detachments of 200 men each. The commander of 4th Tank Army turned over operational control of the detachments to his army's Special Sections (OO). In their first week of employment, between 8 and 14 August, these blocking detachments detained 363 men. Of these, 93 were escapees from encirclement and had to be filtered, 146 were stragglers from their units, 52 claimed to have lost their units, 12 had fled from prison, 54 had fled from the battlefield, and 2 were thought to have wounded themselves. After investigating these men, the OO returned 187 to their units and sent another 43 to understrength units without charges. It sent 73 to special NKVD filtration camps, sent 27 to penal battalions, and arrested 6 who were turned over to higher authorities. The 2 wounded soldiers were sent to a medical commission to determine whether their wounds had been self-inflicted. Finally, it executed 24 men in front of their fellow soldiers from the units they had fled.[37]

Overall, during the German advance on Stalingrad and the Caucasus between 1 August and 15 October 1942, in the entire Red Army, blocking detachments detained 140,755 servicemen who had absented themselves from the front lines. More than one-third (nearly 52,000) came from the retreating Stalingrad and Don fronts. The vast majority of men detained, 131,094, were returned to their units or reassigned to different units. The authorities arrested less than 3 percent (3,980) of those detained. Subsequently, of the arrested, 2,776 sergeants and soldiers were assigned to penal companies, and 185 officers were assigned to penal battalions. Finally, by the decrees of military tribunals, 1,189 soldiers were shot by firing squads.[38] The lethality of these blocking detachments, as shown by this example, was extremely low, with less than 1 percent of those detained (0.84 percent) executed—and this during a period when the regime was desperately trying to intimidate its soldiers.

Although Order No. 227 was viewed as extremely harsh, even by the standards of Stalinist discipline, the formation of penal combat battalions—where the army sent men convicted of cowardice, desertion, or other combat-related infringements—actually saved many lives. Men who previously could have been summarily shot now had a second chance to redeem themselves and survive. Although these battalions were often given the most dangerous tasks and were sent into the worst fighting to prepare the way for regular units, they were not suicide units, and service in them was always brief. The men who survived combat in these units were pardoned and released to regular units when their sentences had been served, or earlier if they performed exceptionally well or were wounded in combat.[39]

Lieutenant P. S. Amosov, for example, remembered standing before a tribunal to hear his sentence read: "For negligence you are demoted to the ranks and sentenced to two months in a penal battalion." His crime: during his division's forcing of the Dnepr, the engineer platoon he commanded had gotten lost and missed the battle. He reported to the *shtrafbat* on 31 December 1943 and spent New Year's Eve peeling potatoes and telling jokes and stories with other *shtrafniki*. They went into combat on 5 January. Amosov was wounded that same day and was evacuated to a field hospital. Upon his recovery, he was reassigned to a regular rifle division at his former rank.[40] He had served all of six days in the penal battalion.

It is difficult to gauge the effectiveness of the threat of assignment to a penal unit. In 1943, 2.7 percent of men in the combat zone were serving in penal units; in 1945, that was down to 1.3 percent. Ironically, the prospect of being sentenced to a penal unit was probably the least threatening for *frontoviki*, the men Stalin most wanted to intimidate. Matvei Gershman, an infantry sergeant, said that in his battalion, the men saw no difference between service in an infantry company and service in a penal company.[41] They mistakenly thought their chances of being killed were pretty much the same. In fact, from 1942 into 1944, penal units had on average 50 percent higher casualties (killed and wounded) than regular infantry units. In the last year of the war, they had three to six times as many losses. By the end of 1944, for example, 346,144 men had served in *shtraf* units, and 50 percent (170,298) had become casualties.[42]

There were two types of penal units: companies for soldiers (*shtrafroty*) and battalions for officers (*shtrafbaty*). Officers and men typically did not serve together. At first, it took court-martial proceedings to have a soldier sent to a penal company, and sentences usually ran for three months. In August 1943 Stalin granted regiment, division, and separate brigade commanders the right to sentence sergeants and soldiers to penal companies without recourse to military tribunals for the crimes of desertion, disobeying orders, infringement of guard duty, and unlawful absence from the unit.[43] In theory, a decision of a military tribunal was always required to sentence an officer to a penal battalion. Some generals were known to ignore this provision if the mood struck them, however, and they would arbitrarily remand subordinates to penal battalions without due process. On release, officers' ranks were restored, they were reassigned to duties commensurate with their preconviction status, and their records were expunged. The army likewise gave soldiers a clean slate and sent them to line units. Soldiers remained eligible to receive medals for courageous acts performed as *shtrafniki*. At the end of the war, the Red Army had 65 *shtrafbaty* and 1,048 *shtrafroty* in which 427,910 men had served.[44] The German army also created penal units, but it did not employ them in combat. The Allied armies had no equivalent and tended to incarcerate cowards, deserters, and other miscreants in military prisons.

Not only individuals but also whole units could be remanded to penal battalions. In November 1944 Stalin sent the entire 214th Cavalry Regiment—officers and men—to penal battalions and companies for losing their regimental flag in battle. He first reduced the rank of the regiment commander from lieutenant colonel to major so that if he survived the penal battalion and resumed normal duties, he would not have his former rank. The problem was not so much that the regiment had lost its colors but that it had not fought hard enough to keep or retrieve them.[45] In contrast, when the 8th and 10th Guards Airborne Regiments lost their colors in combat the next month—but held their ground and were overrun and nearly annihilated in the process—Stalin simply decreed that they be issued new flags.[46]

In addition to punishing officers and men with the hope of intimidating them into conformity, penal units were a means of mobilization. Civilians were recruited—often with threats and intimidation—from the Gulag camps and prisons directly into penal companies. The regime offered convicts a straightforward swap of prison time for *shtraf* time, followed by service in the regular forces for the duration of the war. Criminals with prison sentences of up to five years could exchange that time for one month in a penal company. Men with sentences of five to seven years could trade that for two months *shtraf* time; those serving seven to ten years could opt for three months in a penal company. Political prisoners were not normally recruited to *shtraf* units because their sentences generally exceeded ten years. V. G. Sorokin's penal company consisted of 95 percent camp inmates when it was formed in May 1944.[47] Of the nearly 1 million men in state custody who were sent to the armed forces, it is not known how many began their service in penal units, but probably tens of thousands did. Therefore, we cannot gauge the intimidation factor of Order No. 227 simply by the number of men who served in *shtraf* units.

The state took a host of other measures to deter desertion and empower the military to punish various forms of behavior it labeled betrayal. In dire circumstances, commanding officers were allowed to shoot cowards on the spot; they sometimes used this threat to enforce compliance in combat. Ivan Shelepov witnessed this and said, "Our company commander warned us right away, that if we lay down, he shoots all of us. He really did shoot some. After that we never tried to lie down again."[48] Officers and *politruki* who resorted to such drastic measures had to be prepared for retaliation. A veteran officer told Catherine Merridale, "Oh yes it happened quite often. You had to win the friendship of the men, or else you would not know which way they would shoot."[49]

Conversely, the fear of being shot by their own officers could encourage soldiers to desert to the enemy. Private Ostapenko said on 7 December 1941: "I'm going to desert this place, it's better to flee to the Germans, you can stay alive with them, but if you flee to our rear, you know you'll be shot. The Germans only shoot communists and Komsomolets."[50] Another private recalled a rather telling series of incidents in the summer of 1941 when the use of on-the-spot executions in lieu of sound leadership worked against effectiveness. When his regiment was surrounded for the second time, soldiers began to freely express their defeatist opinions. In one instance, the company *politruk* threatened to shoot a soldier and pulled out his pistol to do so, but before he could fire, the soldier shot him with his rifle. The soldier's comrades helped hide the *politruk*'s body, and no one said a word about it to the chain of command. Two days later, the regiment suffered 50 percent casualties after heavy fighting. The company was ordered to attack, but the men balked, prompting another *politruk* to threaten to shoot anyone who held back. Somebody shot this *politruk* too, and the men then allowed themselves to be captured.[51]

Frontline officers who were reluctant to shoot subordinates were subject to pressure by their superiors. In the summer of 1942, Lieutenant Gol'braikh, while manning the telephones of a mortar company, overheard a conversation between his regiment and division commanders about a company commanded by a friend of Gol'braikh's who was thought to be soft on his men. The company had twice assaulted a German position and failed to take it. The division commander asked, "Have you shot anyone?" The regiment commander paused, then replied, "No." The division commander responded, "Then get to shooting. This is not a trade union meeting. This is war!" That evening, the company commander was executed in front of the other officers of the battalion.[52]

Because of Stalin's suspicion that reversals at the front were caused by more than Soviet incompetence or German ability, and because the situation at the front constituted an emergency, the Politburo agreed on 17 August 1941 to a set of revised procedures for handling accusations of treason to the motherland. The new procedures stipulated that cases must be tried within ten days by a military tribunal. Previously, there had been no set time period for trial. Once a case was presented, the tribunal had only two days to conclude the hearing. The Military Collegium of the Supreme Court of the USSR would then review the verdict and sentence and either confirm or reject them. It would also evaluate whether the families of the convicted traitors had any criminal responsibility. Copies of the decisions were to be delivered to the NKVD for action. Subsequently, verdicts of the Military Collegium would be announced to the units in which the traitor had served before his conviction.[53]

It was not until a year after the start of the war, and on the eve of the issuance of Order No. 227, that the GKO added punishment of the families of traitors to the repressive measures already in existence. The definition of *family* included father, mother, wife, children, brothers, and sisters if they lived with the traitor at the time of the treason or if they had lived with him or her at the time of the traitor's mobilization into the army.[54] This statute was not unique; it was a reiteration of the June 1934 "treason statute" added to the 1926 Soviet Criminal Code. The 1942 statute added a mandatory death sentence for the traitor and five years in the camps for members of the traitor's family.[55] In practice, however, it was not unusual for death sentences to be commuted to imprisonment in the Gulag.

It is not surprising that, given the political insecurity of the Stalinist regime, treason became rather loosely interpreted during the war to encompass what previously might have been considered incompetence, negligence, or poor performance due to a lack of training. For example, in the early months of the war, a military tribunal sentenced to death Major Gaev, an artillery officer, for failure to support an attack with artillery fire. Gaev protested that he did not have adequate signals equipment to coordinate fire with the attack. Many of Gaev's peers considered him innocent, but the tribunal declared him guilty and ordered him to be shot. His conviction and sentence disturbed the other officers, who could see the same thing easily happening to them.[56] It is as though the regime had decided that it could intimidate officers into competence.

In practice, application of the death penalty for desertion and cowardice was inconsistent, arbitrary, and capricious, which may have undermined its potential for deterrence. For example, in the first three and a half months of the war, the NKVD apprehended 657,364 men who were away from their units without authorization or who had fled the front lines. Of these men, Special Sections detained 249,969; blocking detachments and security patrols under NKVD auspices detained the other 407,395 soldiers. The army identified most of them, 632,486, as AWOL, stragglers, or lost. It organized them into units and sent them back to the front. The NKVD arrested 24,878 as deserters, traitors, spies, and criminals. After subsequent investigation, 8,772 of these soldiers were labeled deserters. Military tribunals, under pressure to stem the tide of desertion and panicked flight, condemned to death 10,201 of those arrested. Without exception, they were all executed by firing squads; 3,321 of them were shot in front of their comrades as examples.[57]

Clearly, some sense of justice and compassion was at work here; the authorities in this crisis situation limited themselves to arresting only 3.7 percent of the 657,364 miscreants detained, and it sentenced only 1.5 percent to death. It is evident, then, that the operative mentality was not simply to kill men who avoided combat but to execute only traitors, criminals, and those who determinedly sought to avoid service altogether. Thus, in cases in which due process was involved, soldiers who absented themselves from the front stood a good chance of prolonging their lives. The real danger for soldiers in 1941 and early 1942 was the potential of being shot out of hand by panicked, overwrought officers and commissars acting under the authority of Order No. 270.

As it turned out, not everyone caught away from his unit was declared a deserter, and not all deserters or cowards were treated as traitors. Infantry lieutenant Aleksei Shilin admitted to fleeing from battle on two separate occasions. He was caught both times, arrested, and put into NKVD camps, and twice he returned to the front.[58] Likewise, seven Tadzhiks deserted from Semen Ravinskii's regiment. They were caught after two months and returned to the regiment with no punishment at all—to the amazement of the rank and file.[59]

At the other extreme, men were shot for helping others desert, even though they themselves did not. Vasily Grossman noted in his diary: "19 October. Red Army soldier shot in the 8th Company for collaborating in a desertion to the enemy."[60] So, despite the harsh sanctions that hovered over the *frontoviki*'s heads, what really mattered was the character or mood of the authorities who wielded the power of life and death and the soldiers' perception of their officers' ruthlessness. For example, in December 1941, of ten fronts and armies that reported arrests and executions during the first six months of the war, the Reserve Army was fifth in number of arrests but eighth in executions (35 percent of those arrested), while the Leningrad Front was seventh in the number of arrests but first in executions (82 percent).[61] It has been reported that over the course of the war, tribunals sentenced around 158,000 soldiers to death for desertion, cowardice, treason, and a variety of criminal acts.[62]

As a consequence of the mass surrenders and costly defeats in 1941, which some suspected were the result of treason, the armed forces assigned additional NKVD personnel to army units, augmenting the lone NKVD officer present in each regiment during peacetime. In 1943, following a reorganization of the security services and their functions, the OO of the NKVD merged with the Main Administration of State Security (GUGKB) and became a directorate designated the Main Administration for Counterintelligence (GUKR) of the NKO. The new organization was renamed *Smersh*, an acronym derived from *smert' shpionam* ("death to spies").[63] Any kind of failure, retreat, or loss of vital equipment had the potential to be deemed treason and was investigated by *Smersh*. Its other tasks were to investigate suspected cases of self-inflicted wounds and sabotage, to fight cowardice, and to bolster discipline in battle, primarily through intimidation. *Smersh* officials had the power to arrest officers and soldiers and send them before a military tribunal. If any failure was judged to be due to incompetence or negligence, the punishment could be demotion, transfer, or assignment to a penal battalion. Treason merited shooting or time in the Gulag. The mere presence of *Smersh* men in the unit kept people nervous, especially leaders.

After the war, Vladimir Khokhlov, a member of a scout detachment, was asked if he had ever failed a mission. He replied: "We always accomplished missions. If you fail—you can shoot yourself right away. Both Germans won't welcome you and our *Smersh* would get you skinned anyway."[64] *Smersh* also engaged in counterespionage work to uncover Soviet citizens and soldiers working on behalf of the German army and its intelligence services. Soldiers missing in action were presumed to have gone over to the enemy until proved otherwise. If they made it back to friendly lines, the burden was on them to prove to *Smersh* that they were not in the employ of the enemy.

In comparison, the Wehrmacht, whose professionalism and cohesiveness have been overstated for the past seventy years, also resorted to severe punitive measures to keep its men in the line, and not just on the Eastern Front. Manfred Messerschmidt's figure of 13,000 to 15,000 executions for desertion, cowardice, or criminal activity on the Eastern Front as a consequence of the "barbarization of warfare" is well known, but less well known are the thousands of German soldiers executed on the supposedly more civilized Western Front in 1944 for the same cause. German soldiers were shot out of hand for desertion, and, like their Soviet counterparts, the Nazi state threatened the families of deserters with dire consequences.[65] An additional 23,000 German soldiers received long prison terms at hard labor; more than 84,000 men were sentenced to more than a year in prison, and 320,000 received less than a year's time in prison. Thousands were sentenced to serve in penal battalions. Omer Bartov claims that fear of punishment was effective in keeping German soldiers in the line, but he provides no objective proof.[66]

In comparison, the U.S. armed forces, which numbered 12 million during the war, recorded 348,217 cases of draft evasion. The United States also recorded about 21,000 cases of desertion, most of which occurred in the U.S. Army in Europe between 6 June 1944 and June 1945.[67] The U.S. Army's Articles of War contained provisions for executing soldiers for desertion in the face of the enemy, but the army executed only one man during the war.

The British army's attitude toward the death penalty as a deterrent was diametrically opposite that of the Soviet army. The British abolished the death penalty for desertion in 1930 after a study concluded that it had failed to deter desertion during World War I. In that war, 3,080 soldiers had been condemned to death, but only 346 were actually executed.[68] In the first year of the war, 1 October 1914 to 30 September 1915, 40,375 soldiers deserted, or 20.7 percent of the army. That was the worst year ever. In the best year, 1916–1917, 6.03 percent deserted, and this was when casualties were at their heaviest. In total, there were 137,773 cases of desertion in the British army during World War I. In World War II, the worst twelve months for desertion were 1 October 1940 to 30 September 1941, when 22,248 men, or 10.05 percent of the army, deserted. All told, 100,350 British soldiers deserted in World War II. Thus, with the death penalty in force during World War I, the annual average rate of desertion was 10.26

percent of the total manpower, but without the death penalty in World War II, the annual average rate of desertion was only 6.8 percent.[69]

In comparing these two averages, the British researchers concluded, "It would, therefore, seem that the 'deterrent' value of the death penalty for desertion in the First World War was, at the least, somewhat dubious." They also thought that the "problem of desertion is primarily a problem of selection and morale. By attention to morale, i.e. by careful training, suitable employment, good leadership, adequate welfare, etc., it is also possible to avoid many of the precipitating factors which contribute to mental breakdown or desertion." Further, "without attention to these fundamental prophylactic measures, in vain may the Army hold this sword of Damocles—as it were, a suspended death sentence—over the heads of fighting men already laboring under the intense stresses of modern warfare: they will prevent neither psychiatric breakdown nor desertion and other lesions of morale." In conclusion, they declared, "the alleged 'deterrent' effect of the death penalty for desertion is no more than a delusion."[70]

The experience of desertion in the Italian army during the First World War was rather different from the British in terms of motivation, but analogous to the Soviet experience in terms of the authorities' attitude. Although the historical record is still incomplete, and contradictions abound, there may have been as many as 350,000 men tried for desertion, resulting in 210,000 convictions and 750 executions—more executions than any other Allied army in the war. Like the Soviets, the Italian civilian and military leadership equated desertion with treason, yet postwar studies revealed that soldiers overwhelmingly deserted from the rear—not the front—for family-related reasons and usually returned to duty of their own volition. A substantial number of men were charged with desertion simply for returning late to their units from leave, yet they were prosecuted as though they had abandoned their comrades under fire.[71] As with other armies, there is no indication that the severity of the punishment had any deterrent value; instead, it was more likely to cause ill feelings among soldiers, officers, and the military system.

Despite the death penalty, the presence of blocking detachments, and potential assignment to *shtraf* units, men continued to desert or to otherwise illegally absent themselves from the front. During the 1943 battle of Kursk, for example, which finally turned the tide of war irrevocably in favor of the USSR, blocking detachments behind three of the armies facing the Germans' assault picked up 6,965 errant soldiers in just one week (8 to 14 July). This was after Order No. 227 had been in effect for nearly a year. More than half these men (3,745) had fled from eight different Guards divisions. The 93rd Guards Rifle Division, for example, lost around 10 percent of its strength (969 men) to soldiers absconding to the rear. A single panicked flight from the southern sector of the front on 8 July yielded 734 detainees.[72]

For all of 1943, in the immediate rear area (the zone from the front line with the enemy to twenty-five kilometers rearward), the NKVD apprehended 42,807 men for unauthorized departure from the front lines and 158,585 for straggling. Upon further investigation, 23,418 of these men were declared to be deserters. Most of the remaining detained soldiers were subsequently returned to the front. An additional 18,086 detainees were determined to be escapees from the encirclements of 1941 who had elected not to return to Soviet lines. They were sent to filtration camps.[73] Those who failed filtration ended up in either penal units or the Gulag.

Overall, in 1942 and 1943, the NKVD caught nearly 1.25 million men who were away from their units without documents, and it rounded up and sent back to their units another 200,000 stragglers.[74] Complete data for 1944 and 1945 are not yet available, so wartime totals are uncertain. For instance, in spring 1944, NKVD rear security detachments rounded up 25,979 men behind the lines. Investigators determined that 7,573 of the soldiers were deserters and charged them accordingly. They labeled the rest stragglers and sent them back to their units.[75] Desertion remained a problem until the very end of the war. In the Belorussian republic, from its liberation in July 1944 to September 1945 (up until the surrender of Japan), the NKVD apprehended 82,752 Red Army soldiers who were inappropriately away from their units.[76]

During the course of the war, the Soviet armed forces recorded 2,846,000 instances of men and women deserting and dodging the draft (some people were multiple offenders). Of these, 1,543,000 eventually turned themselves in; the authorities rounded up another 837,000 and sent them back to their units without taking punitive measures. An additional 212,400 deserters were never caught.[77] In total, those who attempted to avoid either service or fighting and those who actively sided with the enemy add up to a minimum of 4,384,859.[78] Of these, the military judicial system punished only 8.6 percent—251,408 men for evading the draft and 126,956 soldiers for desertion. Punishments included sentences in *shtraf* units, time in labor camps, and execution.[79] All told, 158,000 men were executed and 436,600 were sentenced to time in the Gulag; however, these numbers include not only deserters and draft evaders but also soldiers who committed criminal acts. It is not known whether the number executed includes those shot without recourse to military tribunals in 1941.

Regardless of these unknowns, we have to reconsider the deterrent effect of the death penalty, if only for the fact that it was not widely used, and soldiers knew it. The idea that soldiers were machine-gunned by blocking detachments and arbitrarily executed by officers and NKVD men en masse—and thus kept in the line by fear of such treatment—is essentially a myth. That fact that the rate of dereliction of duty through desertion or draft evasion for the Soviet armed forces was 8.2 percent, compared with 3 percent for the British and the American armed forces, which did not use the death penalty, casts serious doubt on the effectiveness of fear as a motivating factor for the majority of *frontoviki*. It also raises the issue that the execution of deserters and cowards was unnecessary and unjustified.

There is no doubt that some soldiers went into the attack partly out of fear of their own government, and despite their fear of enemy fire. But this does not explain the compliance of the majority of the army. Millions of men risked death to avoid fighting, and millions more were committed to fighting without compulsion or threats. Furthermore, the regime's lack of trust in its soldiers sometimes undercut the morale of those who knew themselves to be trustworthy and loyal. One *frontovik* expressed his resentment in a song that he shared with his trusted friends out of earshot of *Smersh*.

> The first shell punctured my gas tank.
> I jumped out of the tank—how, I do not know.
> So they called me over to the special section:
> "Why didn't you burn up with your tank, you son of a bitch?!"
> So I answered, and this is what I said:
> "I'll be sure and do that the next time we attack."[80]

8

Discipline, Hate, Ideology, and Propaganda

Because of widespread disorganization, chronic mission failure, and grievous casualties, the military and the Soviet state strove doubly hard to maintain and enhance motivation. The fundamental task was to get the soldiers to invest in the idea that the Soviet state was worth saving and that victory was possible; failing that, the goal was to make soldiers fear the consequences of noncompliance. Morale and motivation, the two key factors in sustaining foxhole-level military effectiveness, were intertwined in the Red Army, as they have been throughout much of military history. Motivation determined the soldiers' commitment to the success of the unit and its mission. Morale—the soldiers' emotional state and general feeling about life at the moment—largely determined how much effort they would put forth to accomplish the mission. In this context, it is important to distinguish the motivation of the soldier at the front from that of the civilian weighing the decision whether to join the military. John Lynn suggests that there are three types of motivation: initial, sustaining, and combat. Initial motivation is the impulse to leave civil society behind and enter the armed forces. Combat motivation is obviously the motivation that enables soldiers to endure under fire and perform their tasks. Sustaining motivation is what soldiers feel between battles that keeps them in the ranks and prepared to enter the hell of combat once again.[1]

Initial motivation, seen in the mobilization of society, meshes closely with sustaining and combat motivation. For some men and women, particularly volunteers, intrinsic motivations compelled their entry into the army and continued to fuel their desire to fight and kill. Conscripts, however, who were not necessarily motivated to serve at all, reported for duty more out of extrinsic motivations, so their sustaining and combat motivations would likely be extrinsic as well. The sources of motivation proved malleable, and their effects fluctuated with morale, unit cohesion, and conditions of service, all of which were inextricably intertwined and subject to manipulation by both the state and the military.

Any attempt to define or analyze combat motivation must include a strong awareness that, at the most basic level, soldiers had to overcome a deep and natural fear of crippling wounds or violent death in order to perform their duties. In fact, 44 percent of all Soviet soldiers, nearly 15.3 million, were wounded or injured in the line of duty, and 25 percent, or 8.7 million, were killed or went forever missing.[2] The following analysis is based on a rejection of both draconian punishment and love of country as primary elements of Red Army effectiveness in the Great Patriotic War. It assumes that the Soviet soldier required extrinsic influences such as sound leadership, thorough training, morale boosts, and social support from both the primary group and society at large, as well as the reinforcement of intrinsic motivations such as patriotism, hate, and moral justification, to succeed at his task.

Finally, the amount of effort and resources the Soviet state dedicated to motivation and morale is noteworthy. The reason for this effort was the inherent insecurity of the Stalinist regime. The Soviet leadership did not assume that the purges had eliminated all its internal enemies. It also assumed that its repressions of the previous decade would generate a backlash, now that its authority and power had been seriously eroded by the severe setbacks following Operation Barbarossa. It became more important than ever to win the heart and mind of the Soviet soldier.

Extrinsic Means of Bolstering Morale and Motivation

One psychological tactic employed by the Soviet state and military high command to enhance motivation was to combine hate for the German army with the desire for a just revenge and the need to liberate the *rodina* from occupation. Hate between the belligerents was mutual. For the German soldier, hate was almost completely ideologically derived before the onset of combat. The threat of Judeo-Bolshevism trumpeted in Hitler's *Mein Kampf* and the victimization of Germany through the

Treaty of Versailles—which thoroughly permeated Nazi propaganda and the Hitler Youth indoctrination undergone by most German soldiers during their school years—convinced them that their opponents were subhuman and evil and that they were the sworn enemies of Germany. German troops had been inoculated with hatred and disdain for Slavs and Jews; some senior Wehrmacht generals had collaborated with Nazi ideologues in the distribution of virulent propaganda well before Barbarossa. The hate felt by Soviet soldiers had twin sources: ideologically based anti-Nazi propaganda, which blended truth and fiction, and the reality of German (and other Axis) excesses on Soviet soil.[3]

Stalin's speeches set the tone for the Soviet propaganda machine. His speech commemorating the twenty-fourth anniversary of the October Revolution, given in Moscow on 6 November 1941, sought to raise the ire and indignation of the Soviet soldier. Stalin proclaimed: "The German fascist invaders are plundering our country, destroying the cities and villages built by the labor of the workers, peasants, and intelligentsia. The Hitler hordes are killing and violating the peaceful inhabitants of our country without sparing women, children or the aged."[4] In his May Day 1942 speech, he blatantly and unequivocally endorsed hatred, saying: "Red Army men have become more bitter and ruthless. They have learned really to hate the German fascist invaders. They realize that one cannot defeat the enemy without learning to hate him with every fiber of one's soul."[5] Stalin encouraged the men to hate; to not do so was an act of disobedience.

Four days later, Ilya Ehrenburg, writing for *Krasnaia zvezda*, elaborated on Stalin's hatred theme, justifying it almost as a moral imperative:

> The idea of vengeance does not satisfy our outraged reason. We do not speak of spite but of hatred; not of revenge but of justice. These are not shadings of word—these are entirely different feelings. Hatred, as love, is inherent to pure and warm hearts. We hate Fascism because we love people, children, the earth, trees, horses, laughter, books, the warmth of a friend's hand, because we love life. The stronger the love of life is within us, the firmer is our hatred.[6]

Ehrenburg sought to make hating easier by dehumanizing the enemy: "To us the Hitlerites are not simply enemies; to us the Hitlerites are not people, to us they are murderers, executioners, moral freaks, cruel fanat-ics, and we therefore hate them." He concluded, "For us the German soldier with a rifle in his hand is not a human being, but a Fascist. We hate him."[7]

At its most basic and functional level, dehumanizing the enemy, practiced routinely by belligerents, was designed to make it easier for soldiers to overcome their inhibitions and kill other human beings. Ehrenburg, though he later denied authorship, is credited with writing the famous "Kill" pamphlet in 1942. "Now we understand the Germans are not human," it states. "Now the word 'German' has become the most terrible curse. Let us not speak. Let us not be indignant. Let us kill. If you do not kill a German, a German will kill you. He will carry away your family, and torture them in his damned Germany. If you have killed one German, kill another."[8]

Junior Lieutenant Fedor Bachurin remembered that hate served as a motivation for him and his men: "During the war we saw villages and gallows both burned. We saw guerrillas and civilians hanged. So the ha-tred for the Germans was immensely strong."[9] From the perspective of experience, it seems soldiers had no need for Stalin's or the press's urg-ing to hate their enemies, so the propaganda may have done more to validate their hate than induce it. Ehrenburg wrote on 13 August 1943:

> Yesterday I received a letter from a Ukrainian, Lieutenant Suprunenko, who writes, "I did not know before that one could hate someone like this. I am an artillerist, and I am only sorry that I cannot kill a Fascist with a bayonet, or with a rifle butt, or strangle him with my own hands." A sacred sentiment! It was born out of the blood of Russian women and children tortured to death by the Hitlerites, it was born out of the smoldering ruins of our cities.[10]

In fact, Nazi atrocities were a godsend to the Soviet state. Many anti-Soviet citizens claim they fought not for Stalin, for socialism, or for Rus-sia but against fascism—not its ideology, but the behavior of German soldiers who were its physical manifestation. A Harvard Refugee Project interviewee stated explicitly that he had been looking for a way to escape to the West well before the war. At first, the German invasion seemed to offer a way out, until the reality of the Nazi racial policy hit home. He decided that going over to the Nazis was not the equivalent of defecting to the West. Psychologically, he fell back on Russian patriotism and military honor to make it through the war. He fought hard, being wounded four times, all the while harboring the hope of getting to the West. He succeeded in defecting in 1945, at war's end.[11]

Boris Ol'shanskii, in an unpublished memoir written shortly after his defection to the West in the 1950s, dismissed the idea that the state's antifascist propaganda had any lasting effect. Far more compelling was the experience of liberating one's hometown and learning the fate of one's friends and family. Some found their families intact, but some did not. He writes:

> Many found only carbonized debris. "They have all perished. Our hut was burned down as a reprisal. Father and mother were shot. Little sister has been taken to Germany for slave labor. Brother was hanged for cooperation with the partisans. My wife was beaten with a stick by order of the German commandant on account of allegedly lack of respect towards a policeman. Soon after that she died on consequence of the beating. The children were taken by other people. I do not know where they are now. I must search in the neighborhood. Perhaps they have come back from the woods." A mother told her son: "We believed that you were dead. Your wife married Ivan Khromich. When you were approaching, they packed and left. They could not stay here because they had worked at the commandantura."[12]

There were thousands of such tidings in 1943 and 1944 as the Red Army moved westward. Ol'shanskii saw that these reunions had a much stronger effect on his fellow soldiers than any newspaper propaganda or "fiction" made up by the commissars.

> They were much more effective than the photos in the newspapers of the "body of the Red Army officer, Lieutenant N. whom the fascist barbarians burned alive," than the ghost stories about bloody stars having been cut into the foreheads of the Russian soldiers or about wells filled with bodies of killed babies. Neither I nor those whom I met have at any time seen such things or heard of such things.

Therefore I did not care much when again a propagandist told me about them. But it made a very deep impression on me when on a scrap of gray paper were . . . wrote [sic] a few words . . . in an [sic] handwriting known to us: "Nobody is alive anymore at home."[13]

Another officer who would later defect expressed what was likely felt by many who had reservations about Stalinism and what it meant in their lives: "We were in a tragic dilemma: we did not want to defend the Soviet regime yet we did not want to fight with the Germans."[14] Like Ol'shanskii, it was Nazi atrocities that convinced him to fight.

Still, hate is a powerfully negative emotion that some men resisted. Georgii Khol'nyi, a Red Army private, looked back on the war and recalled, "In 1942 Ehrenburg wrote his big article 'Kill Germans'—but I did not want to kill Germans. And all my friends didn't want to."[15]

A certain amount of hatred is useful in motivating soldiers to fight and overcome whatever inhibitions they might have about killing. It is also nearly inevitable that the combat experience will generate hate as soldiers' friends are killed or wounded. In the heat of battle, hatred and the thirst for revenge can even distract soldiers from fear and motivate superior combat performance. Such "naturally arising" hate might actually be healthier in the long run for an army and its soldiers than the type of extrinsically inspired hate promoted by the Stalinist state. The years of hate-filled propaganda likely contributed to the scale of violence against German civilians after the war and indiscipline among the occupying soldiers.

The issues of hatred and revenge, both spontaneous and deliberate, and their usefulness to combat motivation were not unique to the Red Army. The German citizen-cum-soldier had been inculcated with hatred for the Jewish-Bolshevik horde since 1933, and the atrocities this led to in Russia are well known. The leadership of the U.S. Army, during its first campaign against the Germans in North Africa in 1942 through 1943, worried that the men did not hate the Germans but decided to let combat generate such hate organically. The British army, at its first battle school for new officers, formed in 1942, included a period of instruction in hate, which it hoped would raise morale. But a psychiatrist observing the course advised that it be abandoned immediately. In his opinion, "the training in 'Hate'. . . [was] not only socially undesirable but liable to increase rather than decrease the incidence of [psychological] breakdown in the Army." Members of Parliament and religious leaders also objected to it on psychological and ethical grounds. Field Marshal Bernard Montgomery raised objections because, in his opinion, artificially induced hate and bloodlust were not part of the British character.[16]

Given the testimony of hundreds of contemporaries and veterans on the subject, it seems that Stalin's call to hate was unnecessary. The Germans' horrendous treatment of civilians and prisoners of war, combined with the soldiers' anger when comrades were killed, is cited most often by veterans as the source of their hatred during the war, not Stalin's order to hate. When Soviet soldiers committed atrocities in the heat of battle, they followed the same pattern of excesses committed by armies whose troops were not instructed to hate.

Nikolai Dupak, a cavalry lieutenant, recalled what happened when a platoon of his battalion was wiped out by some soldiers of the Waffen SS division "Viking." Dupak's company turned the tables on the SS, killing nine or ten in close combat, then killed six they had taken prisoner. He described the captives as "big, well-built men. [They had] families, children. It was a very unpleasant moment and I'd rather not remember it, but it was revenge for specific guys." The murder of these prisoners was not an isolated incident. "We shot those whom we captured on the spot of their crimes. War is a brutal thing."[17]

Another appeal to soldiers' emotions and intellect was to portray the war as just. By extension, their sacrifices were honorable, and the cruel retribution they inflicted on the Germans was justified. Setting the tone in his May Day 1942 speech, Stalin told the army: "Comrades, we are waging a just and patriotic war of liberation. We have no such aims as seizing foreign lands or subjugating foreign peoples. Our aim is clear and noble. We want to rid our Soviet land of the German fascist scum. We want to liberate our brothers, Ukrainians, Moldavians, Belorussians, Latvians, Estonians, Karelians, from the shame and humiliation to which the Nazi-fascist beasts subject them."[18]

Similarly, the U.S. armed forces relied heavily on the "just war" theme, which was the basis of Frank Capra's "Why We Fight" film series. Essentially, it was not how right the Allies were but how wrong the Nazis were, along with the need to answer the high calling of justice; indeed, destroying such an evil regime was presented as a duty to humanity.

Even the Nazis used the "just war" theme. In Hitler's order to the troops announcing the invasion of Russia, he justified it as a preemptive attack to fend off an imminent Soviet assault on Germany.

Another technique to raise morale, again spearheaded by Stalin, was to promote pride among the soldiers as defenders of the USSR. On 3 July 1941, in his first radio address to the nation and the army after the German invasion, Stalin said: "Our troops are fighting heroically against an enemy armed to the teeth with tanks and aircraft. Overcoming innumerable difficulties, the Red Army and the Red Navy are self-sacrificingly disputing every inch of Soviet soil. The men of the Red Army are displaying unexampled valor."[19] He followed up on this theme on 6 November, saying: "Defending the honor and freedom of the country, courageously repelling the attacks of the brutal enemy, setting examples of valor and heroism, the fighters of our army and navy have compelled the enemy to shed streams of blood." Furthermore, "There can be no doubt that the idea of defense of one's country, or the sake of which our people are fighting, must produce and is actually producing in our army heroes who are cementing the Red Army."[20]

The effectiveness of Stalin's speeches in bolstering morale and resolve cannot be quantified, but some soldiers referenced them in conversations and letters and mentioned the inspiration they drew from Stalin. Writer and military correspondent Vasily Grossman reported that one soldier, after hearing Stalin's 6 November 1941 speech, said, "Comrade Stalin's report gave me more strength." Another Red Army soldier declared, "I give you my word, Comrade Stalin, I'll go on fighting the enemy as long as my heart beats."[21] In 1942 Grossman reported that a soldier wrote this note to his commanders: "Let Comrade Stalin know that I will sacrifice my life for the sake of the Motherland, and for him. And I won't regret it even for a second. If I had five lives, I would sacrifice them all for his sake, without hesitating, so dear is this man to me."[22]

A year later Stalin praised the soldiers, saying: "I think that no other country and no other army could have withstood this onslaught of the savage gangs of German fascist brigands and their allies. Only our Soviet country and only our Red Army are capable of withstanding such an onslaught. And not only withstanding it, but also overpowering it."[23] Six months later he continued to appeal to his army's ego: "The peoples of our country meet May First in the stern days of Patriotic War. They have entrusted their destiny to the Red Army and their hopes have not been misplaced."[24]

In this vein, Ilya Ehrenburg wrote to the soldiers on 3 November 1943: "Kiev is waiting. Paris is waiting. The Czechs are waiting. Thus the battle for the Ukraine becomes the battle for humanity. Thus the Russian infantry becomes the hope of the world."[25] A week later, Ehrenburg wrote, "The Red Army has become the army of freedom in the eyes of all nations."[26] This was rather heady stuff for an army of many semiliterate or illiterate peasants whose world and worldview before the war did not extend far beyond their village.

Another source of motivation—but one that was not sponsored by the state, at least not officially—was hope for change after the war. Rumors abounded that the collective farms would be dismantled and political repression would end after the victory. A veteran who later defected recalled:

> From my twelfth to fourteenth year I was already a passive enemy of the Soviet Union and in the beginning of the war had no desire to protect her. Had I been at the front in the beginning of the war, I would have surrendered to the Germans. In the second half of the war I was supported by my belief that after the end of the war everything would be better. Officers' shoulder pieces, the opening of the churches—we thought that these were the first steps and that the rest would follow. I hoped that the kolkhozes were to be abolished.[27]

The Red Army and the Communist Party were well aware of the positive effects of these rumors and did nothing to dispel them.

One tactic to increase motivation that was rejected by Stalin was referencing the experience of the last two tsarist-era wars. V. E. Markevich, who identified himself as a veteran, wrote to Stalin in May 1942 to say that calling on the distant memories of Aleksandr Nevskii, Suvorov, and the patriotic war of 1812 was all well and good, but the Russo-Japanese War and Great War had a certain relevance that ought to be exploited to motivate the soldiers. After all, many current soldiers were the sons or grandsons of veterans of those conflicts. Markevich suggested that the state promote the experience of those wars and call on veterans, especially those who had fought the Germans and Austrians, to talk to the men, sharing their recollections of combat and campaigning.[28] The fact that Russia lost those wars was not lost on Markevich, but he stressed that Red Army men should feel like they were part of the living heritage of defenders of the *rodina*. We will never know for sure, but it is likely that Stalin refused to equate defense of imperial Russia—fought under the tsar overthrown by the February Revolution—or defense of the bourgeois Provisional Government—overthrown by the October Revolution—with defense of the socialist homeland. It was bad enough that he had to resort to the memory of 1812.

Overall, the Stalinist regime's attempts to motivate and bolster the men's fighting spirit produced uneven, inconsistent, weak, or ineffective results in the face of sagging morale. Historian Nikita Lomagin, in his study of morale during the battle of Leningrad, notes that the state got a late start in addressing some of the more important issues that affected morale, and there were some subjects that the authorities were fairly helpless to address. For instance, Lomagin states that the soldiers wanted explanations of why Soviet aircraft did not support them, why there were no tanks to counter the Germans', why their officers proved to be so inept, and what role treason played in the recent defeats. Furthermore, soldiers began to think the Germans were unbeatable.[29]

As a result of German propaganda leaflets showing captured Red Army men eating bread and drinking beer, many soldiers began to believe that the Nazis treated prisoners well, or at least they doubted the claims of their *politruki* to the contrary.[30] Rather than address these questions, the army, security, and political authorities ordered all Nazi propaganda leaflets immediately destroyed and criminalized the possession of them. Furthermore, they suppressed discussion of the Red Army's shortcomings and treated complaints and doubts as subversion. Not until November 1941, with a barrage of hate propaganda detailing the Germans' barbarous behavior toward civilians and POWs, did morale begin to rise.

When the Germans found themselves in a similarly desperate situation, they responded with nearly identical propaganda, delivered by *Nationalsozialistische Führungsoffizieren* (NSFOs), the Nazi equivalent of commissars, established in December 1943. The Nazi Party charged the NSFOs with raising morale and bolstering motivation through political indoctrination and by assuring the German soldiers that their faith in

Hitler was warranted.[31] Although Hitler did not make speeches to the troops after 1943, high-ranking officers delivered tirades of their own that were thoroughly consistent with the Nazi Party line. For example, when the U.S. Army was at Germany's border in November 1944, General-Feldmarschall Model sent this order to the men at the front, anticipating an Allied offensive at Aachen:

> Disappointed peoples stand behind the mercenaries of America and England, peoples who had been promised Germany's collapse this year. Behind them stand the greedy Jew, lusting after gain, and the murderous, bloodthirsty Bolshevist. Capture of the Ruhr, the collapse of the Reich, the enslavement of all Germans are but stages of their will to destroy. We must shock these hypocritical benefactors of mankind out of their expectations of a cheap victory. With terror they shall realize that here German soldiers battle stubbornly and tenaciously for German home soil.[32]

Just as the Soviet press had invoked paternal responsibility, Model reminded his soldiers that "our women and children look on us." He called on the men to fight with "hatred and unceasing courage" and commanded, "Every combat squad must be a repository of fanatic battle spirit in our holy struggle for life." Finally, and in contrast to the often ambiguous position Stalin took in Soviet propaganda, Model invoked the person of Hitler as inspiration for German soldiers, claiming, "Faith in the Führer will guarantee our victory."

The Place of Ideology in Motivation and Morale

From the moment Lenin and Trotsky conceived of creating armed forces for their revolutionary socialist state, they assumed that ideology would provide their army with a winning edge over traditional armies. One cannot be sure if they genuinely continued to believe this after their civil war and the war with Poland, even though they and their successors professed that they did. So, during the Great Patriotic War, was there a connection between communist ideology and combat effectiveness?

In examining what constitutes or passes for ideology during war, H.

Wayne Moyer concludes, "ideology is defined as a set of integrated beliefs about the nature of man, his place in the universe and the requisite actions which flow from these things."[33] In the Soviet case, the state sought to explain and justify prosecution of the war and soldiers' tasks in terms compatible with prewar ideology and designed to motivate compliance, resolve, and feelings of moral superiority. To balance the selective revival of Russian (*rossiiskii*) nationalism, ideology was used as a tool to create common ground and a common language among the diverse nationalities of the Soviet Union. As Moyer suggests, "A supportive national ideology and the absence of serious domestic ideological conflict clearly promote the national consensus requisite for military cohesion." To this end Stalin, and the Soviet propaganda machine, within the army and without, sought to define the USSR's war aims beyond mere defense of the nation, as observed in most of Stalin's speeches.[34] Thus, the formulations of wartime ideology were as follows: Soviet patriotism united all the peoples, socialism was superior to fascism, the USSR was a union of equal peoples, the USSR was a democratic and socially egalitarian state, and the communist system embodied in the Soviet Union represented the destiny of the world. All this was set against a backdrop of a renaissance of Russian nationalism.

In analyzing the role of Soviet ideology, it is useful to compare it to the Nazi case. In contrast to Shils and Janowitz's groundbreaking work, which downplayed the role of ideology among German soldiers during the war, recent work on the Wehrmacht suggests that Nazi ideology was quite significant in maintaining morale, motivation, and cohesion. It formed a common bond among soldiers in pursuit of a "higher" purpose—a purpose higher than soldiering.[35] If Nazi ideology could inspire fanatical behavior by German soldiers, we need to consider that communist ideology might have done the same for Soviet soldiers. Nazi ideology, however, had a distinct advantage over the Soviets' communist ideology, in that it appealed to German nationalism, history, race identity, and a broad inclusiveness of the German people.

In contrast, communist ideology and socioeconomic policy under Stalin was necessarily internationalist, multiracial, and multiethnic and therefore challenged national group identities. Also, because it was class based, it sought to exclude and victimize "former people" (those privileged under the tsarist autocracy) and their children. It created millions

of outcasts (primarily peasants) by changing the rules of property own-
ership and wealth accumulation. Furthermore, the internationalist appeal was challenged by pervasive xenophobia and a "Russia first"
mentality, whereby people identified the well-being and defense of historic Russia as an empire as being most important. This attitude alienated non-Russian peoples such as Balts, Caucasians, and Central Asians,
who considered themselves captive nations. Nevertheless, the ideological appeal was made and adapted to the times.

As noted during the discussion on mobilization, some Soviet citizens
closely identified the socialist system with their feelings of patriotism
when they enlisted. For some, this identification sustained their motivation throughout the war, especially as the Germans' brutality toward the
civilian population became associated with fascist ideology. With regard
to combat motivation, however, it is difficult to find evidence that ideological attachment affected behavior under fire in the same way it likely
did for German soldiers. There were numerous reasons to fight that had
ideological facets. For one, the *rodina* was not just the motherland; the
regime identified it as the socialist motherland. Therefore, not only was
the USSR in danger; as the only socialist country, socialism itself and its
potential for saving humankind were threatened. Fascism, as a false socialism, would set back humanity's progress and destroy its hope for a
better world; the lofty goals of the October Revolution would never be
attained with a Soviet defeat. The Stalinist regime, however, presented
all these issues as secondary reasons why soldiers should fight tena-
ciously and loyally. Patriotism and hatred took the top places. The state
included ideological factors only as a supplementary rationale for those
soldiers who might be persuaded as a result of their personal outlook.

When interviewed in 1997, noted historian Lev Pushkarev, who had
served as a private at the front, was asked what, if any, ideological motivations drove him during the war. He freely admitted to being a Ger-
manophile before and after the war. When confronted with Stalin's
command to hate the enemy, Pushkarev tried to conform, but without
giving up his love for things German. He rationalized his hate by saying
that he hated the fascists, not the Germans. So in his case, ideology provided the psychological means necessary for him to kill Germans. He
could hate the fascist enemy and do his duty to kill, but he did not have
to hate Germany or any non-Nazi German soldiers. In combat, he said,

"I had no pity for him. But I have to say, I also had no contempt or repugnance either."[36]

The Western Allies, in contrast to both Nazi Germany and Stalinist Russia, only touched lightly on democratic values as motivating factors. Fighting to make the world safe for democracy was a rather discredited philosophy by 1941 and did not fit well with the Soviet alliance. As determined by many correspondents as well as social scientists in uniform, American servicemen in the combat zones seemed to be motivated by a relentless pragmatism: because they were serving for the duration of the war—or until they were killed or wounded—the sooner they gained what President Roosevelt called "the inevitable victory," the sooner they could escape the ordeals of service or battle and go home.[37]

Establishing definitively whether soldiers were inspired by communist ideology is tricky. That the Soviet regime had to defend its socialist ideology to them, however, cannot be questioned. The Germans, believing National Socialism to be superior, brought ideology to the forefront of Red Army soldiers' minds in the hope of weakening their resolve to fight. The Nazi propaganda campaign to persuade Red Army soldiers to lay down their arms and come over to the German side often used ideological themes. Many pamphlets cited Lenin's promises of freedom and prosperity to the peasants and accused Stalin of perverting them. One leaflet dropped on Soviet soldiers in July 1941 said that Stalin was the enemy of all workers, an *uberbandit* and enemy of the people. It ended by stating: "Down with Stalinist Power!"[38] In his study of German propaganda, Lomagin points out that "'Nazi' or 'real' socialism was constantly contrasted with Stalinist socialism, which was depicted as being 'perched at the edge of the abyss.'"[39]

Stalin's 6 November 1941 speech addressed the issue of socialism as an idea worth fighting for and attacked the Nazis' claim of being socialists: Stalin asked, "Can the Hitlerites be considered socialists?" Then he answered, "No, they cannot. In fact, the Hitlerites are the avowed enemies of socialism, the bitterest reactionaries and blackguards who have deprived the working class and peoples of Europe of their elementary democratic liberties." He characterized the Nazis as "the most rapacious and plunderous imperialists among all the imperialists of the world."[40]

The following spring, Stalin reiterated that their enemies were not really socialists, thereby implying that the Soviets were the true socialists fighting for the worthy socialist cause. He called the Nazis' claim to have the true interests of workers and peasants at heart a lie. He said, "Only liars can assert that the German fascists, who have introduced slave labor in the factories and mills and resurrected serfdom in the German villages and in the vanquished countries, are champions of the workers and peasants. Only brazen deceivers can deny that the slave and serf system set up by the German fascists is advantageous to the German plutocrats and bankers and not to the workers and peasants." Stalin maintained that, "in actual fact, the German fascists are reactionary feudal barons and the German army is an army dominated by feudal barons and shedding its blood to enrich German barons and re-establish the rule of landlords."[41]

In May 1942 Ehrenburg followed up on Stalin's ideological theme in his aforementioned article on hatred. He reinforced the idea that fascism was a capitalist phenomenon, and he attributed the Germans' evil behavior to it. Soviet socialism was held up as superior when Ehrenburg stated, "Fascism is a monumental attempt to halt the course of history."[42] All soldiers with a Soviet education knew that the course of history progressed through socialism to communist utopia. In an article written in July 1942, Ehrenburg promoted communist ideology and Soviet national pride, praising the USSR for being the first nation to take the path to socialism.[43] Thus, the soldiers of the Red Army should feel unity not only for the national cause but also for a historical cause.

The Propaganda Machine at Work

The Main Political Administration of the Red Army (GlavPUR), headed until June 1942 by Lev Mekhlis, had overall responsibility for soldiers' morale, motivation, and political education. Contrary to its title, an insignificant amount of its work involved ideological education. Instead, it mostly promoted and justified the party line on regime policies. It tended to take a holistic approach to matters of morale, from quality-of-life issues to entertainment, political education, and party work, and it generally tried to keep the soldiers informed of war news in ways that would develop and cement their dedication to fighting the war to a successful conclusion. Those efforts included denying military disasters or falsifying information about their scale. It encouraged soldiers to do their duty, obey their officers, and kill the enemy. GlavPUR headquarters regularly issued slogans to inspire the men and provided themes and talking points to commissars and *politruki*.

GlavPUR played an important role in shaping the heroic imagery, symbols, and myths of the Great Patriotic War. Along with other central party organizations and even Stalin himself, GlavPUR decided whose heroic acts would be publicized for others to emulate. In doing so, it disregarded the truth and freely manipulated the names, circumstances, dates, and other details of the deeds in order to create a script for the rest of the army and future conscripts to follow. Although dozens or even hundreds of soldiers might perform a certain kind of heroic deed, such as throwing themselves on the embrasures of a German bunker, only one (Aleksandr Matrosov), whose life story best fit the image desired by the state, would become a national hero. With rare exception, only those who conformed—or could plausibly be fashioned as conforming—to the Stalinist ideal would receive the coveted Hero of the Soviet Union award, and only a handful would be held up as examples or martyrs (such as Zoia Kosmodemianskaia) for the rest of the nation to emulate or avenge. Elena Seniavskaia's research indicates that many young, impressionable (and mostly Russian) youths responded to the regime's hero-making propaganda, motivating them to become heroes too.[44]

Besides going to great lengths to shape the Red Army soldier's view of himself, GlavPUR had the vital task of shaping his image of the enemy. It needed to deflect German propaganda, prevent the men from identifying with the supposed liberationist goals of the Nazis, and convince them that killing the enemy was in the best interest of not just the USSR but also the individual soldier. Seniavskaia highlights the salient point that soldiers' perception of the enemy is an important if not foundational element of motivation. Soldiers must be convinced that the enemy not only needs to be but also deserves to be killed, and that they should risk their own lives to do so.[45] Red Army soldiers had to be prevented from empathizing with German soldiers as fellow victims of the "bosses." In this effort, GlavPUR politicized the war, affecting the way soldiers talked and thought about the enemy. At the start of the war, it was normal for Soviet soldiers to refer to enemy soldiers as "Fritz" or "Gans" (Hans), which cast them in the mold of ordinary human beings. The more unsophisticated soldiers, not realizing that Fritz and Hans were personal names, referred to Romanian soldiers as "Romanian Fritzes" and Italians as "Italian Fritzes." Within a year, GlavPUR, through its *politruki* and *Krasnaia zvezda*, successfully changed the men's vocabulary so that the term *fascist* largely displaced *Fritz* and *Hans* as the men's identifier for the German soldier. To promote hatred, it also inundated the troops with the descriptors *marauders, occupiers,* and *invaders* for the German army, usually coupled with the adjective *fascist.*[46]

Before it could demonize the enemy, GlavPUR had to completely reverse its depiction of Nazi Germany. From the signing of the Nazi-Soviet Nonaggression Pact in August 1939 until 22 June 1941, the party line was one of peaceful coexistence with the Nazis and sympathy for the German working class. In the decade before the signing of the pact, the Soviet media had portrayed the Nazis as a malignant threat to peace in Europe that had to be opposed.[47] The abrupt switch to a favorable or neutral stance in August 1939 caught the Soviet people by surprise and cost the state a great deal of credibility. There was a virtual alliance between the USSR and the Third Reich from late August 1939 to June 1941. For its part, the Stalinist propaganda apparatus supported the Nazis against the Western Allies; in particular, it railed against Britain as it stood alone for a year against the Axis. This pro-Nazi shift raised doubts in the minds of many Soviet citizens. The second reversal, in June 1941, deepened the skepticism of the average Soviet citizen and soldier, who— if they had not done so before—now read the papers with scorn.

The shock of the invasion reversed attitudes toward Britain, but it was not so easy to erase the effects of prewar Soviet propaganda, which portrayed the German workers and, by implication, the rank and file of the Wehrmacht as victims of the Nazis who shared class solidarity with the Soviet proletariat and therefore would not fight their Soviet "brothers." When it turned out that German soldiers really did support the Nazi cause, it came as a shock to some of the more politically literate soldiers.[48] After the German invasion, it took GlavPUR a few weeks to react, omitting any class-based reference to German soldiers and instead identifying them all as Nazis. In 1945 GlavPUR once again had to differentiate between Nazis and Germans to avoid the mass slaughter of German civilians and POWs and somehow justify an accommodation with the newly conquered population.

This raises the unanswerable question of how effective Soviet propaganda was in influencing the outlook of the average soldier.[49] From its inception, communist propaganda conflicted with the reality that many citizens experienced, so even before the major reversals of the party line, many Soviets, particularly those of the prerevolution generation, had a healthy skepticism about what they read. Soldiers at the front openly scoffed at the inaccurate reports of supposed Soviet successes and German weaknesses and took a jaundiced view of whatever GlavPUR had to say. Private P. Smolinov told his friends: "Our newspapers write untruths. The Red Army suffers large losses and high tails it from the Germans, but they write it the other way around. I don't believe this."[50] Private Rozhkov told his comrades in December 1941: "Our newspapers lie. Take 7 and 8 November, it was related that we captured ten villages, but in a practical sense it was the opposite—we gave up [some villages] and lost 3,000 soldiers. On our front alone in one battalion there are only forty men left. During the attack forty men were captured."[51] Clerk Makarov told his friends: "I do not believe what the newspapers tell us about the success of our units at the front. My eyes have seen our regiment endure defeat after defeat. I read that our forces inflicted a major defeat on the enemy to the west of the Dvina and occupied a new line," which they had supposedly taken some time earlier.[52]

GlavPUR found it hard to keep the men informed and their morale up when the news was all bad. Worse still was the fact that in many units, the political personnel (commissars, *politruki*, and party and Komsomol organizers—partorgs and Komsorgs) did not try at all. Time after time the political hierarchy was taken to task, with little or no result. Its personnel were sometimes as demoralized as the men they were supposed to encourage and inspire. An investigation of the political organs of 43rd Army in November 1941 revealed especially poor work. Men did not get propaganda materials, especially newspapers, and *politruki* did not hold political education meetings. When meetings were called, the men often did not come, and the *politruki* did not go to the men. Private Khodzhitaev complained: "It's been a month since our company has had a newspaper, we do not know about the situation at the front and in the country, about life, we're in the dark, and no one [in authority] is concerned about it."[53]

Sergeant Shvernikov, serving in 43rd Army, wrote to the editor of *Pravda*:

With respect to propaganda the commissar gives us nothing, nothing is explained about the tactics of the enemy, nothing whatever is understood about the spirit of the soldier. Is it possible there will be no victory? The soldiers are not able to understand anything about this war. One talked about surrendering, others about fleeing from the front, nothing good is expected. It's the same with most of the officers. If this is the sense of the commanders then what are the soldiers to do without leadership?[54]

The report by 43rd Army concluded that because of the poor political work, soldiers could not counter anti-Soviet agitation. They tended to believe rumors and were prone to accept German propaganda as truth—most notably, that they would be treated well if they surrendered. Nevertheless, the opinions of reporters and writers were not without effect, and soldiers craved news about world and diplomatic events and about the war effort in general. Their references to news stories and propaganda messages in their letters home attest to the fact that they paid attention to them. Whether and how it affected them, however, is unquantifiable.

In mid-July 1941 GlavPUR excoriated the military's party, political, and Komsomol organizations for their poor job of raising the combat effectiveness of the Red Army, practically blaming them for the battlefield reverses. It directed the Main Administration for Political Propaganda (GUPP) to start raising soldiers' political consciousness, buck up their confidence, and communicate the seriousness of the war and related issues.[55] In fact, the quality of propaganda work in the army had always been inconsistent. Thousands of civilian party officials who knew nothing about army life were drafted for military propaganda work. It took months for most of them to adapt to their new environment—if they adapted at all. In addition to having to adjust to army life, they had to learn to do their jobs in combat—something civilian party work had not prepared them for. Very few received special training for work among soldiers.

For their part, the higher echelons of GlavPUR often failed to give meaningful guidance or supervision to unit-level political workers. *Politruki* were supposed to follow the themes sent down by GlavPUR to inspire the troops. However, propaganda materials were often scarce, and even the delivery of *Krasnaia zvezda, Pravda,* and *Izvestiia*—essential sources of news—was irregular.[56] Political workers often had no idea how to respond to soldiers' criticism of their officers' leadership, supply shortages, or various changes in political policies. Worse still for the average *politruk* was the expectation that he would share in combat command and logistical duties. He often acted as second in command to battalion and company commanders or served as platoon leader in a pinch. These duties put his life in even greater danger, which was something most had not volunteered for, and these combat duties interfered with political education duties.

The party never supplied GlavPUR with enough trained political workers. It therefore relied heavily on ordinary soldiers or junior officers who were communists or Komsomolets. Like civilian communists thrust into the army, soldiers dragooned into political work received little or no preparation. Gennadii Shutz remembered his stint as a battalion Komsorg. "Any time I had a free minute," he said, "I visited our batteries, talked about the situation at the front, about the actions of our allies."[57] He did not attempt to impart a political message, and it is not clear that it even crossed his mind that he ought to. Because of the low level of education and illiteracy of the majority of soldiers, Shutz, like most of his contemporaries, conducted political work verbally, face-to-face.

During the course of the war, GlavPUR used three major propaganda themes in sequence as the fortunes of war first ran against the USSR and then turned in its favor. First, it promoted heroic deeds on the defensive to encourage soldiers to stem the tide of the German advance. Second, it inculcated an offensive mind-set to attack and take revenge on the Nazis. Third, it encouraged acceptance of a liberating mission to free Europe from the "fascist beast."[58]

Each phase of the war and corresponding propaganda campaign had its particular slogans. The initial thirty-one slogans issued to commissars and *politruki* in the first weeks of the war simplistically focused on practical issues related to defensive frontline combat—for example: "Soldiers of the Red Army do not go into prison camps. The fascist barbarians torture, torment, and brutally murder prisoners. It is better to die than to become a prisoner of the fascists." Another advised, "Soldiers! If you find yourself surrounded, fight to the last drop of blood. Fight in the enemy's rear, destroy his communications, strew panic in the enemy camp." Finally, "There is no place for whiners, cowards, and those who panic in the ranks of the Red Army. Do not know fear in battle, each soldier of the Red Army must self-sacrificingly go into battle against the fascist enslavers!"[59] The military press also published slogans, such as, "Our fathers and brothers selflessly fought the landowners and capitalists to found Soviet power. Hitler wants to bring back the landowners and capitalists, to enslave and Germanize our people. Stand and defend each inch of Soviet land!"[60]

At the beginning of 1942, Stalin, emboldened by his army's success in defending Moscow and pushing the Germans back in the winter offensive, as well as the United States' entry into the war, unwisely ordered GlavPUR to promote the idea that victory could be had in 1942. He declared that 1942 would be the year the "fascist scum" would be driven out of the USSR. The official propaganda themes, distributed on 1 May, obediently supported this line. Talking points and slogans included the following: "A new period of the Patriotic War—the period of liberation of the Soviet land from Hitlerite scum;" "The Red Army has all it needs in order to defeat the German-fascist army in 1942;" and "1942 will yield the final defeat of the German-fascist forces."[61]

With the failure of the Soviet spring offensive and the vast success of the German spring offensive—which continued into summer 1942 and took the German army all the way to Stalingrad and the Caucasus—GlavPUR's propaganda turned from optimism to desperation. The list of agitprop themes and slogans issued in August 1942, in the aftermath of Order No. 227, included, "Cowards and men who panic betray the *rodina*. The first bullet is for cowards!" and "Whoever panics helps the enemy. Whoever is a coward betrays the *rodina*! Death to cowards and panic mongers!"[62] GlavPUR also prominently publicized Nazi atrocities toward Soviet civilians and soldiers in 1942 and 1943 as part of the hate campaign.[63]

In the first two years of the war, the vital theme of eventual victory was the most unconvincing message GlavPUR tried to sell to the men. Until as late as January 1945, some soldiers continued to doubt that the USSR would completely defeat Nazi Germany. In 1943 Stalin and GlavPUR did not repeat their mistake of predicting victory; rather, they focused on the theme of liberating the occupied territories. The theme changed again in mid-1944 to the need to chase the "Nazi beast" into his lair for his final destruction. Simply liberating the USSR was not enough because the beast could return. Fascism as a political force had to be completely liquidated.

In mid-1944, with the survival of the USSR assured, GlavPUR could finally direct some of its efforts to real political education. GlavPUR recognized that most of its new recruits—soldiers who had joined since the beginning of the war—were fundamentally "politically illiterate." Giving them the appropriate instruction would, GlavPUR hoped, make them better socialists, better servants of the party, and better soldiers. What passed as political education actually contained little that related to Marxist ideology. The major instructional themes included Lenin and Stalin as the organizers and leaders of the Bolshevik Party; the Bolshevik Party as the inspiration for and organizer of the international struggle against the fascist invaders; the organizational structure of the Bolshevik Party and the special party structure in the Red Army; how candidates become party members; what the party requires of communists in the Red Army; the rights and obligations of party members; the indissoluble bond with the masses as the party's source of strength and power; the focus of party work to strengthen the fighting capacity of units; propaganda and agitation themes as the activity of agitation; and Stalin as the supreme commander, marshal of the Soviet Union, and leader (*vozhd*) and organizer of the glorious victories of the Red Army in the Great Patriotic War.[64] Conspicuous by their absence were the fundamentals of Marxism—the topics of class struggle and world revolution of the proletariat against capitalist oppression.

In addition to official propaganda, the state sought to sustain morale by tapping into the Russian proclivity for song and poetry. When GlavPUR abruptly dropped the motifs of the October Revolution, class struggle, and socialism to unify the soldiers and promoted nationalism instead, it also encouraged the soldiers to send songs to army newspapers to be printed for the benefit of their fellow soldiers. Soldiers sent not only songs but also poems. Their essence tended to emphasize the individual over the collective and the local over the national. Historian Suzanne Ament observes that, in this arena, the state consciously gave up its ascendancy over the creative process in order to elicit genuine support for the war on the people's terms.[65] Some songs became army-wide favorites; others served to unite men from a particular region or locale. As long as they helped sustain the war effort, the state was willing to let soldiers' songs reflect what they would. Songs abounded about home and the girl left behind, but there were also songs about immediate circumstances, army life, and even soldiers' equipment, weapons, and uniforms.[66]

Motivating the National Minorities

An important point about GlavPUR's motivation and morale work is that it was directed primarily at Russians, secondarily at other Slavic peoples, and at the non-Slavic national minorities only as an afterthought. As early as 12 August 1941 the war was identified as Hitler's effort to annihilate the Slavic races.[67] In another list of topics for propaganda lectures, talks, and other presentations issued in November 1941, the themes were generally the bad things about fascism and Hitler, the surety of victory for the USSR, and the elements and foundations thereof. Propaganda emphasized Russian nationalism and such heroes as Nevskii, Donskoi, Suvorov, and Kutuzov. One theme, for instance, "The Heroic Past of the Russian People," typifies the Russocentric nature of most propaganda.[68]

Morale-building political work with national minorities was hit or miss for two basic reasons. First, the need to motivate non-Russians tended to escape the attention of GlavPUR; second, the language barrier inhibited communication. For example, in May and June 1942, 11,418 Kazakhs, Uzbeks, Tadzhiks, and Turkmen were assigned to reserve brigades in the Moscow, Volga, South Urals, and Central Asian military districts. Not until the men reported for duty did GlavPUR realize it would need personnel who could speak the native languages, because none of the new recruits spoke Russian. The district political authorities belatedly began to search among non-Russian party members for bilingual men to work in agitprop, as they had none on staff. GlavPUR's Russocentrism was reflected in its constant complaints that the minorities did not speak Russian; it was never seen as a problem that the Russians did not speak the languages of the minorities, and the army never established a school to teach *politruki* minority languages.

The talking points of agitprop directed toward Central Asians were as follows: the great inviolable brotherhood of the peoples of the USSR, the Leninist-Stalinist nationality policies of the Soviet government, and the nationality policies of the "ogre" Hitler. Rather than take responsibility for the language issue, GlavPUR shifted the task to the military district political organs, instructing them to create posters in the languages of the non-Russian soldiers—which the central authorities had failed to do after nearly a year of war. GlavPUR also cited the need to create newspapers and films in the native languages, which would strengthen the brotherhood of the non-Russian and Russian people and improve the political-moral knowledge of the non-Russians.[69]

In September 1942 GlavPUR added eight themes for armywide agitprop among the national minorities, including: "The Red Army is an army of brotherhood between peoples and nations," "What Soviet power gives to the peoples of the USSR," and "The fronts of the Great Patriotic War defend the independence of all nationalities and republics." The dominant role of the Slavs was reflected in this instructional topic: "The role of the great Russian people in the struggle for freedom and independence of the peoples of the USSR and in establishing socialism in the brotherly Soviet republics."[70]

Expectations of Party and Komsomol Members

Beginning during the Russian civil war, the party in general, and the army's political administration in particular, counted on communists and their organizations in the military to set a positive tone for morale and to exhibit a higher degree of motivation than the ordinary recruits. Overall, the party expected its members to set shining examples in all areas of endeavor for their nonparty comrades to follow. The Great Patriotic War was different only because the Komsomol would also be expected to provide exemplary soldiers.

In July 1941 GlavPUR called on communists and Komsomolets to set the example of courage and discipline for other soldiers and to promote the party line among their peers. They were given special instructions to fight panic and cowardice. Unfortunately, in some cases, communists and Komsomolets were the ones responsible for panic and cowardly flight from the field of battle. GlavPUR reported two examples of communist junior lieutenants who fled: one ran at the very first shot, and the other abandoned his platoon, which fought on without him and did not lose a single man. Both officers were caught and arrested. GlavPUR headquarters chastised unit political organs for not working with party members and Komsomolets during combat operations. The insinuation was that party members were wanting in courage and that the lack of moral support made officers and men susceptible to panic. As a result, GlavPUR called for the quick expulsion of any party members who showed cowardice, panicked, deserted, or sought only to save themselves.[71]

Communists and Komsomolets proved to be just as prone to human frailties as other soldiers—to the constant exasperation of the party, which unrealistically expected superhuman efforts and results. A GlavPUR report in January 1944 complained that communists and Komsomolets in 7th Separate Army were not living up to the high calling of their party status; nor were they serving as models for other soldiers. In the last months of 1943, communists and Komsomolets in this army perpetrated 33 percent of all violations of military regulations and discipline. In November 1943 the 272nd Rifle Division of 7th Separate Army had five "extraordinary events" of indiscipline—all committed by communists.[72] Overall, the performance of communists and Komsomolets was mixed, but, of course, only their heroic acts were made public.

9
Leadership, Rewards, Morale, and the Primary Group

Leadership

In studies of Western armies, it is a given that leadership is a crucial element of combat effectiveness, and it is similarly useful to include that factor in this analysis of the Red Army. In April 1942, looking back over the previous nine months of war, Panteleimon K. Ponomarenko, First Secretary of the Belorussian Communist Party and member of the military council of the 3rd Shock Army, summed up his views on the soldiery in a letter to Stalin. Perhaps drawing on his experience as a teenaged soldier in the civil war, or perhaps just derived from his common sense, Ponomarenko did not join Stalin or his cronies in blaming any of the misfortunes of 1941 on treason or cowardice. Instead, he hinted that weak leadership at the troop level and insufficient preparation of soldiers were the major problems. He thought the officers and soldiers were insufficiently aware of the higher principles underlying their military duties. The men, it seemed to him, did not understand or had not been taught their professional obligations as soldiers. This was the fault of the officers. Ponomarenko viewed the average Soviet citizen as sound material for making a soldier, but "only an authoritative commander is able to educate soldiers, to develop their self-control and to force them to overcome fear and the instinct for self-preservation, he is able not only to appeal for steadfastness, but also to compel steadfastness." He thought officers needed to be self-disciplined and strong-willed, with a pronounced superiority over the men in order to subordinate the latter's free spirits in combat. Soldiers needed to be taught iron discipline, but officers needed discipline first, before they could demand it of their men. He concluded, "Fighters entering the army today, the overwhelming majority, are patriotic, but regrettably are poorly educated as soldiers." The determining factor in the propensity for officers to shoot their men, he thought, was poor leadership skills. Institutionally, the Red Army had inadequately prepared most of its junior officers, so on an institutional basis, the army needed to accept the blame for facilitating the descent to summary execution.[1]

If we assume that good leadership at the company and platoon level makes a significant difference in the men's morale, their ability to cope with fear, and their willingness to obey, then leadership must be defined. Basically, leadership is securing the willing cooperation of others in a course of action. Good leadership, from the viewpoint of the soldier, is characterized by those actions that minimize his risk in battle and maximize his well-being with regard to food, shelter, and other necessities. Competence and level of experience affect leadership. Like Ponomarenko, veterans of the Abraham Lincoln Battalion felt strongly that leaders needed to instill discipline in their men and that it was essential for leaders to teach soldiers why discipline was necessary. "Explaining to the men how discipline is useful in battle, how it saves lives, achieves results, is unanimously held to be important." Conversely, "training for automatic obedience by never explaining the reasons for commands is believed . . . to produce poorer soldiers."[2]

In close combat and in arduous conditions, sergeants and officers with good leadership skills could make a soldier's life more bearable. Mansur Abdulin held the opinion that, "strictly speaking, it doesn't matter who your commander is: a soldier is simply expected to observe army regulations, period! But regulations aside, the rank and file want to love their commander. This love is rarely expressed or mentioned, but it helps the soldier endure the hard front line existence."[3] During the battle of Kursk, Abdulin remembered reporting to his commander that the new recruits appeared to be on the verge of being psychologically overwhelmed. The battalion commander mounted his horse and galloped into the no-man's-land between the lines. He raced back and forth under the noses of the enemy. The Germans not only held their fire but even cheered in admiration of his courage. The men of Abdulin's unit forgot their fear and also began to cheer wildly for their captain.[4] By his positive example, this commander restored the morale of his unit by acting in the spirit of civil war heroes such as Chapaev, Budennyi, and

Voroshilov. Perhaps he was hoping to evoke the spirit of that war, which the soldiers would have remembered from the history lessons of their school days.

It was not simply winning the love or friendship of the men that kept officers alive and the men obedient; more often it was good leadership that got the job done. In the 1941 battle of Kiev, Lieutenant Cherkasov ordered his company—in combat for the first time—to conduct a hasty counterattack to retake positions lost to the Germans. He and the *politruk* jumped up and ran forward, shouting, "For the *rodina*, For Stalin!" When he looked back, he saw only four or five of his ninety men following. The rest stayed in their holes. He crawled back to the company, but rather than curse and threaten the men, as was the norm, he realized that he had failed to lead them properly. In preparing for another try, he explained the mission, laid out a plan, and made sure everyone knew their assignments. The second time, the entire company went forward and retook the lost ground. Despite suffering twenty casualties in the process, the men were cheerful and as a result gained confidence in Cherkasov—and themselves.[5]

For a decade before the outbreak of war there had been a shortage of officers, with a consequent negative effect on the training and leading of soldiers. The army had had little success in recruiting sufficient numbers of officers and had resorted to compelling *politruki*, NCOs, civilian and enlisted Communist Party members, and Komsomolets to serve as officers. They were given short periods of training before assuming their duties. In the prewar expansion of the army, tens of thousands of junior and midlevel officers had been promoted to higher rank and responsibility without commensurate training.[6] Massive casualties among frontline leaders hindered the improvement of leadership as the Red Army lost more than 973,000 officers who were killed, wounded, captured, or went missing during the war.[7] In desperation, by 1942, it had begun to commission almost anyone with at least six years of education and no known criminal record.

Because of the continuous turnover of officers, many did not serve long enough to gain either leadership experience or the trust of their men, so they led poorly until their demise. Others had simply received inadequate training or lacked the intelligence, social skills, maturity, personality, or character to lead well. In such cases, officers often undermined morale and discipline by resorting to threats, intimidation, and execution, and their units often incurred high casualties. It stands to reason that these officers were most likely to be murdered by their men. Partly because of poor preparation and low standards of selection, the army demoted or punished with terms in penal battalions or prison more than 20,000 officers for negligence, incompetence, or dereliction of duty during the course of the war.[8]

In many instances, soldiers could legitimately question whether their officers were qualified to lead them. The training of officers in military schools during the war was generally quite good, but not all officers came through these schools; some who did manifested attitudes and conduct unbecoming an officer, which suggested a lack of seriousness or commitment to their responsibilities. For example, an NKO investigation in January 1943 exposed shortcomings in military district and front-level courses intended to train officers to be company, battalion, and regiment commanders. The inspectors criticized the level of instruction for not being rigorous, and they questioned the seriousness of the student officers. The report condemned self-inflicted wounds, drunkenness, and desertion among students. It ordered the military councils of military districts and of fronts to get tough with school commanders and their charges, invoking the penalties available under Order No. 227.[9]

An inspection in February 1943 of the South Urals Military District yielded reports of hooliganism among military school students and offenses against the civilian population. Students and officers stole crops and livestock from collective farms and seized apartments from civilians. Some officers went so far as to murder a local policeman who tried to stop their activities. Others took potshots at policemen with their army-issued rifles.[10] Men who exhibited such antisocial behavior discredited the Red Army and were unlikely to show great concern for their men.

Not surprisingly, soldiers' lack of confidence in their officers' ability and commitment to their welfare often undercut morale and motivation. Because they were poorly prepared to lead, officers often performed badly and caused many unnecessary casualties. It was not rare for platoon- and company-level officers—or even those at battalion and regiment levels—to flee the battlefield in fear, abandoning their subordinates and leaving the men to their own devices. This sort of behavior caused soldiers to question the courage and competence of all officers. It also made them less likely to take risks in combat, lest they be betrayed and die for their commanders' mistakes or cowardice. For example, in November 1941 Captain Shutov, a communist and commander of an antitank battery, failed to carry out orders to position his guns to support a tank attack. During the attack, Shutov fled his battery, as did the battery's *politruk*, Barashnikov, who returned only when the attack was over. The men and junior officers fought the battle without them. For their cowardice, Shutov was sentenced to be shot, and Barashnikov was relieved of his duties, expelled from the party, and remanded to a military tribunal.[11]

Aleksandr Bodnar' remembered the failed summer offensive of 1942 as an example of bad leadership:

> I went one or one and a half kilometers behind our combat formation and suddenly saw a field dotted with our dead and wounded soldiers. Young guys, with Guards badges, in brand new uniforms. . . . A German machine gunner sat in a pillbox and wiped out our soldiers. This was such an inept surmounting of the no-man's-land. The soldiers were ready for anything, but the commanders did not know how to attack properly. They needed to bring up the mortars, some artillery, suppress this machine gun, but no, the commanders urged, "Onward! Onward!"[12]

Threats to officers were neither uncommon nor idle. Vasily Grossman noted, "Red Army soldier Kazakov said to his platoon commander: 'My rifle has been loaded for a long time waiting to shoot you.'"[13] Competent officers were also well aware of the shortcomings of their brothers in arms. On 31 October 1941 an ordnance officer told his unit's assistant political officer, "We are going to lose this war, because our officers are untalented, their skill is to drive Red Army men into the enemy's hell."[14]

Some incompetent officers got drunk in the presence of their men, or sometimes with their men, and they fraternized with women in the battle zone with the full knowledge of their men. All these actions destroyed their moral authority over their soldiers and invited disrespect, death threats, resentment, and disobedience. Disrespect for officers led to comments such as those of Private Koval', a twenty-seven-year-old

Komsomolets: "Our generals and officers are incapable, they don't know how to fight. Our infantry, when it attacks goes straight into captivity. If we give up Moscow, I'll be the first to surrender."[15]

Positive Motivation: The Use of Rewards

In modern history, as national armies moved away from plunder as material incentive, they almost universally used medals, badges, and other forms of symbolic commendation as rewards to raise morale and motivate soldiers. Despite its initial forswearing of bourgeois and feudal symbols and practices, the Red Army was no exception; however, unlike Western armies, it extended its reward system to include the material as well. Cash payments first became standard for snipers, and in June 1943 they were also given for downing enemy planes and destroying tanks. For example, antitank gunners and riflemen were paid 500 rubles for destroying a tank; their assistants got 200. For tankers, the commander, gunner, and driver each got 500 rubles; other crewmembers got 200. If artillery knocked out a tank, the gun commander and gunner received 500 rubles each; the rest of the crew got 200 each. If a group of soldiers or several tanks were involved in the destruction of a tank, they split 1,500 rubles among them. The same formula applied to antiaircraft gun crews and pilots who shot down airplanes.[16]

Support soldiers could earn cash awards for retrieving knocked-out Soviet tanks under combat conditions and removing them to the rear for repair. In May 1942 the NKO formalized the reward structure as follows: KV tanks or other heavy tanks, 5,000 rubles for each retrieved; for T-34s or other medium tanks, 2,000 rubles; for T-60, T-70, or other light tanks, 500 rubles to be split among those who recovered the tank.[17] Mention of cash rewards as a motivating factor is extremely rare in memoirs and interviews, and one has to wonder if they had the effect the regime intended. Destroying enemy tanks and aircraft was usually a matter of necessity, not choice, and money was simply unnecessary at the front. There was no time to spend it and nowhere to shop, and even if there had been, there was nothing to buy, because the production of consumer goods had completely ceased. Most men sent their pay home in automatic monthly allotments or committed it to purchase war bonds. Given that the odds of survival were already stacked against the *frontoviki*, it is hard to imagine men taking undue risks simply for a wad of rubles.

Still, some Soviet soldiers were positively effusive in their claims of "destroying fascists," for which they received decorations and cash awards. When Mikhail S. Tsushba, a sniper, shot his 125th German in 1942, he wrote home that his commander had rewarded him with 300 rubles and some gifts.[18] One can question whether the money or the notoriety served as a motivator, or whether the soldiers were just happy to be recognized for their efforts.

Although its exact origins are murky, the idea to reward soldiers for knocking out tanks was suggested as early as November 1941 in a letter to Stalin by one comrade Velichko. Velichko advocated giving soldiers a medal for destroying one tank, the Order of the Red Star for destroying three tanks, the order of the Red Banner for destroying five, the Order of Lenin for ten, and the Hero of the Soviet Union for twenty.[19] Why Stalin opted for cash over a system of medals and orders is unknown, but if soldiers performed such deeds, they were relatively certain to receive an award from the unit commander.

Another suggestion brought to Stalin's attention, and one that might have stimulated some truly heroic acts, was the granting of furloughs. In October 1942 military correspondent V. Ardov wrote to Stalin and suggested, among other things, that besides medals or cash, the promise of a two- or three-week furlough for soldiers exhibiting outstanding performance after six months at the front would highly motivate them to both fight well and behave themselves. General Zhukov and two other high-ranking officers endorsed Ardov's suggestion.[20] Stalin, however, did not. In contrast, the Wehrmacht had a regular system of furloughs throughout the war. The U.S. Army began to grant three- to five-day passes to soldiers once most of France had been liberated.

The widespread use of medals came late to the Red Army because the leftist revolutionaries who founded the army in 1918 saw them as bourgeois. Until the Winter War, the army had only four major awards: Hero of the Soviet Union, Order of Lenin, Order of the Red Banner, and Order of the Red Star. The first two were also conferred on civilians for outstanding performance of duties. The Winter War saw the introduction of two medals, one for valor and one for meritorious service in wartime. With the German invasion and the call for mass heroism from the troops, the idea took hold among the leadership to promote medals as incentives. In 1942 the aforementioned P. K. Ponomarenko wrote a detailed proposal to Stalin about expanding the number and type of commendations and other morale-boosting incentives for soldiers. At the top of his list was the introduction of shoulder boards as part of the insignia of officer rank, arguing that it was a tradition of the Russian people and the Russian army.

Ponomarenko also recommended the introduction of military orders exclusively for officers and others just for soldiers in various grades, such as first class, second class, and third class. In addition, he suggested the introduction of a wound badge. He proposed that the army create titles for officers of Guards units, such as Guards captain, Guards major, and so forth. Finally, he recommended giving unit awards to regiments and name designations to regiments and divisions that distinguished themselves in battle. All these ideas were implemented in 1943, with the exception of the wound badge.[21] To mitigate any protest against the obviously tsarist era–like elevation of officers' status, sergeants were also given shoulder boards for their rank.

The number of medals and military orders proliferated over the next two years, including some that Ponomarenko had not anticipated. The navy adopted unique orders for its officers (the Order of Nakhimov and the Order of Ushakov), and there was even an order reserved for Ukrainians—the Order of Khmel'nitskii. The army also created an order reserved for staff officers—the Order of Kutuzov. These orders referenced Russia's heroic past to reinforce patriotic sentiment. Soldiers could receive the Order of Glory (in three classes), and officers were eligible for the Order of Suvorov and the Order of the Patriotic War. Campaign medals for the defense and liberation of major cities or regions were struck as the occasion arose.

In many frontline units, medals were given almost automatically for certain deeds. In the infantry, for example, men were virtually guaranteed a medal or badge for capturing an enemy officer, knocking out a tank, or shooting down an airplane. Still, as a result, it was the exceptional rather than the ordinary soldier who set out to earn medals. Some Soviet soldiers were quite cynical about medals. Natalia Peshkova's thoughts on medals are characteristic:

It must be said that they started awarding us only after the Kursk Operation and the capture of Kiev. And then, they only gave us "The Star," "The Banner," "For Fighting Merits," and "For Bravery," but only senior officers received other decorations. I have "For the Capture of Kiev" and "For the Defense of Moscow," but I don't have anything real besides the Red Star. Mainly the awards were given out according to distribution lists, and not for actions. There was an assignment to every unit for a defined quantity of such and such medals. Well, somebody is killed, a medal remains unclaimed and gets passed on to another. Our commander, Lieutenant Uglovskii, when he was asked why he didn't recommend anyone for a decoration for such and such battles, replied; "Because I wasn't recommended. They remained alive and became heroes because I was in charge of them. I wasn't recommended and I'm not recommending anyone." He said that to the superiors in front of us.[22]

Mansur Abdulin had a similar experience. He wrote that at a reunion of the regiment thirty years after the war, the regimental adjutant told him that Abdulin had been on a list of people recommended for the Hero of the Soviet Union. The regiment commander, however, would not sign or forward the list because his own name was not on it. In another instance, Abdulin was dismayed when a *politruk* offered to recommend him for a medal in exchange for a wristwatch Abdulin had taken from a German POW.[23]

Semion Aria supports Peshkova's assessment, but in a slightly less negative tone.

You know, decorating for specific actions was practiced rather rarely at the front. Especially in artillery units, it was impossible to connect a specific person to a given successful strike of a shell, therefore, if a person participated in combat, displayed the necessary persistence, courage, then at some point they started making things up, wrote something specific in the award sheet, but in reality all that was fantasies. And so I was well regarded in the regiment, so at some point they added me to the decoration list. Then started making things up: "In fighting for such and such block displayed courage, disregarded mortal danger. . . ." Such folklore.[24]

Private Evgenii Mazo exhibited a cynical but lighthearted appreciation for medals for valor. He was on the Leningrad Front in 1942, in a sector where the Soviet trenches were only fifty meters from the Germans. During lulls in the fighting the Germans would play martial music on a gramophone directed toward the Soviet lines. Mazo and his comrades countered by playing balalaikas and singing Russian songs.

> We would get tired, but they just cranked their gramophone and it would go on forever. One night I and two other guys snuck across the lines into their trench. We grabbed a German soldier and asked him where the gramophone was. He pointed the way and we found it and snatched it up and ran back across to our lines. The German began yelling and chased us. The whole German line then opened up with fire. The German jumped into our trench with us demanding the gramophone back. We tackled him and put a gun to his head and asked him if he wanted to live. Yes, he did. We then tied his hands and led him to our company command post. We presented our "tongue" to the commander, not saying anything about the gramophone. I got a medal for that.[25]

In Western armies, loyalty and bonding as means of getting men to fight are usually tied to the military unit in which the soldier serves, be it a company, battalion, regiment, division, or branch, which encompasses a mix of history, traditions, and reputations of units and leaders. Dread of disgracing their units can cause men to disregard risks and do unbelievable things. In keeping with the egalitarianism of the Soviet state and Marxist-Leninism, during the Great Patriotic War and the years prior to it, the Red Army did not promote unit identity and loyalty along the lines of Western norms. Instead, loyalty was first and foremost directed to the Soviet regime. Therefore, during the war the emphasis was on the soldiers' and the Red Army's loyalty to the state, Stalin, and the *rodina*. This could be construed to mean that failure to do one's duty was an act of disloyalty to the nation and the government. Rather than encouraging pride in their individual units, which no doubt many felt, the Soviet state appealed to the soldiers' pride in their status as defenders of the state.

Awarding the title "Guards" to regiments and larger units was also a method of motivating soldiers. This was another tradition from the tsarist era, when only the most elite regiments were designated Guards of the Emperor and were given special status within the military. During the Second World War, with Stalin's permission, the army bestowed the distinction of the Guards title on entire divisions for exceptional performance in combat. They were given new division numbers and new flags, and they were grouped together in Guards Corps or even Guards Armies. The Guards title was attached to the officers' and men's ranks, and they received higher pay. The idea to reintroduce the Guards title had first surfaced immediately after the Winter War, but Stalin had brushed it aside, along with the suggestion to resurrect the title of sergeant, saying that the Red Army had no need for such tsarist trappings. The disasters of 1941 and 1942 must have convinced him that it was a small price to pay if it would inspire the men to fight.

As a result of its performance in the battle of Stalingrad, Mansur Abdulin's 1034th Rifle Regiment became the 193rd Guards Rifle Regiment. When the announcement of the Guards title was made, he remembered thinking, "This was a great honor." The members of his regiment received their Guards badges a few months later, in June 1943. "Finally," he recalled, "each of us had one! In those days soldiers rarely had medals, let alone orders. For many Guardsmen the badge was the only decoration on their blouse, and it often seemed to a soldier that he did not need anything else." After that, "everyone became especially enthusiastic about winning the war and returning home!" The men painted Guards signs on tanks, guns, cars, trucks, and even two-wheeled carts. They wanted everyone to know they were a Guards unit. Abdulin's pride in that honor lasted long after the war.[26]

Abdulin's response was exactly what the Red Army sought. The Guards title was not intended merely to reward a unit's outstanding combat behavior; it was also meant to elicit a higher level of performance thereafter and set an example for the non-Guards units. Nikolai Barzakovskii also felt energized and proud when he became a Guards soldier. He wrote home in 1942, "On 1 May we had great joy! Our regiment was awarded the title Guards! You should be proud of this award."[27]

Toward the end of the war, when the Red Army was in Eastern Europe, the state adopted another premodern material incentive to motivate the men to keep fighting—legalized looting. Officers and men were allowed, and even encouraged, to send home booty from liberated Europe. The NKO issued an order in December 1944 that stipulated the weight allowances for packages of "liberated" goods. Soldiers and sergeants could send five kilograms per month, officers ten, and generals sixteen.[28]

Morale and Sustaining Motivation

The study of morale and sustaining motivation adds to our understanding of the challenges to the Red Army's combat effectiveness related to noncombat situations—those not usually affected by coercion or propaganda. Because morale is largely emotional and based on the situation at the moment, fluctuations are to be expected. Of the many things that can affect morale, those mentioned most often by soldiers were food, the weather, and the situation of their families. When the bullets were flying, these issues quickly receded from consciousness, as survival and mission accomplishment came to the forefront. The great importance of morale is its effect on sustaining motivation—the feelings that keep a soldier from desertion, suicide, depression, or acts of indiscipline in the periods between combat. In their quiet moments, soldiers had time to reflect on their personal situations, which could either depress them or cheer them, prepare them to fight again or not.

Inadequate or low-quality food was a constant source of poor morale in the Red Army. The censors of 33rd Army reported numerous negative comments in letters written in November 1941. One soldier wrote: "The food is bad, twice a day we get bread, sometimes 400 grams, sometimes 600, we never see more. The soup is like water . . . everything is bad."[29] From 15 through 31 October 1941, the 6th NKVD Military Censor Detachment of 34th Army reported 1,266 letters reflecting the soldiers' depressed mood, of which 848 complained about living conditions, especially the food.[30] A year later, things were no better. An NKVD report from November 1942 notes many failings of the supply apparatus to provide adequate food to soldiers on the Stalingrad Front. Many units went unfed for two or three days at a time. Private Kirillov of the 15th Guards Rifle Division wrote home: "We don't eat here, we will die not from bullets, but from hunger." Private Agapov, a machine gunner in the 1045th Rifle Regiment, wrote: "We have a bad situation here. I have not eaten for three days. . . . I lay hungry in a trench, behind a machine gun, without the strength to shoot. I want to eat and eat."[31]

One of the major problems was the food shortage throughout the USSR due to the loss of Ukraine. Another was transportation; the lack of trucks was severe, and the railroads had been disrupted, but they would have been inadequate in number and capacity in any case. Finally, inept and disorganized logistics played a part. Early in the war, Stalin became so exasperated by the ineptitude of his supply officers that on 1 August 1941 he dismissed and replaced every general working in front-level supply services.[32] The sacking, demoting, reassigning, and prosecution of supply officers kept the Commissariat of Defense busy the entire war.

The Red Army never fully overcame its food problems. The NKO continually inspected military supply organs from front down to division level to see if they were doing their best to serve the soldiers. Time after time, inspectors found that negligence, ineptitude, and corruption were creating problems that eventually affected the health, well-being, and morale of frontline soldiers. In the last quarter of 1942, the men of the 8th Guards Rifle Division often went hungry because the supply chief and his minions were too lazy or incompetent to procure the food authorized for the division.[33] In November 1942 twenty-five men of the 279th Rifle Division died of the effects of malnutrition, and the health of the rest of the men was seriously impaired.[34]

An inspection in January 1944 revealed widespread dystrophy in the 103rd Rifle Division due to malnutrition and unhealthy living conditions. Because of faults in the supply system, men were being fed only 300 to 350 calories per day, when 2,500 to 3,000 would have been appropriate. Due to illness associated with malnutrition, 410 men were hospitalized in October 1943, 1,551 in November, 1,416 in December, and 1,433 in January 1944. The inspectors declared the division unfit for combat.[35]

Mikhail Kuznetsov remembered: "The hunger was awful! Six hundred grams of bread and water with dumplings. In the winter, the bread was frozen. We just talked about food all the time. We shot rooks and crows. We ate horse. We were barely able to walk."[36]

Later, in the spring of 1943, Soviet forces on the offensive outran their supply lines and did not eat for days. When they finally received rations, some men overate and died because their systems could not handle it. In all these cases, the men were so demoralized by hunger that they lost, or were on the verge of losing, their will to fight.

And then there was the bitter cold. Soldiers certainly did not expect the army to change the weather, but they did expect to be provided with adequate clothing to protect them from the elements. Unfortunately, army logistics sometimes fell short. Men froze to death and suffered from frostbite and trench foot. They complained to their officers and to their families in letters home that their hands and feet were freezing. A junior lieutenant wrote in November 1941: "Today it got cold. There are no warm clothes or boots."[37] On the Kalinin Front in December 1941, 30 percent of the censored letters were negative. Overwhelmingly the men listed inadequate food and the lack of warm clothing as their biggest problems.[38]

Other fronts suffered shortages of winter gear due to breakdowns in distribution, which led to thousands of casualties. For example, in December 1942 the Caucasus Front reported 1,600 frostbite cases, the Southwest Front reported 1,340, and the Northwest Front 1,277.[39] Occasionally, morale was restored, if only temporarily, by the arrival of provisions and cold-weather gear. These soldiers regained their motivation to fight, but it was never far from their minds that the "system" did not care enough to ensure adequate supplies—as though they truly were cannon fodder.

Liberating their fellow citizens who had suffered under German occupation improved morale and sustained many men's commitment to keep fighting. Mikhail Kuznetsov described a boost to his morale in 1944, as his unit moved forward swiftly on the offensive and entered a village it had just freed: "The residents saw us, their own people—how they rejoiced! How they kissed us: 'Just now the last German went by on a motorcycle. They set the village on fire. You are a little late.' 'You want something to eat?'" As the soldiers walked through the village, the residents brought out food to share. The effect of that brief encounter was so powerful that more than fifty years later he exclaimed, "Gosh, I simply cannot forget this meeting."[40]

War weariness was another morale problem, which in many cases proved to be insurmountable. Some men reached their breaking point not in combat but during the lulls or in the hospital, when they had time to reflect on their experiences and their dwindling chance of survival if they returned to battle. Mansur Abdulin was an enthusiastic soldier in

Soldiers in a recently liberated village, 1944.

the beginning and grew into a battle-hardened veteran. Yet he was one of those men who eventually lost his motivation to fight. In November 1943, after spending a year at the front hating the Germans and actively avenging his dead comrades, Abdulin was wounded and evacuated to a hospital in Siberia, where he recuperated for five months. "The wound on my buttock healed and the medical board decreed that I was fit for active service. But I, a former volunteer, no longer had any desire to return to the battlefield. 'I'm fed up and sick of fighting!'"[41] At the last minute, a sympathetic medical officer declared him unfit for duty, which, much to Abdulin's relief, kept him from the front.

To raise morale between battles, the regime entertained the soldiers with traveling shows of civilian and military performers. The army treated the men to dramas, comedy and variety shows, orchestras, bands, and singers to take their minds off the war for a moment or two. A wide variety of films was also shown, not only to entertain but also to inspire the men. Before one major offensive, Aleksandr Pyl'syn remembered watching war movies that glorified the Red Army's deeds in the civil war and heroism in the current war, as well as historical epics such as Eisenstein's *Aleksandr Nevskii*. Pyl'syn claimed that he and his comrades went into combat with those war movies fresh in their minds.[42]

To help sustain morale, the political administration promoted the idea that all of Soviet society supported the war effort. This idea was translated into reality through drives among the population to collect gifts for *frontoviki*. GlavPUR started the drives in 1941, on the twenty-fourth anniversary of the October Revolution, and garnered nearly 400 boxcars full of gifts. The items most commonly donated were gloves, mittens, socks, scarves, and food. The success of the first drive led GlavPUR to conduct drives to celebrate New Year's Day, Red Army Day (23 February), May Day, and the anniversary of the start of the war. With each drive, the number of boxcars filled with gifts increased by the hundreds.[43] One soldier remembered: "These parcels cheered us up. We felt that our whole country was with us in the trenches."[44]

Unfortunately, despite the vast amount of effort and goodwill poured into these drives, they did not make as big a contribution to morale—or as big an impact in ameliorating conditions for the soldiers—as intended. Only a minuscule number of parcels made it into the hands of *frontoviki*. For example, in 1942, of 172,839 packages donated and shipped to the Leningrad Front, infantry units received only 1,813 parcels, tank units 1,045, motorized units 840, artillery 130, and aviation squadrons 2,560. The remaining 166,451 parcels of gifts were either filched or distributed to rear area troops, whose needs were less urgent and whose morale was less strained by the rigors of campaigning. Investigations revealed similar results at the Transcaucasus Front, the Southern Front, and the Moscow defense region. The authorities were clearly exasperated by this situation because the explicit intent of these drives was to boost morale by getting food and clothes to the frontline forces that determined the outcome of combat operations.[45] Especially scandalous was that in 1942, donations of goods and money produced close to 5 million gift parcels for the troops, nearly one for every *frontovik*.

Role of the Primary Group

One factor not determined by the political or military authorities, yet very important in maintaining motivation and morale, was the primary group. The basis of primary group theory is that loyalty to comrades keeps men fighting, especially in desperate situations when one would expect organizational collapse. Shils and Janowitz's theory, derived from interviews of German soldiers immediately after the Second World War, posits that loyalty among comrades and to the leaders in small (platoon-to company-sized) groups was the key to combat effectiveness in the Wehrmacht in both victory and defeat. This idea has received much attention in the last sixty years and has been successfully challenged as being too limited and a bit naïve in terms of assigning credibility to the interviewees' denial of the unifying role of Nazi ideology.[46] Nevertheless, primary group theory has yielded valuable insights into how social relations among men and leaders in small groups help maintain individual and group motivation, morale, and cohesion in and out of combat. Primary groups, essentially circles of friends and acquaintances one can rely on, can help soldiers overcome fear, loneliness, and separation from family and can motivate them to fight to preserve the group and fulfill their missions.

Aside from Shils and Janowitz's work, other work on the German army, particularly on the Eastern Front, is worth referencing. Omer Bartov and Stephen Fritz address the viability of the primary group and ideology as motivating factors that kept the Wehrmacht from disintegrating in 1944 and 1945 under the same pressures experienced by the Red Army in 1941 through 1943.[47] Bartov challenges primary group theory, claiming that the scale of casualties obliterated primary groups and that a shared belief in Nazi ideology and draconian discipline held the men together. Fritz agrees with Bartov that ideology was very important, but he disagrees that the primary group was a minor factor. He argues that the primary group need not be based solely on a large military unit; it can be extremely small—perhaps a bond among just a few men who psychologically and emotionally sustain one another through the worst of times. On a squad or smaller basis, primary groups continually reconstituted themselves, and ideology was often a common denominator. Bruce Newsome also maintains that Wehrmacht replacement policies, which was based on groups rather than individuals (as Bartov incorrectly assumes), continually replenished depleted units with primary groups.[48]

Primary group theory and ideological sources of motivation have not been used in any previous work assessing the Red Army. In contrast to Shils and Janowitz's study, which identifies the platoon as the smallest primary group and the company as the largest, my research on Soviet soldiers indicates that a much smaller primary group functioned in the Red Army. When asked, or when they offer information that can be construed as a reference to the primary group, Soviet veterans almost always mention the names of five or fewer wartime comrades who made a difference in their lives. Soldiers infrequently mention platoon or company commanders; when they do, it is almost never in the same context of mutual support that characterizes their discussions of fellow privates or the occasional sergeant. Similarly, junior officers include other lieutenants in their companies as part of their primary group; they sometimes include their company commanders, but seldom sergeants and almost never privates or officers above their company commanders. Even the most cohesive Soviet infantry and armor companies and artillery batteries were likely to be fragmented along the lines of primary groups. The overwhelming majority of Soviet soldiers managed to contain their fear and fulfill their duties; of the several things that helped them (as well as their German foes) do so, the primary group was probably the most significant.

The numerous preconditions and variables that contributed to forming and maintaining primary group ties in the Red Army in World War II were the social background of unit members, the more homogeneous the better; the personality of unit members; the protectiveness and competence of immediate leaders; military discipline and professionalism; patriotism and commitment to the social-political system and ideology; war indoctrination; exigencies of military life and the combat situation; technical aspects of weapons systems; the replacement system and rotation policy; and the social prestige of the soldierly profession. Obviously, the closer the primary group identifies with the larger military organization, the better it functions.[49]

Like the German army, the Soviet army tried to recruit and man regiments from as small a locality as possible. The reasons had nothing to do with cohesion—it is unlikely the Soviet state appreciated the dynamics of the primary group—but had to do with convenience. Transportation was often a difficult prospect in the USSR, so when a few thousand men were processed by a local *voenkomat*, it made sense to form them into a unit, bring in a few leaders, and transport them as an organized body. With the common bond of geography and regional dialect, primary groups formed more easily than when men from all over the USSR were thrown together.

In the Red Army, the primary group was strongest at the squad or platoon level. Semion Chumanev, a *frontovik*, remembered that he and his platoon "were like one family. We not only fought together, but also loved to sing, and some had 'problems of the heart.'"[50] The family atmosphere helped a soldier keep his sanity; it gave him a sense of belonging and acceptance that both kept up his spirits and motivated appropriate behavior under fire. Sergei Abaulin remembered: "At the end of 1944, at his post, my friend Andrei Babich was fatally wounded by mortar shrapnel. I had to bury him on an anonymous hill in an unfamiliar wood. It is a bitter and hard thing to say goodbye to true comrades."[51] The depth of sorrow at the death of a comrade reflects the strong level of attachment these men had to one another.

Stories abound of wounded men fleeing field hospitals to get back to their units to avoid being evacuated to the deep rear, where, once healed, they would be reassigned to different regiments. In their reminiscences, men refer to the desire to get back to their units, but what they really mean is that they wanted to get back to their friends. The fear of going to a different unit was actually the fear of becoming an outsider thrust among strangers. Private Georgii Minin was so attached to his friends that he disobeyed orders to report for training to become a tank officer and was willing to accept whatever punishment he got if it meant he could stay with his platoon.[52] One element of Minin's attachment to his unit, besides comradeship, was the fact that he had gained some status in the company as an old-timer and expert to whom new recruits often turned for advice and instruction; all that would have been lost by a transfer and promotion. Minin also knew that tankers had a short life expectancy in combat.

Quite often, soldiers referred to their squad or crew in family terms. In this environment, letting down a comrade meant disgrace and social isolation. For most men, such considerations were far more significant than their view of the Stalinist state, as Viktor Leonov's experience as a scout platoon leader suggests:

> Actually, we were all one family. Like the time we carried Lieutenant
> Fedor Shelavin from Cape Mogilny. . . . He was the reason we stayed

there; both of his legs were wounded. He wanted to shoot himself . . . to lighten our hands. But I knew—if we abandoned Shelavin, on the next raid someone would have thought, "That's it, if we've abandoned a wounded commanding officer, I would be abandoned for sure." If this thought gets into a soldier's head, he can't fight. He's not a real fighter anymore. This thought will persecute and depress you, whether you want it or not.[53]

He added: "I always hated to lose people. Ask any one. They all knew I would fight for every man's life until the end." Leonov understood very well the need for trust among his men. He knew that this bond gave the men courage and made them feel responsible for one another.

In a similar vein, Ivan Iakushin, speaking of one of the gun crews in his antitank platoon, said: "The crew had been together for a long time and had grown close during many marches and battles. They knew that a mistake by one man in the crew could cost the lives of them all, and this is what knitted them together. In battle, they acted as one. They knew exactly what to do: they understood each other without words and always obeyed every order of the gun leader."[54]

Not wanting to let a comrade down is a significant part of the primary group dynamic. Similarly, genuine courage strengthened the primary group, as acknowledged by the adage "courage is contagious." Examples of courage or coolness under fire are legion in the annals of military history and can make a huge difference in men's behavior. The Red Army promoted several heroic examples early in the Great Patriotic War. The first was Lieutenant I. I. Ivanov, who rammed his fighter plane into a German bomber on 22 June 1941, sacrificing himself in the process. Later, during the battle for Moscow, the state held up the "Panfilov Twenty-eight," who fought as a unit to the last man to stop the Germans. Sergeant Iurii Koriakin wrote to his brother about his admiration for a fellow soldier: "The guys in our team are cool, there is one who was also in combat, the battalion in which he served was completely destroyed, only 21 men left, including him with a radio set, and for several days he dragged the radio and managed to bring it back safely, although it's not light, designed for two. For saving military equipment he was recommended for a decoration."[55]

When asked about heroism, Natalia Peshkova recalled her tank battalion's chief accountant, who had to visit every unit once a month to fill out forms so the soldiers could send money to their relatives. "That man, he was an awful coward, he was trembling from fear—but he never missed a day. He kept himself together and crawled there to fill out the papers. Isn't it heroism?"[56] Although it appears paradoxical to label a man a coward and then to say his acts were heroic, it actually makes sense in the mind of the *frontovik*: it was regrettable that the man showed his fear, but he accomplished his mission in spite of it.

A certain level of courage was expected of superiors as well as peers. Gennadii Shutz was assigned to take over an experienced antiaircraft battery as a junior lieutenant. He recalled that during the first air attack, "Everyone was looking at me—to see how I was going to command. We had a law—while a raid continues no one, from ammo carriers to the battery commander, could even bend down. You had to keep doing your duties. The main thing was not to lose your nerve."[57] Ivan Kobets, a scout platoon leader, told his interviewer: "Did you know that men sense their leader just as a horse senses the rider? If the horse feels the rider's fear, it won't come near the obstacle! Same here, if the commander is brave, the soldier feels it: 'Uhuh! You won't be done for with this one! This leader won't fail you!'"[58]

The penalty for cowardice was social and sometimes physical exclusion from the primary group. Naum Orlov remembered that in one battle "at Bukrin some people were not able to rise up out of the trench and go into the attack. They clung to the ground in the literal sense. They could not raise themselves to meet the bullets and had no moral strength." He acknowledged that "everyone was afraid to die," but "some just stepped over the line and ran away." His response was to scorn and physically separate himself from the "weak willed." Orlov accepted that the instinct for self-preservation was strong and that the option of running away was in the back of everyone's mind. What kept him going? "In the course of combat, although I was a communist, I would sometimes whisper prayers. I relied on myself, loyal comrades, and yes, God."[59]

The two most disruptive factors that undermined the efficacy of primary groups were the use of NKVD or *Smersh* spies in the ranks and casualties. Each division had between fifteen and twenty *Smersh* officers, including one on each regiment and battalion staff, whose duty was to ferret out spies and traitors.[60] The battalion *Smersh* officers recruited informants among the soldiers whom they relied on to report treasonous behavior and speech by their fellow soldiers and officers. By having soldiers spy on one another and their leaders, *Smersh* functionaries undermined the trust necessary for the success of the primary group.

The men were well aware that the NKVD recruited soldiers as informants, and this added to the tension they faced with every mission and every battle. Boris Ol'shanskii, an engineer officer, remembered his brigade's chief *Smersh* officer, Kotov, as a cancer. He considered him a low-life coward who was always looking to do someone in. Kotov tried to recruit him as an informer, but Ol'shanskii declined. He thought Kotov and men like him did a lot of damage to the army by arresting so many innocent men. Contrary to many veterans who claimed that they talked freely at the front, Ol'shanskii believed people were afraid to speak openly of things that might get them arrested, such as the prospect of defeat and the incompetence of the military and political leadership.[61]

Some, such as reconnaissance platoon leader Leonov, took measures to eliminate this internal source of stress. Leonov claims that after he became platoon leader, he worked to keep the *Smersh* officer's informants out of the unit: "By that time I knew almost all of the informers in the unit, because they were recruiting me, and I said 'no' to the deal. I gathered them all and told them: 'Write whatever you want, think up any imaginable illness . . . but I want all of you out of here in 24 hours.' That's how I got rid of them."[62]

Soldiers did their best to determine who was trustworthy, but it was not always possible. A steady stream of denunciations based on soldiers' idle comments and defeatist attitudes occurred throughout the war. Men making these denunciations were sometimes motivated by patriotism, but they could just as easily fabricate the charges out of spite or to settle personal grudges and scores. Ol'shanskii lamented that the political department of his engineer brigade thrived on denunciations of soldiers and officers. He observed that for *politruki* to advance or gain the favor of the brigade commissar, they had to denounce men in their commands. He and his fellow officers generally had nothing but disdain for *Smersh* and the *politruki* and commissars, most of whom had been sent into the military from civilian party jobs.[63]

Maintaining the primary group was sometimes difficult because of excessive casualties. Armies' personnel replacement policies have attracted much scholarly interest, with special attention paid to primary group theory and the effects on morale, motivation, and casualties. The Wehrmacht's policy in the early years of the war—to replace men only in the rear areas, after a unit had been withdrawn from the front—has been held up as the most effective method. Primary groups could form without the stress of combat, and the new men could be assimilated into the unit and trained to its standards. By the time they went into combat, these men had bonded with their units and shared the same level of morale as their veteran comrades. At times, beginning in 1944, heavy casualties in defensive operations required that line units be reinforced while in combat. Whenever possible, those replacements were delivered to divisions as whole companies or battalions and were employed as such.

The U.S. Army's individual replacement policy during World War II was considered the worst. Truckloads of men were taken from replacement detachments and often transported directly to units in combat to replace casualties. There, they were parceled out among the platoons and squads as individuals and thrust as strangers into groups of surviving veterans. New to war, rarely able to attach to primary groups in the turmoil of combat, and ignorant of informal unit customs and procedures, these replacements suffered notoriously high losses.

The Red Army's formal replacement policy (discounting field mobilizations) fell between the German and American extremes. Replacements were delivered to regiments as march companies (so called because they marched to the front to join their regiments). There were two types of march companies—those formed of already trained soldiers being sent back to the front after medical recuperation or after separation from their original units for various reasons, and those formed of new recruits being trained in the rear by reserve regiments. Once they arrived at the receiving regiment, the march companies could be assigned as whole units, broken up into platoons, or parceled out as individuals. If the regiment was in reserve, the new men could meld with the veterans, but if the regiment was in battle, they were sent straight into combat.

As in other armies, circumstances played a huge role in a Red Army replacement soldier's chance of survival. Joining a regiment at rest offered the best chance, while being thrown into combat as a stranger, or with only a handful of friends, and no experience offered the worst. In some battles, regiments went through a dozen or so march companies in just a few weeks. Knowing that march companies were slaves to fortune, wounded soldiers made every effort to return to their original units rather than be assigned to a march company as a replacement.

The link between replacement dynamics and morale is obvious. Whenever men could form primary groups in safety and train with the men they would later fight alongside, morale (and subsequently motivation) was higher. When men were thrust into battle as strangers, morale was correspondingly lower, and they were more prone to straggle, shirk, surrender, or desert. Soviet recruits, however, never knew what their lot would be, so a certain amount of anxiety pervaded their training in the reserve regiments.

The new men who arrived in the march companies did not necessarily bond with a unit's survivors based on ideology; most often, the bond was based on necessity and on a shared commitment to defeat the Nazi invader. Common sense dictates that the replacements knew they needed to learn from the veterans if they hoped to survive the next battle, and the social nature of human beings compels them to seek companionship. It is absurd to think that hundreds of men, thrown together in life-and-death situations, would not form subgroups for security and emotional support. Therefore, although primary groups were destroyed during battle as men died or were wounded and evacuated, once the battle ceased, the process of forming new primary groups commenced immediately as a matter of nature—not by conscious design. The breakout attempts in 1941 and 1942 were examples of the primary group at its best under stress. During these breakouts, units divided into small groups and tried to exfiltrate encirclements. They devolved to the smallest organized fighting units, including squads and sections of fewer than a dozen men, and, in many cases, membership was the result of self-selection by the primary group.

Several things shaped the composition of primary groups, including age, class, ethnicity, and nationality. *Frontoviki* ranged in age from seventeen to fifty years, so generational differences often came into play both positively and negatively. On the positive side, older men were looked up to as examples of seasoned manhood and were respected for their maturity and experience. On the negative side, older men from the peasantry often had a jaundiced view of the state and were less likely to risk their lives for it. For example, a young soldier told Vasily Grossman: "A corporal from the 4th Company called Romanov has let us down on the battlefield. We, the young soldiers who are properly brought up and conscientious, we endure all this with patience, but the moods of older soldiers are worse than ever."[64] Infantry private G. I. Losev told his fellow soldiers: "I am 41 years old, did I live just so I could pound on the Germans? I am not going to shoot." Losev was later caught trying to cross over the lines and desert to the Germans and was arrested.[65] Young, urban Russians might consider themselves proper socialists, but the older generation could compare their lot in life to prerevolutionary days—a comparison in which the Stalinist state often suffered.

The multiethnic composition of the army also had an effect on the formation of primary groups. Shared language was a prerequisite for camaraderie, followed closely by cultural and social compatibility. Iakov Grichener, a Romanian (Bessarabian) conscript in a division of Russians, Romanians, and Central Asians, remembered that the different races did not get along or mix with one another. "We didn't speak to them and they didn't talk to us. No one trusted each other. It was Romanians versus Central Asians versus Russians." The language barrier kept the men divided and forced primary groups to form along both national and racial lines. Grichener's Russian officers made matters worse by treating the nationalities differently—or at least the minorities perceived that they received different treatment. "They gave us Romanians and Central Asians the worst jobs and the most dangerous assignments," he said. "We couldn't complain because we couldn't speak Russian."[66]

Nikolai Blizniuk's artillery battery was an example of how the grouping of small numbers of minorities worked within small units. His battery had twenty to twenty-five Azeris and five to seven Armenians. The rest were Russian. Only one Azeri and one Armenian spoke Russian well, so they served as interpreters for their countrymen, who formed two distinct primary groups.[67]

Ivan Garshtia, a Moldavian conscripted into the Red Army in 1944, claimed that the multiethnic makeup of the army did not create any problems at all, parroting the old Soviet line: "At the front line all of us were like brothers . . . there was nothing to cause division among us."

Table 9.1. *Shift in ethnic and racial composition of the 38th Rifle Division due to replacement of casualties during 1943–1944*

Nationality	1 July 1943	1 January 1944	1 July 1944
Russian	4,114 (52%)	1,959 (40%)	2,796 (30%)
Ukrainian	663 (8%)	2,265 (46%)	5,784 (63%)
Belorussian	88 (0.1%)	145 (3%)	95 (1%)
Armenian	164 (2%)	45	57
Georgian	174 (2%)	35	44
Azeri	338 (4%)	17	26
Uzbek	726 (9%)	62	46
Tadzhik	820 (10%)	47	9
Kazakh	198 (2.5%)	47	59
Kirgiz	84	14	11
Jewish	85	33	54
Marii	37	6	17
Tatar	52	21	15
Bashkir	46	15	20
Ossetian	51	43	9
Others	335	138	137
Total	7,975	4,892	9,179

Source: Iuri Mukhin, *Po povestke i po prizyvu. Nekadrovye soldaty Velikoi Otechestvennoi Voine* (Moscow: Iauza/Eksmo, 2005), 10.

Yet his own words suggest otherwise: "While training in the reserve regiment, we, Moldavians, didn't socialize with numerous recruits of the Baltic Republics origin: both sides didn't know Russian language. At the front we couldn't socialize with reinforcements from the Caucasus region because they knew not a word in Russian. The same situation took place when reinforcements from the Central Asian republics arrived. I didn't rub shoulders with soldiers of Jewish origin."[68] In such situations, language-based primary groups unified subgroups at the expense of the cohesion of the larger military organization. Unlike Grichener, Garshtia claimed to be a loyal Soviet citizen; however, Garshtia remembered his buddies referring to their company as a *shtraf* company because they were assigned the most dangerous tasks.

Table 9.1 shows how casualties in the 38th Rifle Division created turnover numerically as well as ethnically and racially. This affected the personality of the division and the shape of the primary groups. The division went from being a Russian-dominated unit with strong Central Asian representation in 1943 to a mostly Ukrainian division with strong Russian representation and insignificant numbers from minority groups in mid-1944. With minorities represented in such small numbers, there is no doubt they tried to group themselves together, lest they be isolated by language and cultural differences.

In the final analysis, the Red Army and Stalinist state did not simply rely on coercion to get men to fight, but neither did they trust their men to stand fast out of simple intrinsic patriotism. The army hoped its leaders would maintain discipline, but it made no special efforts to train them in the psychology of leadership. Simultaneously, the army rewarded compliance with medals, commendations, and other individual and group honors that appealed to pride, vanity, and a sense of military professionalism. The primary group, which functioned as a social mechanism outside the military's formal methods of control, held the army together at its most basic level. However imperfectly, the primary group served to informally maintain the morale and motivation of masses of individual soldiers, despite the corrosive effects of *Smersh*. In the end, across the front and rear, morale and motivation were in constant states of flux that affected performance on a daily basis. The fact that the Red Army persevered and prevailed against all obstacles—what von Clausewitz labels the frictions of war—or held them in check is a testament, if not a monument, to its overall military effectiveness and the victory of 1945.

10
Failures in Effectiveness

Despite the efforts of the state and the army, hundreds of thousands, if not millions, of soldiers turned out to be ineffective in combat for varying periods of time. This ineffectiveness manifested itself in various acts, such as straggling, shirking, avoiding frontline service, self-inflicting wounds, fleeing the battlefield in panic, deserting to the rear, and going over to the enemy. Other manifestations of ineffectiveness were emotional burnout and psychiatric breakdown. This chapter examines the nature and causes of combat ineffectiveness to show that the army's and the state's actions to improve morale and motivation were responses to a real crisis at the foxhole level.

Initially, the Red Army's official response to men giving in to their fear at the front was not to terrorize them with the threat of execution but to encourage them to be brave and fight heroically. Indeed, it was not the army but the state, through the OO and later *Smersh,* that quickly ratcheted up the penalty for ineffectiveness to death. Officers generally tended (with exceptions) to be more lenient with their men in that respect. There is no doubt that coercion became pervasive as a tool to keep the men fighting; however, as shown in chapter 7, the effectiveness of the death penalty and other punitive measures was highly questionable. I argue here that the draconian punishment imposed by the Red Army was in many ways counterproductive. Because the punishment for failure and transgressions could be unreasonably severe, men sought to cover up problems rather than admitting them and seeking solutions. Sometimes they committed even graver offenses to avoid the consequences of the first.

Desertion

The intent of the death penalty in any army is to coerce compliance in combat and to deter desertion. In the case of the Red Army, the evidence related to desertion leads me to conclude that the death penalty failed as a deterrent, which is contrary to the accepted wisdom of Soviet historiography. Problems with desertion surfaced in the first few weeks of the war and continued throughout. The years of defeat, when the death penalty was used most widely, saw the highest numbers of deserters and men illegally absent from the front. For example, between 22 June and 10 October 1941, 657,364 men were detained for being away from their units without authorization.[1]

It was at the higher levels of the Stalinist regime, far removed from the front, where men, always unsure of popular support, quickly jumped to the conclusion that desertion was both political and moral in nature; that is, deserters were either traitors or cowards, or both. It was these authorities who declared cowardice to be treason. However, it is highly unlikely that much desertion was politically motivated, if only because there were so many other, very human reasons for *frontoviki* to desert. The primary reasons were the desire to survive in an environment of mass slaughter, lack of faith in victory, and lack of confidence in their ability to fight successfully. For example, during the entire war, the Siberian Military District, far from the violence, had only 146 cases of desertion among the 2,641,000 men it mobilized for the front. When one includes the neighboring Urals and Krasnodar *krai,* the number of desertions rises to only 302 out of more than 3 million men.[2] Most desertions occurred in proximity to the front, where danger was a real factor. In the autumn of 1941, one memoirist recorded: "The country was flooded with deserters. In the district of Dobrinka, in the area of Voronezh, alone, there were 30,000 of them. The women hid their returned husbands in the baking ovens or under the floor."[3] There, some desperate deserters resisted arrest or used their rifles to deter the authorities from pursuing them into the woods. A more stark contrast from the calm in Siberia could not be drawn.

The situation on the Leningrad Front is also a case in point. Between 16 and 22 August 1941, 4,300 soldiers were detained for leaving the front without authorization and attempting to make their way into Leningrad.

Of these, 1,412 were determined to be officer and enlisted *opolchentsy*—whom, based on Soviet historiography, one would expect to be the most intrinsically motivated.[4] As the situation deteriorated in the face of renewed German attacks, desertion increased. Between 13 and 17 September 1941, 3,566 soldiers were detained in Leningrad on suspicion of deserting the front. Presaging Order No. 227 by nearly a year, the Leningrad Front military council ordered on 19 September that unit commanders and officers of the Special Sections were to shoot on sight any men fleeing the field of battle. This seems to have been only a minor deterrent because the number of "traitors" remained rather high. In October 1941 the Leningrad Front reported 967 instances of "treason" by desertion, followed by 552 in November.[5] The most likely reason for the decline in desertions was that the German advance had been stopped and Leningrad was now cut off from the rest of the USSR.

The causes of desertion can be inferred from the types of complaints and anti-Soviet agitation recorded on the Leningrad Front, which would be repeated in the battle for Moscow that December and again in the battle for Stalingrad in the latter half of 1942. Soldiers expressed doubts about ultimate Soviet victory, and they overestimated German strength. Many blamed the failing war effort and the war itself on the Communist Party's misguided policies and, echoing Nazi propaganda, Jews—two groups many men were not willing to die for. Some hoped the USSR would sue for peace on whatever terms the Germans might offer. Despite the potentially fatal consequences if caught, some advocated desertion to the Germans among their comrades, thinking they would be well treated and reunited with their families in occupied territory.[6]

With the war going badly into late 1942, morale was visibly low all across the front lines. Given that desertion is closely related to low morale, it is not surprising that the number of men deserting their units was rather high. Among veterans of the Spanish Civil War's Abraham Lincoln Battalion, the major factors affecting morale that drove men to desert were fear, ignorance or uncertainty about how the war was really going, hunger, inadequate protection from the elements, prolonged fatigue, boredom, antagonism toward their own leaders, and obvious enemy superiority in armor and aircraft.[7] All these factors affected the Red Army as the Germans pushed them back with heavy losses and no respite. Stalin and the media lied about the true state of affairs, and most soldiers knew it. Logistics were in shambles, leaving the men inadequately armed, provisioned, and clothed.

A study of British deserters in Europe in 1944–1945 showed that the lack of morale-building factors and the presence of morale-destroying factors were precursors to desertion and absenteeism. The lack of morale-building factors included such things as inadequate training, which undermined self-confidence; a general failure to adapt to military life and discipline; and weak identification with a given group due to transfer from one unit to another or the adverse effect of waiting in replacement depots. Morale-destroying factors included the inevitable externalities, such as stress from combat, as well as internally produced emotional stress caused by changes in or separation from the familiar group, death of a comrade or beloved leader, personal guilt, or wounds. Personal worries also ate away at morale.[8]

A temptation among Soviet soldiers that neither British nor American soldiers in Europe experienced was the idea that desertion could take them home. In the disastrous days of the summer of 1941, Ukrainian soldiers were highly likely to succumb to the lure of home; their motivation to fight in defense of their homes, now under German occupation, was gone. Many deserters crossed the enemy lines to go home. A report from 33rd Army in November 1941 showed that the majority of the fifty-nine men who had recently deserted across the lines were from territories occupied by the Germans.[9] This phenomenon was not limited to Ukrainians and Belorussians, however; it also began to affect Russians once the German army advanced into the RSFSR. The high command recognized yearning for home as an armywide problem in December 1941.

The pull of home manifested itself frequently when men went on patrol behind enemy lines and did not come back. A GlavPUR report gave the following examples, all of which occurred in December 1941 in units defending Moscow: Junior Lieutenant Dvorianchinov, 920th Rifle Regiment, took sixteen men on a mission behind enemy lines on the Kalinin Front (north flank of Moscow), and not one came back with him. All had family in occupied territory. For "allowing" their defection, Dvorianchinov was court-martialed and given ten years in prison. Two NCOs and three soldiers of the 529th Rifle Regiment of the Northwest Front went over to the enemy on a reconnaissance mission. Five men of the 774th Rifle Regiment went over to the enemy, and the remaining member of the patrol, who did not defect, chose not to shoot at the deserters; all were condemned as traitors in the report. Finally, junior *politruk* Beliaev shot and wounded his platoon leader while on patrol and went over to the Germans. Investigation revealed that all the men who failed to return from these patrols had family behind German lines.[10] Obviously, the threat of punishing the families of traitors was no deterrent in these cases. GlavPUR instructed commissars and *politruki* to henceforth check the political reliability of men selected for reconnaissance duties.

Efim Gol'braikh, deputy commander of a penal battalion, reported problems with *shtrafniki* going over to the Germans. Gol'braikh and his fellow officers considered victims of dekulakization and men with families who had been repressed in the 1930s to be the most likely to cross the lines to the Germans. Gol'braikh himself was the son of an enemy of the people (his father had been arrested and shot in 1937), but he was not so inclined. His battalion experienced one incident in which an entire patrol of *shtrafniki* went behind enemy lines and never came back. They never knew for sure whether they had been killed, captured, or defected, but because several of the leaders of the patrol were experienced scouts, they suspected the last.[11]

One of the major obstacles to the Red Army's rational handling of desertion was the state's conception of cowardice. According to the British Army Act, as related by Lord Moran in his book on the psychological effects of war, "a man is guilty of cowardice when he displays 'an unsoldierlike regard for his personal safety in the presence of the enemy' by shamefully deserting his post or laying down his arms."[12] In the British and American armies, it was generally accepted that cowardice was a character flaw and had no external or situational causes; cowards were cowards all the time. Based on this reasoning, the U.S. Army used preinduction psychological testing to weed out men of insufficient character and thus avoid such problems as desertion and fleeing under fire. The Stalinist state did no such testing and made no allowance for weak character; instead, it assumed that external factors, especially sociopolitical ones, motivated cowardly behavior. This resulted in untold numbers of men who were psychologically unfit for combat being sent to the front, where they endangered their units, undermined morale, and "confirmed" Stalin's fear that the army was full of traitors.

Not everyone in the Red Army leadership accepted the state's version of cowardice, and many officers sought to mitigate punishment for supposedly cowardly actions. As Lord Moran points out, there are many external factors that can break otherwise combat-worthy men. These include overexposure to combat, malnutrition, health and weather issues, loss of comrades, and other problems that, in combination, would lead men to succumb to the natural fear of violent death. The British had discovered, through their experiences in the First World War, that if men were treated with rest and time away from the front as soon as symptoms of psychological stress appeared, they could be fully rejuvenated.[13] Institutionally, the Red Army never came to this conclusion, and one can only speculate that the mental stress of combat, exacerbated by the loss of one's friends, likely contributed to desertion and other methods of avoiding further service at the front. Men in an irrational state would be less able to comprehend the reasons why they should stay in the line and less likely to appreciate the consequences of getting caught. It is not hard to imagine that many dazed and shell-shocked soldiers ended up in front of firing squads, labeled traitors and cowards.[14] When possible, individual officers, on their own initiative, often tried to cycle long-serving soldiers out of the front line to preserve their mental health.

Although some officials in Moscow assumed the worst of their soldiers, Panteleimon Ponomarenko, First Secretary of the Belorussian Communist Party and the political member of the military council of 3rd Shock Army, dismissed the idea of mass cowardice and treason. In August 1941 he went to the front to personally conduct what turned out to be a remarkably clear-headed study of the causes of desertion and combat ineffectiveness. In the end, he did not ascribe the desertions to anything political. Instead, he correctly concluded that the normal conditions of modern industrial war and soldiers' inadequate preparation for the shock of combat were to blame for their succumbing to fear. In his report to Stalin he explained that no political education work was being done among the soldiers, and this led to unreliability, especially among recently called up reservists and conscripts reporting as replacements. They had heard wild rumors of impending doom and German invincibility. He noted, "Many days on the road are spent under the power of fantastic inventions about matters at the front. When the first bombs fall the echelons disperse." Men would run and hide in the woods and not rejoin their units as they prepared to move to the front. Ponomarenko noted, "The woods in the immediate rear of the front are full of such refugees. Many abandon their weapons and go home."[15]

To make matters worse, units that rotated back from the front had acquired inferiority complexes, which they spread to the new, untested men. But, as Ponomarenko assured Stalin, "this matter is easy to correct." He assigned ten groups of ten combat-tested political workers to a series of march companies destined for the front. The political workers worked with the soldiers for five days, not politicizing them but telling them about the reality of combat and how to cope with being under fire. When these men got to the front, they performed better than units that had not had such instruction. Ponomarenko observed that military districts, which made the mistake of not preparing the men for the front, yielded large contingents of deserters. His conclusion was, "These people should be accompanied by men who already have combat experience." As sensible as Ponomarenko proved to be, he still believed that some coercion might be necessary and recommended to Stalin, "It is better to shoot one as an example, than to threaten them all."[16]

Ponomarenko's remedy corresponded to the conclusions of the Abraham Lincoln Battalion soldiers, who believed that when combat veterans explained the reality of the dangers of battle to untested troops, it made them less afraid and better able to handle their first battle. Men who have an idea of what to expect are less likely to invent mental images of disaster. Also, if soldiers expect to be afraid and prepare for it, they are less prone to flee.[17]

Unfortunately, Ponomarenko's counsel was not institutionalized. A year later, in October 1942, the 299th Rifle Division, which had never seen combat, was sent on a 200-kilometer march to the Stalingrad Front. The inexperienced staff failed to coordinate provisioning in advance, so the division often went hungry. On the basis of hunger alone, the men were demoralized before ever reaching the front. When the division finally launched its attack, the staff, owing to its lack of experience and poor training, did not coordinate with the accompanying artillery or tank brigades. At the outset, the Germans bombed the attacking regiments from the air, and the attack failed.[18] This outcome validated the men's fears and doubts and deepened their feelings of inferiority.

Avoiding Combat by Other Means

Besides desertion, men avoided combat by straggling, holing up during combat, or leaving frontline units to find safe jobs in the rear. Also, during the first year of the war, hundreds of thousands of Red Army men decided to sit out the war behind enemy lines. In the great battles of encirclement of 1941 and 1942, captured soldiers chose to either attempt to escape or not. Those who escaped or eluded capture then had to choose whether to evade the Germans in an attempt to rejoin the Red Army, join partisan detachments, or hide out in towns and villages. How many opted out of the war will never be known for sure, but, according to one set of official figures, the NKVD processed 582,515 former servicemen and officers in newly liberated areas in 1943.[19] Between 1 January and 1 October 1944, another 304,151 soldiers and 50,441 officers were processed by the NKVD. Another source claims that during the course of the war, 939,700 men were drafted for a second time after the advancing Red Army liberated their hiding places or freed them from German captivity.[20]

Upon investigation, if any of these men were determined to be deserters rather than survivors of encircled or destroyed units, they were usually assigned to penal battalions; some were sent to the Gulag, and a few were summarily executed for treason. In 1944, for example, of the 354,592 men processed in filtration camps, 231,034 soldiers and 27,042 officers were reenlisted in the active army. Another 16,163 officers and 2,219 soldiers were sentenced to time in *shtraf* battalions and companies when they could not provide good explanations for being in the enemy rear. *Smersh* arrested another 11,556 officers and men and charged them with being enemy agents.[21] G. M. Dubinin recalled that when he was assigned to a *shtrafbat* in May 1944, an overwhelming number of battalion members were officers who had been "reconscripted" in the liberation of Ukraine.[22]

Privates Gabriel Temkin and Aleksandr Goncharov are two examples of men who took a break from the war. Temkin, a Polish Jew who had sought refuge in the USSR before the war and had been drafted into a labor battalion, experienced the destruction of his unit in the battles of encirclement in the spring of 1942 and witnessed the choices presented to the soldiers. He recalled: "Abandoned by all our officers, our labor battalion quickly disintegrated. People were going in all directions, those from territories already occupied by the Germans heading mostly home."[23] Temkin, being Jewish, decided to head east to Soviet lines, but he was captured. After he escaped from German captivity, peasants took him in and incorporated him into their collective farm.

When his unit disintegrated in 1941, Goncharov, wounded in the foot, chose not to surrender and sought out his grandparents. They took him into their home in a small village in Ukraine. After his foot healed, he decided to stay in the village. Both men could have sought out partisan units or continued east to rejoin the army, but instead they chose to live quietly as peasant farmers. Only when the Red Army liberated their areas in 1943 did both soldiers get back into the war.[24]

Men taken back into the army from liberated areas sometimes turned out to be less than motivated to resume soldiering. Boris Mikhailov, a mortarman in an infantry regiment, recalled that the replacements in his unit in 1944 were almost exclusively former Red Army men from recently liberated areas. The soldiers referred to these men as *okruzhentsy*—"the surrounded." In their first major engagement, the majority of these replacements broke and ran for the rear at the first sign of a German counterattack. Another veteran recalled that he and hundreds of other *okruzhentsy* in his reserve regiment had very poor morale due to bad officers, low-quality food, and inadequate training. On the eve of deploying in march units, numerous men intentionally drank contaminated water, hoping to get dysentery and avoid being shipped to the front.[25]

In Georgii Minin's experience, such replacements were no worse than the regular soldiers were. He recalled, however, that they were not well received when they were first assigned in late 1943. The men's attitude was, "You were sitting here, eating *galushki* (Ukrainian dumplings) while we were fighting against the Germans." After they proved themselves in combat, attitudes softened.[26] Why hundreds of thousands of men opted out of the war is unknown. It could have been any number of reasons, from personal to political.

During an attempt at desertion, Private Vladimir Dolmatov made the acquaintance of another soldier he at first labeled a deserter. The man corrected him, saying he was a straggler who somehow managed to "get left behind" whenever his unit deployed to the front.[27] Straggling was a generally safe way to avoid the dangers of combat because the regulations prescribed no punishment for it. It was not fleeing from battle, because the soldier never got to the battle. It was not desertion, because the soldier was always "on his way to the unit"; either "accidentally" or for reasons out of his control, he had fallen or been left behind. Individuals who did this were usually not part of a primary group. They were willing to accept the disdain of their peers and the curses of their officers with a shrug of their shoulders, a weak smile, and endless excuses.

It did not take the army long to figure out that intentional straggling (which was hard to prove) was becoming a serious problem, and it identified the movement of units by train as a major venue for this phenomenon. In April 1942 GlavPUR instructed political officers assigned to train stations to be on the lookout for men "left behind" when troop trains passed through, citing the 41st Reserve Rifle Brigade as an example. In April the brigade passed through one station in several echelons. One troop train lost forty-three men who "got left behind," and another train lost twenty-nine. In addition to these stragglers, police detained thirty-nine brigade members at the station for criminal behavior. The brigade commander and commissar were unaware that they had lost any men until personnel at the station telegraphed them.[28]

One of the more egregious examples of mass straggling happened in the 35th Guards Rifle Division in August 1942. With an estimated strength of less than 10,000 men, 1,815 men (close to 20 percent) became stragglers during five days of battle. They avoided being rounded up and returning to their regiments until after the battle was over.[29] For some reason, morale had hit rock bottom in this division. In the battle for the city of Poznan in February 1945, a political report noted that one battalion could muster only 15 or 16 men for the firing line out of 157. The rest were unaccounted for and were thought to be drinking in the homes of the local Polish inhabitants. In contrast, the corps headquarters to which this battalion belonged had 85 infantrymen for defense and fatigue duties. Without a doubt, soldiers eagerly sought these kinds of assignments away from the front lines. One of the report's conclusions was that urban warfare provided soldiers with many opportunities to shirk fighting by hiding out in apartments, fraternizing with the local population, and getting drunk.[30]

The emotional environments of these two episodes were exactly opposite. In August 1942 the Germans were at the height of their summer offensive, driving to the Volga and the Caucasus. Despite the successful defense of Moscow the previous winter, morale had plummeted, and Order No. 227 had just been issued. A feeling of hopelessness pervaded the units reeling from the German onslaught. The cause seemed lost, and there was no point dying for it. In February 1945 soldiers were finally convinced that the war was won, and hope abounded. With the war about to end in victory, nobody wanted to die and miss out on a long and peaceful life.

A dangerous and illegal method of getting away from the front was inflicting a wound on oneself. The practice was dangerous not just because such a wound might prove fatal; if a soldier was suspected of intentionally injuring himself, a guilty sentence would likely result in the death penalty. Attitudes toward men who injured themselves to avoid combat were mixed. Some soldiers were repulsed by the presumed cowardice that motivated the act and considered death an appropriate consequence. Others felt indifference or even sympathy. One soldier recalled that a man in his battalion was executed for shooting himself in the hand to avoid combat. The reaction of most of the men was that the soldier was just plain stupid. He was ten kilometers behind the front when he "accidentally" shot himself while cleaning his rifle. The consensus was that he should have waited until they got to the front.[31]

One soldier who gave himself a self-inflicted wound and got away with it remembered being inspired to do so by his platoon leader. The officer, in a private moment, confessed his fear of death to the soldier and said he was going to shoot himself in the hand. The soldier, empathetic and like-minded, suggested hand grenades instead. Together, they held a hand grenade in their outstretched hands and let it go off, resulting in the loss of several fingers. They were evacuated to a field hospital and later discharged as invalids.[32] Others also thought through their self-wounding; one soldier recalled, "If you put a piece of dark bread and a wet rag against the skin on the place of the wound—I did it myself, I know—then you can't tell that the wound is self inflicted, that the shot was fired from close distance."[33]

An army doctor, a division medical chief, professed that he and most of his doctors looked the other way in cases of even obvious self-inflicted wounds, if they thought they could get away with it. They felt sympathy for the frontline soldiers. However, they had to watch out for political officers and a few patriotic zealots on the staff who would denounce them and the injured soldier. He claimed that self-inflicted wounds were especially prevalent among the intelligentsia who wanted to get out of frontline service.[34]

Training

Good training helped minimize desertion and other behaviors that took men out of the firing line. Soldiers who are confident in their ability to succeed at a task are usually more willing to accept the risks involved than are raw recruits with little or no training. Training helps overcome fear, and fighting alongside the men one has trained with imparts cohesion.[35] Soldiers are also less fearful if they have confidence in their weapons and equipment. How well, then, did the Red Army train its soldiers, and how well did the soldiers who trained together fight together? Obviously, as in other major armies, the quality of performance varied wildly from unit to unit, case to case, and year to year. In 1941 many units in western USSR proved to be vastly underprepared in terms of training, despite their experience in the Winter War and the invasion of Poland. One reason was the vast expansion of the army in 1940 and 1941, which caused tremendous personnel turnover as divisions and regiments broke up and re-formed two or three times to absorb new men and form new units. The armed forces doubled in size from 1.7 million men in 1938 to 3.4 million in mid-1940. Another million would be added by June 1941.

The relocation of scores of divisions into the Baltic States, western Ukraine, and Bessarabia and northern Bukovina threw all their normal routines, including training, into chaos for the better part of a year.[36] In the interval between the movement west and the outbreak of war with Germany, cohesion waned, and training slowed or halted altogether. Units were often formed weeks or months before they were issued arms and equipment, so precious training time was wasted waiting for rifles, artillery pieces, and even boots to be delivered. Veterans who had been in the army before the German invasion generally agreed that the army was unprepared. For instance, Semen Matveev recollected: "The main problem with our army before the war was that, in my opinion, combat training really only got going when things heated up. When France quickly capitulated."[37] The training his tank battalion received was amateurish and unrealistic, and he sarcastically noted that the only combined arms instruction they received was at the hands of the Germans.

Once the war started, training became even more haphazard, and competent instructors, weapons, and equipment were hard to come by. The many *opolchenie* units were cases in point. Generally manned by motivated men and women with above-average education and thus easily instructed, they waited months for weapons, and morale suffered for it.[38] When equipment and arms did arrive, the quantities were often shockingly insufficient. Where thousands of rifles were needed, a division might have only a hundred or so. Where a unit required hundreds of machine guns, the army supplied only a handful. Uniforms and footwear were also in short supply and sometimes were not delivered before a unit headed for the front.[39] Regular units also suffered weapons and equipment shortages, though usually not as severe as the *opolchenie* divisions.

Despite their inherent advantages in unit cohesion and motivation to defend their homes, the combat record of the *opolchenie* divisions was as mixed as that of regular army units. Some performed well enough to eventually become Guards divisions, while others were annihilated in their first fight. It is virtually impossible to unearth the reasons for success or failure because the variables of leadership, training, supply, and battlefield circumstances all played roles. Two Moscow *opolchenie* divisions, the 21st and 17th, provide contrasting examples of success and failure in the battle for that city. The 21st DNO performed well. In its first fight, its forward regiments suffered nearly 600 casualties and a heavy loss of equipment. The division was forced to withdraw to a new defensive line, which it accomplished in good order without panic, malingering, or straggling.[40] The 17th DNO, however, crumbled under the weight of German firepower. The division broke and ran to the rear, allowing the Nazis to cross a major river unopposed. By the time the division's flight was stopped, it was down to 558 survivors, having suffered 94 percent casualties. Marshal Zhukov ordered that the division commander, Colonel Kozlov, be executed for leaving his post—he had been drunk and safely ensconced in the rear area during the battle. The division commissar shared Kozlov's fate.[41]

Opolchenie divisions were not the only ones to suffer massive casualties owing to inadequate training and equipment and poor cohesion. Regular army units that were formed early in the war under emergency conditions and quickly thrust into combat faced the same fate. For example, formation of the 289th Rifle Division in Kiev was completed on 30 July 1941. On 6 August, on the eve of going into combat, the division commander pleaded with his superior to grant him at least five more days to prepare. To convince his superiors that he needed more time, he listed all the personnel and equipment shortages and training problems of his division: It had 13,460 men aged nineteen to forty-five, but half the soldiers were only partially trained or completely untrained. Only half the NCOs had any training, and the majority of the officers had recently been recalled from the reserves. They did not have enough uniforms: 7,000 men had new uniforms, 2,700 had no uniforms and still wore civilian clothes, and the rest had worn-out or partial uniforms; 2,000 needed new boots. In terms of weaponry, the division was short on just about everything except rifles. There were no 120mm or 82mm mortars and only twenty-nine 50mm mortars. It was short 240 light machine guns, and the machine gunners had never fired a shot. It did not have enough artillery or ancillary equipment for artillery fire, and artillery forward observers lacked binoculars. The division did not have enough horses or vehicles to move the men and the equipment it did have. The division bakery was inoperable.[42] Given the state of Red Army logistics, it is unlikely that these shortages were made up in five days. The division had little chance to succeed under these conditions, and with failure in their first battle, the men would carry a sense of inferiority that might take years to overcome.

The training of conscripts during the war was hit or miss. Some reserve brigades and regiments conscientiously devoted the necessary time and equipment to train newcomers, but other units did not. At the highest levels, recruiting was the first consideration; planning for training usually came as an afterthought. For example, as the regime faced a manpower shortage in 1943, it launched a special recruitment effort directed at Komsomol youth and set a target of 166,000 men to be distributed among ten different military districts and fronts. These recruits would be trained not by army reserve regiments but by the Directorate of Universal Military Training (*Vsevobuch*), which had been in charge of preconscription training before the war.

The handicaps *Vsevobuch* faced in preparing the recruits for war is illustrated by the weaponry set aside for their instruction. *Vsevobuch* in the Moscow Military District, for example, was to train 6,000 snipers but had only 106 sniper rifles; it was to train 6,000 antitank riflemen but had only 121 antitank rifles and 6,000 rounds of ammunition. It was asked to train 12,000 submachine gunners, and although it had 120,000 rounds of ammunition, it had no submachine guns. In the army's ten military districts, eight *Vsevobuch* detachments had no submachine guns at all for training 30,000 men; one district had nine weapons, and another had eight. Six military districts had no sniper rifles, four had no heavy machine guns, and four had no antitank rifles. The order for this training went out on 30 January, and training was to begin on 15 February.[43] The trainees would then be sent straight to the front as replacements.

Given the example of the Khar'kov and Orel military districts, there is no guarantee that these men would have been better trained if they had been sent to the army's training units. When they were inspected in January 1944, numerous deficiencies were uncovered in the 11th and 16th Reserve Brigades that affected the morale, motivation, health, and training of soldiers headed to the front. The inspectors found that the men were poorly fed, living in unhealthy conditions, and lacking in discipline due to poor supervision. Desertion and ill health among the trainees were common. The NKO deemed the situation so serious that it relieved of command Colonel General Chervichenko of the Khar'kov Military District. It also reprimanded Lieutenant General Popov, commander of the Orel Military District, and the political members of the military councils of both military districts. The commander of the 16th Reserve Brigade was arrested, relieved of command, and ordered to be courtmartialed. The heads of the supply administration of both military districts were relieved of their duties.[44]

At the beginning of the war, the loss of military bases in the western part of the USSR and the relocation of training facilities to the east required soldiers to become laborers, which consumed valuable training time. Units had to build their own housing, training facilities, firing ranges, and everything else needed on a military base. This all had to happen before training began. In contrast, divisions in the Russian interior or the Far East were more cohesive and better trained before heading into battle because they had, for the most part, escaped the turmoil prevalent in the west. They were also better armed because they had been equipped since the mid-1930s to repel an expected Japanese invasion. They had not been subjected to the variety of distractions from training experienced by their brothers in arms in the newly occupied western Ukraine in 1939 through 1941. Their training bases were well established and equipped, and personnel turnover was substantially lower.

Soldiers drafted in 1941 were the least prepared of all and were most likely to suffer a lack of confidence in themselves and their leaders. The British army deserters mentioned earlier often cited inadequate training as a factor in their decision to desert. Likewise, many Soviet soldiers felt incompetent and therefore lacked confidence in their ability to fight or defend themselves.[45] In any event, millions of men were thrust into the fight inadequately trained.

Uncertain Victory and Lack of Commitment to a Higher Cause

For the first two years of war, into the summer of 1943, many Soviet soldiers held the opinion that German soldiers were better trained to fight and that their technology outclassed that of the Soviets. They thought German tanks and German aircraft were superior, and they admired the Germans' ability to supply these vehicles in quantity. Any comparison with the Germans usually found the Soviets' equipment wanting, causing soldiers to lose confidence and their morale to fall. They also envied the German soldiers' food.[46] This sense of inferiority led to a lack of faith in victory, which posed a serious challenge to combat and sustaining motivation until, at the earliest, the victory at Kursk in midsummer 1943.

The first six months of the war were the worst with regard to hope for victory. The next year was not that much better, even after the victories at Moscow and Stalingrad. In 1941 Vasily Grossman recorded in his notes: "24 October. Squad Commander Marchenko isn't certain of the Red Army winning. He says, 'Hitler is going to push us back to Siberia.'"[47] In September a Komsomolets soldier in an NKVD rifle brigade at the front was reported as saying: "In our newspapers they write that at the front the Red Army destroys German regiments, but they don't write anything about how the Germans destroy whole Red Army corps. Why do the

Germans keep going forward and look like they will go farther?"[48] Another bemoaned that if things kept up like they were, the Germans would win, and all Russia would have left would be Siberia.[49] His thoughts were echoed two months later by Private Kholodov, who read a German propaganda leaflet to his fellow soldiers and added: "The enemy will defeat us and be victorious, but not before driving us into the taiga." Kholodov had been a member of the Communist Party, but he tore up his party card when his unit first went into combat.[50] Like many other party members in those months, he wanted to avoid being executed under the Germans' "Commissar Order," which mandated the murder of captured commissars and party members.

The rampant defeatism spreading throughout the army was reflected in the query of Private Marchev on 5 November 1941: "Why did I bother escaping from encirclement? We are still very weak, clearly the Germans will break through us. Soon they will push on to Moscow and the war will end." Likewise, Senior Lieutenant Karadkov, commander of a machine gun squadron, told his men, "We can't beat the Germans."[51] In the autumn of 1941, Private Tkachev was not sure how things were going to work out, but he was rather pessimistic. He had thought about surrendering in October but decided to wait another month to see how things went. He did not act quickly enough and was arrested before he could steal away.[52]

An important source of motivation failure was many soldiers' alienation from the regime and its goals. The massive propaganda efforts of the Stalinist regime sometimes failed to overcome the estrangement felt by many soldiers. For example, the call to fight for the *rodina*, which was central to so much of Soviet wartime propaganda, turned out to be a two-edged sword when soldiers interpreted the *rodina* to be local. Despite the regime's intense efforts to get the men to see the war as being fought for the whole union, many non-Russian soldiers remained unconvinced and unmoved. Getting the soldiers to commit to causes higher and more abstract than their families, villages, or towns was not easy. For this reason, Stalin's speeches were important vehicles to broaden the men's perspective. Fighting to defend one's home area was an almost natural impulse, but what if a soldier's village had been captured by the Germans? If it looked as if the USSR would win the war, the call for liberation would have an effect; however, if victory was in doubt, the desire to go home became stronger.

As we have seen, the desire to return home hit Ukrainian and Belorussian soldiers hardest in 1941 and 1942, when it seemed like the Soviet Union might actually lose the war. In November 1941 the NKVD detachment of 33rd Army noted the poor attitude of soldiers defending the approaches to Moscow who were not native to Moscow province. For example, Private Suvorov from Mogilev province, Belorussia, abandoned his post and went into a dugout, saying, "Why should I be sorry that I don't want to be killed by a German bullet."[53] Private V. P. Pavlov from Smolensk province, which was occupied by the enemy at the time, said, "I fled from my home region when it was surrounded by the Germans, which I thought was for the best. In reality our own have treated us worse than the Germans. Life with the Germans is much better, easier, than under our Soviet power. When I get some *valenki* I'm going home to my *rodina* where I live. There will be meat, potatoes, and other food."[54]

With Soviet defeat a real possibility, soldiers took stock of where their faith and loyalty lay, and it was not always with Stalin, the state, or Soviet socialism. Private Poichenko told two of his fellow soldiers: "Now there is no need to fight. Our areas have been taken by the Germans. The fight now is only for Stalin. We don't have reserves or weapons. The Germans are stronger, there's only one thing left for us—go into captivity."[55]

In December 1941, when his home province was lost to the enemy, Private Korotkov lost all motivation to fight. He told his platoon leader: "It's good for you to talk about fighting when you are not from occupied territory. The Germans occupy my oblast, to whom will I return after the war? That won't be such a victory for me." Referring to rumors about the promise of rewards for service after the war, he said to his squad mates: "It is well for the officers . . . they will receive one thousand rubles, not a bad sum. . . . I would pay 500 rubles a month to get out of being made to fight."[56]

Officers also had their doubts. On 31 October 1941, as the Germans bore down on Moscow, one replied to a colleague: "No, the peasants fight for Russia, they want the kolkhozes broken up. You know Bukharin was right about the peasants' attitude about this, they needed to keep private property. Russia has stayed the same, but people are all corrupted by policies of the party."[57] Filipov, an artillery officer, said: "Now the question of the war has been decisively resolved. Socialism has lost, victory has gone to fascism, the Germans have good technology (*teknik*) and well-disciplined personnel. We have said much about vigilance, jabbered about discipline, but our people do not want to fight and spill their blood for workers of the NKVD."[58]

Some officers who shared their men's doubts and fears merely made things worse by admitting this, rather than trying to remedy the situation. In October 1941 a platoon commander, Lieutenant Kriukov, told his men: "I read a German leaflet on which it was written that the NKVD oppresses workers and peasants. This activity does happen. I don't know what I'm fighting for, what we lay down our heads for. The armed forces of the Soviet Union send people to fight without weapons."[59]

Lack of information and distrust of official information undermined morale and motivation and weakened attachment to the regime. The civilian and military presses tried to hide the extent of the early disasters from the people and distorted the reality of conditions at the front. This turned out to be a mistake, at least in the case of the soldiers, who could see the truth for themselves; inaccurate and dishonest information only heightened their uncertainty and fear. Knowing that they were being lied to fed the latent mistrust of the Soviet regime that many soldiers had been feeling for some time. Stalin also distorted the truth in his speeches in an attempt to bolster morale, but this too backfired. Private Tsarev remarked in September 1941 that, according to the Soviet press, German casualties were 2 million, and the Red Army's were only 800,000. He wanted the papers to be truthful about the real cost of the war, and he thought that soon the Red Army's casualties would be 8 million.[60]

Just as in the Winter War, heavy casualties contributed to low morale. Military censors reported that letters written by soldiers fighting in the battle for Moscow revealed a certain level of demoralization because of the high loss of life. Private Malov wrote home: "On 24 January we had a big fight with the Germans, we came to within fifteen meters of each other, and I don't understand how I stayed alive. Twenty-five men of our company died in this fight, and there are only ten men left." A. F. Sorikin wrote: "The company started with 160 men but there remain only nine who were not killed or wounded." A. I. Bogomazov, an antitank gunner, wrote: "In our battery there were 57 men, but now there are only ten, the rest have been killed or wounded. Our battery doesn't have a single gun left, they were all captured by the Germans, and now we have to serve as infantrymen."[61]

Morale was particularly bad among the infantry, which felt it was not adequately supported by the other combat arms, especially the Red Air Force. On the subject of Soviet airpower, which was a sore point among soldiers for years, a soldier named Ivanov said, "Everything that is written in the newspapers about the combat feats of aviation is a big lie. Our pilots need to make a raid on Germany. Instead we're flying around the Ukraine, which is lost, and the press is saying that 'victory will be ours.'"[62] Likewise, Private Loginov told soldiers in his unit: "The newspaper writes that our airplanes destroy German infantry by the thousands, but who has seen our airplanes yet this whole war? In all the units I've been in at the front so far in this war I've seen only one airplane, and he did a bunk, really, you can believe me."[63]

Private Tret'iakov's outlook after nearly three months of war reveals his and other soldiers' feelings about the army and the regime. He summed up his attitude about the party by saying, "It is very well for the communists to go to the front, that way they can all be killed." On the course of the war, the truthfulness of the media, and the causes of defeat, he said:

> Soviet newspapers write that the Red Army is strong, but here the city of Kremenchug is weak and all have given up and surrendered the city, and from here we need to conclude that the Red Army is weak, and only because it . . . is composed exclusively of kolkhozniks, and in the kolkhozes life is very bad. For the last three years the kolkhozniks have received nothing for their labor, clearly, what do they have to fight for? For this reason Red Army men do not go into battle, as a result it happens that city after city is handed over to the Germans.[64]

Every Red Army unit had officers and enlisted men with similar opinions, and they sometimes shared them openly; therefore, every soldier had to decide for himself whether the regime was worth fighting for, whether victory could be had, and what alternatives might be available.

The one thing that finally turned the tide of morale to the positive once and for all was the realistic prospect of victory in the near future. Pinpointing the exact time is difficult, and it is largely anecdotal. Some soldiers claim that the victory at Moscow in 1941 was the turning point for them; others say it was Stalingrad in 1943. The scale of deserters, stragglers, and AWOLs, however, suggests a much later date. Oral testimony, however unscientific, indicates that the final and overwhelming psychoemotional change did not come until December 1944 or January 1945. At that time, all but the Baltic States had been liberated from the Nazis, and the Red Army was conquering foreign territory. Although desertions never ceased, they dropped dramatically at this time, if only because it was much harder to get home from Germany, Poland, Hungary, or the Balkans, and the language barrier and the hostility of local inhabitants served as deterrents. Furthermore, the end of the war seemed imminent, and the prospect of returning home soon was realistic.

The case of Vladimir Dolmatov is perhaps the most useful for illustrating the fluctuations of motivation and morale and the problematic nature of man's relation to the state during wartime. He began his wartime service as a teenaged volunteer in an *opolchenie* unit; then, though still underage, he manipulated the system to enlist as a regular Red Army soldier. Still later he risked prosecution to illegally transfer himself to a safer assignment; he subsequently deserted, risking death. At no point in his story does Dolmatov mention his relation to the state. Did he start out as a patriotic or pro-Stalin citizen who became a traitor in the end? Neither extreme is likely. All his actions seem to be personally motivated. The war was exciting at first, and he went off and volunteered with his friends. Later, in a unit with strangers, he experienced the true horrors of modern war; later still, the urge for self-preservation and homesickness won out. Soon after he deserted he turned himself in to the authorities because his parents had threatened to do so, fearing punishment if he were caught. Dolmatov exemplifies the idea that for some citizen-soldiers, feelings about the state were not their primary concern; such feelings were less likely to affect their behavior than were concerns related to survival. Yet many of the examples cited earlier show that some soldiers, when it came time to live or risk death, definitely considered their feelings about Soviet socialism.

The Motivation and Morale of Ethnic and National Minorities

If the motivation of Russians and other Slavs could falter, then it should come as no surprise that national and ethnic minorities who wound up in uniform had even less commitment to the war and greater difficulty maintaining their motivation. In September 1942 GlavPUR reported desertions, betrayal, and disobedience throughout the army, but especially among troops from the Caucasus and Central Asia. In the classic self-delusional style of the Soviet bureaucracy, the army hierarchy ascribed those problems to the fact that political education work with non-Russian soldiers was hampered by language difficulties. GlavPUR and the NKO were completely blind to the possibility that the non-Russian minorities might be disaffected by their historical maltreatment at the hands of the Russians.[65]

During the battles of encirclement of 1941, Bessarabian Petr Margulis was mobilized into a construction battalion and witnessed unit disintegration along national lines. His construction battalion was composed primarily of Moldavians and Ukrainians—presumably from western Ukraine. They had been retreating for several days when their commander announced that they were surrounded. Shortly thereafter, the Ukrainians and all the Moldavians except for Margulis abandoned the battalion and went home. There were only forty men left, including the officers, NCOs, and *politruki*. Because he was Jewish, Margulis wisely thought it best to stay with the remnants of the battalion. They evaded capture for a month before finally rejoining the Red Army.[66] A Belorussian soldier whose unit disintegrated in encirclement in 1941 said: "I went to the forest but as hunger set in I left the forest and went home. I remained at home and when the Russians came [in 1943] they drafted me."[67] During his interview, whenever he spoke of issues related to communism or Soviet power he referred to it as "Russian," as something distinctly alien to his world.

Georgii Minin uncritically accepted the Russocentric Soviet propaganda, and fifty years after the fact, he still did not recognize the condescending attitude he and his Russian friends had toward minorities. Of Central Asians in his battalion he said, "We treated them indulgently as if they were our younger brothers and never despised them."[68] In contrast, an Armenian Red Army officer observed, "The Red Army is the best place to notice the contempt and suspicion of the Russians to the Caucasians and other minorities."[69]

Given Central Asians' reluctance to volunteer, it is no surprise that the service of such conscripts was often lackluster. Specific nationality-based statistics on desertion are not available, but Russians in the Red Army believed that many minorities deserted, straggled, and shirked their duties. There was no reason to expect them to be more motivated than the Russians. A dramatic case of a national minority putting his interests before that of the nation involved Allonov Dzhumaev, one of Turkmenistan's deputies to the Supreme Soviet. The NKVD arrested him for deserting the Red Army in April 1943. To the chagrin of the Turkmenistan Communist Party, the facts of Dzhumaev's case ended up on Stalin's desk.[70]

That the average Central Asian conscript was unenthusiastic—to say the least—about serving the Soviet state was an unspoken truth among Russian officers. One Harvard University interviewee reported witnessing "an occasion upon which a general, a very good one too, was informed that he was to be in command of Turkmen and Uzbek troops, and he grabbed his head between his hands, shaking it back and forth and cried out, 'I'm finished. There is no more for me.'"[71] Another Russian officer, a young lieutenant who had managed to avoid frontline service until a falling out with his commander landed him at the front in 1944, had an experience that validated the general's apprehension. When he arrived at his regiment, the lieutenant was assigned a platoon of eighteen Uzbeks, fifteen of whom did not speak Russian. He had only a few hours to train them before going into their first fight, and he was supplied with only a handful of rifles in various states of disrepair. "After four hours we attacked, and all of my men either were wounded or just ran away," the lieutenant recalled. "I reported them as killed—they might have shot me without much questioning for not stopping the deserters."[72] Sometimes, Stalinist repression not only prompted disloyalty but also facilitated it, as in the case of the Turkmen. In the 1930s the state had internally exiled to Ukraine nearly 15,000 Turkmen accused of being kulaks. In the summer of 1941 their communities became havens for deserting Uzbek soldiers.[73]

Men from areas recently annexed by the USSR—western Ukraine and western Belorussia, taken from Poland in 1939, and Bessarabia and northern Bukovina, taken from Romania in 1940—served reluctantly or avoided service altogether. Before the war had been on for a full month, the NKVD informed the high command that there had been mass desertions and betrayals by soldiers from these regions. The high command in turn warned the military councils of fronts to examine the political reliability of such people under their commands.[74] These fears were well-founded. Iakov Grichener, from recently annexed Bessarabia, was conscripted from a labor camp with several thousand other Romanian teenagers in 1941. He remembered being distinctly unpatriotic: "I did not feel like I was a Soviet. I did not speak Russian. I never believed in Stalin."[75]

The attitude of many men from the Baltic States was similar. A soldier who was half Russian and half Estonian was drafted in 1940. Later that year, when the Red Army discharged all Estonians from the service, he tried to use his half-Estonian heritage to get out, but the authorities denied his request because he had a Russian name. Later on, he deserted to the enemy. "The fact that the whole army was falling back on all sides and that there were so many deserters," he said, "strengthened me in my view. When I saw people openly shot after being tried in court martial before all our eyes, I knew that the Soviet government was not interested in the welfare of the people. I decided that the Russian army could not last long in this harsh punishment based on pistols, with the NKVD behind the line, with guns ready to shoot soldiers who retreated."[76] He had heard how badly the Germans treated prisoners and claimed he did not believe it, but he was still apprehensive. Even so, he decided the risk was worth it. In contrast, three years later, when the tide of war had turned and the resurgent Red Army approached Estonia, 38,000 Estonian men voluntarily joined the German army in defending their homeland from the Russians.[77]

The Soviet historiography of the Latvian division formed in 1942 is presented as one of patriotic success and a shining example of the unity of the Soviet peoples. The story of the other Latvian division, the 50th Latvian Reserve Rifle Division, formed in 1944, was not only excluded from the story of the war; it was suppressed. Formed in part by Latvians conscripted from liberated areas, it lost 1,000 men to desertion between October and the first half of December. Most of the deserters, 830, were Latvian. An NKO report asserted that, from its founding, the division had not been inculcated with a fighting spirit. Living conditions were stark, and poor-quality and inadequate food had depressed morale and led to rampant sickness, including multiple cases of typhus. On Stalin's order, the division commander was reassigned; Stalin reprimanded the commander and military council of the Belorussian-Latvian Military District. The division kept the best regiment but disbanded the other two and reassigned the men to march companies to reinforce other divisions. The division was stripped of the title "Latvian" and re-formed with two new regiments of non-Latvians.[78] The Latvians conscripted for this division had spent the war years under German occupation and had avoided joining partisan units. Their commitment to the USSR was essentially nil, and this was evident when they were called on to sacrifice for a regime to which they felt no loyalty. In contrast, between February 1943 and July 1944, 146,000 Latvians volunteered to serve in the German armed forces against the Soviets.[79]

Effects of the Home Front

Just as in the war with Finland, morale at the front was often affected by news from home. Many soldiers were bolstered in their resolve by exhortations from their families to persevere; the justice of their cause and the necessity of their sacrifices were reaffirmed. But when civilian morale wavered, this too was transmitted to the front. Families' doubts about the war, the regime, and the party convinced some soldiers to desert or shirk their duties. Quantifying causal links between soldiers' and civilians' morale on the basis of the documentary evidence is virtually impossible because both were shaped by the dialogue between front and rear; likewise, both were affected by the course of the war and the privations it caused. One must keep in mind that Soviet civil society suffered more deaths than the army did. The number of wounded, maimed, or traumatized civilians has never been tallied.

Millions of civilians were relocated to the east to work in factories seven days a week for the duration of the war. Most lived in shoddy, makeshift housing at best; some had nothing but holes in the ground. The vast majority of the population routinely suffered from hunger. Thus, the soldiers at the front did not always have the right to complain to their civilian friends and family. Knowing that their families shared their suffering was no consolation. Red Army soldiers could not expect much good news from home to cheer them. In contrast, American servicemen and soldiers of the British Commonwealth were assured of their families' safety and general well-being (with the exception of Londoners subjected to German V-1 and V-2 rockets until early 1945).

Just as morale fluctuated up and down at the front according to living conditions and the prospects of victory or defeat, so it did in the rear. In Moscow, for example, at the start of the war there were some who expected victory in short order, but others were deeply pessimistic.[80] Reactions to Stalin's 3 July 1941 speech reflected those mixed expectations. Some people were encouraged by his candor and felt a deepened resolve to fight or to do their part at work. Others became cynical or became more entrenched in their cynicism and defeatist attitudes, and some even hoped the regime would fall.[81] People in Leningrad and other regions exhibited defeatist and anti-Soviet attitudes early in the war, which only undermined morale and resolve at the front.[82]

Shortly after the war, a myth arose that Stalinist repression had declined during the war, bringing the Soviet people together in a way they had never experienced before or since. In fact, the security organs were as active as ever during the war years, and they relied as heavily as ever on denunciations and informers. During the war the People's Commissariat for State Security (NKGB) arrested 452,292 people. The most common charge was anti-Soviet agitation.[83] Defeatist talk and criticism of the Soviet government, shared between the front and the rear, consistently challenged the state's version of affairs and contributed to soldiers' doubts about victory and their reasons for fighting.

In the end, the vast majority of soldiers remained loyal and did their duty, but it was not always an easy choice to make. For its part, the regime often made poor or ignorant choices and did sloppy work in trying to motivate and compel compliance. Combat motivation at the front mirrored the initial motivation of the volunteers and nonvolunteers, discussed previously in the context of mobilization. Young, urban, working class, or student, Russians were more likely to stick with the fight and maintain their motivation. The older generation, non-Russians, and peasants were more likely to opt out of the war in the short or long term and to exhibit lower morale.

Part 5

RUSSIA'S FEMALE SOLDIERS

11

Perspectives on Women's Motivation in the Great Patriotic War

What motivated women to volunteer or to serve willingly in the Soviet armed forces at war? What compelled the men running the Soviet state and the Red Army not only to let women serve but even to require their uniformed service? Most historians agree that patriotism motivated women to volunteer or to serve when called, and in so doing, they have either discounted or ignored altogether the possibility of gender-based responses. Historians disagree on whether it was necessity or ideology that prompted the Soviet regime to use large numbers of women in the armed forces. I agree that in many ways, women's motivations to serve, such as patriotism and vengeance, paralleled those of men, yet they were not identical to men's. The long-standing ideology of the women's liberation movement in Russia, elements of which had been amalgamated into Bolshevik ideology, influenced many women.

It is well known that women participated in the Soviet armed forces during the war. Around 800,000 served in the ranks of the *opolchenie*, *istrebitel'nyi*, communist, and Komsomol battalions and in the regular army as combat medics, doctors, nurses, radio operators, snipers, infantry soldiers, members of tank and artillery crews, pilots, and air and ground crews, as well as in myriad unglamorous support jobs, such as censors, drivers, laundresses, and cooks. Less than half the female soldiers (310,000) volunteered, and in some cases the voluntary nature of their enlistment is suspect. The Communist Party and the Komsomol pressured many of these women into serving by holding hostage their membership, good standing, and potential benefits in what historian Evelin Wittig characterizes as a "voluntary draft."[1] Like the men, many of these female volunteers would not have enlisted if the state had not come to them and asked them to join. The Red Army, with the aid of the Komsomol, conscripted the other 490,235 women.[2] Like their male counterparts, the female volunteers were predominantly young, single, urban students or working-class Russians. In contrast to male draftees, whose demographics ran the gamut of Soviet society, female conscripts were largely from the same demographic group as female volunteers. At least half were Komsomol members at the time of induction.[3] A much smaller percentage were party members.

Historical Background

When explaining female participation in the Red Army, historians of the Soviet period routinely claim that it was based on postrevolutionary changes in society and the large-scale involvement of women in the workplace in the era of the Five-Year Plans. During this time, women became a numerically significant factor in the workplace and took on occupations previously reserved for men. Many historians make the unfounded assumption that women joined men in the Stalinist socialist workplace as equals, which made their choice to join the army at the time of the German invasion all the more natural and easy. In fact, women had been part of the industrial workforce since the formative years of Russian industrialization in the late nineteenth century, and as historian Laurie Stoff points out, women holding "men's" jobs in the industrial workplace was not exactly a new phenomenon. Large numbers of women voluntarily performed war work during the First World War. By 1917, women constituted 50 percent of the nonfarm labor force and, through necessity, had branched into traditionally male jobs in steel mills, coal mines, and armaments factories.[4] Stoff and historian Melissa Stockdale have shown that the precedent of women working in the previously exclusive male sphere, combined with socialist, democratic, and feminist ideology, was a factor in some women's expression of patriotism through active military service in World War I, well before the Bolshevik takeover and even before the February Revolution. In fact, women disguised as men served in the Imperial Russian Army as far back as the eighteenth century, and women are known to have served in all the major wars of the nineteenth century—the Napoleonic Wars, the Crimean War, and the Russo-Turkish War of 1877–1878.[5]

Both Stoff and Stockdale have thoroughly documented women's military service to Russia in World War I. Based on their evidence and arguments, it is clear that, in many ways, the Russian female experience in World War I was a precursor to that of World War II. In the first weeks and months of World War I, women petitioned to serve but were allowed to do so only as nurses. Around 18,000 of these "sisters of mercy" were accepted into military service. Some of these women found themselves in forward aid stations and were killed in combat. Hundreds of others were turned away because the army did not have the capacity to train or administer so many women.[6] But the traditional role of nursing was not for every woman. Some began petitioning to participate in frontline combat early in the war. Nearly all were rejected, but some local draft boards allowed women to serve as soldiers, most notably those who volunteered with their brothers or fathers. Surprisingly, some who appealed directly to the tsar were given imperial permission to enroll openly as female soldiers in rifle regiments.

Other women worked for the army as cooks, supply clerks, and drivers, but most of these were recruited by civilian organs of local government, not by the army, and they were considered contract labor, not soldiers. Hundreds of others disguised themselves as men to join regiments bound for the front, where they engaged in combat. Many fought well, even earning the St. George's Cross, Russia's highest medal for valor. When their gender was discovered, most were sent home or redirected to nursing. A small number were allowed to remain in their units and fight openly as women.[7]

Motivation to Volunteer

Before the February Revolution, the primary motivation to serve, according to Stoff, was simple patriotism. As an example, she cites a petition a woman wrote to her local draft board: "I have a strong, passionate desire to become a volunteer in the active army for the defense of our dear tsar and Fatherland." Another said, "I must stand up for the motherland . . . my heart burns for this." Yet another was conscious of the ideals of the women's liberation movement and wrote: "Women also can fight, and just as well as men. Why are men given all the important responsibilities while women are assigned to kitchen work? Why does society so mistrust the intentions of women? Thousands of women could be fighting in the ranks of the Russian army. Why don't they trust that we, like men, can also take up arms and go to the defense of our motherland with honor and pride?"[8]

After the February Revolution swept away the tsarist government in 1917, female voluntarism increased, this time with more overt political and feminist content, both socialist and democratic. According to Stockdale, "the experience of war and revolution in Russia revolutionized conceptions of patriotism, citizenship, and gender, as well as class identity."[9] Now that Russia had proclaimed itself a democracy with definite socialist tendencies, women being allowed to serve in the military openly and in large numbers became a real possibility.

Almost immediately after the tsar's abdication, progressive women's organizations began to petition for the creation of female combat units. A "women's military movement" emerged and had organizations across Russia. It began recruiting women for military service in sixteen cities even before the Provisional Government could respond to the request for women's combat units. The movement, which Stoff argues constituted a genuine social movement, took on a national character when, in the summer of 1917, the Organizational Committee of the Petrograd Women's Military Union convened a Women's Military Congress. The congress sought not only to organize the movement but also to pressure the Provisional Government to accept women for uniformed service. The meeting was "suffused with the spirit of feminism and Socialist Revolutionary style patriotism," according to Stoff. "Speakers invoked images of self-sacrifice for the nation, coupled with progressive achievement for women."[10]

Eventually, the Provisional Government did agree to create women's battalions, but not for their fighting capacity. Given the desperate military situation, the majority in the Provisional Government saw that the acceptance of women's units could potentially shame the men in the disintegrating army to fight harder. Other, more progressive thinkers in both the Provisional Government and the Petrograd Soviet approved of women serving, based on socialist and democratic principles. For them, the acceptance of women in uniform and in combat was the logical outcome of decades of leftist pro–women's equality work on the part of the Russian women's liberation movement. Besides allowing female volunteers, the Provisional Government went so far as to conscript female doctors into the military medical service. By the time of the October Revolution in 1917, as many as 6,000 women were serving as soldiers, 5,000 in the four women's "Battalions of Death."[11] The army turned away thousands of others as physically or otherwise unfit. Only one of the battalions saw combat in the line, but it performed quite well. Its example, unfortunately, only temporarily galvanized some of the men in neighboring units. The army as a whole remained unmoved.

The women who volunteered for these units in no way shared the Provisional Government's belief that their primary mission was to shame men. If men were shamed into fighting or fighting harder, so much the better, but post–February 1917 female volunteers—from all classes and all walks of Russian life—were far more likely to be politicized or to have higher motives. Although some women continued to volunteer out of patriotism and the desire to avenge the deaths of family members, the revolution inspired others to serve the Provisional Government and a "free Russia." They served alongside women who detested the revolution but whose patriotism transcended politics in favor of defending the *rodina*. Such was the case of one young woman who clashed with her monarchist father over her enlistment. She remembered the incident thus: "'Who are you going off to defend,' he shouts, 'that riff-raff that threw the tsar off the throne?' 'No, Dad,' I say, 'I'm going to defend Russia!'"[12] Whether monarchist or democrat, Russian women understood the close ties between citizenship and soldiering because of the work of feminist organizations—especially those involved in creating the Battalions of Death. According to Stockdale, "Women's new identity as full citizens was part of larger egalitarian processes unleashed by the revolution."[13]

In a description that closely foreshadowed the voluntarism of 1941, Stockdale writes of the spirit of 1917: "The way some of Russia's women responded to the new national emergency was to take up arms, on a scale that surprised the country and the world. Their self-mobilization for combat was not solely or even primarily a 'bourgeois' or intelligentsia outpouring, although it appears to have been more urban than rural. The movement's transcendence of class and social status reminds us that class conflict and class identity, as important as they became, existed alongside and sometimes yielded to other powerful loyalties." She notes that patriotism cut across political boundaries. The women were democrats, monarchists, republicans, liberals, and socialists. Others were politically neutral. They had in common a readiness to take up arms and "swear an oath that proclaimed, 'my death for the Motherland and for the freedom of Russia is happiness.'"[14]

The desire to serve in all capacities had been fermenting since the origin of the radical movement in the 1860s, and women finally saw the opportunity to exercise their ideals in real form. Writing years later, one veteran of a Battalion of Death expressed a feminist outlook: "Each of us felt ourselves not just a Russian woman defending her own country (as every she-wolf defends her den) but also a representative of half the population of the whole planet, going into an examination, to prove that even in military matters a woman can be a worthy soldier."[15] Thus we have conflicting outlooks: some women were "simple" patriots, others were gender-conscious patriots, and others were gender- and politically conscious patriots. This pattern would be repeated in 1941. There was also a significant element of what might be called personal motivation. Some served not only to avenge the deaths of loved ones but also to escape from personal sorrows (often unrelated to the war) and, perhaps even more importantly, to escape from controlled lives, to seek opportunity and adventure in ways that were otherwise unavailable to women. This may have included a good deal of unrealistic romanticism about war, but the motivation was present nonetheless.[16]

Soviet Socialism and Women's Military Service

Following the lead of the Provisional Government, the new Soviet regime expanded the participation of women in the armed forces during the Russian civil war. It conscripted female doctors for work in the Red Army and also accepted female volunteers. It is estimated that between 50,000 and 70,000 women served in the Red Army during the civil war. At least 30,000 were employed at administrative and economic tasks, and 20,000 worked in the medical services.[17] While the nascent Bolshevik government waffled over the role of women in war, numerous women, perhaps hundreds, worked their way onto the firing line. Ironically, Aleksandra Kollontai, a prominent Bolshevik feminist, did not believe that women should kill and be killed at the front. Instead, she promoted stereotypical roles for women in the military—as nurses to nurture and heal men.[18]

After their victory the Bolsheviks promptly demobilized the women, explaining that their service had been necessitated by the wartime emergency. Subsequently, only a handful of women served on active duty between the wars. They were assigned almost exclusively to medical or administrative and clerical work.

The Stalinist regime declared women to be equal and, in 1936, pronounced the "women's question" solved. So, when discussing women's service in the armed forces under the Soviet regime after that time, one must choose to either accept or reject the claim that equality had been achieved when asking whether females' motivation differed from that of males. Historian Reina Pennington believes that there may have been differences in the Great Patriotic War, but it is impossible to determine. Her writing highlights the similarities: "Their motivations ranged from following relatives to the front, to avenging the death of a friend or relative, to simple patriotism," which is congruent with the motivations that Soviet historiography ascribes to men. Pennington believes that, like men, women had a self-interested desire to serve in order to restore their families' good names in the aftermath of political arrest. Pennington cites the case of Sergeant Klara Tikhonovich, an antiaircraft gunner, who wrote, "A young person recently told me that going off to fight was a masculine urge. No, it was a human urge. . . . That was how we were brought up, to take part in everything. A war had begun and that meant that we must help in some way."[19] In other words, Pennington suggests that it was a gender-neutral decision made possible in part by the changes in Russian society in the years after the Bolshevik revolution; therefore, women's motivations mirrored those of men. But as we have already established, men's motivations were more complex than heretofore recognized, so we should expect women's motives to be complex as well.

Historian Anna Krylova discounts the role of socialist or feminist ideology as a factor in women's decision making and ignores the precedents women set during the First World War and the civil war. She stresses that changes in the social environment wrought by the revolution made it seem almost normal or even expected for women to want to participate in the war and for the Soviet regime to allow it. She argues, "the conceivability of women's compatibility with combat, war and violence was a product of the radical undoing of traditional gender differences that Stalinist society underwent in the 1930s."[20] In her thinking, the young generation of Soviet women saw themselves as the equals of men and therefore were not restrained by traditional gender boundaries. The fact that they were women played no role in their decision to go to war. For them, women's patriotism was the same as men's, as were their desires for vengeance, to accompany a family member, or to uphold or restore the family name.

This analysis is undermined by several facts. First, we have to remember that less than half the women who served actually volunteered; most were conscripted or were pressured into joining by the Komsomol or the party. Without the efforts of the Komsomol to reach out to women, probably far fewer would have volunteered. Second, such an analysis accepts women like Klara Tikhonovich as the norm, without considering that she might have been exceptional. Third, no one has looked into draft evasion or desertion by women to test the degree of women's resistance to service. It would be extraordinary if there were none.

The historical-literary trope on Soviet women's military participation has affected both veterans' and historical interpretations. The official story line was that, like the men who served, they were all patriots and heroes. Officially, women were required to conform to this paradigm if they wished to be published or to speak on the record. Later, the majority of oral history accounts, published during the Gorbachev era and after the collapse of the USSR, indicated that, for women faced with volunteering or answering the summons of a *voenkomat*, their female identity was a factor in the decision. Many privately evaluated, on a gender basis, their ability to serve in uniform and the desirability of service at all. Despite decades of socialist-feminist rhetoric, they still viewed war and the military as a man's world.

The precedent of women serving in large numbers and in combat organizations in World War I suggests that women choosing to serve cannot be adequately explained by the changes in society since the revolution. It is therefore unclear whether socialist ideology—or, more specifically, the ideology of the Russian Revolution regarding the promised equality of the sexes—played a significant role in the psyche of the volunteers and of those willing to report for conscription. If this egalitarian ideology did play a role, the October Revolution cannot be given sole credit because it was preceded by at least five decades of effort by the women's liberation movement in the industrial workplace; the revolution, however, gave it currency in daily life.

Another challenge to assertions that women's voluntarism in the Great Patriotic War was a product of Soviet socialism and egalitarianism comes from historian Choi Chatterjee, who shows that there was a profound difference between the Bolsheviks' rhetoric of women's liberation and the reality on the workshop floor during the First Five-Year Plan (1928–1932). Rather than treating women as the equals of men, factory management kept them in low-paying, unskilled work and routinely denied them promotion to skilled work. If a woman was promoted into administrative work, it was often at the lowest level, which paid even less than manual labor. When women were put in positions over men, the men routinely made their lives so hard that the women often asked to be demoted. The state also failed to follow through in a meaningful way to provide the social services necessary to compensate women for the additional burdens they shouldered upon entry into the workforce; thus, they continued to bear the double burden of family and workplace duties.[21] It appears, then, that the state drew women into the factories in large numbers less out of ideology than out of necessity. First and foremost, industrial expansion required female workers; it could not succeed without their labor, but it could succeed without making women equal.[22]

That the state was not inherently predisposed to consider women as a source of soldiers, even after the October Revolution, is implied in its mobilization of women for the workplace under the three prewar Five-Year Plans. In arguing for completion of the First Five-Year Plan in four years instead of five, Stalin raised the threat of impending war with capitalism. The regime argued that more women needed to be trained for work to replace the men who would inevitably be called up for military service. This indicates that, in the minds of the Stalinist leaders, women's place in wartime was in the factory, not the army. Furthermore, the big push to employ women in factories in 1931 failed to meet its ambitious goals because factory management and local party officials did not embrace the recruitment of women. According to Chatterjee: "Despite the immense labor shortages, factory managers felt little compunction in disregarding party orders about the mobilization of women."[23] So, if women were not readily welcomed into male spheres of industrial labor in the decades before and after the revolution, only the young and naïve would expect to be welcomed into the Red Army.

The largest pool of potential female volunteers and conscripts for military service was the Soviet peasantry, yet it proved to be the least fertile ground for recruits. In fact, as Matt Oja observes, in the years 1933–1941, the Stalinist regime made a major effort to modernize and raise the status of women in the countryside relative to that of men.[24] This effort was part of the state's goal to add women to the collective farm labor force as tractor and combine drivers and as collective farm chairpersons, mechanics, and other occupations that had previously been reserved for men. The state intentionally promoted women's equality at the expense of male authority to undermine resistance to collectivization. But by the outbreak of war, female participation in these occupations was 10 percent at best, and it was seldom that high. The problem was that rural women consciously rejected these modern roles because of their attachment to traditional roles. So, as one would expect, at the outbreak of the war, peasant women's participation in the armed forces on a voluntary basis mirrored that of peasant men. There were some volunteers, but not nearly as many as from the urban areas.

The ideology of women's equality was much better received by young urban women. If the state followed through on its pretense of equal opportunity for women in any area, it was in higher education. In 1929, 20 percent of admissions to institutions of higher education were reserved for women; in 1930, this was increased to 25 percent.[25] On the eve of the war, owing to quotas and laws giving preferential treatment to women, the number of women in specialized schools and universities had risen to nearly 50 percent of overall enrollment.[26] In 1941 a significant number of the women who volunteered for the military were college educated. These women had benefited most from Stalinist social policy and had remained idealistic.

Chatterjee concludes: "Stalinism did not fulfill the ideals of the October Revolution in that gender parity remained an abstract dream throughout the life of the Soviet Union. But Stalinism did complete one part of the Bolshevik gender project; it managed to semiotically reencode the category of 'woman' in Soviet public discourse."[27] To this end, Article 22 of the first Soviet Constitution of 1918 proclaimed the equality of all citizens in the Soviet Republic, regardless of sex, race, or nationality. Article 64 established the right of women to elect or to be elected to soviets on an equal footing with men. The constitution also declared a universal military obligation for males; women could serve on a voluntary basis.[28] In accord with this spirit, the military conscription regulations of 1925 permitted women to join the army.[29] The social progress intended by the Bolsheviks was spelled out again in Article 122 of the Constitution of 1936, which accorded women equal rights and an equal footing with men in all spheres of political, economic, social, and cultural activity.[30] This was followed by Article 19 of the newly revised Law on Universal Military Obligation of 1 September 1939, which allowed the army to draft women with specialized skills. This law restricted women to "ancillary" and "specialist" noncombat duties. It took until 1942 for the state to cast off this restriction.[31]

Despite the precedents of women's voluntarism for war and the public acclaim of women as equals in the rural and urban workplace, the state and the armed forces were surprised by the number of women who wanted to serve and to fight. Unclear in the Western treatment of women's voluntarism for the Great Patriotic War, and opaque in the Soviet record, was what exactly these women volunteered to do. Of the 310,000 women who joined the military by volunteering or responding to the call of the Komsomol, an overwhelming number ended up joining their local *opolchenie* divisions or *istrebitel'nyi*, communist, or Komsomol battalions. Fewer attempted or were permitted to join the regular Red Army. The patterns of voluntarism and the demographics of female volunteers were identical to those of males. Very few peasants and non-Russians volunteered, but those who did were usually Komsomol or party members.

Initially, in June and July 1941, the Red Army rejected female volunteers; only weeks later, when it was clear that the war would be a long one, did it begin to accept their applications. Female applicants, some of whom had been turned away by the army, deluged the *opolchenie* and other volunteer units, which accepted them by the tens of thousands. By the eighteenth day of war, 10 July 1941, nearly 200,000 women had volunteered for the *opolchenie*. Most of them, as one would expect, were in Moscow and Leningrad; however, considerable numbers of women outside of these metropolises also volunteered. For example, military commissariats in Dnepropetrovsk province received 10,175 requests to volunteer for service, of which 3,602 were from women. Kirovograd province received 2,398 requests to be sent to the front—1,113 from women. In Donets province, 5,314 applications out of 20,000 were from women, and in Odessa province, of the 73,200 Komsomol members who volunteered, 10,000 were female (Komsomolkas).[32] Bear in mind that these numbers represent requests to volunteer, not numbers of women accepted into service. By the time Nikolaev province's *opolchenie* divisions were through forming in the late summer, they had enrolled 70,464 people, including 18,884 females. Chernigov province provided 64,784 people for the *opolchenie,* of whom 13,269 were female. One factory in Lugansk formed an *opolchenie* brigade of 6,000 people, 1,200 of whom were women.[33]

In contrast to the large numbers of volunteers for the *opolchenie,* those seeking to join the Red Army—both women and men—were far fewer. About 20,000 Muscovites volunteered for the Red Army in the first three months after the invasion; of these, 8,360 were women. Farther east of Moscow, voluntarism among both men and women was less widespread and was focused on the Red Army, perhaps because few *opolchenie* divisions were formed in the eastern USSR. For example, in Barnaul, Altai *krai,* military commissariats received only 800 requests to volunteer in the early weeks of the war—more than half, 474, from women. In July 1941 Krasnodar *krai* and Ivanovsk province each saw 4,000 women volunteer for the active army. Chitinsk province had 9,754 female volunteers, of whom 3,754 had been mobilized by the Komsomol. Karagandinskii province produced about 25,000 volunteers, of whom nearly 10,000 were female. The army, however, did not accept all these volunteers.[34]

In Their Own Words: Why Women Served

The trope delivered by the postwar Soviet media and in literature downplayed the conscription of women and included only two motives for women's volunteering for service—patriotism and vengeance. There is absolutely no mention that feminism or the desire to prove women's equality played a role in their decision making. As we have seen, the revolution opened up more opportunities for women than they had had under the tsar; however, contrary to the party line, many women still felt they had much to prove, and they recognized that equality had not really been achieved. This perception comes out most forcefully in the studies of the women's air regiments. Because of a more rigorous selection process, these women were generally better educated than the average male in the armed forces, and the majority were volunteers. Although there is certainly no evidence that all or even the majority of Soviet female soldiers had some sort of a feminist agenda, to deny it completely is to miss the reality behind some women's motivation to serve and persevere. Some of their individual stories reveal a strong desire to excel in what most people still considered a man's world.

To a degree, primary materials support the conventional wisdom that the motivations of women who volunteered were very similar to men's. In line with the official story, they were affected by patriotism, by the desire to do their part or take revenge, or even by their regard for Stalin. A careful reading of memoirs and interviews, however, reveals that women were extremely conscious of their gender as they contemplated military service. Women knew that they were not expected to volunteer, especially not for the front, yet many felt compelled to do so to demonstrate that, as citizens, they were the equal of men.

In addition to their own feelings, women, like men, were subject to external stimuli such as propaganda and family influences. Evgeniia Sapronova, who became an aircraft mechanic, remembered that her parents did not want her to volunteer, but she did anyway. "I, for one, was greatly affected by the posters that are now housed in museums: 'The Motherland Calls You,' 'What Did You Do for the Front?' I thought that women more advanced in age than I should stay behind in the rear, but that I had to go to the front."[35] Sapronova's response to these posters is intriguing, because it is generally assumed that they were directed at men.

The need to be accepted and to conform also played a role. Maria Morozova, who tried to enlist at the offices of the Komsomol Central Committee late in the summer of 1941, said, "Young people from all over the Soviet Union had come to the place, many of them from the occupied areas, seething to avenge the death of their near and dear." She was accepted and observed, "Everybody was fighting and we did not want to be left out." Private Zinaida Palshina also felt the need to belong, writing: "I volunteered for the front. How could it be otherwise? Everybody did. There was no alternative in anyone's mind."[36]

One reason that feminist ideology may have been left out of the historiography of the war is Stalin's proclamation that the women's question had been solved, making it off-limits. Perhaps with this in mind, women did not mention feminist motivations in their letters to state officials. For example, N. M. Nikulina submitted the following petition to her district military commissariat on 23 June 1941:

> I am 16 years old. But I consider myself capable of using weapons. I ask you to allow me to join in the membership of our valiant Red Army. I want to volunteer to go to assault the fascist plunderers who dare to violate our sacred borders.
>
> My friends, Komsomolkas, also strongly desire to go to the front line. I will begrudge neither my blood nor my life for the good of the rodina and to achieve victory over the enemy.[37]

Of all the ideological arguments available to her, including equal rights of citizenship, she chose only love of the *rodina*. Patriotism and vengeance were the only acceptable formulas.

Lidia Aleksinskaia sent an equally nonfeminist letter to her local *voenkomat* after her factory had had several patriotic rallies and several of her male coworkers had volunteered for service. She wrote:

> Many have fathers, brothers, and husbands who have gone to the front. I have no family other than my mother. My father died at the front in the civil war happy to fight for the lives of the working people. I ask to be accepted into the ranks of the active army in the capacity of nurse.
>
> I was born in 1922, am a Komsomolka, and in recent years completed the 10th grade of the Blagodatenskoi middle school. In that time of instruction I was given the badges "GSO," "PVKhO," and "GTO." I can bandage, give first aid to the wounded, I can look after

the wounded, and if necessary, I will go so far as to fight the fascists, with rifle in hand.[38]

She established her credentials as a Soviet patriot by her membership in the Komsomol, her participation in paramilitary training, and her legacy as the child of a veteran. These, she must have known, would satisfy the expectations of the authorities. Had she or Nikulina justified their desire to fight as a means to achieve equality for women, they probably would have been scolded for questioning the state of equality in the USSR.

A sense of family also motivated some women. Esten Kozhemiatnikov wanted to join the army, she said, because "I wanted to be like my parents," both of whom were veterans of the civil war.[39] M. Solovei joined the army alongside her husband. They were allowed to serve in the same regiment, but not together. She was assigned to a medical battalion and he to a rifle battalion. Komsomolka M. Kholdiak asked to be taken into the army because her brother had been serving for five years and had taught her to shoot rifles and pistols. She wanted to defend the *rodina* at his side. O. Motlokh wrote to *Proletarskaia pravda* on 26 June 1941 from Uman: "Now, when the enemy want to take our happy lives, I am not able to sit at home. My two brothers are in the Red Army, I want to go to the front as a medic."[40] These sentiments were no different from those of the women who volunteered during the First World War.

A counterexample of the influence of family is the story of Maria Matveeva. After the outbreak of war, as part of civil defense, she initially became commander of a Komsomol detachment to guard a production facility. She also helped handle evacuees from Leningrad. Later she volunteered in the local hospital as an aide to wounded soldiers. She read their letters to them, wrote letters for them, and read the news to them. She remembered being inspired by the story of Zoia Kosmodemianskaia. Maria wanted to answer the Komsomol's call for women to join the PVO, but her parents did not want her to go. Her father, a soldier, was home convalescing from his wounds. Maria's parents argued that she was their only daughter and they did not want to lose her. They emphasized, "This is war—war!" Her father accused her of not being up to the demands of war, given her soft, "mollycoddled" life. Maria argued that she was up to the task. Her father retorted by noting that whereas her mother was a hard worker, Maria "only read books." Having worked with the wounded in the hospital, she knew that war was no game. But now she felt that she had something to prove to her parents, who had lived through the very difficult times of the civil war, and especially to her father, who doubted her ability. She finally won their consent and volunteered for the regular army through the recruitment efforts of the Komsomol. She was assigned to an antiaircraft artillery regiment in Stalingrad in 1942.[41]

In Maria's story, we see various motivations and pressures at work on her. She felt social responsibility, a sense of duty as a Komsomolka, and a responsibility to the soldiers she helped. She may have felt anger at the suffering of the wounded soldiers and the evacuees from Leningrad. No doubt, she took it as a personal challenge as a "new Soviet woman" to prove her worth to her parents.

In contrast, Natalia Sergeeva's father sent her to the army and to war. He was upset because his sons were too young to join the army, so he volunteered his daughters. "When nurses' courses were organized, father took me and my sister there. He said: 'This is all I can give for the Victory . . . my girls.'"[42]

In some quarters, there was peer pressure among women not only to serve but to serve at the front. Kira Petrovskaia, mobilized to be a nurse in Leningrad in 1941, was envious of an army medic friend because "she looked smart in her uniform with the field-nurse arm band and medical corps emblem on her military cap. She had been assigned to front-line duty immediately, while I had been detained to take an additional course to become a hospital nurse. I wanted to go to the front. All my friends were there, fighting." Petrovskaia's peers reinforced the feeling that she was not doing enough or not doing anything significant. She would occasionally see her field nurse friends (*druzhinnizi*) when they brought casualties to the hospital from the front. They carried submachine guns, which they used in the line of duty to protect the wounded men. Because the hospital nurses were safe and led a comfortable existence compared with the field nurses, Kira felt guilty and unworthy in their presence. She recalled: "To them, we were pampered city girls, well educated and clever enough to escape *real* service by flaunting our college degrees. They all but accused us of cowardice."[43]

Liudmila Popova is an example of someone moved by the desire for vengeance. Her father, a reserve officer called into active service in 1941, was killed at the front. She clearly remembered that, "from the moment I found out he had been killed, I was determined to go into the military and avenge his death."[44] Until then, she had never considered fighting for her country. Likewise, Valentina Tokareva left her children with her mother and enlisted to avenge the death of her husband.[45]

The feeling of having a social responsibility to their fellow citizens, not the state, motivated two other women. Zoia Khlopotina said: "I knew I was needed at the front, I knew that even my modest investment would count in the great common undertaking of the defeat of the enemy."[46] Nina Solntseva spent her free time looking after wounded men in a local hospital. Her interaction with the men convinced her to become a medic and go to the front "in order to help injured men on the field of battle."[47] Even so, Solntseva waited until October 1941 to join the fight. She signed up to serve only when the Germans were literally on Moscow's doorstep and the party started recruiting for communist battalions to defend the city. So, despite being a communist and her supposed sense of social responsibility, it took a particular set of circumstances to get Solntseva, and thousands like her, to come forward.

Some women who harbored doubts about Stalinism were able to separate their feelings about the nation and the state, understanding that the *rodina* was not the equivalent of the Communist Party, its failings, or its evils. In the years after the collapse of the USSR, Natalia Peshkova, a Komsomol organizer in a tank battalion, did not want anyone to think she had fought for Stalin. Fifty years after the fact, she recounted what she did after hearing the news of the German invasion: "Well, I regarded myself as no less than Joan of Arc, so I immediately ran to a regional office of the Komsomol committee and they sent me to a group of medics." She said, "Patriotism was a real thing, it isn't exaggeration. Every one of us fought for our Motherland. I never heard that anybody cried 'Long live Stalin!' or even 'Hurrah!' during the battles."[48] Peshkova, by claiming the Joan of Arc image, equated patriotism with nationalism, intentionally separate from any endorsement of Stalin.

Antonina Kotliarova is another example of a woman who felt a sense of duty to the *rodina* without having respect for the government or its officials. She wanted to join her husband and father at the front but was twice rejected for military service. When Moscow was evacuated in October 1941, she could have left with her factory, but "of course, I didn't go with it," she said. "Why would I go if it was my duty to fight fascists?"[49] During the "great skedaddle" in October, when thousands of government officials shamelessly tried to leave Moscow to save themselves and their families from the German advance, Kotliarova claims to have thrown rocks at fleeing officials in their chauffeured cars. In her case, the idea of having a duty to fight fascists was her own, having been rejected by the state for military service.

Other women identified Stalin with the good things about Soviet socialism and wanted to serve out of a desire to reciprocate what socialism and Stalin had done for them. Raisa Surnachevskaia, a young pilot trainee in the 1930s who would later serve during the war, remembered praying to Stalin like a god: "I know there were terrible things that happened in camps, but it was Beriia who sent the people there. Stalin was against this; he defended the good people."[50] Another, Valentina Ivanova, said of the times and of Stalin: "I became a pilot, one of Stalin's falcons. Me, from a poor village, because Stalin gave us this opportunity. He rid us of traitors."[51]

Although the official record fails to mention it, not every woman the state called on wanted to serve. Zoia Nekrutova-Ket'ko, a Ukrainian living in Central Asia, remembered that in the spring of 1942, she and other girls in Alma-Ata were called to the *voenkomat*. She went with several of her Russian girlfriends in the same spirit that Russian boys joined together. At the *voenkomat*, "One of the girls did not want to go to the front and cried," she recalled. Zoia, in contrast, had to argue her way into the army because the *voenkomat* members thought she was too frail. She also had to defend her decision to her sister (a party member), who was not about to volunteer herself and did not want Zoia to go either. She started out as a medic, but in September 1942 her regimental commander heard that Zoia was a good shot and asked her to accept the job of sniper. She did.[52]

Unexpected Female Volunteers

Just as we saw with men, there were hundreds if not thousands of cases of unexpected female volunteers—women who had suffered at the hands of the Stalinist state and had every reason to reject service to it. For example, Klavdiia Ivanova joined the army in 1942, became a corporal and a sniper, and earned a medal for having shot twelve "Fritzes." She proudly wrote home to her mother about her award. Her father, however, would never know of her feat, having been arrested and, with neither a trial nor an investigation, shot in 1937.[53]

Tat'iana Ershova, a thirty-eight-year-old mother of seventeen- and nine-year-old daughters, joined an *istrebitel'nyi* battalion in Moscow in 1941, which required her to send her children away to a refugee camp. Ershova volunteered for frontline duty as a medic, against the wishes of her children and despite the arrest and disappearance of her husband in the purges in 1938. She was quite torn between her desire to be with her daughters and her sense of duty to help stop the Nazis (and perhaps the chance to rehabilitate her family). Her letters home always responded to the girls' wish to have her return to them, yet she constantly defended her decision to serve. In one letter, she rebuked her daughters for their plea that she leave the army, writing, "Daughters . . . for your information it is a privilege to be the child of a *Krasnoarmeitsa* [Red Army woman]." She died in March 1942 of wounds received on the battlefield while administering first aid to wounded soldiers.[54]

Neither Klavdiia Ivanova nor Tat'iana Ershova had to serve in the army or go into combat. Soviet society in general did not expect women to serve, and, given the treatment of their loved ones by the secret police, these two women would have been justified in not supporting the regime. But like male victims of the terror, women whose families had been persecuted by the state may have sought to prove their loyalty through service. Reina Pennington tells us that Lilia Litviak, a female fighter pilot, was motivated to redeem her family's honor after her father's wrongful arrest in the purges.[55] Nina Popova had been wrongfully arrested and expelled from the Komsomol in the 1930s and was initially refused the opportunity to enlist. Finally, the Komsomol said she could enlist if she first volunteered for an extremely dangerous mission. Popova said, "Those terms sounded as though I had committed a crime and were expiating my guilt, so I couldn't accept them."[56] She continued to appeal and eventually succeeded in serving on her terms. In Popova's case, the Komsomol officials involved unofficially shared the assumption that military service was linked to the redemption of marginalized people.

To become a *frontovik* and overcome the stigma of being the child of arrested parents, Mariana Miliutina lied. After finishing medical school, she said, "I was given the rank of senior lieutenant and immediately called up to the military commissariat, where they had me write an autobiography. I wrote: 'My parents died.' If I wrote that they had been arrested in the purges, they wouldn't have sent me to the front, and I didn't want to remain at the home front."[57] Her father had been shot in 1937, and her mother was incarcerated in the camps—facts she had already concealed in order to attend medical school. Her story conveys that some form of patriotism lay behind the desire to get to the front, but the potential for redemption may have played a part as well.

It seems to have been much less difficult for children of persecuted parents to join the *opolchenie* than the regular army. Tamara Butenko's father had been arrested in 1937 as an enemy of the people and sentenced to ten years in the camps, without the right of correspondence. Tamara was immediately expelled from school, but she had no trouble joining an *opolchenie* artillery regiment in her hometown of Fatash in the summer of 1941, where she served as a medic.[58] Another child of enemies of the people, thirteen-year-old Maia Norkina lived on her own for four years after her parents were arrested. She survived in Leningrad on meager handouts from relatives and food scraps from charitable neighbors, even as she scraped together parcels to send to her incarcerated parents. Finally, at age eighteen, motivated to secure food and an income, having had no formal schooling in her teen years, and possessing no occupational skills, she joined the Leningrad *opolchenie* in 1941.[59]

Continued trust in the regime was another dimension to the thinking of the victims of Stalinist terror that helped them serve the state. One woman, reflecting on her experience, explained: "When my father was arrested, it was very unpleasant but I did not blame the government. It hurt me when my friends turned away from me. But I did not rebel against the regime."[60] She convinced herself that it was all a misunderstanding and that everything would be straightened out. She ended up serving as an army nurse.

Why Did Men Let Women Serve?

An important issue that deserves more attention is the attitude and motivation of the men who dominated the state and why they first allowed and then compelled women to serve. The accepted wisdom is divided into two schools of thought: according to one, women's service was a matter of necessity; according to the other, ideology was the driving force that convinced men to grant women the right to serve. Anne Eliot Griesse and Richard Stites take the position that using women in the armed forces—and especially in combat—was "a stopgap measure used by a desperate regime pushed to its ultimate resource, which it did not hesitate to exploit." In their view, it succeeded in part because it did *not* represent a dramatic reordering of gender roles and relations in Soviet society.[61]

John Erickson acknowledges the manpower needs but recognizes that women, who had been pressing for frontline duties for months, had ideology on their side and that this was necessary for overcoming male reluctance to enlist women.[62] Kazimeira Cottam cites D. A. Zhuravlev, commander of the Moscow Front PVO, who said, "When the matter of the recruitment of women was discussed in the Central Committee, it was justified on two grounds: releasing men for other duty; and acceding to the wishes of the women themselves, since so many, being eager to serve, reportedly wrote to the party, the Komsomol, and Stalin himself."[63] More recently, Krylova argues that even though the egalitarian rhetoric of the 1930s was often contradictory, it had affected men to the extent that many were able to view soldiering in gender-neutral terms and therefore accept women into the ranks. This was supposedly a reflection of their adoption of a changed outlook on gender relations in Soviet society.[64]

A deeper examination of the issue produces a more nuanced insight into the decision making behind the use of women in the Red Army, especially in combat. There are two elements of this issue: the state's and society's willingness to accept and even require female military service on a large scale, and the use of women in combat.

At the outbreak of the war, there were only 1,000 women in the army. The Soviet regime had made no attempt to include women in a meaningful way in the rapid expansion of the Red Army on the eve of war. In

June and July 1941, women began to appear by the thousands demanding to serve. The *voenkomaty*, with no clear instructions from the NKO on the matter, responded in a variety of ways, which Krylova characterizes as "discouragement without prohibition."[65] A minority of draft boards simply turned women away; many redirected them to the *opolchenie*. Still others, like those in the First World War, directed women to Red Cross courses for medical training, in preparation for eventual enlistment in the military medical services. This was exactly the type of service that many of the first female volunteers intended.

The handling of women's voluntarism in Kursk in the first weeks of the war was typical. The provincial authorities reported, "There have been not a few cases when women, in the first days of the war, appeared at the military commissariats requesting to be taken into the active army." By the end of August, at the direction of *voenkomaty*, 687 women had signed up for Red Cross nursing instruction and 783 for instruction as medical orderlies. Large numbers of women also volunteered to help at local hospitals, and 2,600 women gave blood for wounded soldiers. The authorities boasted that, "in the city of Kursk about 5,000 women have joined the *opolchenie* ready to support the Red Army," and "one hundred fifty-two women work at the Kursk State Bank. Of these 63 have enrolled in the *narodnoe opolchenie*, 40 women work in groups of self defense, and 59 women volunteer at hospitals after work." Not a single woman had been allowed to join the army. The traditional attitude of the men in charge of deciding women's "proper" role in wartime comes across clearly. They reported that at the beginning of August, 6,308 women in the province had completed courses to become tractor and combine drivers and combine drivers' assistants, "thus freeing their husbands, fathers, and brothers for the front."[66]

Rather than relegating women's participation in the wartime military to the exceptional individual, after several months, the Stalinist state opted for massive organized female participation. How was the state able to get the traditionally minded, male-dominated military to agree? Even if need were the driving force, we must account for the ideological environment that made it possible for men to consider using so many women to solve the manpower problem. Many armies in history suffered from catastrophic manpower shortages without resorting to the enlistment of women. Therefore, ideology may have provided the final justification for turning to such an innovation; more cynically, it may have given the state the cover it needed to avoid the criticism of those resisting the erosion of male dominance in postrevolution society. Ideology gave female volunteers a moral advantage in their argument for the right to serve.

It is hard to imagine the Soviet state daring to draft or voluntarily mobilize so many women without the ideological and practical preparation of society beforehand. This conditioning included the tsarist regime's use of women in noncombat assignments and the Provisional Government's Battalions of Death, which both occurred in the context of national emergency. Women's recent entry into the industrial workforce in large numbers and their performance of skilled work traditionally reserved for males gave the state the advantage in overcoming objections to the conscription of women for military service. If industry could not keep women out of "men's" jobs, how could the army?

In drawing women into the workforce in large numbers, the state relied on a certain interpretation of ideology to get its way. As historian Mary Buckley notes, "Evidence suggests that ideological lines on women's lives under socialism, the nature of debate about them, and the images of women propagated by the state, have been tailored to the needs of different periods of Soviet history, as defined by their political leaderships."[67] She further observes, once the state has adapted its ideology for one purpose, it cannot abruptly ignore or contradict it for another; it is constrained by its past use of ideology. This last observation is debatable. Instances abound in which the Soviet state said one thing and did another or completely reversed its stance on a subject and promoted the change as progressive. Therefore, we cannot say that the state trapped itself into one course of action simply because of its previous tack. Therefore, when the Stalinist regime recruited women to perform men's work, we cannot assume that it was intending to prepare society for their use in the military—that turned out to be an unintended consequence.

Buckley's observation aptly describes the situation the regime faced in 1941, when women wanted to volunteer for nontraditional roles and some officials sought to accommodate them. Men in the army who held traditional ideas about the military and thought that war should be a man's preserve had to contend with the twin pressures of necessity and precedent, backed by ideology. Still, we have to consider the fact that ideology is malleable and can serve whatever purpose a regime chooses. Thus, we have to stop short of thinking that women's use of ideology forced Stalin's hand; instead, we should consider that the state saw an advantage to using women in the ways it ultimately did.

The idea of women having the right, or even the duty, to serve alongside men in war predates Stalin's Five-Year Plans. During the civil war, the authorities addressed the issue of women serving in the armed forces. In 1920, at the Ninth Party Congress, Nikolai Podvoiskii, head of *Vsevobuch*, campaigned for the compulsory military training of women. He argued that, as equal citizens of the motherland of the proletariat, "the woman worker must know how to use a rifle, revolver, and machine gun, must know how to defend her city, her village, her children, herself from the attacks of the White Guard bands."[68] Whereas most militaries argued that getting women into uniform would release men for the front, Podvoiskii argued just the opposite—that sending women to the front would release men to go back to the factories. At that time, there was a desperate need for skilled workers in defense industries. Many had been drafted and made up the backbone of the army.

However, several prominent Bolshevik women, leaders of the party's short-lived women's section (*zhenotdel*), were against females other than party members and Komsomolkas serving in the army, especially under obligation. They did not want women to be killed. The result of the debate was a resolution calling for the voluntary military training of females aged eighteen and older. Under pressure from his political rivals, Podvoiskii changed his tune and called for women to serve in support roles to free up men for the front.[69]

We also have to consider the long-term effects of the women's liberation movement on men and the support it received from the Bolshevik regime. Richard Stites, commenting on the structure of female liberation, writes: "At its base is the economic and educational equality of the sexes in law, embellished ideologically by a widely if not universally held conviction that woman is as capable as man in almost every field of endeavor now open to mankind. This notion is encased in the official myth that Soviet people of both sexes are better equipped than any other group in the world to cope with the new challenges that science and technology may present to humanity in the near future." This was the

Soviet regime's public stance on the "woman question." Stites continues: "If the active phase of women's liberation accomplished nothing else, it must be credited with having transformed into a national myth the notions that women are capable of great economic wonders, that they must be allowed full play to their faculties, and that men have no right to hinder this process, but rather every obligation to further it."[70]

This line had been perpetuated in the 1930s in part through the portrayal of women fulfilling traditionally male roles. In the countryside, this meant operating machinery and serving as collective and state farm leaders. Elsewhere, women's exploits in aviation and production were lauded. The campaign to promote women, however, was political and economic in nature, not social. Chatterjee shows that the results benefited the state far more than the women, because women depended on the state to uphold their authority in an environment rife with male resistance and hostility. This dependency led women to attach their political allegiance to the state. Because women were marginalized within the very party that professed egalitarianism, they could not exert pressure from within the system, yet, according to Chatterjee, "the fact that they engaged in occupations traditionally reserved for men . . . lent credibility to the alleged Soviet commitment to women's liberation."[71] In 1941 women were able to use this campaign to make their argument for service, and the regime was able to use it to justify to skeptical members in its midst and to society at large its decision to mobilize women.

The decision to mobilize women was made reluctantly, informed by ideology and experience. It was meant to be a temporary measure, and the intent was to keep women out of harm's way. Contrary to Krylova's assertion, women's military participation in the Great Patriotic War in large numbers and in combat did not represent the confirmation of a dramatic reordering of gender roles and relations in Soviet society.[72] Instead, it represented another step forward for the women's liberation movement along a path opened by the emergency of war. Women had another opportunity to prove themselves worthy of the true equality that continued to be denied them. Men had another chance to reevaluate their feelings about the social order and the stereotypes of women. One might even argue that by the time the war began, Soviet society had come to accept that some women could do many of the things men could do, and, if the need arose, they should. However, they did not necessarily think that this was some new preferred gender order.[73] We can summarize the mobilization of females into the armed forces by saying that some women served because they wanted to, many because the regime needed them to, and because socialist ideology and historical precedent made it both feasible and acceptable to most of Soviet society—at least temporarily during the state of emergency.

12

The Female Experience
of Military Service and War

The regime did not induct women into the armed forces to make an ideologically based pro-feminist statement; it did so to get meaningful work
out of them. Thus, the question of their effectiveness is an important
one: did the induction of women serve the army's purposes, and did the
Red Army get the performance it wanted from the women it accepted?
As a matter of perspective, it should be mentioned that women voluntarily served in various noncombat capacities in several other armies
during the war, including the British, American, and German. Only the
Soviet Union, however, conscripted women and allowed them to kill
men. On 1 January 1945, of the 490,000 women who had been conscripted, 463,503 were serving in various combat and support capacities
in the Red Army, 318,000 of them in the frontal zone—within twenty-
five kilometers of the main battle line—qualifying them as *frontoviki*. At
the end of the war in Europe, in May 1945, 246,530 Komsomolkas were
still at the front.[1]

The mobilization of women began only weeks after the German invasion. Once the regime was convinced that the female voluntarism at the
war's onset was no fluke, it decided to use women en masse, but without
a long-term plan. The Stalinist state could not use the ordinary conscription system of the *voenkomaty;* there had been no peacetime registration
of women for the draft (which indicates that the Stalinist regime had no
plans to use women in war), and it would require too much time and effort to collect the names of draft-eligible females. Instead, it called on the
services of the VLKSM. At the time, the Komsomol had more than a million female members, all of military age, on its rolls. In the second month
of the war, the Komsomol was instructed to recruit 30,000 females with
at least seven years of schooling to become nurses and at least 30,000

more who had at least four years of schooling to become medics.[2] The recruits did not have to be Komsomolkas, and they did not necessarily have to be volunteers. With the Law on Universal Military Obligation on its side, the VLKSM could and did compel women to serve. In August 1941 it delivered 10,000 Komsomolets and 10,000 Komsomolkas to the army specifically for signals duty (radio, telegraph, and telephone operators and linemen). The NKO conscripted 5,594 women in 1941, but not until 7 March 1942, the eve of International Woman's Day, did the army announce the regular mobilization of women for military service.[3]

Officially, once the policy to accept women into the active army was established, women, unlike men, would be selected on the basis of education (complete literacy), culture, health, physical strength, and inclination for military specialties.[4] At the point of induction, the army and *opolchenie*, apparently informally and arbitrarily, also added the criteria of being single and childless. These criteria automatically guaranteed that fewer peasants and non-Russians would be accepted, because they usually married younger and bore children earlier than urban Russian women, and they had less access to education and cultural enrichment.

The mobilization took place in five waves between 1942 and 1944. The GKO decreed that the first wave was to produce 300,000 women between 23 March and 13 April 1942 to take jobs in the rear areas and thus free men for the front. The time frame proved to be a bit too ambitious and resulted in the conscription of just 100,000 women aged nineteen to twenty-five.[5] It took several more months to take in the additional 200,000 women, but the goal of 300,000 was met. All told, the good offices of the VLKSM summoned, interviewed, examined, and delivered to the armed forces 235,025 women in 1942, 194,695 in 1943, 51,306 in 1944, and 3,615 in 1945.[6]

Another 300,000 women either enlisted directly into the Red Army or the *opolchenie* and other volunteer units (all of which were later absorbed into the regular army) or were taken into the army through the phenomenon of front "self-mobilization."[7] That is, they volunteered to join units when the war came to them. Usually, such volunteers had skills or services to offer to the unit, such as providing intelligence on the Germans, guiding lost soldiers, or giving first aid to the wounded. Allowing them to join was usually a spontaneous decision by the regiment commander. Once the manpower crises had been overcome in 1944 and it was clear that the USSR would win the war, the state stopped mobilizing women.

Perhaps one of the clearest indications that gender equality had not truly permeated Soviet society was that there was no public stigma attached to women's not serving. In contrast to the mobilization of men, the state neither created a public campaign to convince women to serve nor used peer pressure to compel women to join the armed forces. Only within the Komsomol did a certain level of institutional and peer expectations exist, and then only after the state instituted recruitment quotas. In contrast to its recruitment of men, the regime did not take women from Gulag labor and prison camps or special settlements.

The army's assignment policy, following the law on military service, which decreed that women be used as support personnel, also reflected a traditional male outlook. The army assigned 177,065, the vast majority of conscripted women, to the antiaircraft defense service (PVO); 41,224 to the medical services; 41,886 to the signals service; 14,460 to military instruction institutions; 18,785 to transportation units; 28,500 as cooks; 7,500 as railway guards; 70,458 to the Moscow regional defense administration; and 29,259 to administrative duties at various organizations in the Red Army.[8] The Red Air Force was given 40,209 female conscripts, and the Red Navy 20,889.[9]

The women serving in the PVO worked mostly as ground crews, searchlight operators, observers, radio operators, and *politruki*. The British and Germans had formal policies that kept women out of "trigger-pulling" assignments in antiaircraft units, but the Red Army's intention to keep women from such jobs was apparently only informal.[10] The British and Germans succeeded; the Red Army did not. Hundreds of women insisted on becoming gunners. Some women even managed to convince their regiment commanders to form all-female batteries in which all the officers, NCOs, and gunners were women.[11] The NKO allowed it but never set out a policy to create such units.

Women dominated the signals service at the division level and higher. For example, the signals staff of the 62nd Army at Stalingrad was made up entirely of women. They, along with the men, served under artillery and mortar fire as well as aerial bombardment. The army assigned many of the 10,000 Komsomolkas drafted in early 1942 to all-female signals battalions.[12]

Beginning in 1942 the Red Army formally allowed women to serve in male units as frontline combat soldiers. At that time, the army allowed women who were already in the army and had previously petitioned for combat duty to transfer from the rear to the front. The NKO announced this decision in March, following the devastating losses of the winter offensive, which had pushed the Germans back from Moscow. The offensive bled the Red Army but failed to destroy German Army Group Center as planned. In July of that year, as the German summer offensive captured tens of thousands of Red Army soldiers and killed and wounded hundreds of thousands more, the GKO ordered the Commissariat of Defense to reorganize the logistical services to free 400,000 soldiers—specifically, women and previously wounded soldiers—to transfer to duty in the war zone.[13]

Why did the Stalinist state let women into combat at all? The manpower shortage is not a sufficient explanation. There was no need to put women on the firing line because by assigning a woman to a support job held by a man, that man would be freed up for the front. The U.S., British, and German armies also faced manpower challenges and used women in uniform on a volunteer basis but never assigned them to the front lines.[14] These armies had no ideological influences to push them to use women; however, the Red Army did. Therefore, we have to consider socialist ideology, this time assessing its effect on men and their decision making.

Socialist ideology supported allowing women in combat, just as it supported their motivation to volunteer for military service; the historical precedent of more than a hundred years of Russian and Soviet women fighting successfully made it feasible. Some women had an intrinsic desire to fight and relentlessly pressed their case in military and political circles. Yet, despite years of rhetoric about sexual equality, and in contrast to the progressive thinking of the Provisional Government, there was deep reluctance within Soviet society, the Red Army, the Soviet government, and the Communist Party to allow women into combat. The best analysis is that ideology and history caught up with the Russian male. Once women were required to serve as an obligation of citizenship, the regime was helpless to deny them the right to fight without being utterly hypocritical. Instead, the regime sought to channel women's patriotic ardor into noncombat roles, or at least nonoffensive roles, and it refused to create true combat units composed of females like the Battalions of Death of World War I.

Still, despite communist ideology, the army leadership clearly exhibited a gendered response to women's service. It sought to employ them primarily in traditionally female roles or to assign them noncombat tasks. Every woman who found herself on the firing line in a job that required her to kill men got there by her own devices and in defiance of the military hierarchy's general intent to use women in "safe" assignments. Frontline medic was a notable exception to these "safe" assignments, but it fell within the framework of the stereotypical women's role of healer and nurturer. In the end, the majority of women who ended up in uniform served in noncombat and traditionally female roles, such as cooks, laundresses, and medical personnel. Even those in combat organizations nearly always held support jobs such as radio operators, drivers, and clerks. So far, no evidence has surfaced to indicate that any woman who did not want to fight or to kill was required to do so.

The male military hierarchy, once it decided to allow large numbers of women to serve, proved to be very willing to accommodate women's assumed reluctance to kill. In the *voenkomaty,* where people interacted face-to-face, it was a tough decision for men to allow women to take assignments that involved killing or that put them at risk of serious injury or death. After the war, Klara Goncharova was haunted by the memory of the recruiting officer who had tried to dissuade her from volunteering. "It was not easy for him to send naïve girls into the crucible of war. They did not know what awaited them: he, a regular officer, did. Feelings of guilt towards women because they, too, were involved in the fighting were shared by many men."[15]

In the end, the state failed to establish a policy on women in combat and allowed commanding officers of units to make on-the-spot decisions whether to allow women to take combat roles. Essentially, women were allowed to engage in ground combat on an individual, case-by-case basis. Thus, for the most part, women had to take the initiative and push their way to the front lines to fight with rifle in hand. The timing of the decision to let women fight is hardly coincidental. The manpower losses of the 1941–1942 winter offensive and the Germans' successful summer 1942 offensive caused a crisis that may have led to the army's willingness to greatly expand the participation of women at the front.

The army did not train women for combat. It left that to *Vsevobuch*, which claims to have trained 222,053 women in combat specialties, including the use of mortars, light and heavy machine guns, and submachine guns, as well as in general marksmanship and sniper training. This number included 11,061 traffic controllers and 49,509 signals personnel, which are not normally considered combat personnel.[16] Tens of thousands of Komsomolets and Komsomolkas participated in *Vsevobuch* training on instructions from the VLKSM as a way of showing institutional support for the war, but we cannot presume an individual readiness to fight in all cases. Exactly how many Komsomolkas eventually made it into combat is unknown.[17]

A large number of women received training in basic rifle marksmanship, but few chose to become infantry soldiers. Rather, the Red Army wanted them trained to handle weapons for self-defense—an acknowledgment that a great number of positions that were considered noncombat still put women in harm's way. Additionally, basic military training is an important step in indoctrination that gives support personnel—male and female alike—the feeling of being a soldier. When support personnel have an appreciation of the tasks and the hard life of the infantry, it is hoped that they will be more conscientious in serving the soldiers at the front.

The Red Army and Komsomol provided special training, not available through *Vsevobuch*, to individual women who wanted to become snipers, tank gunners, drivers, mechanics, radio operators, and officers. Once a woman finished her combat training, she had to petition to be assigned to the front and find a unit willing to accept her.

The army did create two all-female ground force units—the 1st Separate Women's Reserve Rifle Regiment and 1st Separate Volunteer Women's Rifle Brigade. The Reserve Rifle Regiment was an instructional unit that primarily trained women seeking leadership positions. This regiment alone was credited with training 5,175 soldiers and sergeants for frontline duties. Women were also trained for leadership positions in regular army schools, such as the Voroshilov Riazan infantry school.[18]

In February 1943 the GKO authorized the formation of the Volunteer Women's Rifle Brigade, the first of fifty proposed women's rifle brigades to assume guard duties in rear areas and release men for the front. The GKO envisioned recruiting up to 162,000 women for these brigades.[19] It is not clear whether the Red Army deliberately misrepresented the brigade's mission as one of frontline combat to attract volunteers. Its structure and armament made it look like a combat-oriented tactical force, as did its training regimen. Perhaps at its inception, there were some who considered it feasible to employ this and other women's brigades in the front lines.

Why the other projected forty-nine brigades were never formed is unknown; however, we can speculate. First, the initial call for women did not yield the expected outpouring of volunteers. It barely attracted the minimum number necessary to form the first brigade, and even then, the VLKSM had to do some arm-twisting and lower its standards. Nearly 400 of the women recruited by Komsomol boards were in ill health or pregnant, causing the army to discharge them later.[20] In fact, despite two and a half decades of socialism, the number of women who volunteered for this all-female brigade was little more than the number who had volunteered for the various women's Battalions of Death in World War I. Second, the pool of women available for service was not bottomless. Millions of women performed work that was vital to maintaining war industries and agricultural production. In addition, millions of these working women had to care for children whose fathers were away at war.

The VLKSM handled recruitment for the Volunteer Rifle Brigade, and it attracted the usual cohort of young, urban, educated Russians. The brigade was authorized at over 9,000 women but fell shy of achieving that number by nearly 2,000. More than 1,000 women already serving at the front in male units volunteered for the brigade, but they were sorely disappointed by the unit's failure to be posted to the front lines. Some of them, once they understood that the brigade was destined for only guard duties, deserted and joined combat units at the front.

Another disappointment was that the majority of officers turned out to be men, and not very good ones. Sexual harassment and exploitation were rampant.[21] The selection process for male officers has not been examined, but it is possible that some commanders used the opportunity of manning the women's brigade to rid themselves of their less desirable subordinates.

When the brigade's training was complete in January 1944, it was transferred from the army to the NKVD, which was responsible for rear-area security. The brigade performed guard duty until July 1944, when it was disbanded without explanation. The details of the women's reassignment are still unknown. The short life of the brigade and the scrapping of plans for more of them indicate some level of conflict in the GKO and NKO over the role of female ground formations. One can only conclude that neither ideology nor need was pressing enough to overcome male reluctance to employ all-female units in ground combat. Furthermore, in contrast to the Battalions of Death in World War I, popular pressure to create and employ them was, as far as we know, wholly lacking.

Sniping was the single major exception to the Red Army's reluctance to use women to kill. Women were not only allowed but also encouraged to volunteer for this task of coolly and calculatingly killing men. Why this killing role was accepted but not others has yet to be explained. There were no tactical sniper units per se, but snipers were sometimes assigned to divisions as platoons. Divisions then assigned snipers to infantry regiments, where they were paired for combat. Women began volunteering to serve as snipers in the summer of 1941. Most were turned away and redirected to the medical service, but some managed to convince army units to accept them. Others who had been turned away and became medics eventually persuaded regiment commanders to let them snipe. Finally, reacting to pressure from below, the VLKSM Central Committee, with the permission of the NKO, created the Central Women's School for Snipers in May 1943. In two years the school graduated 1,468 women; of these, 1,061 became snipers and 407 served as sniper instructors. Other military sources trained an additional 1,000 women to be snipers or instructors. In total, nearly 2,500 women successfully completed sniper training.[22]

There were three exceptional cases of all-female air combat organizations created by the NKO: the 586th Fighter Regiment, 587th Day Bomber Regiment, and 588th Night Bomber Regiment. These units were formed after intense lobbying by prominent female aviators. Stalin personally made the final decision to allow their creation. Why he did so has yet to be explained; however, it cannot be ruled out that his decision was informed by knowledge of the Battalions of Death of 1917.

The 586th and 587th Regiments were not strictly all female; a small number of men served in these organizations as officers, ground crew, and later as commanders after the death of one regiment commander and the reassignment of the other. The fighter regiment was assigned to the PVO and therefore operated behind the front lines to intercept German aircraft intent on bombing the Soviet rear area. It was not allowed to foray forward of the lines to look for Germans to shoot down. The bomber units, however, were used offensively against enemy targets. Not all female aviators served in these three regiments. Some chose to serve in otherwise all-male squadrons, where their assignments involved flying fighter and bomber aircraft behind German lines.[23]

Women's War Experience

The important questions related to women's experience of war are as follows: Was it qualitatively different from men's? What were the general patterns of female-male relations? What do they tell us about the state of gender equality in the USSR more than twenty years after the Bolshevik Revolution?

The idea that "we were raised to do everything together" may have heightened some women's expectations of military service; however, many of the men with whom they were to "do everything together" had not arrived at the same conclusion when it came to accepting women in traditionally male roles in war. Just because the leaders of the regime accepted the idea of women in the ranks and at the front did not mean that the ordinary Soviet male soldier had done so. In fact, the same kind of male resistance to women working on the shop floor arose toward their service in the ranks. This should come as no surprise, because many soldiers had joined the army straight from the factories. Some men did not want women to serve in the army at all; others just objected to women serving in combat or under difficult circumstances. Even before the German invasion, for example, Colonel Raevskii exhibited a fairly common sense of paternalism when he protested that women nurses in field hospitals had to endure the exceedingly harsh winter conditions that prevailed during the Winter War.[24]

Firsthand accounts illustrate how women were received in the ranks and how they interacted with male soldiers. In contrast to the official ideology of female equality, their treatment ran the gamut from good to bad. The most obvious negative reaction by men was sexist resentment and indignation at women performing traditional male roles; condescending, patronizing, and paternalistic attitudes also abounded.[25] Maria Kaliberda expressed her frustration: "We wanted to be equal—we didn't want the men saying 'Oh, those women!' about us. And we tried harder than the men. Apart from everything else we had to prove that we were as good as them. For a long time we had to put up with a very patronizing, superior attitude."[26]

Natalia Peshkova experienced condescending and biased treatment at the hands of her battalion commander from the moment they met. She explained: "You can understand him, even though he used to be a math teacher and not a career officer, he had been fighting for some time already and knew what it was all about, and they sent him a girl, and to such a post! Komsorg—that was the number three person in the battalion. He immediately said to my face: 'Don't expect any advantages or indulgences.'"[27] She felt deeply insulted that he thought she would demand special treatment, and she never developed a good relationship with him.

It was not uncommon for regiment and battalion commanders to refuse to accept women for combat assignments. An engineering battalion commander who refused to accept women into his unit recollected: "When some idiot from the personnel department sent me two girls as platoon commanders, I immediately told them to go back, although they were terribly offended. They wanted to go to the front line as engineering platoon commanders and clear minefields." He continued, justifying his actions:

> In the first place, I had enough fine sergeants who could do what those girls had been sent for; secondly, I knew the girls very well; they were my fellow-students at the architectural college where I had studied. I considered it unnecessary for women to go to the front line. There were enough of us men for that. And I also knew their presence would cause no end of trouble with my men who had their hands full as it was. It would've been necessary to dig a separate dugout for them and, besides, for them to be giving orders would have involved a lot of problems, because they were girls.[28]

This officer, a generational peer of the women assigned to his unit, exhibited many of the traits of the prerevolutionary generation of men.

He was unmoved by his generation's experience of men and women "doing everything together." Not wanting to dig extra dugouts and fearing that his men would be distracted by sexual desire were practical excuses for rejecting the women, but his discomfort with women giving orders was the product of a traditional society that stubbornly persists to this day in Russia.

Just as in the First World War, women faced hostile men who thought they did not belong in the army; however, those who proved themselves adept at their duties often changed the attitudes of their male counterparts.[29] Sergei Abaulin remembered that his artillery battalion was required to conduct many fifty- to sixty-kilometer marches in a twenty-four-hour period so that it would be in position to provide fire for the next engagement. He recalled that the infantry was exhausted to the limit, but "for us artillerymen, it was necessary to roll, carry, and drag our not-so-light guns by hand too, but nobody grumbled or whined. Among us soldiers were many women, who also courageously transcended all the adversity as well."[30]

Vasily Grossman interviewed a field nurse after a vicious battle that had cost the lives of many soldiers as well as the medics who aided them. She told him: "In reserve, we didn't get on well with the soldiers. We checked them for lice and quarreled with them all the time. And now the soldiers are saying: We are very grateful to our girls." In this case, the women's performance under fire profoundly affected the men's attitudes toward them, but this nurse began to feel superior to the soldiers. She recounted how the women went into the attack alongside the men, crawled with them, fed them, gave them water, and bandaged them under fire. She concluded, "We turned out to be more resilient than the soldiers, we even used to urge them on." Yet they were neither fearless nor superwomen. She admitted, "Sometimes, trembling at night, we would think: 'Oh, if I were at home right now.'"[31]

A particular difference between women who served in the Great Patriotic War and those who served in World War I was that in the earlier war, women who served in male units abandoned their femininity. According to Stoff, the women who sought to serve in male units in disguise "almost completely abandoned those behaviors that defined their femininity and surrendered their traditional roles without challenging the social order."[32] In terms of femininity, there was some variation among the several female death battalions. Maria Bochkareva ordered the women in her battalion to cut their hair so they would look like male soldiers and encouraged them to act like men by swearing and smoking. The women in other battalions chose not to follow this example.[33] During World War II, because of the official ideology of equality and because the regime required them to serve, women did not feel the need to deny their femininity, whether they served in male units or all-female units. They usually put soldiering first, but not at the expense of expressing their female identity.

Women were very conscious of themselves as female in what most of them considered a man's world. Sergeant Maria Shchelokova, who served in a signals detachment, remembered that her commander was very handsome and that all the girls were a little bit in love with him. He attempted to downplay their gender, telling them that they were soldiers and nothing more. In her thoughts, she protested: "A soldier was needed. . . . But I wanted to be pretty as well. . . . All through the war I was afraid of being hit in the legs and left a cripple. I had pretty legs."[34]

Private Nonna Smirnova, an antiaircraft gunner, recalled how the women in her unit satisfied their need to feel like women: "We tried to make our uniforms fit well, often washing and ironing them: we wanted to look neat. For the most part we did that at night, while during the day we were taught to crawl on our stomachs, to dig ourselves in and so on. We dried our underwear at night only, we should have been embarrassed to hang things up during the day with the men about, and anyway the sergeant scolded us."[35]

Attempting to retain a semblance of modesty, decorum, and cleanliness sometimes created lighter moments during the war. Mariana Miliutina, an army doctor serving in a field hospital, remembered that they had a special soap to kill the lice that proliferated in the field, and it smelled like kerosene.

One time we got acquainted with the commander and zampolit of a field hospital close to ours, and invited them to [visit] us. I tell my girlfriend: "My head burns." She looked at it, found lice. She said: "Mine also feels wrong." We lathered this soap on our heads, put on kerchiefs, and sat there waiting for our cavaliers. She asked: "Mariana, what if they start crawling out from under the kerchief?" I said: "No, they must drop dead in there." The guys came, asked "Wow, there's a strange smell here. What is it?" We go: "Oh, yes? We don't smell anything!" Oh man, it's funny and it's sad![36]

Not so funny was the army's initial disregard for women's gender-specific needs. More proof that the army never intended to rely on women in wartime, despite the change in service laws, was the absence of uniforms specially tailored for women. Women were simply issued men's uniforms, which did not fit their smaller frames. They were also issued men's boots, which were usually too big and resulted in blisters and sore feet. The army did not issue women undergarments of any kind, so they had to make or procure bras and underwear themselves. Later in the war, special women's tunics and skirts were manufactured. Hygiene was a particular issue for women, which the army was reluctant to address and many commanders refused to acknowledge. Urogenital inflammation was a problem because of a lack of proper supplies, such as soap and cotton batting, and a lack of private spaces for women to attend to their hygiene needs.[37] Not until April 1943 did the army increase the ration of soap for female soldiers to 100 grams per month.[38] Whether they actually got their soap depended on the vagaries of the logistics system.

As soldiers, women's reaction to combat and the stress of war was largely the same as men's. Reina Pennington sees no gender difference in reactions to killing and states, "There was no 'woman's' reaction to killing." However, like men, "women's reaction to killing varied widely, depending on the role they filled and their personality."[39] Nurse Nina Erdman's memory of a German pilot dying in her care speaks volumes about women's ability to be callous in the presence of death, and perhaps their ability to be affected by propaganda and patriotism, too.

At the very beginning, in '41, we shot down a plane. The pilot was wounded and was taken prisoner. He was truly like we had imagined them. Redheaded, healthy, and very tall. He was wounded in his bladder and had to have an operation. We had a remarkable female surgeon. When she came in, he announced: "I don't want a woman to operate on me!" We removed him from the table; we had no other surgeon. What the hell? We should have killed him. They always showed off and wanted some kind of rights here. We tied the

German firmly to the bed. Nevertheless, all night he struggled and cursed. Thank God, he died toward morning.[40]

Antonina Kotliarova, a sniper, called killing "horrible." Yet, as her interview went on, she conveyed a very businesslike attitude toward her task.

> Olga and I lay at arm's length from each other. We spoke quietly because the Germans would be there not far in front of us. They were listening to everything. We tried not to move, to say something quietly, find a target. Everything would grow so numb! For example, I would say: "Ol'a, mine." She would already know—she wouldn't kill that one. After the shot I would only help her observe. I would say, for example, "There, behind that house, behind that bush," and she would already know where to look. We took turns shooting.[41]

She told of another instance, toward the end of the war, when she showed mercy to a German boy-soldier while combing a forest. "He was such a runt, and I had a younger brother, about [the] same as him. I was sorry for him—didn't kill him, and didn't take him prisoner, even though I was supposed to do that. I don't know, maybe someone killed or captured him later, but I didn't touch him." Her kindness and mercy had their limits, however, and were affected by emotion.

> There was another case when we were liberating Deutch-Krony. . . . That town was located in a forest. So, we supposedly liberated it. Took many prisoners and moved on. Suddenly, someone came up from behind and told us, "The city is occupied by the Germans again." We had dispersed them, but they had re-entered the town from the forest. We had to capture it for the second time. But we didn't spare anyone anymore—we were so angry. We killed many there, very many. War is war. There was such business.[42]

When asked how she felt about the Germans, she replied, "Oh, we hated them."

Like men, women had to deal with fear. Olga Omelchenko conveyed the horror she experienced at the battle of Kursk in 1943: "The fighting was very heavy. I saw hand-to-hand fighting. . . . That was awful. A person becomes something . . . it isn't for human beings. . . . Men strike, thrust their bayonets into stomachs, eyes, strangle one another. Howling, shots, groans. . . . It's something terrible even for war, it's more terrible than anything else."[43] Vera Malakhova, who was wounded in an air attack in 1942, remembered: "It was terrifying—I never hid my fright—I was absolutely terrified of the bombings. It was awful!"[44] In contrast to men, women were more likely to admit their fear and not be ashamed of it. Although no one wanted to be thought a coward, there was no code of machismo among women to bolster their courage or help them suppress their fear; however, women's primary groups certainly offered support and exerted social pressure to hold themselves together.

Grossman's notes of his interview with junior nurse Lelia Nikova during the battle of Stalingrad are powerful reading. "Galia Titova's friends told me that once when she was bandaging someone, there was heavy firing, the soldier was killed, and she was wounded. She stood up straight and said: 'Goodbye, girls.'" She fell, mortally wounded. Some women cracked under the pressure, and those who persevered had to do so with the death of their friends weighing on their hearts. Nikova sadly recounted: "There are just three of us left, out of eighteen girls. . . . After the first battle, we lost two girls. We saw the corporal who said that Tonia had died in his arms." Two days later, after the battle had ended, they went out to recover Tonia Egorova's body. Nikova told Grossman: "When we finally got there, we found her lying in the trench. We dressed her, put a handkerchief there, covered her face with a blouse. We were crying. There was myself, Galia Kanysheva and Klava Vasileva. They are both dead now."[45]

Among the female draftees, 94,662, or about 19 percent, died. Some 42,627 were killed in action, 10,491 died of wounds in aid stations or hospitals, 5,960 died of disease or illness, and 3,501 died in prisoner of war camps. Another 32,083 went forever missing in action.[46] Nonlethal losses from wounds, injuries, and illnesses have not been separately calculated for women. Losses of female volunteers have not been calculated either, but, because most women who made it into the firing lines were volunteers, it stands to reason that their losses equaled or exceeded those of the draftees.

Good leadership in moments of crisis helped women overcome their fear and perform their duties, just as it did men. Field hospital nurse Nina Erdman recalled: "There was this doctor, Klikov, and he tried to support us by saying, 'Girls, keep in mind that no bomb will strike me. Stick close to me and don't be afraid.' And indeed, when he was nearby, we weren't afraid of anything."[47]

Women could act as courageously as men, and sometimes more so. Ninety-five women earned the USSR's highest medal for valor, the gold star of the Hero of the Soviet Union. Several nurses and medics who died trying to save men were awarded theirs posthumously. Maria Kukharskaia, a medic, treated 421 wounded men, 277 under fire. For this, the Red Army gave her the Order of Lenin; in the decades after the war, she and fifteen other medics were awarded the Florence Nightingale Medal for their heroic, compassionate service.[48] Among veterans, there are stories of women who were braver than men—women who would run or crawl under fire to rescue soldiers in no-man's-land when their male counterparts refused to do so. Many other female medics, nurses, signalers, and other military personnel died at the front without achieving hero status. Some were as young as fourteen years old when they enlisted.[49]

Even though 70,647 women served capably as officers and 113,990 as NCOs, few were allowed to command men or were promoted to high ranks. One reason was that not many women had been in the armed forces long enough to achieve a high rank.[50] One of the few to rise to the rank of lieutenant colonel was E. S. Kostrikova, daughter of Sergei Kirov, assassinated Politburo member and party boss of Leningrad. She commanded a tank detachment. It was not so unusual, however, to find women commanding mostly female signal companies and battalions and PVO batteries and battalions. Others commanded air squadrons and even regiments. Women also served in GlavPUR as *politruki*, Komsorgs, and even battalion commissars.[51]

Male-Female Social and Sexual Relations

Despite sporadic and unofficial admonishment from on high, romantic relationships abounded, which could complicate individual, small-unit, and even large-unit military performance. The Red Army never established a fraternization policy to govern sexual and social relations between soldiers or between officers and subordinates. Because of this, a wide range of behaviors was exhibited—some healthy, some unhealthy. When women served together (and could form primary groups) and had a feminist consciousness, their interactions with male soldiers tended to be healthier. However, when women served in small numbers or as isolated individuals, they were often sexually exploited by their male superiors.

It became commonplace for commanders—both single and married—to take what was colloquially and disparagingly termed a "marching field wife," usually referred to by the Russian acronym PPZh. Nikolai Chistiakov was asked, "In the active army did all the leaders have PPZh?" He answered:

> It seemed so to me. Commanders of platoons did not have PPZh. We slept together with soldiers in one dugout. There were female medics in all the companies. But the company had a separate dugout for the medics. From company commanders on up to the higher ranks, they all had PPZh. Mostly at the battalion level. In the regiment there was one such, Katia. She was a healthy peasant gal. First she would be with the regiment commander, then the chief of staff. She would be summoned on orders, and never went to the front. That's a PPZh.[52]

Marshal Zhukov, the highest-ranking officer in the Red Army, had a PPZh in the person of Senior Lieutenant Lidia Zakharova, whom he assigned as his personal physician. Soldiers assumed that all the top leaders had PPZh. Among commanders there existed a pervasive mentality that they had a right to them. Some resorted to coercion to get the women they wanted, and there were even rumors of officers creating harems. It was not unusual for the senior officers of a unit to quarrel or fall out over these women. The NKO had no formal procedures to prosecute men for sexual harassment, so women were basically helpless. Grossman felt compelled to write during the war that "the PPZh is our great sin."[53]

In his memoirs, Gabriel Temkin notes that the regiment commander could have his choice of women. "I remember one such girl, she was a telephone operator, skinny, looking unhappy, and sloppily dressed. As the colonel's PPZh, she blossomed, had a smile on her face, and in a very

Female traffic controller. Note the reaction of the soldiers in the trucks.

short time became pregnant and was sent home."[54] According to Semion Aria, a tank sergeant, there were never any women in his tank company, but there were women at the battalion or brigade level: "Only some signaler girls appeared, [and] eventually officers married them. When later there was a reunion of the regiment's veterans in Moscow, I saw these old signalers, who came as our regiment's officers' wives of many years. Back then I had thought they were simply whores, but it turned out these relationships lasted for the rest of their lives."[55]

In the memoir literature and oral histories, stories abound of front-line officers at the company level and higher being unavailable to lead their units at critical moments because they were with their PPZh. In one case, Marshal Zhukov decided that one of his subordinate generals was unable to fulfill his professional duties because of the inordinate amount of time he spent giving amorous attention to his mistress. Zhukov sent this general's superior the following message in February 1945:

> I have reports . . . that Comrade Katukov is completely idle, that he is not directing the army, that he is sitting around at home with some

woman, and that the female he is living with is impeding his work. Katukov . . . apparently never visits his units. He does not organize the operations of the corps and army, which is why the army had been unsuccessful recently. I demand . . . that the woman immediately be sent away from Katukov. If that is not done, I shall order her to be removed by the organs of *Smersh*. Katukov is to get on with his work. If [he] does not draw the necessary conclusions, he will be replaced by another commander.[56]

Clearly, Zhukov was not condemning the practice of officers having PPZh; he objected to this situation only because the man was letting it interfere with his duties. Zhukov's and the high command's failure to institute formal guidelines for proper male-female relations speaks negatively of the male attitude toward women. It indicates a desire to be able to exploit such women, unencumbered by regulations, and it reinforces doubts that men had accepted women as their equals in Soviet society.

Women's reaction to their peers being PPZh was mixed. Vera Malakhova, an army doctor, said: "Well, it seems to me a few even flaunted it. We didn't like them. We were upright, we behaved honorably, we didn't like the PPZh." Malakhova resented women who received special privileges for their "services," such as being kept safe from the front, receiving better food, and having better living conditions. When everyone else had to walk, "wives" got to ride in vehicles with high-ranking officers. Malakhova also remembered with disdain the PPZh of her division commander, Batiuk. The woman was an excellent surgical nurse, but Batiuk would call her to be with him without regard for her work, which the other nurses would then have to do. Besides having sex with him, the nurse washed and ironed his uniforms. No one begrudged her this relationship because they thought she was in love, but when Batiuk was killed, this woman immediately attached herself to the head of the division's Special Section. Then her fellow nurses began to disdain her as a self-serving and promiscuous PPZh.[57]

Decades after the war, Galina Dokutovich, a navigator in one of the female night bomber regiments, still had hard feelings against the men who used their rank to commit sexual depredation. She remembered thinking at the time: "Everything around me is so disgusting. Even the best senior commanders are debauched scoundrels! The way that the best and worst characteristics can be combined in the same person is really terrible and absurd."[58]

Vera Malakhova experienced sexual harassment firsthand. One night the hospital commissar summoned her for a talk. As they sat together on his coat spread out on the ground, "He moved closer and closer; and suddenly—bang! He put his hand under my skirt. I jumped away and said: 'Ah, so that's the kind of conversation you had in mind!'" Angry and indignant, she wanted to slap him across the face but was intimidated by his superior rank. When he realized he was not going to have his way with her, he made a weak attempt to disguise his intent, saying, "I just wanted to test you." She characterized him as "simply disgusting." Later a regiment commander made a similar move on her.[59]

Officers used their rank and status to pressure women for sex, but soldiers could not. Overall, Malakhova thought sergeants and ordinary soldiers treated the women better. Surgeon Vera Shevaldysheva agreed that "[enlisted] men were ennobled by the presence of women. Wherever you appeared their faces would brighten. For example, if they learned that a girl orderly was going to make a medical inspection they would try to clean up their clothes and tidy up their dug-outs."[60] There is virtually no discussion of rape in Soviet primary or secondary sources. It seems implausible that it did not occur, but on what scale and whether it was officially or only informally covered up are impossible to know.

Proximity to the front, where women shared the same danger as men, sometimes made no difference in their treatment. Malakhova saw a case of sexual harassment during the battle of Stalingrad. The women of her medical battalion were bathing in a big dugout using washbasins when a medical company commander got some grenades, threw them around, and shouted, "Air raid!" The girls came running out naked and jumped into the trenches while he watched and laughed. They reported him to higher authorities, and the division commissar insisted that he be sentenced to a term in a penal battalion.[61]

Women were fortunate indeed if they had a commander who would defend their honor. Bella Epshtein remembered that when she and another woman arrived at the Second Belorussian Front, the personnel officer intended to assign them to work as clerks at a division headquarters. When they protested, he asked, "You are women . . . why should you go to the front line?" Epshtein retorted, "No, we are snipers, send us where we are supposed to go." The personnel officer reconsidered and declared, "We'll send you to one regiment, the colonel's a good man, he looks after girls." Epshtein was made to understand that commanders were not all the same, noting, "that was made quite clear."[62]

Just because a woman was in a relationship with a man, of whatever rank, did not mean she was a PPZh or the victim of some sort of pressure. Private Nonna Smirnova fondly reminisced: "We were young, of course, and we wanted to love and be loved. A woman can't do without being noticed. But love was, so to speak, forbidden (if command found out, one of the lovers was, as a rule, transferred to another unit) and we protected and preserved it as something sacred, elevated."[63] An obvious double standard existed, whereby officers believed they had a right to women, but enlisted personnel did not. This certainly did not endear the leaders to their men.

Pregnancy was an ever-present possibility, which normally meant discharge and being sent home without disciplinary action. Women could use this to their advantage, if they chose. For some unknown reason, the army did not send women home until they were seven months pregnant. Lieutenant Aleksandr Bodnar' recalled the following episode from his journey on a medical evacuation train:

And when they loaded us up, we started off; I heard them start to sing songs in the next wagon. I asked an old soldier, "What is that?" "Oh, it's the girls that loaded us up." — "And why are they going to Moscow?" "To give birth." "What do you mean to give birth?" "Well, in October, when they took every one of them away, the mothers said, 'Go and quickly get pregnant and return home.'" And so that's how it worked out. That's the law of life, and I don't condemn them.[64]

Some women who unintentionally became pregnant and did not want to let their friends down by being sent home resorted to abortion. A male army doctor claimed that in his field hospital in the first year of the war, practically every nurse he knew had two or three abortions, although they were strictly forbidden. The doctors who helped them kept the obstetrical instruments hidden from the OO and commissars.[65]

Women's Contribution to Military Effectiveness

In the big picture of women's military effectiveness in the Red Army, the two focal issues are quantity and quality. With regard to quantity, the indisputable fact is that every woman serving at the front fulfilled a role that otherwise would have required a man. Every woman in uniform in the rear area represented an additional man at the front. In the initial wave of voluntarism in 1941, 200,000 women stepped forward for the *opolchenie* or were conscripted by the Red Army. The call-up of women in 1942 and 1943 released about 300,000 men from other duties to go to the front, as did the call-up of 1944.[66] It does not take much of an imagination to see how much less effective the army would have been in those years without the women.

In terms of quality, without a doubt, Soviet women made effective soldiers. This should come as no surprise, given that the regime recruited most of them from the ideal demographic of Soviet society. They were primarily Russian, urban, young, educated, from the industrial workforce or universities and institutes, and Komsomol members. Those who found themselves under fire were there by choice, and they bore that burden well. Statistics on disciplinary problems and desertion are few, but the example of the women's rifle brigade suggests that women were less prone to both than men were. There is precious little evidence of women failing to do their duty. Such failures may have been covered up for political reasons, but it is more likely that the selection process for women, being more rigorous than for men, resulted in more reliable and stable recruits, most of whom served in noncombat jobs. Those women who did serve in combat were all volunteers, and this process of self-selection resulted in more dedicated and determined people—quite the opposite from the situation with the men.

Another reason women performed well is that so many worked in traditionally female tasks. As historian Svetlana Aleksievich notes, these many unheralded tasks, demeaned as "women's work," were critical to the overall effectiveness of the Red Army. She aptly asserts, "War is not just shooting, bombing, hand-to-hand fighting, digging trenches— clothes are washed, porridge is cooked and bread baked as well. If a soldier is to fight well, he must be clothed, shod, fed, his clothes have to be washed. Otherwise he will be a bad soldier." She astutely observes, "As the army advanced it was followed by a 'second front'—laundresses, bakers, cooks."[67] Thus, women's service in the Red Army and their contribution to the final victory took a variety of forms, few of them glamorous, and all involving varying degrees of hardship and suffering.

In an earlier work on Soviet women in the war, Griesse and Stites ask the question, "Did women help win the war for Russia?" They answer it by writing:

> Women's role in the armed forces is a variable that cannot be detached and measured in terms of its effectiveness in the total picture any more than the performance of all junior officers, all artillerymen, all Ukrainians, or all imported American vehicles could be assessed in the overall war effort. The evidence assembled here should be sufficient to convince anyone that [Soviet] women played an important role in World War II, far in excess of all of the belligerent nations. And that is all that can be said with assurance.[68]

This is too modest an assessment. Women, by their sheer numbers and demonstrated competence, were a *vital* part of Soviet success in the war. Of course, there is no way to determine whose role was most vital, nor should one try; however, no one can deny that without those 800,000 women—the equivalent of about eighty rifle and tank divisions—the Soviet war effort would have been seriously compromised.

Furthermore, we can say that, in general, the wartime experience was harder for women than for men. The expectation that they would perform at the same level as men meant that it was physically harder for them. Because of their nature and upbringing, it was psychologically and emotionally harder for most women to be in proximity to death and killing. Above all, the sexual demands made on many women created psychoemotional stress and sometimes led to a state of social isolation, which compounded the hardships of service. This, men did not have to suffer.

Conclusion

Five major conclusions can be drawn from this rather brief foray into perspectives on the Soviet soldier's military effectiveness and popular attitudes about service in the Great Patriotic War. First, the Red Army was at all times militarily effective, if inconsistent in degree, even though it simultaneously fought quite inefficiently. Second, morale and motivation fluctuated dramatically during the war, varying by circumstance, nationality, and social group. Third, the state and Stalinism did not always figure prominently in people's decision to fight or not. Instead, a wide variety of factors based largely on personal circumstances played the greatest role in voluntarism or compliance with conscription. Fourth, although the state was determined to enforce compliance, its ability to do so was limited, and people's willingness to challenge it directly through draft evasion and desertion was fairly persistent and widespread. People's willingness to risk the consequences of resistance, however, was based primarily on a weighing of the lethality of the battlefield against the lethality of the state. Thus, coercion was a far less important factor in maintaining effectiveness than it has been made out to be. Fifth and finally, Soviet patriotism was real, but it did not equate directly with support for the Stalinist system. Fighting for the *rodina* meant different things to different people; however, wartime letters and postwar and post-Soviet interviews provide stable and similar accounts of why people responded to the war as they did, with a fairly narrow range of meanings attached to patriotism.

The main schools of the historiography of the war lie at the extremes: they maintain that people either rejected Stalinism or actively supported it. My analysis does not propose a meet-in-the-middle compromise. There are indeed hundreds of thousands of cases that support each of the two conflicting interpretations; however, there are millions more that fall at various points in between. There was a wide range of popular responses to the Nazi invasion, and although the state wielded tremendous coercive power, people exerted significant agency in determining their own fate. Ironically, the decisions of many to fight the Nazi invaders, which served the state's purposes, were often made with no reference to the state at all, or they were sometimes made with conscious hostility to the state. People adopted an astoundingly wide variety of reasons and rationalizations to justify serving or not. Personal or family circumstances, ideology, life experience, the immediate war situation, social factors, institutional factors, and many others, usually in combination, all affected people's thinking.

The power of the state was manifest in the penalties it imposed on the population for noncompliance, but the power of the people was evident in their attempt to avoid service or to escape the dangers of the front. Still unresolved is the issue of whether the early surrenders equated to a rejection of Stalinism or whether fighting the Germans and their allies meant support for Stalinism; however, it is clear that blanket statements one way or the other are untenable. It is well established that the Soviet people expected their participation in the war to result in a moderation of the Stalinist state's oppressive policies. Peasants expected an end to collectivization, and workers anticipated an end to strict labor discipline. Intellectuals expected more freedom of thought and expression. Party apparatchiks and government officials expected greater latitude in decision making at the lower levels. A sense that the state owed the people something pervaded popular attitudes, which shows that many people fought for a state they did not endorse in its current form.

Soviet patriotism was real but certainly not universal; it resonated most deeply among Russians and least among the non-Slavic ethnic and national minorities. For many, patriotism did not equate with support for the Stalinist system; instead, it was an elemental urge to defend what they understood to be their homeland, sometimes coincidental with the socialist ideals inherent in the revolution and professed by the Communist Party and Stalin. The state, for the most part, failed to generate patriotism; rather, it took advantage of inherent or latent patriotic feelings and harnessed them. In non-Slavic and non-Russian areas of the USSR, where there was no inherent *russkii, rossiiskii,* or *Sovetskii* patriotism, the state not only failed to generate significant levels of voluntarism and struggled to enforce conscription but also faced outright resistance.

In the end, the Stalinist state succeeded in mobilizing, through inspiration and coercion, just enough of the population for military service to ensure its survival. The numbers are actually quite impressive, yet in the end, it was a rather close run to keep enough men in the field to get the job done. The armed forces began the war with nearly 5 million officers and men, and in the first week of September 1941, having already lost millions who were captured, killed, missing, and discharged due to wounds, it had a ration strength of 7.4 million service members.[1] People from all social classes and milieus, age cohorts, nationalities, and ethnicities, including both party members and nonparty citizens and both victims and beneficiaries of Stalinism, volunteered to serve or reported for conscription. Simultaneously, people in all the same categories rejected service; they refused to volunteer and evaded the draft. Still, mobilization, with all its flaws and obstacles, proved to be the bedrock of Soviet military effectiveness, and it provided the military with the essential element for eventual victory—the Soviet soldier.

The Red Army's effectiveness in the Great Patriotic War was foreshadowed by its performance in the Winter War. Although unappreciated at the time, rather than revealing *ineffectiveness*, the war with Finland showed the Red Army to be highly *inefficient* in its operations against a well-organized, well-trained, and determined foe. Reacting to this inefficiency, the military fell back on the methods of intimidation first adopted in the chaotic days of its founding during the civil war— shooting officers and commissars for cowardice. It also employed blocking detachments and combat penal (*strafnyi*) battalions, all of which would be used again in 1941. The examples of poor personnel administration, insufficient logistical planning and support, inept strategic and tactical planning, and underestimation of the enemy would all be repeated in the war with Germany, as would examples of resourceful and energetic means to overcome them.

During the Winter War, at all levels of assessment, the Red Army passed the test of military effectiveness, but not in equal measure. It proved to be most tenuous at the individual level; at the level from battalions to armies, effectiveness was much stronger, marked by organizational commitment to the task and a willingness to purge unfit officers from command. The highest level was clearly the most effective. The state and the Communist Party apparatus rallied to overcome weaknesses and problems, supported the military, and clearly indicated their intention to persevere until an acceptable outcome was achieved. Finally, to reiterate the most important lesson derived from the Winter War: the Red Army proved that despite catastrophic personnel and equipment losses and incompetent logistic and administrative personnel and leaders in the field, it could regroup and, with the support of the state, mobilize society and deliver victory on the battlefield.

There were numerous major differences in effectiveness between the Winter War and the Great Patriotic War. In the latter, the state undertook significant efforts to improve morale and motivation, including Stalin's speeches, propaganda posters, newspaper articles, and films. Defeatism, both military and civilian, did not exist in the fight with Finland, but it was a serious challenge to morale and motivation in the war with Germany. Unlike the war with Finland, the German invasion caused many to question the viability of the Stalinist system. The Winter War did not generate the inferiority complex that the war with Germany did, nor did it involve the issue of soldiers having family in occupied territory, which could tempt them to desert and go home or to fight fanatically for its liberation. The Winter War did not generate widescale and officially publicized coercion, such as Order Nos. 270 and 227. Finally, the Great Patriotic War saw the problematic mobilization of large numbers of minorities. All these issues indicate that the state confronted a much more difficult process as it strove to maintain effectiveness during the Great Patriotic War. The similarities of the Great Patriotic War to the Winter War, such as high casualties, supply problems, shortages of food and equipment, poor leadership, and questionable training, make it even more impressive that the Red Army did not disintegrate but held on to achieve complete and total victory.

In reconsidering the question of whether the capture of millions of Soviet soldiers by the Germans in 1941 and 1942 was the result of superior German generalship or anti-Stalinist sentiment among Red Army soldiers, it now seems clear that neither was the dominant causal factor. Instead, we have to consider that the loss of millions of Soviet soldiers to captivity and death in German POW camps was due to massive failures in the *efficiency* of the Soviet military, which then led to localized situational failures in *effectiveness*. At the strategic level, the Red Army lacked a coherent doctrine for dealing with encirclement and failed to recognize that breaking out was not always the best option. At the tactical level, the Red Army had not prepared its officers to lead their men out of encirclement. Consequently, a lack of training and cohesion, compounded by the leadership failures of unit commanders, left the common soldier and the junior officer with little or no guidance in battle. As a result, units often disintegrated, and it became every man for himself.

At the foxhole level, the factors affecting soldiers' decisions to fight or surrender in 1941 were different from those in 1939, and the strategic situation in the summer of 1941 was dissimilar from that in the winter of 1939–1940. The social and demographic basis of the army had changed markedly. The "repeasantization" of the army and the conscription of large numbers of non-Slavic men and recruits from recently annexed or conquered territories brought in large numbers of potentially disaffected soldiers and minorities with little or no attachment to the Russian concept of *rodina*. In contrast, the army that fought the Winter War in 1939 relied more on Russian workers and students, who were potentially more attached to the success of the socialist experiment.

The soldiers' perception of the strategic situation also played a role in whether they chose to fight, surrender, or escape and evade capture. Despite the highly visible tactical failures in the first months of the Winter War, on a strategic level, it was always certain that the USSR would defeat Finland; however, in the Great Patriotic War, success against the Axis and even national survival were in doubt for some time. In the Winter War, the continued existence of the USSR was never questioned, and the state's authority was as strong as ever, but in 1941 and 1942, soldiers could not be so sure. The soldiers recognized that they were up against a larger, better armed, and better equipped army in 1941 than they had been in 1939. This opened the door to individual thoughts of self-preservation, true allegiance, family and home, and personal well-being.

Ascribing motives and attitudes to the collective actions of encircled soldiers is methodologically challenging, to say the least. In general terms, there is little concrete evidence that politics motivated behavior. Many units or individuals were captured simply due to the fog of war, the failure of commanders, surprise, fatigue and physical collapse, and unpredictable battlefield conditions. Even Stalin's son Iakov was captured in the first few weeks of the war, much to his father's embarrassment. Most soldiers did fight, but without a doubt, some chose to quit. All the reasons why are still not clear. The intricacy of motive and situation casts a haze over any attempt by historians or military analysts to draw a precise chart of motive and causation in war in general, and especially in the case of the massively complex events of the summer and fall of 1941.

Despite those limits, looking back at that time can cast light on several aspects of the surrender debate. We are aware of the issues surrounding why men fought so hard against Finland, which posed no real danger, yet went into captivity en masse to the Nazis, who were a genuine threat to the existence of the USSR. Doctrinal and practical matters came into play, which were unrelated to ideology or social issues. It is unlikely that anything extraordinary happened between 12 March 1940 and 22 June 1941 to turn the soldiers against the regime. Besides the alteration in the social composition of the army, the most important change may have been the Red Army's increased commitment to the offensive in the coming war with Germany, at the expense of studying and training for defensive operations.

The Stalinist regime employed a variety of methods to motivate the soldiers and keep up their morale, including emotional and logical appeals by Stalin and the media to hate the enemy, defend the innocent, and kill without remorse. Once at the front, the majority of men and women found ways to convince themselves to do their duty and remain at their posts, even under the most brutal circumstances of war and primitive living conditions. The effort and resources the Soviet state poured into shoring up morale and motivation during the Great Patriotic War were unprecedented up to that point in its history. Just how important propaganda and agitation were to the eventual victory is impossible to determine, but there is no doubt that it was necessary. The doubt and resentment of vast numbers of Soviet citizens needed to be assuaged, deflected, or buried under an avalanche of pro-Soviet propaganda to keep them from giving up in hard times and to encourage them to continue risking their lives even when victory was certain. In the process, the Stalinist state astutely and successfully used the war to reinvent its image. It dropped its revolutionary rhetoric and attached itself to the legacy of historic Russia, thereby establishing a more durable legitimacy beyond that of the October Revolution. Nostalgic Russians continued to refer to it even after the collapse of the USSR.

The Soviet Union fought and won the Great Patriotic War with an army that continuously suffered from low morale and motivation problems. Despite the Red Army's best efforts to intimidate soldiers into compliance with the death penalty and to promote obedience through patriotic propaganda and pecuniary and symbolic rewards, the Soviet soldiers' commitment to the fight often wavered. To some extent, the disaffection and reluctance to fight resulted from opposition to Stalinist political, social, and economic policies, but most problems were directly related to soldiers' fear of death. They often felt they lacked a fighting chance to survive because of poor leadership, insufficient equipment and weaponry, and inadequate training. Low morale and lack of motivation manifested in self-preserving behaviors such as desertion, shirking, straggling, and self-inflicted wounds to avoid or escape combat. One of the few things we can say with certainty is that non-Russians were less motivated to serve and less apt to risk their lives in the service of the USSR, which a great many identified as an exploitative, repressive, hegemonic Russian invention. The bulk of the credit for holding the army together belongs not to the party or the state but to the Russians, the young urban workers and students, the communists, the Komsomolets and Komsomolkas, and the professional soldiers who formed the core of the nation's fighters.

The participation of large numbers of women in the Red Army during the Great Patriotic War, in both support and combat positions, did not represent some dramatic reordering of gender roles in Soviet society. Nor was it a clear-cut validation of socialist gender egalitarianism. It was inextricably linked to the historical precedents of women's participation in Russia's wars under the tsars, Russia's nineteenth-century women's liberation movement and socialist ideology, and the experiences of the First World War and the Russian civil war. The Bolshevik men who first decided to use women in the Red Army in 1918 had firsthand knowledge of women serving in the armies of the tsar and the Provisional Government. It was they who promulgated legislation in 1918 that, for the first time, codified women's right to serve and the state's right to compel them to serve. Women's service began, without a doubt, as a push from below, but it expanded and was sustained mainly as a pull from above. The state conscripted nearly half a million women and set recruitment quotas for the VLKSM.

Women's participation in the war was acceptable to Soviet society at large in part because of the steady incursion of women into the male-dominated workplace since the emancipation of the serfs in 1861 and the subsequent industrialization of the imperial Russian economy. The Stalinist recruitment of women into the rapidly expanding industrial workplace built on this trend and reinforced the notion that women need not be relegated to traditional female economic roles. The ideology of the women's liberation movement was an integral part of the revolutionary socialist movement adopted in the Bolshevik program. This made it conceivable and possible for the state to accept women's service in the military—or even to require it. But it also made it virtually impossible for men to overtly and officially use gender-based arguments to keep women from serving. Nevertheless, men were often successful in preventing women from taking up arms; it was the remarkable and persistent woman who secured a place on the firing line.

Without the war, women would not have served in the armed forces in large numbers. Despite all the precedents and ideology and their constitutional right to serve, only a minuscule number of women had chosen to join the peacetime army. It simply did not occur to most women to enlist; nor did the regime consider it necessary or desirable to encourage women to do so. A handful of women had served in the Spanish Civil War as military interpreters for Red Army advisers, and some had served in medical units during the Winter War, but this service was officially ignored. The great emergency caused by the scale and success of the German invasion led women to pressure the state to allow them to exercise their right to serve.

Despite decades of socialist-feminist rhetoric, some soldiers and officers overtly resisted the presence of females in the army, and especially in combat. Although some women may have assumed that the experiences of the 1930s logically led them to the front, their male counterparts by and large did not. In the end, necessity did not fully trump chauvinism—women were given noncombat assignments that mostly replicated traditional roles. The United States, Britain, and Germany all used women in noncombat assignments, but only the Soviet Union consciously allowed women to undertake tactical assignments in which their job was to kill men. Snipers were a particular case in point because these women went out, identified individual male targets, and killed them. Yet in nearly all cases, only the exercise of personal initiative led women to the firing lines as combatants. So, although the Soviet state mobilized women by the hundreds of thousands, they were mobilized primarily to serve, not to fight, to risk death but not to kill. In the end, Russia's Provisional Government was actually more progressive, setting the precedent of creating all-female combat units and sending them into the fray.

Finally, women's participation in war and the historical appreciation of it will find a small audience. The common wisdom is that war is bad enough for men, and it is even worse to involve women in it; no one should be waging war, so no nation ought to boast about getting women into it.[2] In the twentieth and twenty-first centuries, political debates and the popular press have focused on the male versus female aspect of soldiering, but the postmodern world at large has deep misgivings about war and would rather see it limited, not expanded. Therefore, to date, even most women would not readily embrace going off to war or sending their daughters, sisters, and mothers into battle, so this subject may attract scholarly attention but will probably not find a wide audience among the general public. The right to fight and die at the front is more commonly seen as a step backward for humankind than as an advance for women. Still, the sacrifices made by so many Soviet women deserve to be studied, understood, and appreciated to the same degree that men's have been. Their contribution to the effectiveness of the Red Army should not be ignored, belittled, or forgotten.

Notes

ABBREVIATIONS

AP RF	Archives of the President of the Russian Federation
GAKO	State Archives of Kursk Oblast
GARF	State Archives of the Russian Federation
PASO	Public Archives of Sverdlovsk Oblast
RGANI	Russian State Archives of Contemporary History
RGASPI	Russian State Archives for Social and Political History (formerly RTsKhIDNI)
RGVA	Russian State Military Archives
RTsKhIDNI	Russian Center for the Collection and Preservation of Contemporary History (later renamed RGASPI)
TsA FSB RF	Central Archives of the Federal Security Bureau of the Russian Federation
TsAMO	Central State Archives of the Ministry of Defense
TsDNI KO	Central Repository for Contemporary History, Kursk Oblast
TsDNI SO	Central Repository for Contemporary History, Saratov Oblast
TsGAOO RB	Central State Archives of the Republic of Bashkira
TsGA RD	Central State Archives of the Republic of Dagestan

PREFACE

1. Mark Von Hagen, *Soldiers in the Proletarian Dictatorship: The Red Army and the Soviet Socialist State, 1917–1930* (Ithaca, N.Y.: Cornell University Press, 1990); Roger Reese, *Stalin's Reluctant Soldiers: A Social History of the Red Army, 1925–1941* (Lawrence: University Press of Kansas, 1996); Roger Reese, *The Soviet Military Experience: A History of the Soviet Army, 1917–1991* (London: Routledge, 2000); Catherine Merridale, *Ivan's War: Life and Death in the Red Army, 1939–1945* (New York: Metropolitan, 2006).

2. See Amir Weiner, "Saving Private Ivan: From What, Why, and How?" *Kritika: Explorations in Russian and Eurasian History* 2, 2 (spring 2000): 305–336, for his take on the benefits of studying the Soviet people at war.

3. In this vein, it is amazing that the Harvard University Refugee Interview

Project, undertaken in the 1950s, neglected to inquire about the refugees' wartime experiences and focused exclusively on the prewar period. All the information gathered about the war years was derived incidentally to the objectives of the interviews.

4. Seweryn Bialer, *Stalin and his Generals* (New York: Pegasus, 1969); John Erickson, *The Road to Stalingrad: Stalin's War with Germany* (New York: Harper and Row, 1975); *The Road to Berlin* (Boulder, Colo.: Westview, 1983); David Glantz and Jonathan House, *When Titans Clashed: How the Red Army Stopped Hitler* (Lawrence: University Press of Kansas, 1995); Richard Overy, *Russia's War: A History of the Soviet War Effort, 1941–1945* (New York: Penguin, 1998); Albert Seaton, *The Russo-German War* (New York: Praeger, 1971).

5. Vladlen S. Izmozik, "Voices from the Twenties: Private Correspondence Intercepted by the OGPU," *Russian Review* 55, 2 (1996): 287–308. See also V. A. Somov, "Pis'ma uchastnikov Velikoi Otechestvennoi voiny 1941–1945 gg.," *Voprosy istorii* 7 (July 2007): 131–135, for an analysis of the content of wartime letters.

6. See Amir Weiner, *Making Sense of War: The Second World War and the Fate of the Bolshevik Revolution* (Princeton, N.J.: Princeton University Press, 2001); Elena Zubkova, *Russia after the War: Hopes, Illusions, and Disappointments, 1945–1957* (Armonk, N.Y.: M. E. Sharpe, 1998); Elena Seniavskaia, *Frontovoe Pokolenie 1941–1945* (Moscow: RAN, 1995); and Susan J. Linz, ed., *The Impact of World War II on the Soviet Union* (Totowa, N.J.: Rowman and Allanheld, 1985).

7. Vasily Grossman, *A Writer at War: Vasily Grossman with the Red Army 1941–1945,* ed. and trans. Antony Beevor and Luba Vinogradova (London: Harvill Press, 2005).

CHAPTER 1. PERSPECTIVES ON MILITARY EFFECTIVENESS

1. Sam C. Sarkesian, "Introduction: Combat Effectiveness," in *Combat Effectiveness: Cohesion, Stress, and the Volunteer Military,* ed. Sam C. Sarkesian (Beverly Hills, Calif.: Sage Publications, 1980), 9; John E. Jessup, "The Soviet Armed Forces in the Great Patriotic War, 1941–5," in *Military Effectiveness,* vol. 3, *The Second World War,* ed. Allen R. Millet and Williamson Murray (Boston: Allen and Unwin, 1988), 256–276.

2. Sarkesian, "Introduction," 12.

3. Roger A. Beaumont and William P. Snyder, "Combat Effectiveness: Paradigms and Paradoxes," in Sarkesian, *Combat Effectiveness,* 36.

4. Allan R. Millet and Williamson Murray, "The Effectiveness of Military Organizations," in *Military Effectiveness,* vol. 1, *The First World War,* ed. Allan R.

Millett and Williamson Murray (Boston: Unwin Hyman, 1988), 1–4; H. Wayne Moyer, "Ideology and Military Systems," in Sarkesian, *Combat Effectiveness*, 108.

5. John Lynn, *Bayonets of the Republic: Motivation and Tactics in the Army of Revolutionary France, 1791–94* (Urbana: University of Illinois Press, 1984), 21–40; quote from 21.

6. Josh Sanborn, *Drafting the Russian Nation: Military Conscription, Total War, and Mass Politics 1905–1925* (De Kalb: Northern Illinois University Press, 2003), 1–17; Mark Von Hagen, *Soldiers in the Proletarian Dictatorship: The Red Army and the Soviet Socialist State, 1917–1930* (Ithaca, N.Y.: Cornell University Press, 1990), 1–9.

7. Stephen D. Wesbrook, "The Potential for Military Disintegration," in Sarkesian, *Combat Effectiveness*, 247, 266.

8. Carl Van Dyke, "The Timoshenko Reforms: March–July 1940," *Journal of Slavic Military Studies* 9, 1 (March 1996): 84–85.

9. The first three categories are taken from Lynn, *Bayonets of the Republic*, 22; the last, the state system, is my own.

10. E. A. Shils and Morris Janowitz, "Cohesion and Disintegration in the Wehrmacht in World War II," *Public Opinion Quarterly* 12 (1948): 280–315; Omer Bartov, *Hitler's Army* (Oxford: Oxford University Press 1992); Stephen G. Fritz, *Frontsoldaten: The German Soldier in World War II* (Lexington: University Press of Kentucky, 1995). Thousands of Soviet veterans, mostly officers, have written memoirs, and, in the last decade, a number of them have been translated; in addition, there is a plethora of books on the war in the east with a Soviet emphasis. However, only Elena Seniavskaia has done any work on the psychology of the Soviet soldier in wartime.

11. J. Stalin, "Speech Delivered by J. V. Stalin at a Meeting of Voters of the Stalin Electoral District, Moscow, February 9, 1946," in *Speeches Delivered by J. V. Stalin at Meetings of Voters of the Stalin Electoral District, Moscow* (Moscow: Foreign Language Publishing House, 1950), 27. Historian Robert Thurston supports Stalin's viewpoint in his recent works: "Cauldrons of Loyalty and Betrayal: Soviet Soldiers' Behavior, 1941 and 1945," in *The People's War: Responses to World War II in the Soviet Union*, ed. Robert W. Thurston and Bernd Bonwetsch (Chicago: University of Illinois Press, 2000), 235–241, and *Life and Terror in Stalin's Russia, 1934–1941* (New Haven, Conn.: Yale University Press, 1996), chap. 7.

12. Robert Conquest, *The Great Terror: A Reassessment* (New York: Oxford University Press, 1990), 456, 468; George Fischer, *Soviet Opposition to Stalin: A Case Study in World War II* (Cambridge, Mass.: Harvard University Press, 1952), 5–6.

13. Josh Sanborn, "The Mobilization of 1914 and the Question of the Russian Nation: A Reexamination," *Slavic Review* 59, 2 (summer 2000): 267–275.

14. Jeffrey Brooks, *Thank You, Comrade Stalin! Soviet Public Culture from Revolution to Cold War* (Princeton, N.J.: Princeton University Press, 2000). The veterans I interviewed claimed they did not know of Stalin's crimes until the Khrushchev era.

15. John Barber, "Popular Reactions in Moscow to the German Invasion of June 22, 1941," in *Operation Barbarossa: The German Attack on the Soviet Union June 22, 1941,* ed. Joseph L. Wieczynski (Salt Lake City: Charles Schlacks, 1993), 10–11.

16. Alexei Gorchakov, "The Long Road," in *Thirteen who Fled*, ed. Louis Fischer (New York: Harper and Brothers, 1949), 73–74; John Erickson, "Red Army Battlefield Performance, 1941–45: The System and the Soldier," in *Time to Kill: The Soldier's Experience of War in the West 1939–1945*, ed. Paul Addison and Angus Calder (London: Pimlico, 1997), 236. The role of alienation to Soviet power and how that affected choices and behavior detrimental to the Soviet regime are prevalent in the interviews of the Harvard University Refugee Interview Project.

17. Hubertus F. Jahn, *Patriotic Culture in Russia during World War I* (Ithaca, N.Y.: Cornell University Press, 1995), 2.

18. Earl L. Hunter, *A Sociological Analysis of Certain Types of Patriotism* (New York: 1932), 22–26, cited in Jahn, *Patriotic Culture,* 2, n. 4.

19. Geoffrey Hosking, "The Second World War and Russian National Consciousness," *Past and Present* 175 (May 2002): 163.

20. Ilya Ehrenburg, "On Patriotism," in *In One Newspaper: A Chronicle of Unforgettable Years* by Ilya Ehrenburg and Konstantin Simonov, trans. Anatol Kagan (New York: Sphinx Press, 1985), 174.

21. Serhy Yekelchyk, "Stalinist Patriotism as Imperial Discourse: Reconciling the Ukrainian and Russian 'Heroic Pasts,' 1939–1945," *Kritika: Explorations in Russian and Eurasian History* 3, 1 (winter 2002): 51–80.

22. Lisa A. Kirschenbaum, "Local Loyalties and Private Life in Soviet World War II Propaganda," *Slavic Review* 59, 4 (2000): 828.

23. Jahn, *Patriotic Culture,* 3.

24. Harvard University Refugee Interview Project, #395, Hoover Institution Archives, Stanford University, Stanford, Calif.

25. Sheila Fitzpatrick, *Stalin's Peasants: Resistance and Survival in the Russian Village after Collectivization* (New York: Oxford University Press, 1994); Sheila Fitzpatrick, *Everyday Stalinism: Ordinary Life in Extraordinary Times: Soviet Russia in the 1930s* (New York: Oxford University Press, 1999); Moshe Lewin, *The*

Making of the Soviet System: Essays in the Social History of Interwar Russia (New York: Pantheon, 1985); Moshe Lewin, *Russian Peasants and Soviet Power: A Study of Collectivization* (New York: W.W. Norton, 1968); Lynne Viola, *Peasant Rebels under Stalin: Collectivization and the Culture of Peasant Resistance* (New York: Oxford University Press, 1996); Robert Thurston, *Life and Terror in Stalin's Russia, 1934–1941* (New Haven, Conn.: Yale University Press, 1996).

26. Vera Sandomirsky, "Soviet War Poetry," *Slavic Review* 4, 1 (spring 1944): 47–66.

27. Amir Weiner, "The Making of a Dominant Myth: The Second World War and the Construction of Political Identities within the Soviet Polity," *Russian Review* 55, 4 (1996): 658–659.

28. David Brandenburger, "Soviet Social Mentalité and Russocentrism on the Eve of War, 1936–1941," *Jahrbücher für Geschichte Osteuropas* 48 (2000): 388–406.

29. Ehrenburg, "On Patriotism," 178.

30. Stephen Kotkin, *Magnetic Mountain: Stalinism as a Civilization* (Berkeley: University of California Press, 1995), 21.

31. Igal Halfin and Jochen Hellbeck, "Rethinking the Stalinist Subject: Stephen Kotkin's 'Magnetic Mountain' and the State of Soviet Historical Studies," *Jahrbücher für Geschichte Osteuropas* 44 (1996): 457.

32. Sarah Davies, *Popular Opinion in Stalin's Russia: Terror, Propaganda and Dissent, 1934–1941* (Cambridge: Cambridge University Press, 1997), chaps. 1, 2, 11.

33. Igal Halfin, "From Darkness to Light: Student Communist Autobiography during NEP," *Jahrbücher für Geschichte Osteuropas* 45 (1997): 210–236.

34. Anna Krylova, "Soviet Modernity in Life and Fiction: The Generation of the 'New Soviet Person' in the 1930s" (doctoral diss., Johns Hopkins University, 2000), chap. 4.

35. Natalia Peshkova interview, http://www.iremember.ru/content/view/289/89/lang,en/ (accessed 25 July 2006). Oleg Sheremet and Artem Drabkin created this website with the support of a grant from the Russian Federation Ministry of Print Media, Television, and Radio. Neither is a historian, but they conducted their interviews using an instrument prepared by scholar Aleksandr Samsonov, who heads a Russian World War II memory project, and eminent social psychologist Elena Seniavskaia of Moscow State University, who studies the effects of war on soldiers. The instrument is available for viewing at the website. Seniavskaia did several of the interviews herself. Despite the fact that the interviews were conducted forty or more years after the war, I believe they are valid indicators of the interviewees' experiences and thoughts because the war was the most significant experience of their lives and made an indelible impression on them.

36. Alexander Hill, in his study of the partisan movement, shows that many of those who collaborated with the Germans or sought positions of local influence in the occupied areas had been victims of Stalinism. Alexander Hill, *The War behind the Eastern Front: The Soviet Partisan Movement in North-West Russia 1941–1944* (London: Frank Cass, 2005), 47–68.

37. O. B. Mozokhin, "Statistika repressivnoi deiatel'nosti organov bezopasnosti SSSR (1943gg.)," *Voenno-istoricheskii arkhiv* 9 (2005): 187–188.

38. Fischer, *Thirteen Who Fled*, 12–17. This is also a recurrent theme in many interviews of the Harvard University Refugee Interview Project.

39. James M. McPherson, *For Cause and Comrades: Why Men Fought in the Civil War* (New York: Oxford, 1997).

40. One of the more recent sources of oral history is http://www.iremember.ru.

41. Katharine Hodgson, *Written with the Bayonet: Soviet Russian Poetry of World War Two* (Liverpool: Liverpool University Press, 1996), 11.

42. Kirschenbaum, "Local Loyalties and Private Life," 836; Brooks, *Thank You, Comrade Stalin*, 185–188.

43. Lisa Kirschenbaum, *The Legacy of the Siege of Leningrad, 1941–1995: Myth, Memories, and Monuments* (Cambridge: Cambridge University Press, 2006).

44. J. V. Stalin, "Order of the Day of the People's Commissar of Defense, May 1, 1942, no. 130," in *On the Great Patriotic War of the Soviet Union* (Moscow: Foreign Language Publishing House, 1946), 58.

45. Alexander Werth, *Russia at War 1941–1945* (1964; reprint, New York: Carroll and Graf, 1984), 416–419.

46. Letter from Valentin Nikolaevich Shikanov to his mother, 28 May 1942, in "*Byla voina . . .*": *Sbornik dokumentov i vospominanii o Rostove v period Velikoi Otechestvennoi voiny 1941–1945 godov* (Rostov: Rostovskii kreml', 2001), 301.

47. Letter from Georgii Ivanovich Eremin to his family, 30 May 1942, ibid., 302.

48. Mark Edele, "'Paper Soldiers': The World of the Soldier Hero according to Soviet Wartime Posters," *Jahrbücher für Geschichte Osteuropas* 47 (1999): 89–108.

49. Serge Schmemann, *Echoes of a Native Land: Two Centuries of a Russian Village* (New York: Alfred A. Knopf, 1997), 12.

50. Brooks, *Thank You, Comrade Stalin*, 194.

51. Ibid., 167–173.

52. Nina Tumarkin, *The Living and the Dead: The Rise and Fall of the Cult of World War II in Russia* (New York: Basic Books, 1994).

53. Elena S. Seniavskaia, *Frontovoe Pokolenie 1941–1945* (Moscow: Institut Rossiiskii Istorii-RAN, 1995), 1–21.

54. Vladimir A. Somov, "Pis'ma uchastnikov Velikoi Otechestvennoi voiny 1941–1945 gg.," *Voprosy istorii* 8 (2007): 131–135; Catherine Merridale, *Night of Stone: Death and Memory in Twentieth-Century Russia* (New York: Viking, 2000), 220–223.

55. Mansur G. Abdulin, *Red Road from Stalingrad: Recollections of a Soviet Infantryman* (Barnsley, South Yorkshire: Pen and Sword, 2004), 9.

56. Ibid., 67, 75.

57. Ibid., 109.

58. Ibid., 141.

CHAPTER 2. THE WINTER WAR AS PREDICTOR OF MILITARY EFFECTIVENESS IN THE GREAT PATRIOTIC WAR

1. Alexander Werth, *Russia at War, 1941–1945* (1964; reprint, New York: Carroll and Graf, 1984), 74–80; Sergei Shtemenko, *The Soviet General Staff at War, 1941–1945* (Moscow: Progress, 1985), 23–25; Seweryn Bialer, *Stalin and His Generals: Soviet Military Memoirs of World War II* (New York: Pegasus, 1969), 130–137.

2. John Erickson, *The Soviet High Command: A Military-Political History, 1918–1941*, 3rd ed. (London: Frank Cass, 2001), 541–548; David Glantz and Jonathan House, *When Titans Clashed: How the Red Army Stopped Hitler* (Lawrence: University Press of Kansas, 1995), 18–23; Albert Seaton, *The Russo-German War, 1941–45* (New York: Praeger, 1971), 47.

3. N. I. Baryshnikov, ed., *Istoriia ordena Lenina Leningradskogo voennogo okruga* (Moscow: Voenizdat, 1988), 126–131.

4. O. Manninen, "Pervyi period boev," in *Zimniaia voina 1939–1940*, book 1, *Politicheskaia istoriia*, ed. O. A. Rzheshevskii and O. Vekhviliainen (Moscow: Nauka, 1998), 145–147; N. N. Voronov, *Na sluzhbe voennoi* (Moscow: Voenizdat, 1963), 136–137; Kirill Meretskov, *Serving the People* (Moscow: Progress, 1971), 100–101.

5. Meretskov, *Serving the People,* 105–106.

6. Allen F. Chew, *The White Death: The Epic of the Soviet-Finnish Winter War* (East Lansing: Michigan State University Press, 1971), 7–9; Baryshnikov, *Istoriia ordena Lenina Leningradskogo voennogo okruga,* 130–131; RGVA f. 37977, op. 1, d. 233, ll. 1–4, in *Tainy i uroki zimnei voiny, 1939–1940* (St. Petersburg, Russia: OOO Poligon, 2000), 76–79.

7. RGVA f. 25888, op. 11, d. 76, ll. 16, 17; f. 33987, op. 3, d. 1240, ll. 88, 89, in *Tainy i uroki zimnei voiny, 1939–1940*, 48, 49, 50–52.

8. RGVA f. 33987, op. 3, d. 1376, l. 26, ibid., 170.

9. RGVA f. 34980, op. 10, d. 7, ll. 1–2; op. 1, d. 69, l. 62.

10. Erickson, *Soviet High Command*, 547.

11. This estimate is limited to ground forces. If one includes all naval and air force personnel, aviators, and their support crews, the number, according to Aptekar' rises to roughly 1.3 million Soviet servicemen involved in the war. This would drive the casualty rate down to 40 percent, which would be deceptive because aviation support personnel were not in the line of fire and suffered no casualties, and few naval personnel came under fire. Pavel A. Aptekar', "Opravdanny li zhertvy? O poteriakh v sovetsko-finliandskoi voine," *Voenno-istoricheskii zhurnal* 3 (1992): 43–45.

12. RGVA f. 34980, op. 15, d. 6, ll. 200, 203, 204, 206, 208, 211, 213, 215, 217, 219; G. F. Krivosheev, *Grif sekretnosti sniat: Poteri Vooruzhennykh Sil SSSR v voinakh, boevykh deistviiakh i voennykh konfliktakh: Statisticheskoi issledovanie* (Moscow: Voenizdat, 1993), 93–126; "O Nakoplenii Nachal'stvuiushchego sostava im Raboche-Krest'ianskoi Krasnoi Armii: Iz spravki-doklada Upravleniia po nachal'stvuiushchemu sostavu RKKA Narkomata Oborony SSSR E. A. Shchadenko, 20 Marta 1940 g.," *Izvestiia TsK KPSS* 1 (1990): 181; Evgenii Balashov, *Prinimai nas, suomi-krasavitsa! "Osvoboditel'nyi" pokhod v Finliandiiu 1939–1940 gg.*, pt. 1 (St. Petersburg, Russia: Galeia Print, 1999), 176, 180; O. Manninen, "Moshchnoe sovetskoe nastuplenie," in Rzheshevskii and Vekhviliainen, *Zimniaia voina 1939–1940 gg.*, 324–335; Georgi Dimitrov, *The Diary of Georgi Dimitrov 1933–1949* (New Haven, Conn.: Yale University Press, 2003), 128; Aptekar', "Opravdanny li zhertvy?" 43–45.

13. Balashov, *Prinimai nas, suomi-krasavitsa*, 55.

14. E. N. Kulkov and O. A. Rzheshevskii, eds., *Zimniaia voina 1939–1940 gg.*, book 2, *I. V. Stalin i finskaia kampaniia: Stenogramma soveshchaniia pri TsK VKP (b)* (Moscow: Nauka, 1998), 36, 52–53, 61, 91.

15. RGVA f. 34980, op. 5, d. 269, l. 15, in Manninen, "Pervyi period boev," 149.

16. Mikhail Lukinov interview, http://www.iremember.ru/artillerymen/lukinov/lukinov6_r.htm (accessed 4 April 2002).

17. RGVA f. 34980, op. 10, d. 1242, l. 25; d. 2935; d. 2990, l. 14.

18. Ibid., op. 9, d. 32, ll. 4–18.

19. Ibid., op. 14, d. 283, l. 32; op. 5, d. 292, l. 34; op. 5, d. 212, l. 12.

20. Kulkov and Rzheshevskii, *Zimniaia voina 1939–1940 gg.*, 21, 72.

21. Aleksei G. Maslov, "I Returned from Prison," *Journal of Slavic Military Studies* 19, 4 (December 2006): 752. Tsar Nicholas II set the precedent for punishing soldiers for voluntary surrender in 1915. Soldiers' families lost all state benefits related to their man's service, and, upon repatriation, former POWs

deemed to have betrayed their tsar and country were shipped to Siberia. Soldiers taken prisoner against their will were not punished. See Melissa K. Stockdale, "United in Gratitude: Honoring Soldiers and Defining the Nation in Russia's Great War" *Kritika: Explorations in Russian and Eurasian History* 7, 3 (summer 2006): 464–465.

22. After repatriation in 1940, Red Army tribunals ordered the summary execution of 350 of the more than 5,000 Red Army men captured by the Finns and sentenced 4,354 to hard labor in the camps for five to eight years. The majority of these men came from the destroyed 44th and 163rd Rifle Divisions. See Manninen, "Moshchnoe sovetskoe nastuplenie," 326; Mikhail Semiryaga, *The Winter War: Looking Back after Fifty Years* (Moscow: Novosti, 1990), 29–30; and Aptekar', "Opravdanny li zhertvy?" 45.

23. Those soldiers who opted to place their fate in the hands of a court rather than fight to the death may have made a reasonable choice. Of the 350 men executed, it is likely that they were shot not for their act of surrender but for their behavior in prison camp. The case of Leonid I. Levin, a medic in the 18th Rifle Division, is illustrative. Levin was tried by a military tribunal after the war and convicted under articles 58-4 and 58-10 of the RSFSR criminal code for counterrevolutionary anti-Soviet agitation and propaganda. He was found guilty of writing anti-Soviet articles in a POW camp newspaper. In peacetime, this activity was punishable by six months in jail; in wartime, by death. See A. V. Churakov, "Za 'Prekrasnoe Suomi' . . . ," *Voenno-istoricheskii arkhiv* 8 (August 2005): 74–91, and 1 (January 2006): 174–191.

24. Ivan N. Iudin, "Finskii pokhod glazami ochevidtsa: Vospominaniia I. N. Iudina," *Russkoe proshloe* 9 (2001): 158–160.

25. Chew, *White Death*, 137–138; V. Zenzinov, *V strecha s Rossiei: kak i chem zhivut v sovetskom soiuze: pis'ma v Krasnuiu Armiiu, 1939–1940* (New York, 1944), 39–40. Zenzinov incorrectly refers to the unit as the 34th Tank Battalion. Soviet sources identify it as a brigade. A battalion would have had only 700 members, not 2,100.

26. Kulkov and Rzheshevskii, *Zimniaia voina 1939–1940 gg.*, 248–249; Eino Luukkanen, *Fighter over Finland* (1963; reprint, London: Macdonald, 1992), 34–35; Ivan S. Chetyrbok interview, http://www.mannerheim-line.com/veterans/chetyrboke.htm (accessed 3 March 2006).

27. Dmitrii Krutskikh interview, http://www.mannerheim-line.com/veterans/krutskih.htm (accessed 4 April 2005).

28. Aleksei Shilin interview, http://www.iremember.ru/content/view/128/76/lang,en/ (accessed 23 May 2005).

29. Vasilii Davidenko interview, http://www.mannerheim-line.com/veterans/davidenkoe.htm (accessed 25 January 2004).

30. Nikolai A. Ponomarenko interview, http://www.mannerheim-line.com/veterans/ponomarenko.htm (accessed 25 January 2004).

31. "Pis'ma s finskoi voiny," *Istoricheskii arkhiv* 1 (2008): 220.

32. Lukinov interview.

33. Ibid.

34. Nikolai Shishkin interview, http://www.iremember.ru/shishkin/shishkin_r.htm (accessed 30 July 2006).

35. Kulkov and Rzheshevskii, *Zimniaia voina 1939–1940 gg.*, 22.

36. Gregory Ugryumov, "Faith Betrayed," in *Thirteen Who Fled*, ed. Louis Fischer (New York: Harper and Brothers, 1949), 215–218.

37. Ibid., 219–220.

38. "Prodolzhaem prodvigat'sia v glob' Bezuiutnoi Strany," *Istochnik* 3 (1993): 40–42.

39. Kulkov and Rzheshevskii, *Zimniaia voina 1939–1940 gg.*, 29.

40. Vasilii Davidenko interview, http://www.mannerheim-line.com/veterans/davidenkoe.htm (accessed 25 January 2004).

41. "Meteousloviia vo vremia voennykh deistvii na Karel'skom peresheike," in Balashov, *Prinimai nas, suomi-krasavitsa*, 181.

42. RGVA f. 34980, op. 9, d. 1174, ll. 23–33.

43. Nikolai A. Guzhva interview, http://www.iremember.ru/content/view/82/75/lang,en/ (accessed 14 March 2007).

44. Lukinov interview. The excerpt is also in Balashov, *Prinimai nas, suomi-krasavitsa*.

45. "L. Z. Mekhlis—E. I. Smirnovu, 14 Ianvaria 1940 g.," "L. Z. Mekhlis—E. A. Shchadenko, F. F. Kuznetsovu, 14 ianvaria 1940 g.," "L. Z. Mekhlis—M.V. Zakharovu, 21 ianvaria 1940 g.," "L. Z. Mekhlis—V. I. Vinograodovu, Paramonovu, 14 ianvaria 1940 g.," "L. Z. Mekhlis—A. V. Khrulevu, N. I. Trubetskomu, marta 1940 g.," *Istoricheskii arkhiv* 2 (2005): 95–100.

46. Krutskikh interview.

47. Lukinov interview.

48. Kulkov and Rzheshevskii, *Zimniaia voina 1939–1940 gg.*, 16–17.

49. Krutskikh interview.

50. Shilin interview.

51. Kulkov and Rzheshevskii, *Zimniaia voina 1939–1940 gg.*, 21–22.

52. Ibid., 26–27, 244, 254–255.

53. Krutskikh interview.

54. Kulkov and Rzheshevskii, *Zimniaia voina 1939–1940 gg.*, 242.

55. Harvard University Refugee Interview Project, #15, 6, Bakhmeteff Archive, Rare Books and Manuscript Library, Columbia University, New York.

56. RGVA f. 33987, op. 3, d. 1386, ll. 150, 151, in *Tainy i uroki zimnei voiny, 1939–1940*, 283.

57. Kulkov and Rzheshevskii, *Zimniaia voina 1939–1940 gg.*, 236.

58. N. F. Ksenofontova, "Sovetsko-Finliandskaia voina v osvenshchenii sovetskoi propagandy (1939–1940 gg.)," in *Velikaia Otechestvennaia voina v otsenke molodykh: Sbornik statei studentov, aspirantov, molodykh uchenykh* (Moscow: Ros. Gos. Gumanit. Un-t., 1997), 38–45; Semiryaga, *Winter War*, 61.

59. Georgi Prusakov interview, http://www.mannerheim-line.com/veterans/Prusakov.htm (accessed 21 June 2007).

60. Shishkin interview.

61. Zenzinov, *V strecha s Rossiei*, 126–127, 172–175.

62. Balashov, *Prinimai nas, suomi-krasavitsa*, 131.

63. Chetyrbok interview. Sarah Davies reports similar skepticism among the population in Leningrad and their doubts that tiny Finland would have provoked a war with the USSR. Sarah Davies, *Popular Opinion in Stalin's Russia: Terror, Propaganda and Dissent, 1934–1941* (Cambridge: Cambridge University Press, 1997), 100.

64. Balashov, *Prinimai nas, suomi-krasavitsa*, 124–127, 128–129.

65. Zenzinov, *V strecha s Rossiei*, 164–167.

66. Shishkin interview.

67. Semiryaga, *Winter War*, 57.

68. Davies, *Popular Opinion in Stalin's Russia*, 100–101.

69. Valerii Sudakov, ed., *Kniga Pamiati Vologodskoi oblasti: Sovetsko-Finliandskaia Voina 1939–1940 gg.* (Vologda: Izd-vo VIPK i PPK, 1995), 9, 25–27.

70. Zenzinov, *V strecha s Rossiei*, 128–131.

71. Balashov, *Prinimai nas, suomi-krasavitsa*, 131–135.

72. Semiryaga, *Winter War*, 57; Zenzinov, *V strecha s Rossiei*, 128–131; Davies, *Popular Opinion in Stalin's Russia*, 41–43.

73. Davies, *Popular Opinion in Stalin's Russia*, 95.

74. RGVA f. 9, op. 31, d. 292, l. 318, cited in Catherine Merridale, *Ivan's War: Life and Death in the Red Army, 1939–1945* (New York: Metropolitan, 2006), 51.

75. RGVA f. 25880, op. 4, d. 4, ll. 16–20.

76. Ibid., ll. 196–197.

77. Ibid., ll. 268, 270.

78. RGVA f. 9, op. 36, d. 4282, l. 148, cited in Merridale, *Ivan's War*, 71.

79. RGVA f. 34980, op. 6, d. 39, ll. 226–228, in *Tainy i uroki zimnei voiny, 1939–1940*, 319–321.

80. Ibid.

81. Balashov, *Prinimai nas, suomi-krasavitsa*, 2.

82. Pavel Aptekar', "Vystrelov ne bylo," *Rodina* 12 (1995): 53–55.

83. Viktor Iskrov interview, http://www.mannerheim-line.com/veterans/iskrove.htm (accessed 18 May 2007).

84. Israel Peltzman interview by the author; Anatolii Muzhikov interview, http://www.iremember.ru/content/view/206/69/lang,en/ (accessed 24 July 2006).

85. Muzhikov interview.

86. RGVA f. 40442, op. 1a, d. 1798c, ll. 176–181; "O sformirovanii iz dobrovol'tsev lyzhnykh batal'onov dlia deistvuiushchikh armii," in V. P. Serdiukov, *Kniga pamiati: Sovetsko-finliandskaia voina 1939–1940* (St. Petersburg, Russia: Vesti, 2004), 24. All told, the Red Army formed ninety-three ski battalions from both civilian volunteers and regular army units. Four were specially designated Komsomolets ski battalions.

87. Prusakov interview.

88. Shiskin interview.

89. Lukinov interview.

90. Baryshnikov, *Istoriia ordena Lenina Leningradskogo voennogo okruga*, 145; Carl Van Dyke, *The Soviet Invasion of Finland 1939–40* (Portland, Ore.: Frank Cass, 1997), 120.

91. Lukinov interview.

92. "Prodolzhaem prodvigat'sia v glob' Bezuiutnoi Strany," *Istochnik* 3 (1993): 40, 43.

93. Mekhlis is universally blamed for the executions, yet it was probably to Chuikov's advantage to have his subordinates executed and thus shift the burden of failure from him. Prior to the disaster, the *Stavka* categorically ordered Chuikov to relieve the 44th Rifle Division and not leave a single piece of heavy equipment or machine gun behind, and Chuikov failed miserably. All the reports on the matter are signed by both Chuikov and Mekhlis. RGVA f. 37977, op. 1, d. 233, l. 104; f. 33987, op. 3, d. 1386, ll. 119, 120; f. 33987, op. 3, d. 1385, ll. 127–132, in *Tainy i uroki zimnei voiny, 1939–1940*, 259–260, 270–271, 271–277.

94. G. A. Kumanev, "Besslavnaia voina, ili pobeda, kotoroi ne gordilic," paper presented to a seminar at the Institute of the History of Russia, Moscow, 29 January 1992, 6, quoted in Van Dyke, *Soviet Invasion of Finland*, 77.

95. Kulkov and Rzheshevskii, *Zimniaia voina 1939–1940 gg.*, 17, 24; Van Dyke, *Soviet Invasion of Finland*, 197.

96. RGVA f. 37977, op. 1, d. 233, ll. 125, 126, in *Tainy i uroki zimnei voiny, 1939–1940*, 282–283.

97. Merridale, *Ivan's War*, 80.

98. Kulkov and Rzheshevskii, *Zimniaia voina 1939–1940 gg.*, 242; Van Dyke, *Soviet Invasion of Finland*, 88.

99. "Krasnoarmeets Malashikhin I. P. to his wife," in "'Esli sud'ba budet vernut'sia domoi': Pis'ma s finskoi voiny," *Istochnik: Dokumenty russkoi istorii* 3 (1999): 82.

100. RGVA f. 34980, op. 9, d. 82, l. 2.

101. N. I. Baryshnikov, "The Soviet-Finnish War of 1939–1940," *Soviet Studies in History* 29, 3 (1990–1991), 52–53; V. M. Molotov, *Soviet Foreign Policy: The Meaning of the War in Finland* (New York: Workers Library, 1940), 10–11.

CHAPTER 3. NEW PERSPECTIVES ON THE GREAT ENCIRCLEMENTS OF 1941

1. Evgenii Balashov, *Prinimai nas, suomi-krasavitsa! "Osvoboditel'nyi" pokhod v Finliandiiu 1939–1940 gg.*, pt. 1 (St. Petersburg, Russia: Galeia Print, 2000), 176, 180.

2. John Erickson, *The Road to Stalingrad: Stalin's War with Germany* (New York: Harper and Row, 1975), 150–153; David M. Glantz and Jonathan House, *When Titans Clashed: How the Red Army Stopped Hitler* (Lawrence: University Press of Kansas, 1995), 52–53.

3. "Postanovlenie GKO SSSR, no. GOKO-169ss," *Istoricheskii arkhiv* 2 (2006): 55–57.

4. RTsKhIDNI f. 644, op. 1, d. 3, ll. 95–96, in *Voenno-istoricheskii zhurnal* 4–5 (1992).

5. TsAMO RF f. 33, op. 725588, d. 36, ll. 304–310, in *Istoricheskii arkhiv* 2 (2006): 57–62; Erickson, *Road to Stalingrad*, 175.

6. "Postanovlenie 3-go Upravleniia NKO SSSR na arest Pavlova D.G.," in *Organy gosudarstvennoi bezopasnosti SSSR v Velikoi Otechestvennoi voine: Sbornik dokumentov*, vol. 2, book 1, *Nachalo, 22 iiunia—31 avgusta 1941 goda* (Moscow: Rus', 2000), 210–213.

7. "Prikaz Stavki verkhovnogo glavnogo komandovaniia krasnoi armii no. 270, 16 avgusta 1941 goda," *Voenno-istoricheskii zhurnal* 9 (1988): 26–28; Erickson, *Road to Stalingrad*, 176.

8. Erickson, *Road to Stalingrad*, 181–182; Glantz and House, *When Titans Clashed*, 58–61.

9. "Oborona Kievskogo ukrepraiona, Telegramm iz Kieva," in *Leto 1941*.

Ukraina: Dokumenty i materialy. Khronika sobytii, ed. V. A. Zamlinskii (Kiev: Ukraina, 1991), 190.

10. "Direktiva Stavki Verkhovnogo glavnokomandovaniia," in Zamlinskii, *Leto 1941,* 457.

11. Erickson, *Road to Stalingrad,* 199–210; Glantz and House, *When Titans Clashed,* 75–77.

12. TsAMO f. 48a, op. 3408, d. 36, ll. 326, 327, in *Russkii arkhiv: Velikaia Otechestvennaia. General'nyi shtab v gody Velikoi Otechestvennoi voiny: Document i materialy. 1941 god,* vol. 23 (12-1), ed. Vladlimir A. Zolotarev (Moscow: Terra, 1998), 213.

13. Erickson, *Road to Stalingrad,* 213–219; Glantz and House, *When Titans Clashed,* 78–81.

14. Glantz and House, *When Titans Clashed,* 119–120.

15. E. N. Kulkov and O. A. Rzheshevskii, eds., *Zimniaia voina 1939–1940 gg. Kniga 2: I. V. Stalin i finskaia kampaniia: Stenogramma soveshchaniia pri TsK VKP (b)* (Moscow: Nauka, 1998), 188.

16. Ibid., 129.

17. "Stenogramma plenarnogo zasedaniia komissii GVS po voprosu voennoi ideology," in *"Zimniaia voina": rabota nad oshibkami (aprel'–mai 1940 g.): Materialy komissii Glavnogo voennogo soveta Krasnoi Armii po obobshcheniiu opyta finskoi kampaniia* (Moscow: Letnii sad, 2004), 360.

18. RGVA f. 34980, op. 5, d. 211, l. 400, in *Tainy i uroki zimnei voiny, 1939–1940* (St. Petersburg, Russia: OOO Poligon, 2000), 225.

19. RGVA f. 37977, op. 1, d. 233, l. 104, ibid., 259–260.

20. RGVA f. 33987, op. 3, d. 1386, ll. 119, 120, ibid., 270–271.

21. RGVA f. 33987, op. 3, d. 1377, l. 51, ibid., 314–315.

22. Kulkov and Rzheshevskii, *Zimniaia voina 1939–1940 gg.,* 120–122.

23. Pavel A. Aptekar', "Opravdanny li zhertvy? O poteriakh v sovetsko-finliandskoi voine," *Voenno-istoricheskii zhurnal* 3 (1992): 43.

24. Pavel Aptekar', "Tragediia okruzhennykh," *Voenno-istoricheskii arkhiv* 2 (2007): 179.

25. V. Zenzinov, "Diary, Found on the Corpse of a Slain Under-Officer. Near Lake Ladoga, on the Spot Where the 34th Soviet Tank Division [*sic*] Was Destroyed," V. Zenzinov Collection, "Excerpts from Letters and Diaries, 1939–1940," 3, Hoover Institution Archives, Stanford University, Stanford, Calif.

26. Kulkov and Rzheshevskii, *Zimniaia voina 1939–1940 gg.,* 219.

27. RGVA f. 4, op. 15, d. 30, ll. 336–356, in ibid., 397.

28. A. I. Starunin, "Boi v okruzhenii," *Voennaia mysl'* 10 (October 1940):

86–96, cited by Jacob Kipp, "Barbarossa and the Crisis of Successive Operations: The Smolensk Engagements, July 10–August 7, 1941," in *Operation Barbarossa: The German Attack on the Soviet Union, June 22, 1941*, ed. Joseph L. Wieczynski (Salt Lake City: Charles Schlacks, 1993), 134.

29. For an analysis of the development of Soviet operational doctrine in the interwar years, see Richard W. Harrison, *The Russian Way of War: Operational Art, 1904–1940* (Lawrence: University Press of Kansas, 2001).

30. Carl Van Dyke, "The Timoshenko Reforms: March–July 1940," *Journal of Slavic Military Studies* 9, 1 (March 1996): 69–96.

31. TsAMO f. 48a, op. 3408, d. 15, l. 46, in Zolotarev, *Russkii arkhiv,* vol. 23 (12-1), 53.

32. Ruslan S. Irinarkhov, *Kievskii osobyi* (Minsk: Kharvest/AST, 2006), 428–429, 475–485, 546.

33. For an overview of the battle, see A. I. Eremenko, *V nachale voiny* (Moscow: Nauka, 1964), 73–78.

34. *Krasnoznamennyi Belorusskii voennyi okrug*, 2nd ed. (Moscow: Voenizdat, 1983), 131–142.

35. TsAMO f. 48a, op. 3408, d. 16, ll. 185, 186, in *Russkii arkhiv,* vol. 23 (12-1), 252–253.

36. Klaus Schüler, "The Eastern Campaign as a Transportation and Supply Problem," in *From Peace to War: Germany, Soviet Russia and the World, 1939–1941*, ed. Bernd Wegner (Providence, R.I.: Berghahn Books, 1997), 212.

37. Ibid., 214.

38. Eduard V. Kharitonov, "Byla li oborone Kieva geroicheskoi?" *Voenno-istoricheskii arkhiv* 4 (2009): 52–67.

CHAPTER 4. THE SMALL-UNIT AND INDIVIDUAL EXPERIENCES OF ENCIRCLEMENT

1. Stephen D. Wesbrook, "The Potential for Military Disintegration," in *Combat Effectiveness: Cohesion, Stress, and the Volunteer Military*, ed. Sam C. Sarkesian (Beverly Hills, Calif.: Sage Publications, 1980), 244.

2. John Bushnell, "Peasants in Uniform: The Tsarist Army as a Peasant Society," *Journal of Social History* 13, 4 (1980): 565–572.

3. Anatolii S. Khoniak interview, http://www.iremember.ru/content/view/273/87/lang,en/ (accessed 25 July 2006).

4. Aleksei Vladimirskii, "Ob'iasnitel'naia zapiska ob obstoiatel'stvakh okruzheniia 5 armii Iugo-Zapadnogo Fronta v sentiabre 1941 goda i moego vykhoda iz okruzheniia," *Voenno-istoricheskii arkhiv* 7 (July 2006): 19–22.

5. Israel Peltzman interview by the author.

6. Nina Erdman interview, http://www.iremember.ru/content/view/286/88/lang,en/ (accessed 25 July 2006).

7. Vasily Grossman, *A Writer at War: Vasily Grossman with the Red Army 1941–1945*, ed. and trans. Antony Beevor and Luba Vinogradova (London: Harvill Press, 2005), 12.

8. Ibid., 118.

9. Konstantin K. Rokossovskii, *Soldatskii dolg* (Moscow: Voenizdat, 1980), 31, 41.

10. RGANI f. 89, op. 40, d. 1, ll. 218–223; Natalia Peshkova interview, http://www.iremember.ru/content/view/289/89/lang,en/ (accessed 25 July 2006). Filtration camps were established only in late December 1941 on Stalin's orders to check for traitors, spies, and deserters. Prior to this, the army just accepted these soldiers and returned them to duty.

11. V. A. Matrosov, ed., *Pogranichnye voiska SSSR v Velikoi Otechestvennoi voine 1941: Sbornik dokumentov i materialov* (Moscow: Nauka, 1976), 763–764.

12. Vasilii Kotov interview, http://www.iremember.ru/content/view/184/82/lang,en/ (accessed 24 July 2006).

13. Alexei Gorchakov, "The Long Road," in *Thirteen Who Fled*, ed. Louis Fischer (New York: Harper and Brothers, 1949), 73, 74.

14. Grossman, *Writer at War*, 71.

15. Harvard University Refugee Interview Project, #118, 42, Hoover Institution Archives, Stanford University, Stanford, Calif.

16. Aleksei G. Maslov, "I Returned from Prison," part 3, *Journal of Slavic Military Studies* 19, 2 (June 2006): 378–379.

17. Georgii A. Khol'nyi interview, http://www.iremember.ru/content/view/382/85/lang,en/ (accessed 6 September 2006).

18. Iurii Mukhin, *Po povestke i po prizyve: Nekadrovye soldaty Velikoi Otechestvennoi* (Moscow: Iauza/Eksmo, 2005), 142, 144–146.

19. Boris Gavrilov, *Cherez "Dolinu smerti" podvig i tragediia voinov Volkhovskogo fronta Ianvar'–iiun' 1942 g.*, vol. 1, *Vospominaniia i materialy* (Moscow: RAN, 2002), 3–22; Iu. A. Siakov, "Liubanskaia nastupatel'naia operatsiia 1942 goda," *Voprosy istorii* 12 (2005): 48–69.

20. TsAMO f. 48a, op. 3408, d. 4, l. 47, in Zolotarev, *Russkii arkhiv*, vol. 23 (12-1), 90.

21. John Bushnell, *Mutiny amid Repression: Russian Soldiers in the Revolution of 1905–1906* (Bloomington: Indiana University Press, 1985).

22. E. I. Baranovskii and V. D. Selemenev, eds., "Tolko avtoritetnyi komandir

smozhet zastavit' preodolet' strakh i instinkt samosokhraneniia': Dokladnye zapiska sekretaria TsK KP(b)B P. K. Ponomarenko I. V. Stalinu. 1940–1942 gg.," *Istoricheskii Arkhiv* 6 (2004): 55.

23. Richard W. Stewart, "The 'Red Bull' Division: The Training and Initial Engagements of the 34th Infantry Division, 1941–1943," *Army History* 29 (winter 1993): 1–10.

24. Charles Whiting, *Death of a Division* (New York: Stein and Day, 1980), 74–121.

25. Ibid., 122–128.

CHAPTER 5. THE GREAT PATRIOTIC WAR: THE MOBILIZATION OF SOCIETY FOR ARMED SERVICE

1. John Erickson, "Red Army Battlefield Performance, 1941–45: The System and the Soldier," in *Time to Kill: The Soldier's Experience of War in the West 1939–1945*, ed. Paul Addison and Angus Calder (London: Pimlico, 1997), 235. All told, 34,476,700 men and women served in the Soviet armed forces during the war; 4.5 million were already in uniform at its start. It is likely these numbers include noncitizens, such as Poles impressed into Soviet service.

2. Robert Conquest, *The Great Terror: A Reassessment* (New York: Oxford University Press, 1990), 456, 468; George Fischer, *Soviet Opposition to Stalin: A Case Study in World War II* (Cambridge, Mass.: Harvard University Press, 1952), 5–6.

3. "V politsiiu prinimaiutsia tol'ko Ukraintsy," *Istochnik: Dokumenty russkoi istorii* 3 (1995): 137.

4. Bruce Newsome, "The Myth of Intrinsic Combat Motivation," *Journal of Strategic Studies* 26, 4 (December 2003): 24. Newsome limits his analysis to combat motivation, but it seems obvious that it can be applied to initial motivation to serve as well.

5. For a general overview of the USSR's mobilization of society during the war, see John Barber and Mark Harrison, *The Soviet Home Front 1941–1945: A Social and Economic History of the USSR in World War II* (London: Longman, 1991), chap. 4.

6. Valentina Galagan, *Ratnyi podvig zhenshchin v gody Velikoi Otechestvennoi voiny* (Kiev: Vyshche Shkola, 1986), 30.

7. Anna Krylova, "Soviet Modernity in Life and Fiction: The Generation of the 'New Soviet Person' in the 1930s" (doctoral diss., Johns Hopkins University, 2000), chap. 4.

8. Aleksandr Bodnar' interview, http://www.iremember.ru/content/view/96/76/lang,en/ (accessed 4 May 2008).

9. Julianne Fürst, review article, *Kritika: Explorations in Russian and Eurasian History* 7, 3 (summer 2006): 675–688.

10. Sarah Davies, *Popular Opinion in Stalin's Russia: Terror, Propaganda and Dissent, 1934–1941* (Cambridge: Cambridge University Press, 1997).

11. Vasilii V. Gradosel'skii, "Komplektovanie Krasnoi Armii riadovym i serzhantskim sostavom v gody Velikoi Otechestvennoi voiny," *Voenno-istoricheskii zhurnal* 3 (2002): 11.

12. "Zaiavlenie brat'ev Shalashkovykh—zhitelei Marmyzhskogo s/s v Konyshevskii raivoenkomat ot otpravke ikh na front dobrovol'tsami," in *Surovaia pravda voiny: 1941 god na Kurskoi zemle v dokumentakh arkhivov,* vol. 1 (Kursk: MIR Kurskaia gorodskaia tipografiia, 2002), 31.

13. Catherine Merridale, *Night of Stone: Death and Memory in Twentieth-Century Russia* (New York: Viking, 2000), 226.

14. Catherine Merridale, "Culture, Ideology and Combat in the Red Army, 1939–1945," *Journal of Contemporary History* 41, 2 (2006): 315.

15. TsDNI KO P-2878, op. 1, d. 739, ll. 100–101, in *Surovaia pravda voiny,* vol. 1, 168–169.

16. Arsenii Rodkin, personal narrative, http://www.iremember.ru/content/view/104/76/lang,en/ (accessed 30 July 2006).

17. Nina S. Solovei, personal narrative, http://www.iremember.ru/content/view/26/74/lang,en/ (accessed 20 July 2006).

18. Menache Borochin interview by the author.

19. *Poslednie pis'ma s fronta,* vol. 2, *1942* (Moscow: Voenizdat, 1991), 424.

20. Nikolai Zheleznov interview, http://www.iremember.ru/content/view/101/76/lang,en/ (accessed 20 July 2006).

21. Olga Iu. Vasil'eva, *Russkaia Pravoslavnaia Tserkov' v politike sovetskogo gosudarstva v 1943–1948 gg.* (Moscow: IRI RAN, 2001), 50.

22. Tatiana A. Chumachenko, *Church and State in Soviet Russia: Russian Orthodoxy from World War II to the Khrushchev Years,* ed. and trans. Edward E. Roslof (Armonk, N.Y.: M. E. Sharpe, 2002), 4.

23. Davies, *Popular Opinion in Stalin's Russia,* 147–154, 155–167.

24. Daniil Zlatkin interview, http://www.iremember.ru/content/view/8/75/lang,en/ (accessed 15 July 2006).

25. Anne Noggle, *A Dance with Death: Soviet Airwomen in World War II* (College Station: Texas A&M University Press, 1994), 117.

26. John Barber, "The Image of Stalin in Soviet Propaganda," in *World War 2 and the Soviet People: Selected Papers from the Fourth World Congress for Soviet*

and East European Studies, Harrogate, 1990, ed. John Garrard and Carol Garrard (New York: St. Martin's Press, 1993), 42–43; Jeffrey Brooks, *Thank You, Comrade Stalin! Soviet Public Culture from Revolution to Cold War* (Princeton, N.J.: Princeton University Press, 2000), 165–175.

27. Konstantin Simonov, "June–December," 31 December 1941, in *In One Newspaper: A Chronicle of Unforgettable Years* by Ilya Ehrenburg and Konstantin Simonov, trans. Anatol Kagan (New York: Sphinx Press, 1985), 99–110.

28. Maurice Hindus, *Mother Russia* (Garden City, N.Y.: Doubleday, 1942), 114.

29. *"Byla voina . . .": Sbornik dokumentov i vospominanii o Rostove v period Velikoi Otechestvennoi voiny 1941–1945 godov* (Rostov: Rostovskii kreml', 2001), 302.

30. Noggle, *Dance with Death*, 145.

31. *Vse dlia fronta! Sverdlovskaia oblastnaia organizatsiia KPSS v gody Velikoi Otechestvennoi voiny (1941–1945): Dokumenty i materialy* (Sverdlovsk: Sredne-Ural'skoe knizhnoe izdat, 1985), 53.

32. Ibid., 36.

33. Vladimir I. Shliakhterman interview, http://www.iremember.ru/content/view/27/75/lang,en/ (accessed 20 July 2006).

34. Nina A. Solntseva, personal narrative, http://www.iremember.ru/content/view/305/89/lang,en/ (accessed 24 July 2006).

35. *Poslednie pis'ma s fronta,* vol. 2, *1942,* 79.

36. Catherine Merridale, *Ivan's War: Life and Death in the Red Army, 1939–1945* (New York: Metropolitan, 2006), 23–29.

37. Nikolai D. Nadol'ko interview, http://www.iremember.ru/content/view/52/74/lang,en/ (accessed 20 July 2006).

38. V. N. Khaustov, ed., *Lubianka. Stalin i NKVD-NKGB-GUKR "Smersh" 1939–mart 1946. Arkhiv Stalina. Dokumenty vysshikh organov partiinoi i gosu-darstvennoi vlast* (Moscow: Materik, 2006), 289–290.

39. Ibid., 295–296.

40. Semen V. Bilenko, *Istrebitel'nye batal'ony v Velikoi Otechestvennoi voine* (Moscow: Voenizdat, 1969), 11, 12.

41. The use of *opolchenie* units to capitalize on patriotism predates Napoleon's invasion. They were used in 1611–1613 and 1806–1807 and during the Crimean War and the First World War. Soviet propaganda, however, referred almost exclusively to Napoleon's invasion in its appeals for the formation of these units.

42. E. I. Baranovskii and V. D. Selemenev, eds., "Tolko avtoritetnyi komandir smozhet zastavit' preodeolet' strakh i instinkt samosokhraneniia': Dokladnye za-

piska sekretaria TsK KP(b) Ponomarenko I. V. Stalinu 1940–1942 gg.," *Istoricheskii arkhiv* 6 (2004): 53.

43. Harvard University Refugee Interview Project, #59, 8, Hoover Institution Archives, Stanford University, Stanford, Calif.

44. Bureau of Applied Social Research, War Documentation Project, box 11, 51, Bakhmeteff Archive, Rare Books and Manuscript Library, Columbia University, New York.

45. S. A. Smith, "Citizenship and the Russian Nation during World War I: A Comment," *Slavic Review* 59, 2 (summer 2000): 316–329.

46. Boris Sokolov, *V plenu* (St. Petersburg, Russia, 2000), 9, translated by and quoted in Arthur George with Elena George, *St. Petersburg: A History* (Gloucester, England: Sutton, 2006), 502.

47. T. G. Kirtoraga, "Narodnoe opolchenie Moskvy 1941 g.: Istoriia sozdaniia," *Vestnik Moskovskogo Universiteta* 8, 5 (2005): 51, 52.

48. Anatolii N. Muzhikov interview, http://www.iremember.ru/content/view/206/69/lang,en/ (accessed 24 July 2006). See also Richard Bidlack, "The Political Mood in Leningrad during the First Year of the Soviet-German War," *Russian Review* 59, 1 (January 2000): 96–113.

49. Rodric Braithwaite, *Moscow 1941: A City and Its People at War* (London: Profile, 2006), 116.

50. Harvard University Refugee Interview Project, #382, Bakhmeteff Archive.

51. *Surovaia pravda voiny,* 175–176.

52. Kirtoraga, "Narodnoe opolchenie Moskvy 1941 g.," 40–41.

53. Georgii V. Il'in, "Podmoskov'ie—frontu," *Voprosy istorii* 6 (1999): 136.

54. L. N. Pushkarev, "Uchastie voinov-dobrovol'tsev v oborone Moskvy v 1941 g.," *Voprosy istorii* 10 (2007): 131.

55. *Popu Bitva za stolitsu: sbornik dokumentov,* vol. 1, *Ot oborony k kontrnastupleniiu* (Moscow: UVTII, 1994), 1; John Barber, "Reactions in Moscow to the German Invasion of June 22, 1941," in *Operation Barbarossa: The German Attack on the Soviet Union June 22, 1941,* ed. Joseph L. Wieczynski (Salt Lake City: Charles Schlacks, 1993), 5.

56. Braithwaite, *Moscow 1941,* 104.

57. Kirtoraga, "Narodnoe opolchenie Moskvy 1941 g.," 48–49.

58. Pushkarev, "Uchastie voinov-dobrovol'tsev v oborone Moskvy v 1941 g.," 132.

59. *Vse dlia fronta,* 47–48.

60. Aleksandr D. Kolesnik, *Opolchenskie formirovaniia Rossiiskoi Federatsii v gody Velikoi Otechestvennoi voiny* (Moscow: Nauka, 1988), 35.

61. *Kommunisticheskaia Partiia Belorussii v rezoliutsiakh i resheniiakh s'ezdov i plenumov TsK*, vol. 3, *1933–1945* (Minsk: Belarus', 1985), 416–418.

62. "Sobshchenie UNKVD BSSR po Vitebskoi oblasti no. 48/3 v NKVD i NKGB Belorusskoi SSR o sostoianii istrebitel'nykh batal'onov," in *Organy gosudarstvennoi bezopasnosti SSSR v Velikoi Otechestvennoi voine: Sbornik dokumentov*, vol. 2, book 1, *Nachalo, 22 iiunia–31 avgusta 1941 goda* (Moscow: Rus', 2000), 180.

63. *Organy gosudarstvennoi bezopasnosti SSSR v Velikoi Otechestvennoi voine*, 173–175.

64. AP RF f. e, op. 50, d. 477, l. 6, in *1941 god*, vol. 2, ed. L. E. Reshin (Moscow: Mezhdunarodnyi fond 'Demokratiia', 1998), 453.

65. *Kievskii Krasnoznamennyi* (Moscow: Voenizdat, 1974), 188, 193–194.

66. Valentina Ia. Galagin, *Ratnyi podvig zhenshchin v gody Velikoi Otechestvennoi voiny* (Kiev: Vyshche Shkola, 1986), 30.

67. N. S. Kudrin, "Semeinaia pamiiat'," *Voenno-istoricheskii arkhiv* 7 (2008): 91.

68. Vladimir Dolmatov interview, http://history.vif2.ru/atwar/dolmatov/dolmatov.htm (accessed 14 May 2001).

69. Boris Ol'shanskii Papers, 34, Bakhmeteff Archive.

70. Ruslan S. Irinarkhov, *Kievskii osobyi . . .* (Minsk: Kharvest, 2006), 343.

71. TsA FSB RF f. 3, op. 8, d. 193, l. 180; f. 3, op. 9, d. 226, ll. 99–101, in *Lubianka v dni bitvy za Moskvu: Materialy organov gosbezopasnosti SSSR iz Tsentral'nogo arkhiva FSB Rossii*, ed. V. K. Vinogradov (Moscow: Evonnitsa-MG, 2002), 97, 131.

72. Aleksandr D. Kolesnik, *Opolchenskie formirovaniia Rossiiskoi Federatsii v gody Velikoi Otechestvennoi voiny* (Moscow: Nauka, 1988), 37.

73. *Poslednie pis'ma s fronta*, vol. 2, *1942*, 120.

74. RTsKhIDNI f. 17, op. 88, d. 122, ll. 120–123.

75. V. A. Isupov, "Sotsial'no-demograficheskaia politika Stalinskogo pravitel'stva v gody Velikoi Otechestvennoi voiny (na materialakh Sibiri)," in *Zapadnaia Sibir' v Velikoi Otechestvennoi voine (1941–1945 gg)* (Novosibirsk: Nauka-Tsentr, 2004), 120.

76. PASO f. 4, op. 18, d. 17, ll. 145–147; f. 2128, op. 1, d. 497, l. 49, in *Vse dlia fronta*, 334, 335.

77. PASO f. 4, op. 39, d. 81, ll. 15–16, ibid., 336–339.

78. PASO f. 483, op. 3, d. 96, ll. 1–2; f. 4, op. 38, d. 119, ll. 38, 39, ibid., 339–341, 348.

79. V. A. Zolotarev, ed., *Russkii arhiv: Velikaia Otechestvennaia: Prikazy*

Narodnogo komissara oborony SSSR (1943–1945 gg.), vol. 13 (2-3) (Moscow: Terra, 1997), 44–45.

80. Barber, "Popular Reactions in Moscow," 8.

81. *Poslednie pis'ma s fronta*, vol. 2, *1942*, 518–522.

82. Ibid., vol. 4, *1944*, 257, 532–534.

83. Ibid., vol. 2, *1942*, 233.

84. Orlando Figes, *The Whisperers: Private Life in Stalin's Russia* (London: Penguin, 2007), 345.

85. Ibid., 342–343.

86. RGVA f. 4, op. 18, d. 46, ll. 178–182.

87. Yuri Koriakin interview, http://www.iremember.ru/content/view/229/85/lang,en/ (accessed 24 July 2006).

88. See Sheila Fitzpatrick, *Tear off the Masks! Identity and Imposture in Twentieth-Century Russia* (Princeton, N.J.: Princeton University Press, 2005), chap. 1, for a discussion of the remaking of identity through changes in the "file-self."

89. Steven Barnes, "All for the Front, All for Victory! The Mobilization of Forced Labor in the Soviet Union during World War Two," *International Labor and Working-Class History* 58 (fall 2000): 242.

90. See Golfo Alexopoulos, "Soviet Citizenship, More or Less: Rights, Emotions, and States of Civic Belonging," *Kritika: Explorations in Russian and Eurasian History* 7, 3 (summer 2006): 500–501, 517–518, 522–523, for the relationship of military service to citizenship under the Soviet regime.

91. Melissa K. Stockdale, "United in Gratitude: Honoring Soldiers and Defining the Nation in Russia's Great War," *Kritika: Explorations in Russian and Eurasian History* 7, 3 (summer 2006): 459–485; Mark Von Hagen, *Soldiers in the Proletarian Dictatorship: The Red Army and the Soviet Socialist State, 1917–1930* (Ithaca, N.Y.: Cornell University Press, 1990).

92. Alexander V. Pil'cyn, *Penalty Strike: The Memoirs of a Red Army Penal Company Commander 1943–1945* (Solihull, England: Helion, 2006), 128.

93. Petr A. Malikov, "Talisman," in *Zhiviaia Pamiat': Velikaia Otechestvennaia: Pravda o voine v trekh tomakh*, vol. 1, ed. V. L. Bogdanov (Moscow: Sovet veteranov zhurnalistiki Rossii Soiuz Zhurnalistov, 1995), 284–286.

94. *Poslednie pis'ma s fronta*, vol. 4, *1944*, 182.

95. Teodor A. Klein narrative, http://www.iremember.ru/content/view/317/89/lang,en/ (accessed 30 July 2006).

96. Timothy P. Mulligan, "Escape from Stalingrad: Soviet Nationals with the German Sixth Army," *Journal of Slavic Military Studies* 20, 4 (2007): 739–748.

CHAPTER 6. MOBILIZING THE NONVOLUNTEERS

1. Vasilii V. Gradosel'skii, "Komplektovanie Krasnoi Armii riadovym i serzhantskim sostavom v gody Velikoi Otechestvennoi voiny," *Voenno-istoricheskii zhurnal* 3 (2002): 11.

2. TsA FSB RF f. 9401, op. 2, d. 64, ll. 9–13, in *Lubianka. Stalin i NKVD-NKGB-GUKR "Smersh" 1939–mart 1946. Arkhiv Stalina. Dokumenty vysshikh organov partiinoi i gosudarstvennoi vlast,* ed. V. N. Khaustov (Moscow: Materik, 2006), 407.

3. GARF f. 9401, op. 2, d. 65, ll. 325–327, ibid., 438.

4. GARF f. 9401, op. 2, d. 66, l. 60, ibid., 442.

5. Grigorii F. Krivosheev et al., *Velikaia Otechestvennaia bez grifa sekretnosti. Kniga poter'* (Moscow: Veche, 2010), 41; Alexander Statiev, "The Nature of Anti-Soviet Armed Resistance, 1942–44: The North Caucasus, the Kalmyk Autonomous Republic, and Crimea," *Kritika: Explorations in Russian and Eurasian History* 6, 2 (spring 2005): 290–291.

6. Amnon Sella, *The Value of Human Life in Soviet Warfare* (New York: Routledge, 1992), 194.

7. Fedor Bachurin interview, http://www.iremember.ru/content/view/45/73/lang,en/ (accessed 15 July 2006).

8. E. A. Shils and Morris Janowitz, "Cohesion and Disintegration in the Wehrmacht in World War II," *Public Opinion Quarterly* 12 (1948): 280–315.

9. Mikhail M. Kuznetsov interview, http://www.iremember.ru/content/view/28/75/lang,en/ (accessed 15 July 2006).

10. Lev Sh. Kolodenko interview, http://www.iremember.ru/content/view/66/69/lang,en/ (accessed 16 July 2006).

11. Valentin G. Kukhtin, "Kak ia stal komandirom strelkovogo otdeleniia na fronte," *Voenno-istoricheskii arkhiv* 10 (2005): 181.

12. Pavel M. Rogozin interview, http://www.iremember.ru/content/view/75/75/lang,en/ (accessed 20 July 2006).

13. Nikolai I. Blizniuk, "Eto vam ne 41-i!" in *Po povestke i po prizyvu. Nekadrovye soldaty Velikoi Otechestvennoi Voine,* ed. Iurii Mukhin (Moscow: Iauza/Eksmo, 2005), 217–218.

14. Mikhail Kalashnikov with Elena Joly, *The Gun that Changed the World,* trans. Andrew Brown (Cambridge: Polity Press, 2006), 105.

15. Harvard University Refugee Interview Project, #385, 27, Bakhmeteff Archive, Rare Books and Manuscript Library, Columbia University, New York.

16. Mikhail V. Chistiakov, letter to his wife, 8 June 1942, in *"Byla voina . . .": Sbornik dokumentov i vospominanii o Rostove v period Velikoi Otechestvennoi voiny 1941–1945 godov* (Rostov: Rostovskii kreml', 2001), 302.

17. Boris V. Viaznikovtsev, letter to a friend , 22 August 1941, ibid., 276.

18. Ivan I. Kopiistov, letter to his wife, 3 May 1942, ibid., 298.

19. *Poslednie pis'ma s fronta*, vol. 2, *1942* (Moscow: Voenizdat, 1992), 135–136.

20. Ibid., vol. 4, *1944,* 321.

21. Evgenii D. Moniushko, *From Leningrad to Hungary: Notes of a Red Army Soldier, 1941–1946,* trans. Oleg Sheremet (London: Frank Cass, 2005).

22. Toivo M. Kattonen interview, http://www.mannerheim-line.com/veterans/ Toivo.htm (accessed 1 June 2005).

23. V. A. Zolotarev, ed., *Russkii arhkiv: Velikaia Otechestvennaia: Prikazy Narodnogo komissara oborony SSSR (1943–1945 gg.),* vol. 13 (2-3) (Moscow: Terra, 1997), 216, 219.

24. B. V. Sokolov, "The Cost of War: Human Losses for the USSR and Germany, 1939–1945," trans. Harold S. Orenstein, *Journal of Slavic Military Studies* 9, 1 (March 1996): 180.

25. Natalia Peshkova interview, http://www.iremember.ru/content/view/289/ 89/lang,en/ (accessed 25 July 2006).

26. *KPSS o vooruzhennykh silakh Sovetskogo Soiuza: dokumenty 1917–1968* (Moscow: Voenizdat, 1969), 309–310.

27. "Doklad o rabote Glavnogo upravleniiam ispravitel'no trudovykh lagerei i kolonii NKVD SSSR za gody Otechestvennoi voiny," *Istoricheskii arkhiv* 3 (1994): 64–65; Krivosheev et al., *Velikaia Otechestvennaia bez grifa sekretnosti,* 41.

28. Evgenii Mazo, *Bryzgi Shampanskogo (nevydumannye istorii)* (Minneapolis, Minn., 2002), 24–26.

29. "Doklad o rabote Glavnogo upravleniiam ispravitel'no trudovykh lagerei," 62.

30. Fedor I. Gorb memoirs, 60–61, Bakhmeteff Archive.

31. TsA FSB RF f. 3, op. 8, d. 193, l. 180; op. 9, d. 226, ll. 99–101, in *Lubianka v dni bitvy za Moskvu: Materialy organov gosbezopasnosti SSSR iz Tsentral'nogo arkhiva FSB Rossii,* ed. V. K. Vinogradov (Moscow: Evonnitsa-MG, 2002), 97, 131.

32. TsGA RD f.p. 3, op. 1, d. 423, ll. 58–60, in *Narody Dagestana v gody Velikoi Otechestvennoi voiny (1941–1945 gg.) (Dokumenty i materialy)* (Makhachkala: Tipografiia DNTs RAN, 2005), 321–322, 723.

33. TsGA RD f.p. 1, op. 1, d. 5163, l. 372, ibid., 378–379.

34. "Predstaviteliu General'nogo shtaba o zaprose mneniia chlena Gosudarstvennogo Komiteta Oborony i komanduiushchego voiskami Zakavkazskogo fronta otnositel'no prizyve v deistvuiushchuiu armiiu Ingushei i Chechentsev," in *Russkii arkhiv: Velikaia Otechestvennaia: General'nyi shtab v gody Velikoi*

Otechestvennoi voiny: dokumenty i materialy 1942 god, vol. 23, 12 (2), ed. Vladimir A. Zolotarev (Moscow: Terra, 1999), 318.

35. TsGA RD, f.p. 1040, op. 1, d. 1, l. 25, in *Narody Dagestana v gody Velikoi Otechestvennoi voiny,* 601–602.

36. TsGA RD, f.p. 1, op. 1, d. 5275, ll. 55–57, ibid., 616.

37. TsGA RD, f.p. 1, op. 1, d. 5615, ll. 161–162; d. 5892, ll. 54–66, ibid., 339–342, 529–530.

38. Statiev, "Nature of Anti-Soviet Armed Resistance," 292–293.

39. Harvard University Refugee Interview Project, #86, 55, Hoover Institution Archives, Stanford University, Stanford, Calif.

40. Statiev, "Nature of Anti-Soviet Armed Resistance," 296–300.

41. Aleksei V. Basov, *Krym v Velikoi Otechestvennoi voine 1941–1945* (Moscow: Nauka, 1987), 20, 23, 24.

42. "Acts of the Crimean Tatars during the Second World War and Their Subsequent Punishment," State Committee of Defense Decree no. 5859ss—on the Crimean Tatars, 11 May 1944.

43. AP RF f. 3, op. 58, d. 207, l. 176, in Khaustov, *Lubianka. Stalin i NKVD,* 389.

44. Ibid.

45. Roza A. Bazarova, *Sovetskii Turkmenistan-frontu* (Askhabad: Ylym, 1978), 46–50.

46. *Kazakhstan v period Velikoi Otechestvennoi voiny Sovetskogo Soiuza 1941–1945: sbornik dokumentov i materialov* (Alma-Ata: Nauka, 1964), 10, 12, 186–189.

47. Nikolai A. Kirsanov, "Natsional'nye formirovaniia Krasnoi armii v Velikoi otechestvennoi voine 1941–1945 godov," *Otechestvennaia istoriia* 4 (1995): 122–123.

48. TsGAOO RB f. 122, op. 21, d. 104, ll. 17–18; f. 651, op. 11, d. 333, ll. 185–186; f. 122, op. 21, d. 104, l. 56, in G. D. Irgalin and G. R. Mukhametdinov, *Bashkiria v gody Velikoi Otechestvennoi voiny 1941–1945: Sbornik dokumenty i materialy* (Ufa: Kitap, 1995) 15–17, 19–20, 21.

49. TsGAOO RB f. 122, op. 21, d. 17, l. 4; d. 7, l. 43, ibid., 34–35, 378–379.

50. TsGAOO RB f. 788, op. 1, d. 108, l. 50; f. 122, op. 23, d. 622, ll. 103–105, ibid., 31, 417–418.

51. Nikolai Pak, *Sovety Tadzhikistana v gody Velikoi Otechestvennoi voiny* (Dushanbe: Donish, 1985), 36–37.

52. "Ukazanie NKVD SSSR no. 687/14190 Narkomatam vnutrennikh del

Uzbekskoi, Turkmenskoi, Tadzhikskoi, Kazakhskoi i Kirgizskoi SSR o meropriiatiiakh po presecheniiu antisovetskoi deiatel'nosti basmacheskikh elementov," and "Iz ukazaniia NKVD Uzbekoi SSR no. 36672 oblastnym upravleniiam NKVD respubliki ob aktivizatsii raboty po vskrytiiu organizovannoi deiatel'nosti basmacheskikh elementov," in *Organy gosudarstvennoi bezopasnosti SSSR v Velikoi Otechestvennoi voine: Sbornik dokumentov*, vol. 2, book 2, *Nachalo, 1 sentiabria–31 dekabria 1941 goda* (Moscow: Rus', 2000), 21, 67–68.

53. Stepan P. Zubarev, *Materialy k istorii Udmurtii v gody Velikoi Otechestvennoi voiny: sbornik statei* (Izhevsk: Udmurtski' nauchno-issledovatel'skii institut istorii, ekonomiki, literatury i iazyka, 1982), 3–5.

54. "Direktiva GlavPU RKKA secretariu TsK KP(b) Uzbekistana o meropriiatiiakh po ukrepleniiu sviazi boitsov Krasnoi Armii—Uzbekov so svoim narodom," in *Russkii arkhiv: Velikaia Otechestvennaia: Glavnye politicheskie organy Vooruzhennykh sil SSSR v Velikoi Otechestvennoi voine 1941–1945 gg.: Dokumenty i materialy*, vol. 17-6 (1-2), ed. Vladimir A,. Zolotarev (Moscow: Terra, 1996), 227–228.

55. Harvard University Refugee Interview Project, #60, 5, Hoover Institution Archives.

56. Ibid., #116, 3.

57. O. F. Zhemaitis, "Pervyi boi 16-i litovskoi strelkoi divizii na fronte Velikoi Otechestvennoi voiny," *Voenno-istoricheskii arkhiv* 6 (June 2005): 25, 29–31; Kirsanov, "Natsional'nye formirovaniia Krasnoi armii," 117.

58. Kirsanov, "Natsional'nye formirovaniia Krasnoi armii," 118–119.

59. *Oni srazhalis' za Rodinu: Predstaviteli repressirovannykh narodov SSSR na frontakh Velikoi Otechestvennoi voiny* (Moscow: Novyi khronograf, 2005).

CHAPTER 7. THE FEAR FACTOR

1. Stephen D. Wesbrook, "The Potential for Military Disintegration," in *Combat Effectiveness: Cohesion, Stress, and the Volunteer Military*, ed. Sam C. Sarkesian (Beverly Hills, Calif.: Sage Publications, 1980), 247.

2. RGASPI f. 644, op. 1, d. 3, l. 118, in A. I. Kokurin and N. V. Petrov, *Lubianka organy VChK-OGPU-NKVD-MGB-MVD-KGB 1917–1991: spravochnik* (Moscow: Materik, 2003), 616–617.

3. James Lucas, *War on the Eastern Front, 1941–1945: The German Soldier in Russia* (New York: Stein and Day, 1979), 31–33.

4. Ibid., 193.

5. Basil Liddell Hart, *The German Generals Talk* (New York: Quill, 1979), 223.

6. Ibid., 225.

7. John E. Jessup, "The Soviet Armed Forces in the Great Patriotic War, 1941–5," in *Military Effectiveness,* vol. 3, *The Second World War,* ed. Allan R. Millet and Williamson Murray (Boston: Allen and Unwin, 1988), 264.

8. Semion Aria interview, http://www.iremember.ru/content/view/98/76/lang,en/ (accessed 20 July 2006).

9. Daniil Zlatkin interview, http://www.iremember.ru/content/view/8/75/lang,en/ (accessed 15 July 2006).

10. Gennadii Shutz interview, http://www.iremember.ru/content/view/186/84/lang,en/ (accessed 24 July 2006).

11. Ivan I. Shelepov, "A la guerre comme ala guerre" interview, http://www.iremember.ru/content/view/10/75/lang,en/ (accessed 15 July 2006).

12. Aria interview.

13. Ivan Kobets interview, http://www.iremember.ru/content/view/14/71/lang,en/ (accessed 15 July 2006).

14. Konstantin Simonov, *Soldatskie memuary: Dokumental'nye stsenarii* (Moscow, 1985), 297, quoted by Elena S. Seniavskaia, "Psikhologiia voennogo byta kak istoricheskaia problema," *Voenno-istoricheskii arkhiv* 8 (1999): 203.

15. Nikolai Dupak interview, http://www.iremember.ru/content/view/308/89/lang,en/ (accessed 25 July 2006).

16. Mikhail Badigin interview, http://www.iremember.ru/content/view/185/82/lang,en/ (accessed 24 July 2006).

17. Elena S. Seniavskaia, "Chelovek na voine: opyt istoriko-psikhologicheskoi kharakteristiki rossiiskogo kombatanta," *Otechestvennaia istoriia* 1 (1995): 9.

18. Charles McMoran Wilson, Lord Moran, *The Anatomy of Courage: The Classic WW I Account of the Psychological Effects of War* (1947; reprint, London: Robinson, 2007), 67.

19. John Dollard, *Fear in Battle* (1944; reprint, Westport, Conn.: Greenwood, 1977), 40–41, 46.

20. William L. Hauser, "The Will to Fight," in Sarkesian, *Combat Effectiveness,* 188.

21. Aleksandr Bodnar' interview, http://www.iremember.ru/content/view/96/76/lang,en/ (accessed 4 May 2008).

22. Joseph Stalin, "The German Invasion of the Soviet Union, July 3, 1941 Radio Address," in *The Great Patriotic War of the Soviet Union* (New York: International Publishers, 1945), 14–15.

23. TsAMO f. 48a, op. 3408, d. 23, l. 353, in *Russkii arkhiv: Velikaia Otechestvennaia. General'nyi shtab v gody Velikoi Otechestvennoi voiny: Document i materialy. 1941 god,* vol. 23 (12-1), ed. Vladimir Zolotarev (Moscow: Terra, 1998), 61.

24. "Ukaz Prezidiuma Verkhovnogo Soveta SSSR," and "Zapiska A. Ia. Vyshinskogo V.M. Molotovu," *Istoricheskii arkhiv* 3 (2000): 34–35.

25. Josef Finkelshtein interview, http://www.iremember.ru/content/view/238/85/lang,en/ (accessed 25 July 2006).

26. *Organy gosudarstvennoi bezopasnosti SSSR v Velikoi Otechestvennoi voine: Sbornik dokumentov,* vol. 2, book 2, *Nachalo, 1 sentiabria–31 dekabria 1941 goda* (Moscow: Rus', 2000), 164–165; Rodric Braithwaite, *Moscow 1941: A City and Its People at War* (London: Profile, 2006), 165.

27. Mansur G. Abdulin, *Red Road from Stalingrad: Recollections of a Soviet Infantryman* (Barnsley, South Yorkshire: Pen and Sword, 2004), 31.

28. TsA FSB RF f. 14, op. 4, d. 22, ll. 45–46, in *Stalingradskaia epopeia: Materialy NKVD SSSR i voennoi tsenzury iz Tsentral'nogo arkhiva FSB RF* (Moscow: Zvonnitsa-MG, 2000), 180.

29. TsA FSB RF f. 14, op. 4, d. 912, ll. 160–162, ibid., 174.

30. TsA FSB RF f. 14, op. 4, d. 912, ll. 167–168, ibid., 191.

31. TsA FSB RF f. 14, op. 4, d. 912, ll. 163–166, ibid., 187.

32. Ibid.

33. Arsen Martirosian, *100 Mifov o Berii: Ot slavy k prokliatiiam. 1941–1953 gg.* (Moscow: Veche, 2010), 38–39; *Organy gosudarstvennoi bezopasnosti SSSR v Velikoi Otechestvennoi voine,* 20.

34. Harvard University Refugee Interview Project, #118, 35, 39, Hoover Institution Archives, Stanford University, Stanford, Calif.

35. *Organy gosudarstvennoi bezopasnosti SSSR v Velikoi Otechestvennoi voine,* 85.

36. Vladimir Zolotarev, ed., *Russkii arkhiv: Velikaia Otechestvennaia: Prikaz Narodnogo komissara oborony SSSR (1943–1945 gg.)* vol. 13 (2-3) (Moscow: Terra, 1997), 326.

37. TsA FSB RF f. 14, op. 4, d. 22, ll. 45–46, in *Stalingradskaia epopeia,* 181–182.

38. TsA FSB RF f. 14, op. 4, d. 386, ll. 22–24, ibid., 230.

39. S. Khomenko, "Disciplinary Battalion Joins Battle," *Soviet Soldier* 11 (1990): 36–38.

40. "Iz pisem P. S. Amosova," *Istoricheskii arkhiv* 3 (2007): 44–45.

41. Matvei Gershman interview, www.iremember.ru/infantry/gershman/gershman_r.htm (accessed 7 July 2005).

42. Iu. V. Rubtsov, "Put' v nikuda ili shans dlia ostupivshegosia? Shtrafnyi chasti v pis'makh uchastnikov Velikoi Otechestvennoi voiny," *Istoricheskii arkhiv* 3 (2007): 37, 305. G. F. Krivosheev et al., *Velikaia Otechestvennaia bez grifa sekretnosti. Kniga poter'* (Moscow: Veche, 2010).

43. Zolotarev, *Russkii arkhiv,* vol. 13 (2-3), 198.

44. Krivosheev et al., *Velikaia Otechestvennaia bez grifa sekretnosti,* 41; Rubtsov, "Put' v nikuda ili shans dlia ostupivshegosia?" 36, 37.

45. Zolotarev, *Russkii arkhiv,* vol. 13 (2-3), 332–333.

46. Ibid., 338.

47. "Iz pisem V.G. Sorokina," *Istoricheskii arkhiv* 3 (2007): 53.

48. Shelepov interview.

49. Catherine Merridale, "Culture, Ideology, and Combat in the Red Army, 1939–45," *Journal of Contemporary History* 41, 2 (2006): 318.

50. TsA FSB RF f. 14, op. 4, d. 287, ll. 150–154, in *Lubianka v dni bitvy za Moskvu: Materialy organov gosbezopasnosti SSSR iz Tsentral'nogo arkhiva FSB Rossii,* ed. V. K. Vinogradov (Moscow: Evonnitsa-MG, 2002), 305.

51. G. Bukhanstev memoir, 1941–1945, 2–3, Bakhmeteff Archive, Rare Books and Manuscript Library, Columbia University, New York.

52. Efim Gol'braikh interview, http://www.iremember.ru/content/view/57/75/lang,en/ (accessed 16 July 2006).

53. RGASPI f. 17, op. 162, d. 28, l. 73, in *Lubianka. Stalin i NKVD-NKGB-GUKR "Smersh" 1939–mart 1946. Arkhiv Stalina. Dokumenty vysshikh organov partiinoi i gosudarstvennoi vlast,* ed. V. N. Khaustov (Moscow: Materik, 2006), 184.

54. AP RF f. 3, op. 57, d. 59, l. 67, ibid., 350–351.

55. Richard Overy, *The Dictators: Hitler's Germany, Stalin's Russia* (New York: W. W. Norton, 2004), 297–298.

56. Ivan Stadniuk, "Na podstupakh k stolitse," in *Zhiviaia Pamiat': Velikaia Otechestvennaia: Pravda o voine v trekh tomakh,* vol. 1, ed. V. L. Bogdanov (Moscow: Sovet veteranov zhurnalistiki Rossii Soiuz Zhurnalistov, 1995), 124–125.

57. RGANI f. 89, op. 18, d. 8, ll. 1–3, in *Lubianka. Stalin i NKVD,* 317–318.

58. Aleksei Shilin interview, http://www.iremember.ru/content/view/128/76/lang,en/ (accessed 19 July 2006).

59. Semen Kh. Ravinskii interview, http://www.iremember.ru/content/view/59/73/lang,en/ (accessed 16 July 2006).

60. Vasily Grossman, *A Writer at War: Vasily Grossman with the Red Army 1941–1945,* ed. and trans. Antony Beevor and Luba Vinogradova (London: Harvill Press, 2005), 71.

61. "Narodnomu komissaru vnutrennikh del SSSR General'nomu komissaru gosudarstvennoi bezopasnosti tovarishchu Beriia," *Istoricheskii arkhiv* 3 (2000): 37–38.

62. Review by Evan Mawdsley, *War in History* 4, 2 (1997): 230.

63. Robert Stephan, "Smersh: Soviet Military Counter-Intelligence during the Second World War," *Journal of Contemporary History* 22, 4 (October 1987): 587–592.

64. Vladimir V. Khokhlov interview, http://history.vif2.ru/library/memoirs2 .html (accessed 24 January 2001).

65. Manfred Messerschmidt, "Deutsche Militärgerichtsbarkeit im Zweiten Weltkrieg," in *Die Freiheit des Anderen,* ed. Hans-Jochen Vogel, Helmut Simmon, and Adalbert Podlech (Baden-Baden: Nomos, 1981); Robert S. Rush "A Different Perspective: Cohesion, Morale, and Operational Effectiveness in the German Army, Fall 1944," *Armed Forces and Society* 25, 3 (spring 1999): 488–489.

66. Omer Bartov, *Hitler's Army: Soldiers, Nazis, and War in the Third Reich* (Oxford: Oxford University Press, 1992), 95–96.

67. George Q. Flynn, *Conscription and Democracy: The Draft in France, Great Britain, and the United States* (Westport, Conn.: Greenwood, 2002), 251, 252.

68. Gerard Oram, "'The Administration of Discipline by the English Is Very Rigid': British Military Law and the Death Penalty (1868–1918)," *Crime, History, and Societies* 5, 1 (2001): 94.

69. Robert H. Ahrenfeldt, *Psychiatry in the British Army in the Second World War* (New York: Columbia University Press, 1958), 271–275.

70. Ibid., 273–274, 275.

71. Paul O'Brien, "Summary Executions in Italy during the First World War: Findings and Implications," *Modern Italy* 11, 3 (November 2006): 353–359.

72. Iurii Konnov, "Voiska NKVD SSSR po okhrane tyla deistvuiushchei Krasnoi Armii v kurskoi bitve (Belgorodskoe napravlenie)," *Voenno-istoricheskii arkhiv* 3 (March 2006): 144–145.

73. GARF f. 9401, op. 2, d. 64, ll. 9–13, in Khaustov, *Lubianka. Stalin i NKVD,* 406–409.

74. RGVA f. 38650, op. 1, d. 313, ll. 10–41.

75. GARF f. 9401, op. 2, d. 65, ll. 325–327, in Khaustov, *Lubianka. Stalin i NKVD,* 438–440.

76. GARF f. 9401, op. 2, d. 99, ll. 167–69, ibid., 537–538.

77. Grigorii F. Krivosheev, "O dezertirstve v Krasnoi Armii," *Voenno-istoricheskii zhurnal* 6 (2001): 94; Krivosheev et al., *Velikaia Otechestvennaia bez grifa sekretnosti,* 41.

78. It is unknown exactly how these data were gathered, so the potential for double counting is high; thus, the numbers should be understood to indicate instances of desertion, straggling, and the like, rather than numbers of individuals.

79. Krivosheev et al., *Velikaia Otechestvennaia bez grifa sekretnosti,* 41.

80. A. A. Kurnosov first heard this song after the war from a relative of a

frontline soldier; he is quoted in Elena S. Seniavskaia, "Heroic Symbols: The Reality and Mythology of War," *Russian Studies in History* 31, 1 (1998): 84.

CHAPTER 8. DISCIPLINE, HATE, IDEOLOGY, AND PROPAGANDA

1. John A. Lynn, *Bayonets of the Republic: Motivation and Tactics in the Army of Revolutionary France, 1791–1794* (Urbana: University of Illinois Press, 1984), 35–36, 177–182.

2. John Erickson, "Red Army Battlefield Performance, 1941–45: The System and the Soldier," in *Time to Kill: The Soldier's Experience of War in the West 1939–1945,* ed. Paul Addison and Angus Calder (London: Pimlico, 1997), 235–236.

3. Argyrios K. Pisiotis, "Images of Hate in the Art of War," in *Culture and Entertainment in Wartime Russia,* ed. Richard Stites (Bloomington: Indiana University Press, 1995), 141–156.

4. Joseph Stalin, "The Twenty-fourth Anniversary of the October Revolution," in *The Great Patriotic War of the Soviet Union* (New York: International Publishers, 1945), 19.

5. Joseph Stalin, "May Day 1942," ibid., 52.

6. Ilya Ehrenburg, "About Hatred," 5 May 1942, in *In One Newspaper: A Chronicle of Unforgettable Years* by Ilya Ehrenburg and Konstantin Simonov, trans. Anatol Kagan (New York: Sphinx Press, 1985), 147.

7. Ibid., 147, 149.

8. http://www.sovlit.com/bios/ehrenburg.html.

9. Fedor Bachurin interview, http://www.iremember.ru/content/view/45/73/lang,en/ (accessed 15 July 2006).

10. Ehrenburg, "August 13, 1943," in Ehrenburg and Simonov, *In One Newspaper,* 332.

11. Harvard University Refugee Interview Project, #470, Bakhmeteff Archive, Rare Books and Manuscript Library, Columbia University, New York.

12. Boris Ol'shanskii Papers, 149, Bakhmeteff Archive.

13. Ibid.

14. Harvard University Refugee Interview Project, #382, Bakhmeteff Archive.

15. Georgii A. Khol'nyi interview, http://www.iremember.ru/content/view/382/85/lang,en/ (accessed 6 September 2006).

16. Robert H. Ahrenfeldt, *Psychiatry in the British Army in the Second World War* (New York: Columbia University Press, 1958), 199, 200.

17. Nikolai Dupak interview, http://www.iremember.ru/content/view/308/89/lang,en/ (accessed 25 July 2006).

18. Stalin, "May Day 1942," 54.

19. Joseph Stalin, "The German Invasion of the Soviet Union, July 3, 1941 Radio Address," in *The Great Patriotic War of the Soviet Union*, 12.

20. Stalin, "Twenty-fourth Anniversary of the October Revolution," 20, 23.

21. Vasily Grossman, *A Writer at War: Vasily Grossman with the Red Army 1941–1945*, ed. and trans. Antony Beevor and Luba Vinogradova (London: Harvill Press, 2005), 71.

22. Ibid., 138.

23. Joseph Stalin, "The Twenty-fifth Anniversary of the October Revolution," in *The Great Patriotic War of the Soviet Union*, 64.

24. Joseph Stalin, "May Day 1943," ibid., 83.

25. Ilya Ehrenburg, "The New Brotherhood," in Ehrenburg and Simonov, *In One Newspaper*, 351.

26. Ilya Ehrenburg, "The Soul of Russia," ibid., 362.

27. Harvard University Refugee Interview Project, #25, Bakhmeteff Archive.

28. "Pis'mo V. E. Markevicha," *Istoricheskii arkhiv* 2 (2005): 16–17.

29. Nikita Lomagin, "Soldiers at War: German Propaganda and Soviet Army Morale during the Battle of Leningrad, 1941–44," *Carl Beck Papers in Russian and East European Studies*, no. 1306 (Pittsburgh: University of Pittsburgh, 1998), 11–12, 13, 18.

30. Lev Anninskii, "Rus, sdavaisia!" *Rodina* 5 (1996): 63–65.

31. Roger Beaumont, *The Nazi's March to Chaos: The Hitler Era through the Lenses of Chaos-Complexity Theory* (Westport, Conn.: Praeger, 2000), 97–130.

32. Quoted in Robert S. Rush, "A Different Perspective: Cohesion, Morale, and Operational Effectiveness in the German Army, Fall 1944," *Armed Forces and Society* 25, 3 (spring 1999): 490.

33. H. Wayne Moyer, "Ideology and Military Systems," in *Combat Effectiveness: Cohesion, Stress, and the Volunteer Military*, ed. Sam C. Sarkesian (Beverly Hills, Calif.: Sage Publications, 1980), 150, n. 1.

34. Ibid. The Spanish Civil War veterans of the Abraham Lincoln Battalion agreed that identification with a cause is a "powerful antidote to fear and that men who understand war-aims are better soldiers." John Dollard, *Fear in Battle* (1944; reprint, Westport Conn.: Greenwood, 1977), 42–43.

35. E. A. Shils and Morris Janowitz, "Cohesion and Disintegration in the Wehrmacht," *Public Opinion Quarterly* 12 (1948): 280–315; Jürgen Fürster, "Motivation and Indoctrination in the Wehrmacht, 1933–1945," in *Time to Kill: The Soldier's Experience of War in the West, 1939–1945*, ed. Paul Addison and Angus Calder (London: Pimlico, 1997), 263–273.

36. Lev N. Pushkarev interview, http://www.iremember.ru/content/view/320/89/lang,en/ (accessed 29 July 2006).

37. Gerald F. Linderman, *The World within War: The American Combat Experience in World War II* (New York: Free Press, 1997), 344–370.

38. RGASPI f. 558, op. 11, d. 181, ll. 1, 11, in *Lubianka. Stalin i NKVD-NKGB-GUKR "Smersh" 1939–mart 1946. Arkhiv Stalina. Dokumenty vysshikh organov partiinoi i gosudarstvennoi vlast,* ed. V. N. Khaustov (Moscow: Materik, 2006), 303–305.

39. Lomagin, "Soldiers at War," 25–26.

40. Stalin, "Twenty-fourth Anniversary of the October Revolution," 27. Prior to the war Stalin forbade use of the term *National Socialists* and insisted the Nazis be referred to as *fascists*.

41. Stalin, "May Day, 1942," ibid., 48–49.

42. Ehrenburg, "About Hatred," 143, 144.

43. Ilya Ehrenburg, "On Patriotism," in Ehrenburg and Simonov, *In One Newspaper,* 177.

44. Elena Seniavskaia, "Heroic Symbols: The Reality and Mythology of War," *Russian Studies in History* 31, 1 (1998): 81–82. See also Rosalinde Sartorti, "On the Making of Heroes, Heroines, and Saints," in *Culture and Entertainment in Wartime Russia,* ed. Richard Stites (Bloomington: Indiana University Press, 1995), 176–193.

45. Elena Seniavskaia, "Obraz germanii i nemtsev v gody vtoroi mirovoi voiny glazami sovetskikh soldat i ofitserov," *Voenno-istoricheskii arkhiv* 13 (2000): 11–58.

46. Lev N. Puskharaev, "Slovesnye istochniki dlia izucheniia mental'nosti sovetskogo naroda v gody Velikoi Otechestvennoi voiny," *Voprosy istorii* 4 (2001): 129.

47. Vladimir A. Nevezhin, "Metamorfozy sovetskoi propagandy v 1939–1941 godakh," *Voprosy istorii* 8 (1994): 164–171.

48. Seniavskaia, "Obraz germanii i nemtsev v gody vtoroi mirovoi voiny glazami sovetskikh soldat i ofitserov," 16–17.

49. For general studies of Soviet propaganda, see Peter Kenez, *The Birth of the Propaganda State, 1917–1929* (Cambridge: Cambridge University Press, 1985), and Jeffrey Brooks, *Thank You, Comrade Stalin! Soviet Public Culture from Revolution to Cold War* (Princeton, N.J.: Princeton University Press, 2000).

50. TsA FSB RF f. 40, op. 10, d. 351/1, ll. 134–43, in *Lubianka v dni bitvy za Moskvu: Materialy organov gosbezopasnosti SSSR iz Tsentral'nogo arkhiva FSB Rossii,* ed. V. K. Vinogradov (Moscow: Evonnitsa-MG, 2002), 263.

51. TsA FSB RF f. 14, op. 4, d. 287, ll. 150–154, ibid., 304.

52. TsA FSB RF f. 14, op. 4, d. 296, ll. 106–110, ibid., 310.

53. TsA FSB RF f. 40, op. 80, d. 351, ll. 74–80, ibid., 230.

54. Ibid.

55. "Direktiva GUPP KA voennym sovetam, nachal'nikam UPP frontov ob itogakh partiino-politicheskoi raboty za tri nedele voiny," in *Russkii arkhiv: Velikaia Otechestvennaia: Glavnye politicheskie organy Vooruzhennykh sil SSSR v Velikoi Otechestvennoi voine 1941–1945 gg.: Dokumenty i materialy*, vol. 17-6 (1-2), ed. Vladimir A. Zolotarev (Moscow: Terra, 1996), 42–44.

56. RGASI f. 17, op. 125, d. 58, ll. 207–208, in A. Ia. Livshin and I. B. Orlov, *Sovetskaia propaganda v gody Velikoi Otechestvennoi voiny: "Kommunikatsia ubezhdeniia" i mobilizatsionnye mekhanizmy* (Moscow: Rossen, 2007), 593.

57. Gennadii Shutz interview, http://www.iremember.ru/content/view/186/84/lang,en/ (accessed 24 July 2006).

58. Seniavskaia, "Heroic Symbols," 67–68.

59. "Direktiva GUPP KA voennym sovetam i nachal'nikam UPP frontov i armii ob ispol'zovanii lozungov, podgotovlennykh GUPP KA," in Zolotarev, *Russkii arkhiv*, vol. 17-6 (1-2), 36–38.

60. "Direktiva GUPP KA voennym sovetam i nachal'nikam UPP frontov o rabote s pamiatkoi krasnoarmeitsu," ibid., 38–39.

61. "Direktiva GlavPU RKKA nachal'nikam politupravlenii frontov, okrugov i otdel'nykh armii o propagande prikaza NKO no. 130 ot 1 maia 1942 g.," ibid., 133–134.

62. "Direktiva GlavPU RKKA nachal'nikam politupravlenii frontov i okrugov o rasprostranenii lozungov dlia voisk RKKA," ibid., 154–158.

63. "Donesenie nachal'niku GPU RKKA A. S. Shcherbakovu," in Livshin and Orlov, *Sovetskaia propaganda v gody Velikoi Otechestvennoi voiny*, 634–643.

64. "Direktiva GlavPU RKKA nachal'nikam politupravlenii frontov, okrugov, nachal'nikam politotdelov armii, soedinenii ob usilenii ideinogo vospitaniia molodykh kommunistov," in Zolotarev, *Russkii arkhiv*, vol. 17-6 (1-2), 274–275.

65. Suzanne Ament, "Reflecting Individual and Collective Identities: Songs of World War II," in *Gender and National Identity in Twentieth-Century Russian Culture*, ed. Helena Goscilo and Andrea Lanoux (De Kalb: Northern Illinois University Press, 2006), 116–117.

66. For the content and variety of poetry, see also Katharine Hodgson, *Written with the Bayonet: Soviet Russian Poetry of World War Two* (Liverpool: Liverpool University Press, 1996), and "The Other Veterans: Soviet Women's Poetry of World War 2," in *World War 2 and the Soviet People: Selected Papers from the*

Fourth World Congress for Soviet and East European Studies, Harrogate, 1990, ed. John Garrard and Carol Garrard (New York: St. Martin's Press, 1993), 77–97. For songs, see Robert A. Rothstein, "Homeland, Home Town, and Battlefield: The Popular Song," in *Entertainment and Culture in Wartime Russia,* ed. Richard Stites (Bloomington: Indiana University Press, 1995), 77–94.

67. "Obrazchenie vseslavianskogo mitinga ko vsem slavianskim narodam," *Izvestiia,* 12 August 1941, ibid., 65–67.

68. "Direktiva GlavPU RKKA nachal'nikam politupravlenii okrgov, frontov, i otdel'nykh armii o soderzhanii propagandistskoi raboty s tematikoi lektsii, dokladov, besed," ibid., 83–84.

69. "Direktiva GlavPU RKKA nachal'niku politupravleniia sredneaziaskogo voennogo okruga russovu, nachal'niku politupravleniia Zakavkazskogo fronta sorokinu ob ulucheshenii kinoobsluzhivaniia voitsov nerusskoi natsional'nost, 10 dekabria 1943 g.," "Direktiva GlavPU RKKA nachal'nikam politupravlenii frontov i okrugov ob uluchshenii ideino-politicheskogo soderzhaniia gazet izdaiushchikhsia na iazykakh narodov SSSR, 4 aprelia 1944 g.," and "Direktiva GlavPU RKKA nachal'nikam politupravlenii MVO, PriVO, IUzUrVO, SAVO, o rabote sredi voinov nerusskoi natsional'nosti v zapasnykh brigadakh okrgov," ibid., 139–140, 243–244, 266–267.

70. "Direktiva GlavPU RKKA nachal'nikam politupravlenii frontov, okrugov o vospitatel'noi rabote s krasnoarmeitsami i mladshimi komandirami nerusskoi natsional'nosti," ibid., 173–174.

71. "Direktiva GUPP KA voennym sovetam i nachal'nikam UPP frontov, okrugov i armii o povyshenii avangardnoi roli kommunistov i chlenov VLKSM v boiu," in Zolotarev, *Russkii arkhiv,* vol. 17-6 (1-2), 40–41.

72. "Prikaz nachal'nika GlavPU RKKA ob ustranenii nedostatkov v partiino-politicheskoi rabote v 7-i otdel'noi armii," ibid., 249–252.

CHAPTER 9. LEADERSHIP, REWARDS, MORALE, AND THE PRIMARY GROUP

1. E. I. Baranovskii and V. D. Selemenev, eds.. "'Tolko avtoritetnyi komandir smozhet zastavit' preodolet' strakh i instinkt samosokhraneniia': Dokladnye zapiska sekretaria TsK KP(b)B P. K. Ponomarenko I. V. Stalinu. 1940–1942 gg.," *Istoricheskii arkhiv* 6 (2004): 60–61.

2. John Dollard, *Fear in Battle* (1944; reprint, Westport, Conn.: Greenwood, 1977), 44–45, 54.

3. Mansur Abdulin, *Red Road from Stalingrad: Recollections of a Soviet Infantryman* (Barnsley, South Yorkshire: Pen and Sword, 2004), 88.

4. Ibid., 94.

5. Petr Cherkasov, "Leto 1941-go: Mezhdu gomelem i brianskom," *Otechestvennaia istoriia* 2 (2005): 37, 38.

6. Roger Reese, *Stalin's Reluctant Soldiers: A Social History of the Red Army, 1925–1941* (Lawrence: University Press of Kansas, 1996), 163–186.

7. John Erickson, "Red Army Battlefield Performance, 1941–45: The System and the Soldier," in *Time to Kill: The Soldier's Experience of War in the West 1939–1945*, ed. Paul Addison and Angus Calder (London: Pimlico, 1997), 236.

8. *Skrytaia pravda voiny: 1941 god* (Moscow: Russkaia kniga, 1992), 342.

9. "Prikaz o boevoi podgotovke slushatelei filialov kursov 'Vystrel' voennykh okrugov i frontov," in *Russkii arkhiv: Velikaia Otechestvennaia: Prikazy Narodnogo komissara oborony SSSR (1943–1945 gg.)* vol. 13 (2-3), ed. Vladimir A. Zolotarev (Moscow: Terra, 1997), 50–52.

10. "Prikaz o merakh po ukrepleniiu distsipliny v chastiakh Iuzhno-ural'skogo voennogo okruga," ibid., 57–58.

11. TsA FSB RF f. 40, op. 10, d. 351/1, ll. 134–143, in *Lubianka v dni bitvy za Moskvu: Materialy organov gosbezopasnosti SSSR iz Tsentral'nogo arkhiva FSB Rossii,* ed. V. K. Vinogradov (Moscow: Evonnitsa-MG, 2002), 263–264.

12. Aleksandr Bodnar' interview, http://www.iremember.ru/content/view/96/76/lang,en/ (accessed 20 July 2006).

13. Vasily Grossman, *A Writer at War: Vasily Grossman with the Red Army 1941–1945,* ed. and trans. Antony Beevor and Luba Vinogradova (London: Harvill Press, 2005), 73.

14. TsA FSB RF f. 4, op. 4, d. 74, ll. 47–58, in Vinogradov, *Lubianka v dni bitvy za Moskvu,* 248–249.

15. TsA FSB RF f. 40, op. 10, d. 100, ll. 358–363, ibid., 270.

16. "Prikaz o pooshchrenii boitsov i komandirov za boevuiu rabotu po unichtozheniiu tankov protivnika" in Zolotarev, *Russkii arhkiv,* vol. 13 (2-3), 186.

17. "Prikaz Narodnogo Komissara Oborony Soiuza SSR o vvedenii denezhnykh nagrad za evakuatsiiu tankov v frontovykh usloviiakh i ustanovleniia premirovaniia za remont boevykh mashin na khozrashchetnykh ABT rembazakh," in *Russkii arkhiv: Velikaia Otechestvennaia. Tyl Krasnoi Armii v Velikoi Otechestvennoi voine 1941–1945 gg.: Dokumenty i material,* vol. 25 (14) 4, ed. Vladimir A. Zolotarev (Moscow: Terra, 1998), 341–342.

18. *Poslednie pis'ma s fronta,* vol. 2, 1942 (Moscow: Voenizdat, 1991), 205–207.

19. "Pis'mo t. Velichko," *Istoricheskii arkhiv* 2 (2005): 6–7.

20. "Pis'mo pisatelia V. E. Ardova," *Istoricheskii arkhiv* 2 (2005): 27–30.

21. "'Tolko avtoritetnyi komandir smozhet zastavit' preodolet' strakh i instinkt samosokhraneniia . . . ,'" *Istoricheskii arkhiv* 6 (2004): 62–63.

22. Natalia Peshkova interview, http://www.iremember.ru/content/view/289/89/lang,en/ (accessed 25 July 2006).

23. Abdulin, *Red Road from Stalingrad,* 96, 86–87.

24. Semion Aria interview, http://www.iremember.ru/content/view/98/76/lang,en/ (accessed 20 July 2006).

25. Evgenii Mazo interview by the author.

26. Abdulin, *Red Road from Stalingrad,* 85.

27. *Poslednie pis'ma s fronta,* vol. 2, *1942,* 351.

28. "Prikaz ob organizatsii priema i dostavki posylok ot krasnoarmeitsev, serzhantov, ofitserov i generalov deistvuiushchikh frontov v tyl strany," in Zolotarev, *Russkii arhkiv,* vol. 13 (2-3), 344–345.

29. TsA FSB RF f. 40, op. 10, d. 100, ll. 228–233, in Vinogradov, *Lubianka v dni bitvy za Moskvu,* 254.

30. TsA FSB RF f. 14, op. 4, d. 318, ll. 98–101, ibid., 275–278.

31. TsA FSB RF f. 14, op. 4, d. 418, ll. 17–18, in *Stalingradskaia epopeia: Materialy NKVD SSSR i voennoi tsenzury iz Tsentral'nogo arkhiva FSB RF* (Moscow: Zvonnitsa-MG, 2000), 265–266.

32. TsAMO FSB RF f. 2, op. 794537, d. 3, l. 39, in Zolotarev, *Russkii arkhiv,* vol. 25 (14) 4, 100–101.

33. "Prikaz o rezul'tatakh proverki sostoianiia material'nogo obespecheniia 8-i gvardeiskoi strelkovoi divizii imeni General-Maiora Panfilova," in Zolotarev, *Russkii arhkiv,* vol. 13 (2-3), 29–30.

34. "Pikaz o nedostatkakh v material'no-bytovom obsluzhivanii boitsov na fronte i v zapasnykh chastiakh," ibid., 36–38.

35. "Prikaz pervogo zamestitelia narodnogo komissara oborony o rezul'tatakh obsledovaniia 103 SD Zabaikal'skogo fronta v sviazi s zabolevaemost'iu alimentarnoi distrofiei," ibid., 268–270.

36. Mikhail M. Kuznetsov interview, http://www.iremember.ru/content/view/28/75/lang,en/ (accessed 15 July 2006).

37. TsA FSB RF f. 40, op. 10, d. 100, ll. 228–233, in Vinogradov, *Lubianka v dni bitvy za Moskvu,* 254.

38. TsA FSB RF f. 14, op. 4, d. 296, ll. 57–65, ibid., 293–301.

39. "Pikaz o nedostatkakh v material'no-bytovom obsluzhivanii boitsov na fronte i v zapasnykh chastiakh," in Zolotarev, *Russkii arhkiv,* vol. 13 (2-3), 37–38.

40. Kuznetsov interview.

41. Abdulin, *Red Road from Stalingrad*, 159.

42. Alexander Pyl'cyn, *Penalty Strike: The Memoirs of a Red Army Penal Company Commander, 1943–45* (Solehul, England: Helion, 2006), 84, 88.

43. RGASPI f. 17, op. 125, d. 80, l. 28, in *Sovetskaia propaganda v gody Velikoi Otechestvennoi voiny: "Kommunikatsiia ubezhdeniia" i mobilizatsionnye mekhanismy*, ed. A. Ia. Livshin and I. B. Orlov (Moscow: Rosspen, 2007), 610–611.

44. Abdulin, *Red Road from Stalingrad*, 57–58.

45. RGASPI f. 17, op. 125, d. 129, ll. 34–36, in Livshin and Orlov, *Sovetskaia propaganda v gody Velikoi Otechestvennoi voiny*, 652–654.

46. E. A. Shils and Morris Janowitz, "Cohesion and Disintegration in the Wehrmacht in World War II," *Public Opinion Quarterly* 12 (1948): 280–315.

47. Omer Bartov, *Hitler's Army: Soldiers, Nazis, and War in the Third Reich* (New York: Oxford University Press, 1991); Stephen G. Fritz, *Frontsoldaten: The German Soldier in World War II* (Lexington: University Press of Kentucky, 1995).

48. Bruce Newsome, "The Myth of Intrinsic Combat Motivation," *Journal of Strategic Studies* 26, 4 (December 2003): 39–41.

49. Alexander L. George, "Primary Groups, Organization, and Military Performance," in *Handbook of Military Institutions*, ed. Roger W. Little (Beverly Hills, Calif.: Sage, 1971), 293–318.

50. Semion A. Chumanev interview, http://www.iremember.ru/content/view/183/82/lang,en/ (accessed 24 July 2006).

51. Testimonial by Sergei Abaulin, http://www.iremember.ru/content/view/188/82/lang,en/ (accessed 24 July 2006).

52. Georgii Minin interview, http://www.iremember.ru/content/view/50/56/lang,en/ (accessed 7 July 2008).

53. Viktor Leonov, "I Spoke to the Germans in Russian," *Russkii Dom* 1, (1997): 13.

54. Ivan Yakushin, *On the Roads of War: A Soviet Cavalryman on the Eastern Front*, trans and ed. Bair Irincheev (Barnsley, South Yorkshire: Pen and Sword, 2005), 68.

55. Yuri Koriakin interview, http://www.iremember.ru/content/view/229/85/lang,en/ (accessed 24 July 2006).

56. Peshkova interview.

57. Gennadii Shutz interview, http://www.iremember.ru/content/view/186/84/lang,en/ (accessed 24 July 2006).

58. Ivan Kobets interview, http://www.iremember.ru/content/view/14/71/lang,en/ (accessed 15 July 2006).

59. Naum A. Orlov interview, http://www.iremember.ru/content/view/65/69/ lang,en/ (accessed 16 July 2006).

60. Robert Stephan, "Smersh: Soviet Military Counter-Intelligence during the Second World War," *Journal of Contemporary History* 22, 4 (October 1987): 595, 597–598.

61. Boris Ol'shanskii Papers, 85–86, 88, 103, Bakhmeteff Archive, Rare Books and Manuscript Library, Columbia University, New York.

62. Leonov, "I Spoke to the Germans in Russian," 13.

63. Ol'shanskii Papers, 71–72.

64. Grossman, *Writer at War*, 139.

65. TsA FSB RF f. 40, op. 10, d. 351/1, ll. 134–143, in Vinogradov, *Lubianka v dni bitvy za Moskvu*, 262.

66. Iakov Grichener interview by the author.

67. Nikolai Blizniuk, "Eto vam ne 41-i," in *Po povestke i po prizyvu. Nekadrovye soldaty Velikoi Otechestvennoi Voine*, ed. Iurii Mukhin (Moscow: Iauza/Eksmo, 2005), 223.

68. Ivan Garshtia interview, http://www.iremember.ru/content/view/567/75/ lang,en/ (accessed 8 December 2007).

CHAPTER 10. FAILURES IN EFFECTIVENESS

1. RGANI f. 89, op. 18, d. 8, ll. 1–3, in *Lubianka. Stalin i NKVD-NKGB-GUKR "Smersh" 1939–mart 1946. Arkhiv Stalina. Dokumenty vysshikh organov partiinoi i gosudarstvennoi vlast*, ed. V. N. Khaustov (Moscow: Materik, 2006), 317–318.

2. V. A. Gashenko, "Organy gosudarstvennoi bezopasnosti Zapadnoi Sibiri v Velikoi Otechestvennoi voine (1941–1945 gg.)," in *Zapadnaia Sibir' v Velikoi Otechestvennoi voine (1941–1945 gg)* (Novosibirsk: Nauka-Tsentr, 2004), 224–225, 230; A. I. Vol'khin, "O kharaktere arestov na urale i v sibiri v gody voiny," *Voenno-istoricheskii arkhiv* 11 (November 2007): 152.

3. Boris Ol'shanskii Papers, 52, Bakhmeteff Archive, Rare Books and Manuscript Library, Columbia University, New York.

4. Nikita Lomagin, "Soldiers at War: German Propaganda and Soviet Army Morale during the Battle of Leningrad, 1941–44," *Carl Beck Papers in Russian and East European Studies*, no. 1306 (Pittsburgh: University of Pittsburgh, 1998), 10, 13.

5. Ibid., 12, 16, 19.

6. Ibid., 27–28.

7. John Dollard, *Fear in Battle* (1944; reprint, Westport, Conn.: Greenwood, 1977), 38–39.

8. Robert H. Ahrenfeldt, *Psychiatry in the British Army in the Second World War* (New York: Columbia University Press, 1958), 204.

9. TsA FSB RF f. 14, op. 4, d. 262, ll. 141–149, in *Lubianka v dni bitvy za Moskvu: Materialy organov gosbezopasnosti SSSR iz Tsentral'nogo arkhiva FSB Rossii*, ed. V. K. Vinogradov (Moscow: Evonnitsa-MG, 2002), 259.

10. "Direktiva GlavPU RKKA voennym sovetam, nachal'nikam politupravlenii frontov, armii voennym komissaram i nachpolitotdelov divizii ob usilenii vospitatel'noi raboty v razvedyvatel'nykh podrazdeleniiakh," in *Russkii arkhiv: Velikaia Otechestvennaia: Glavnye politicheskie organy Vooruzhennykh sil SSSR v Velikoi Otechestvennoi voine 1941–1945 gg.: Dokumenty i materialy*, vol. 17-6 (1-2), ed. Vladimir A. Zolotarev (Moscow: Terra, 1996), 92–94.

11. Efim A. Gol'braikh interview, http://www.iremember.ru/content/view/57/75/lang,en/ (accessed 16 July 2006).

12. Charles McMoran Wilson, Lord Moran, *The Anatomy of Courage: The Classic WW I Acccount of the Psychological Effects of War* (1947; reprint, London: Constable and Robinson, 2007), 19–26.

13. Ibid., 26.

14. The presence of psychiatric disorders in the Red Army is a vastly understudied topic. For the most recent work, see Paul Wanke, *Russian/Soviet Military Psychiatry 1904–1945* (London: Frank Cass, 2005).

15. E. I. Baranovskii and V. D. Selemenev, eds., "'Tolko avtoritetnyi komandir smozhet zastavit' preodolet' strakh i instinkt samosokhraneniia:' Dokladnye zapiska sekretaria TsK KP(b)B P. K. Ponomarenko I. V. Stalinu. 1940–1942 gg.," *Istoricheskii arkhiv* 6 (2004): 53.

16. Ibid., 53–54.

17. Dollard, *Fear in Battle*, 6–7, 8–9, 24–25.

18. "Voennomu sovetu 66-i armii o nedostatkakh v organizatsii marsha i nastupleniia 299-i strelkovoi divizii," in *Russkii arkhiv: Velikaia Otechestvennaia: General'nyi shtab v gody Velikoi Otechestvennoi voiny: dokumenty i materialy 1942 god*, vol. 23, (12- 2), ed. Vladimir A. Zolotarev (Moscow: Terra, 1999), 382.

19. Dmitri Volkogonov, *Stalin: Triumph and Tragedy* (New York: Grove Weidenfeld, 1991), 446.

20. G. F. Krivosheev et al., *Velikaia Otechestvennaia bez grifa sekretnosti. Kniga poter'* (Moscow: Veche, 2010), 37; Vitalii Perezhogin, "Iz okruzheniia i plena—v partizany," *Otechestvennaia istoriia* 3 (2000): 25; Arsen Martirosian, *100 Mifov o Berii: Ot slavy k prokliatiiam. 1941–1953 gg.* (Moscow: Veche, 2010), 158–159.

21. Martirosian, *100 Mifov o Berii*, 158.

22. "Iz pis'ma G. M. Dubinina," *Istoricheskii arkhiv* 3 (2007): 47–48.

23. Gabriel Temkin, *My Just War: The Memoir of a Jewish Red Army Soldier in World War II* (Novato, Calif.: Presidio, 1998), 56.

24. Ibid., 66–84; Aleksandr A. Goncharov interview, located at http://www.iremember.ru/content/view/189/82/lang,en/ (accessed 24 July 2006).

25. Harvard University Refugee Interview Project, #79, 8–9, Hoover Institution Archives, Stanford University, Stanford, Calif.

26. Georgii Minin interview, http://www.iremember.ru/content/view/50/56/lang,en/ (accessed 7 July 2007).

27. Vladimir Dolmatov interview, http://www.iremember.ru/content/view/307/89/lang,en/ (accessed 25 July 2006).

28. "Direktiva GlavPU RKKA nachal'nikam politupravlenii okrugov, nachal'nikam politpravlenii Zabaikal'skogo i Dal'nevostochnogo frontov ob uluchshenii perevozok voisk po zheleznym dorogam," in Zolotarev, *Russkii arkhiv*, vol. 17-6 (1-2), 129–130.

29. TsAMO f. 48, op. 486, d. 35, l. 24, in Iu. N. Semin, Iu. V. Sigachev, and S. I. Chuvasin, "Na linii fronta: Dokumenty Tsentral'nogo arkhiva Ministerstva oborony RF. 1941–1945 gg.," *Istoricheskii arkhiv* 2 (1995): 64.

30. TsAMO f. 233, op. 2374, d. 85, ll. 84–114, ibid., 33, 37, 50.

31. Harvard University Refugee Interview Project, #118, 36, Hoover Institution Archives.

32. Ibid., #121, 5–6.

33. Ibid., #2, 7, Bakhmeteff Archive.

34. Ibid., #40, 18, Hoover Institution Archives.

35. Hew Strachan, "Training, Morale and Modern War," *Journal of Contemporary History* 4, 2 (2006): 211–227; Anthony King, "The Word of Command: Communication and Cohesion in the Military," *Armed Forces and Society* 32, 4 (July 2006): 493–512.

36. RGANI f. 89, op. 74, d. 17, l. 5.

37. Semen V. Matveev interview, http://www.iremember.ru/content/view/88/76/lang,en/ (accessed 20 July 2006).

38. TsAMO f. 388, op. 8719, d. 2, ll. 30–31, in *Bitva za Stolitsu: sbornik dokumentov, vol. 1, Ot oborony k kontrnastupleniiu* (Moscow: UVTII, 1994), 196–197.

39. John Erickson, "Red Army Battlefield Performance, 1941–45: The System and the Soldier," in *Time to Kill: The Soldier's Experience of War in the West 1939–1945*, ed. Paul Addison and Angus Calder (London: Pimlico, 1997), 243.

40. Maksim Mosiagin, "21-ia diviziia narodnogo opolcheniia-173 SD," *Voenno-istoricheskii arkhiv* 10 (October 2006): 156.

41. Valerii Stepanov, "'Sily byli bezbozhno neravny . . . ,'" *Voenno-istoricheskii arkhiv* 4 (April 2007): 139–140; Sergei Ivanov, "Rasstrelian pered stroem: Sud'ba polkovnika Kozlova," *Rodina* 12 (2006): 112–114.

42. "Donesenie komandovaniia 26-i armiei voennomu sovetu Iugo-zapadnogo fronta o sostoianii 289 SD pribyvshei na ukomplektovanie armii," in *Russkii arkhiv: Velikaia Otechestvennaia. Tyl Krasnoi Armii v Velikoi Otechestvennoi voine 1941–1945 gg.: Dokumenty i materialy*, vol. 25 (14), ed. Vladimir A. Zolotarev (Moscow: Terra, 1998), 108–109.

43. "Prikaz o nachal'noi podgotovke v sisteme Vsevobucha chetvertoi ocheredi boitsov-spetsialistov," in *Russkii arkhiv: Velikaia Otechestvennaia: Prikazy Narodnogo komissara oborony SSSR (1943–1945 gg.)*, vol. 13 (2-3), ed. Vladimir A. Zolotarev (Moscow: Terra, 1997), 44–45, 47, 48.

44. "Prikaz o rezul'tatakh proverki sostoianiia 16-i zapasnoi strelkovoi brigady Orlovskogo voennogo okruga i 11-i zapasnoi strelkovoi brigady Khar'kovskogo voennogo okruga," ibid., 243–244.

45. Ahrenfeldt, *Psychiatry in the British Army,* 204–205.

46. TsA FSB RF f. 40, op. 10, d. 100, ll. 74–77, in Vinogradov, *Lubianka v dni bitvy za Moskvu,* 235–237.

47. Vasily Grossman, *A Writer at War: Vasily Grossman with the Red Army 1941–1945,* ed. and trans. Antony Beevor and Luba Vinogradova (London: Harvill Press, 2005), 71.

48. TsA FSB RF f. 14, op. 4, d. 74, ll. 41–46, in Vinogradov, *Lubianka v dni bitvy za Moskvu,* 209.

49. TsA FSB RF f. 40, op. 80, d. 351, ll. 74–80, ibid., 231.

50. TsA FSB RF f. 14, op. 4, d. 262, ll. 141–149, ibid., 257.

51. TsA FSB RF f. 40, op. 10, d. 351/1, ll. 134–143, ibid., 262, 263.

52. TsA FSB RF f. 40, op. 10, d. 100, ll. 358–363, ibid., 270.

53. Ibid., 268.

54. Ibid.

55. TsA FSB RF f. 14, op. 4, d. 287, ll. 150–154, ibid., 305.

56. Ibid., 304.

57. TsA FSB RF f. 4, op. 4, d. 74, ll. 47–58, ibid., 248.

58. TsA FSB RF f. 40, op. 80, d. 351, ll. 74–80, ibid., 230.

59. TsA FSB RF f. 40, op. 10, d. 351/1, ll. 134–143, ibid., 263–264.

60. TsA FSB RF f. 14, op. 4, d. 74, ll. 41–46, ibid., 205.

61. TsA FSB RF f. 40, op. 10, d. 330, ll. 169–173, ibid., 317–318.

62. TsA FSB RF f. 14, op. 4, d. 74, ll. 41–46, ibid., 207.

63. TsA FSB RF f. 14, op. 4, d. 296, ll. 106–110, ibid., 310.

64. TsA FSB RF f. 14, op. 4, d. 74, ll. 41–46, ibid., 205.

65. "Direktiva GlavPU RKKA nachal'nikam politupravlenii frontov, okrugov o vospitatel'noi rabote s krasnoarmeitsami i mladshimi komandirami nerusskoi natsional'nosti," in Zolotarev, *Russkii arkhiv,* vol. 17-6 (1-2), 173–174.

66. Petr S. Margulis interview, http://www.iremember.ru/infantry/margulis/margulis_r.htm (accessed 11 March 2005).

67. Harvard University Refugee Interview Project, #379, 32, Hoover Institution Archives.

68. Minin interview.

69. Harvard University Refugee Interview Project, #504, 4, Bakhmeteff Archive.

70. AP RF f. 3, op. 58, d. 207, 176, in Khaustov, *Lubianka. Stalin i NKVD,* 389.

71. Harvard University Refugee Interview Project, #40, 29–30, Hoover Institution Archives.

72. Ibid., #79, 4–5.

73. Ibid., #221, #262, Bakhmeteff Archive.

74. TsAMO f. 48a, op. 3408, d. 4, l. 47, in Zolotarev, *Russkii arkhiv,* vol. 23 (12-2), 90.

75. Iakov Grichener interview by the author.

76. Harvard University Refugee Interview Project, #111, 91, Hoover Institution Archives.

77. Alan Palmer, *The Baltic: A New History of the Region and Its People* (New York: Overlook Press, 2005), 363.

78. "Prikaz o ser'eznykh nedostatkakh v 50-i Litovskoi zapasnoi strelkovoi divizii i nakazanii vinovnykh," in Zolotarev, *Russkii arkhiv,* vol. 13 (2-3), 341–342.

79. Palmer, *The Baltic,* 360.

80. "Dokladniia zapiska UNKGB i UNKVD po g. Moskve i Moskovskoi oblasti no. 1/344 zamestiteliu narkoma vnutrennikh del SSSR V.S. Abakumovu o polozheniia v g. Moskve v sviazi s nachalom voiny," in *Organy gosudarstvennoi bezopasnosti SSSR v Velikoi Otechestvennoi voine: Sbornik dokumentov: Nachalo, 22 iiunia–31 avgusta 1941 goda,* vol. 2, book 1 (Moscow: Rus', 2000), 68–70.

81. "Spetssvodka UNKGB po g. Moskve i Moskovskoi oblasti 1-my sekretaria MK i MGK VKP(b) A.S. Shcherbakovu o reagirovanii naseleniia na vystuplenie I.V. Stalina," ibid., 167–169.

82. "Smiatenie oseni sorok pervogo goda: Dokumenty o volneniiakh ivanovskikh tekstil'shchikov," *Istoricheskii arkhiv* 2 (1994): 118–136; Richard Bidlack, "The Political Mood in Leningrad during the First Year of the Soviet-German War," *Russian Review* 59, 1 (January 2000): 96–113.

83. A. I. Vol'khin, "O kharaktere arestov na urale i v sibiri v gody voiny," *Voenno-istoricheskii arkhiv* 11 (November 2007): 152–157.

CHAPTER 11. PERSPECTIVES ON WOMEN'S MOTIVATION IN THE GREAT PATRIOTIC WAR

1. Evelin Vittig, "Zhenshchina i voina. 1941–1945. Rossiia i Germaniia," in *Zhenshchina i voina. 1941–1945. Rossiia i Germaniia: Materialy Mezhdunarodnoi nauchnoi konferentsii g. Volgograd, 12–13 maia 2005 g.*, ed. A. V. Shestakova (Volgograd, 2006), 21.

2. G. F. Krivosheev et al., *Velikaia Otechestvennaia bez grifa sekretnosti. Kniga poter'* (Moscow: Veche, 2010), 38; Susanne Conze and Beate Fieseler, "Soviet Women as Comrades-in-Arms: A Blind Spot in the History of the War," in *The People's War: Responses to World War II in the Soviet Union*, ed. Robert W. Thurston and Bernd Bonwetsch (Chicago: University of Illinois Press, 2000), 211–234; Valentina Ia. Galagan, *Ratnyi podvig zhenshchin v gody Velikoi Otechestvennoi voiny* (Kiev: Vyshche Shkola, 1986), 162–163.

3. Kazimeira J. Cottam, "Soviet Women in Combat in World War II: The Ground/Air Defense Forces," in *Women in Eastern Europe and the Soviet Union*, ed. Tova Yedlin (New York: Praeger, 1980), 116.

4. Laurie Stoff, *They Fought for the Motherland: Russia's Women Soldiers in World War I and the Revolution* (Lawrence: University Press of Kansas, 2006), 23–24.

5. Iu. N. Ivanova, "Zhenshchiny v istorii rossiiskoi armii," *Voenno-istoricheskii zhurnal* 3 (1992): 86–93.

6. Stoff, *They Fought for the Motherland*, 26. More recent but as yet unpublished research by Stoff has caused her to raise this number from 18,000 to 25,000.

7. Ibid., 30–33.

8. Ibid., 33, 37.

9. Melissa Stockdale, "'My Death for the Motherland Is Happiness': Women, Patriotism, and Soldiering in Russia's Great War, 1914–1917," *American Historical Review* 109, 1 (2004): 80.

10. Stoff, *They Fought for the Motherland*, 90–113, quote on 141. For the quote, Stoff cites "Vserossiskii zhenskii voennyi s'ezd," *Novoe vremia*, 13 July 1917, 4.

11. Stoff, *They Fought for the Motherland*, 1.

12. Stockdale, "'My Death for the Motherland Is Happiness,'" 88, 100–101.

13. Ibid., 81–82, 88.

14. Ibid., 101.

15. Ibid.

16. I thank Laurie Stoff for this insight. Svetlana Aleksievich gives several examples of unwed women or women with husbands at the front who used their desire to join the army and defend the *rodina* to justify abortions in *War's Unwomanly Face,* trans. Keith Hammond and Liudmila Lezhneva (Moscow: Progress, 1988), 29.

17. Elizabeth A. Wood, *The Baba and the Comrade: Gender and Politics in Revolutionary Russia* (Bloomington: Indiana University Press, 1997), 56; Anne Eliot Griesse and Richard Stites, "Russia: Revolution and War," in *Female Soldiers— Combatants or Noncombatants? Historical and Contemporary Perspectives,* ed. Nancy Goldman (Westport, Conn.: Greenwood, 1982), 67.

18. Josh Sanborn, *Drafting the Russian Nation: Military Conscription, Total War, and Mass Politics 1905–1925* (De Kalb: Northern Illinois University Press, 2003), 153, 157.

19. Reina Pennington, "Offensive Women: Women in Combat in the Red Army," in *Time to Kill: The Soldier's Experience of War in the West 1939–1945,* ed. Paul Addison and Angus Calder (London: Pimlico, 1997), 252. The quote by Klara Tikhonovich is from Aleksievich, *War's Unwomanly Face,* 156. See also Pennington's revised and reissued "Offensive Women: Women in Combat in the Red Army," *Journal of Military History* 74, 3 (July 2010): 786. The quote by Tikhonovich is not included in this version.

20. Anna Krylova, "Stalinist Identity from the Viewpoint of Gender: Rearing a Generation of Professionally Violent Women-Fighters in 1930s Stalinist Russia," *Gender and History* 16, 3 (November 2004): 628.

21. Choi Chatterjee, *Celebrating Women: Gender, Festival Culture, and Bolshevik Ideology, 1910–1939* (Pittsburgh: University of Pittsburgh Press, 2002), 105–112.

22. Mary Buckley, "Soviet Ideology and Female Roles," in *Ideology and Soviet Politics,* ed. Stephen White and Alex Pravda (New York: St. Martin's Press, 1988), 161.

23. Chatterjee, *Celebrating Women,* 124–126.

24. Matt Oja, "From Krestianka to Udarnitsa: Rural Women and the Vydvizhenie Campaign, 1933–1941," *Carl Beck Papers in Russian and East European Studies,* no. 1203 (Pittsburgh: University of Pittsburgh, 1996).

25. Chatterjee, *Celebrating Women,* 131.

26. Richard Stites, *The Women's Liberation Movement in Russia* (Princeton, N.J.: Princeton University Press, 1978), 397–398.

27. Chatterjee, *Celebrating Women,* 160.

28. Wood, *The Baba and the Comrade*, 53.

29. Sanborn, *Drafting the Russian Nation*, 156.

30. Alice Schuster, "Women's Role in the Soviet Union: Ideology and Reality," *Russian Review* 30, 3 (July 1971): 260.

31. John Erickson, "Soviet Women at War," in *World War 2 and the Soviet People: Selected Papers from the Fourth World Congress for Soviet and East European Studies, Harrogate, 1990*, ed. John Garrard and Carol Garrard (New York: St. Martin's Press, 1993), 62; Vera S. Murmantseva, *Sovetskie zhenshchiny v Velikoi Otechestvennoi voine* (Moscow: Mysl', 1974), 119.

32. Galagan, *Ratnyi podvig zhenshchin v gody Velikoi Otechestvennoi voiny*, 28–29.

33. Ibid., 30, 31.

34. Murmantseva, *Sovetskii zhenshchiny v Velikoi Otechestvennoi voine*, 121–122.

35. Aleksievich, *War's Unwomanly Face*, 25–26.

36. Ibid., 14, 22.

37. GAKO f. R-3191, op. 7, d. 53, l. 27, in *Surovaia pravda voiny: 1941 god na kurskoi zemle v dokumentakh arkhivov*, pt. 1, ed. A. T. Strelkov (Kursk: MIR Kurskaia gorodskaia tipografiia, 2002), 24.

38. "Iz pis'ma Komsomolki Lidii Alekrinskoi v kastorenskii raivoenkomat o napravlenii ee v deistvuiushchuiu armiiu v kachestve meditsinskoi sestry," *Kurskaia pravda* 150, 27 iiunia 1941 g., ibid., 30.

39. Aleksievich, *War's Unwomanly Face*, 24–25.

40. Galagan, *Ratnyi podvig zhenshchin v gody Velikoi Otechestvennoi voiny*, 28, 34.

41. Maria Matveeva, *Ia byla na voine*, 2nd ed. (Moscow: Sovetskaia Rossia, 1990), 5, 6–7, 10, 11–13, 20–21.

42. Aleksievich, *War's Unwomanly Face*, 23.

43. Kyra P. Wayne, *Shurik: A Story of the Siege of Leningrad* (New York: Lyons Press, 2000), 3–4, 14.

44. Anne Noggle, *A Dance with Death: Soviet Airwomen in World War II* (College Station: Texas A&M University Press, 1994), 145.

45. Valentina I. Tokareva, personal narrative, http://www.irememember.ru/content/view/286/88/lang,en/ (accessed 25 July 2006).

46. Zoia A. Khlopotina interview, http://www.irememember.ru/infantry/khlopotina/khlopotina_r.htm (accessed 22 April 2002).

47. Nina A. Solntseva, personal narrative, http://www.irememember.ru/content/view/305/89/lang,en/ (accessed 24 July 2006).

48. Natalia Peshkova interview, http://www.iremember.ru/content/view/289/89/lang,en/ (accessed 25 July 2006).

49. Antonina Kotliarova interview, http://www.iremember.ru/content/view/30/74/lang,en/ (accessed 15 July 2006).

50. Jonathan Glancey, "The Very Few" *Guardian*, 15 December 2001, 37.

51. Ibid.

52. Zoia K. Nekrutova-Ket'ko, "Moi oslepitel'nyi mig," in Iurii Mukhin, *Po povestke i po prizyvu: Nekadrovye soldaty Velikoi Otechestvennoi* (Moscow: Iauza/Eksmo, 2005), 40–80; quotes from 51, 59.

53. *Poslednie pis'ma s fronta*, vol. 3, *1943* (Moscow: Voenizdat, 1991), 68–70.

54. *Poslednie pis'ma s fronta*, vol. 2, *1942*, 23–29.

55. Reina Pennington, *Wings, Women, and War: Soviet Airwomen in World War II Combat* (Lawrence: University Press of Kansas, 2001), 136–137.

56. Noggle, *Dance with Death*, 232.

57. Mariana Miliutina interview, http://www.iremember.ru/content/view/284/88/lang,en/ (accessed 25 July 2006).

58. Tamara Butenko, "I rukovoditel', i vospitatel'," in *Bylo u voiny i zhenskoe litso: Zhenshchiny na voine: ocherki, zarisovki, vospominania, fotografii*, ed. Anatolii Panin and Tamara Butenko (Khar'kov: MTK-kniga, 2005), 9–12.

59. Orlando Figes, *The Whisperers: Private Life in Stalin's Russia* (London: Penguin, 2007), 330–331.

60. Harvard University Refugee Interview Project, #41, Bakhmeteff Archive, Rare Books and Manuscript Library, Columbia University, New York.

61. Griesse and Stites, "Russia: Revolution and War," 79.

62. Erickson, "Soviet Women at War," 62.

63. Cottam, "Soviet Women in Combat in World War II," 117.

64. Anna Krylova, *Soviet Women in Combat: A History of Violence on the Eastern Front* (Cambridge: Cambridge University Press, 2010), 14–29.

65. Ibid., 114.

66. TsDNI KO f. P-1, op. 1, d. 2671, ll. 2–4, in Strelkov, *Surovaia pravda voiny*, 66–67, 68.

67. Mary Buckley, *Women and Ideology in the Soviet Union* (Ann Arbor: University of Michigan Press, 1989), 4.

68. Wood, *The Baba and the Comrade*, 53.

69. Ibid., 54.

70. Stites, *Women's Liberation Movement in Russia*, 393–394.

71. Choi Chatterjee, "Soviet Heroines and Public Identity, 1930–1939," *Carl*

Beck Papers in Russian and East European Studies, no. 1402 (Pittsburgh: University of Pittsburgh, 1999), 17.

72. Krylova, "Stalinist Identity from the Viewpoint of Gender," 628.

73. I thank Laurie Stoff for this insight.

CHAPTER 12. THE FEMALE EXPERIENCE OF MILITARY SERVICE AND WAR

1. John Erickson, "Soviet Women at War," in *World War 2 and the Soviet People: Selected Papers from the Fourth World Congress for Soviet and East European Studies, Harrogate, 1990*, ed. John Garrard and Carol Garrard (New York: St. Martin's Press, 1993), 68; G. F. Krivosheev et al., *Velikaia Otechestvennaia bez grifa sekretnosti. Kniga poter'* (Moscow: Veche, 2010), 38. To that number one must add the untold tens of thousands who had been killed, captured, or wounded since June 1941 to get the total women who qualified as *frontoviki*.

2. Vera S. Murmantseva, *Sovetskii zhenshchiny v Velikoi Otechestvennoi voine* (Moscow: Mysl', 1979), 122.

3. Valentina Ia. Galagan, *Ratnyi podvig zhenshchin v gody Velikoi Otechestvennoi voiny* (Kiev: Vyshche Shkola, 1986), 190; Krivosheev et al., *Velikaia Otechestvennaia bez grifa sekretnosti*, 38.

4. Galagan, *Ratnyi podvig zhenshchin v gody Velikoi Otechestvennoi voiny*, 163.

5. Ibid., 137.

6. Ibid., 162, 163; Krivosheev et al., *Velikaia Otechestvennaia bez grifa sekretnosti*, 38.

7. Vera Murmantseva, *Zhenshcheny v soldatskikh shineliakh* (Moscow: Mysl', 1979), 22.

8. Krivosheev et al., *Velikaia Otechestvennaia bez grifa sekretnosti*, 38.

9. Ibid.

10. D'Ann Campbell, "Women in Combat: The World War II Experience in the United States, Great Britain, Germany, and the Soviet Union," *Journal of Military History* 57, 2 (April 1993): 301–323.

11. Murmantseva, *Sovetskii zhenshchiny v Velikoi Otechestvennoi voine*, 166.

12. Sophia Grigor'eva, "Na doliu sekundy operdila vraga," in *Bylo u voiny i zhenskoe litso: Zhenshchiny na voine: ocherki, zarisovki, vospominania, fotografii*, ed. Anatolii Panin and Tamara Butenko (Khar'kov: MTK-kniga, 2005), 59–60.

13. RTsKhIDNI, f. 644, op. 2, Ed. Khr. 83, ll. 70–76, in *Gosudarstvennyi komitet oborony postanovliaet (1941–1945): Tsifry Dokumenty*, ed. Iurii Gor'kov (Moscow: Olma-Press, 2002), 515.

14. Campbell, "Women in Combat," 301–323.

15. Svetlana Aleksievich, *War's Unwomanly Face*, trans. Keith Hammond and Lyudmila Lezhneva (Moscow: Progress, 1988), 157.

16. Murmantseva, *Sovetskii zhenshchiny v Velikoi Otechestvennoi voine*, 128–129.

17. TsDNI SO, f. 4158, op. 7, d. 5, ll. 5–8, 13–16, 23–24, 26–29, in *Saratovskaia oblast' v gody Velikoi Otechestvennoi voiny (1941–1945 gg.): arkhivnye dokumenty*, ed. V. V. Ivanov (Saratov: Izdatel'stvo gubernoskoi torgovo-promyshlennoi palaty, 2005), 62–65.

18. Murmantseva, *Zhenshcheny v soldatskikh shineliakh*, 11.

19. Euridice Charon Cardona and Roger D. Markwick, "'Our Brigade Will Not Be Sent to the Front': Soviet Women under Arms in the Great Fatherland War, 1941–45," *Russian Review* 68, 2 (2009): 243.

20. Ibid., 245–246.

21. Ibid., 245–247, 249–254, 257–261.

22. Galagan, *Ratnyi podvig zhenshchin v gody Velikoi Otechestvennoi voiny*, 182–184; Murmantseva, *Sovetskii zhenshchiny v Velikoi Otechestvennoi voine*, 130; V. M. Mizin, *Snaiper Petrova* (Leningrad: Lenizdat, 1988), 13–36.

23. Reina Pennington, *Wings, Women, and War: Soviet Airwomen in World War II Combat* (Lawrence: University Press of Kansas, 2001).

24. Mikhail Semiriaga, *The Winter War: Looking Back after Fifty Years* (Moscow: Novosti, 1990), 27.

25. Zoia M. Smirnova-Medvedeva, *On the Road to Stalingrad: Memoirs of a Soviet Woman Machine Gunner*, ed. and trans. Kazimiera J. Cottam (Toronto: Legas, 1996), 18; Pennington, *Wings, Women, and War*, 132–142.

26. Aleksievich, *War's Unwomanly Face*, 158.

27. Natalia Peshkova interview, http://www.iremember.ru/content/view/289/89/lang,en/ (accessed 25 July 2006).

28. Aleksievich, *War's Unwomanly Face*, 63.

29. Melissa Stockdale, "'My Death for the Motherland Is Happiness': Women, Patriotism, and Soldiering in Russia's Great War, 1914–1917," *American Historical Review* 109, 1 (2004): 106.

30. Sergei Abaulin testimonial, http://www.iremember.ru/content/view/188/82/lang,en/ (accessed 24 July 2006).

31. Vasily Grossman, *A Writer at War: Vasily Grossman with the Red Army 1941–1945*, ed. and trans. Antony Beevor and Luba Vinogradova (London: Harvill Press, 2005), 184–185.

32. Laurie Stoff, *They Fought for the Motherland: Russia's Women Soldiers in World War I and the Revolution* (Lawrence: University Press of Kansas, 2006), 164.

33. Stockdale, "'My Death for the Motherland Is Happiness,'" 105.

34. Aleksievich, *War's Unwomanly Face,* 147.

35. Ibid., 184.

36. Mariana Miliutina interview, http://www.iremember.ru/content/view/284/88/lang,en/ (accessed 25 July 2006).

37. Erickson, "Soviet Women at War," 69.

38. Order No. 164, "Prikaz ob uvelichenii normy vydachi myla zhenshchinam-voennosluzhashchim," in *Russkii arhkiv: Velikaia Otechestvennaia: Prikazy Narodnogo komissara oborony SSSR (1943–1945 gg.),* vol. 13 (2-3), ed. Vladimir A. Zolotarev (Moscow: Terra, 1997), 115.

39. Reina Pennington, "Offensive Women: Women in Combat in the Red Army," in *Time to Kill: The Soldier's Experience of War in the West 1939–1945,* ed. Paul Addison and Angus Calder (London: Pimlico, 1997), 259, 260.

40. Nina Erdman interview, http://www.iremember.ru/content/view/286/88/lang,en/ (accessed 25 July 2006).

41. Antonina Kotliarova interview, http://www.iremember.ru/content/view/30/74/lang,en/ (accessed 15 July 2006).

42. Ibid.

43. Aleksievich, *War's Unwomanly Face,* 107.

44. Vera I. Malakhova, "Four Years as a Frontline Physician," in *A Revolution of Their Own: Voices of Women in Soviet History,* ed. Barbara Alpern Engel and Anastasia Posadskaya-Vanderbeck, trans. Sonia Hoisington (Boulder, Colo.: Westview Press, 1998), 207.

45. Grossman, *Writer at War,* 184–185.

46. Krivosheev et al., *Velikaia Otechestvennaia bez grifa sekretnosti,* 53.

47. Erdman interview.

48. Galagan, *Ratnyi podvig zhenshchin v gody Velikoi Otechestvennoi voiny,* 33, 169, 197.

49. Zoia Shavruk, a telephone operator, enlisted when she was only fourteen. She lied and said she was sixteen. Aleksievich, *War's Unwomanly Face,* 24–25.

50. Krivosheev et al., *Velikaia Otechestvennaia bez grifa sekretnosti,* 38.

51. Galagan, *Ratnyi podvig zhenshchin v gody Velikoi Otechestvennoi voiny,* 185; Kazimiera J. Cottam, "Soviet Women in Combat in World War II: The Rear Services, Resistance behind Enemy Lines and Military Political Workers," *International Journal of Women's Studies* 5, 4 (September–October 1982): 372–373.

52. Nikolai A. Chistiakov interview, http://www.iremember.ru/content/view/53/75/lang,en/ (accessed 16 July 2006).

53. Grossman, *Writer at War,* 120–121.

54. Gabriel Temkin, *My Just War: The Memoir of a Jewish Red Army Soldier in World War II* (Novato, Calif.: Presidio Press, 1998), 202.

55. Semion Aria interview, http://www.iremember.ru/content/view/98/76/lang,en/ (accessed 20 July 2006).

56. Rodric Braithwaite, *Moscow 1941: A City and Its People at War* (London: Profile, 2006), 114–115.

57. Malakhova, "Four Years as a Frontline Physician," 197–198. In her interview, Malakhova used the term *PPZh,* but the translator rendered this as *FCW* (field campaign wife) in English. For uniformity and to avoid confusion, I have taken the liberty of changing it to *PPZh* in the quotations.

58. Braithwaite, *Moscow 1941,* 114.

59. Malakhova, "Four Years as a Frontline Physician," 187. Krylova asserts that women in combat assignments did not experience sexual harassment and that this phenomenon occurred only among women in support roles. See Anna Krylova, *Soviet Women in Combat: A History of Violence on the Eastern Front* (Cambridge: Cambridge University Press, 2010), 282.

60. Aleksievich, *War's Unwomanly Face,* 148.

61. Malakhova, "Four Years as a Frontline Physician," 199–200, 204–205.

62. Aleksievich, *War's Unwomanly Face,* 151.

63. Ibid., 184.

64. Aleksandr Bodnar' interview, http://www.iremember.ru/content/view/96/76/lang,en/ (accessed 4 May 2008).

65. Harvard University Refugee Interview Project, #40, 24, Hoover Institution Archives, Stanford University, Stanford, Calif.

66. Kazimiera J. Cottam, "Soviet Women in Combat in World War II: The Ground/Air Defense Forces," in *Women in Eastern Europe and the Soviet Union,* ed. Tova Yedlin (New York: Praeger, 1980), 118.

67. Aleksievich, *War's Unwomanly Face,* 127.

68. Anne Eliot Griesse and Richard Stites, "Russia: Revolution and War," in *Female Soldiers—Combatants or Noncombatants? Historical and Contemporary Perspectives,* ed. Nancy Goldman (Westport, Conn.: Greenwood, 1982), 75.

CONCLUSION

1. "Postanovlenie Gosudarstvennogo Komitata Oborony no. GKO-660ss ob ustanovlenii cheslennosti Krasnoi Armii na sentiabr' i IV kvartal 1941 g. i ob otpuske prodovol'stvennykh paikov dlia Narodnogo komissariata oborony," in

Organy gosudarstvennoi bezopasnosti SSSR v Velikoi Otechestvennoi voine: Sbornik dokumentov: Nachalo, 1 sentiabria–31 dekabria 1941 goda, vol. 2, book 2 (Moscow: Rus', 2000), 83–84.

2. Writing in 1940 about Soviet women's participation in the Winter War and their inclusion in the armed forces, Judith Grunfeld, a Polish political activist, notes, "The 'equal opportunity' for women to murder marks a new milistone [*sic*] in totalitarian barbarism." Judith Grunfeld, "Stalin's Amazons" (unpublished manuscript, Hoover Institution Archives, Stanford University, Stanford, Calif.), 2.

Selected Bibliography

ARCHIVAL SOURCES

Archives of the President of the Russian Federation

Central Archives of the Federal Security Bureau of the Russian Federation

Central Repository for Contemporary History, Kursk Oblast

Central Repository for Contemporary History, Saratov Oblast

Central State Archives of the Ministry of Defense

Central State Archives of the Republic of Bashkira

Central State Archives of the Republic of Dagestan

Public Archives of Sverdlovsk Oblast

Russian Center for the Collection and Preservation of Contemporary History
(later renamed Russian State Archives for Social and Political History)

Russian State Archives for Social and Political History (formerly Russian Center
for the Collection and Preservation of Contemporary History)

Russian State Archives of Contemporary History

Russian State Military Archives

State Archives of Kursk Oblast

State Archives of the Russian Federation

BOOKS AND ARTICLES

Abdulin, Mansur. *Red Road from Stalingrad: Recollections of a Soviet Infantry-man.* Barnsley, South Yorkshire: Pen and Sword, 2004.

Addison, Paul, and Angus Calder. *Time to Kill: The Soldiers' Experience of War in the West, 1939–1945.* London: Pimlico, 1997.

Ahrenfeldt, Robert H. *Psychiatry in the British Army in the Second World War.* New York: Columbia University Press, 1958.

Aleksievich, Svetlana A. *U voiny—ne zhenskoe litso.* . . . Minsk: Mastatskaia literatura, 1985. Published as *War's Unwomanly Face,* trans. Keith Hammond and Liudmila Lezhneva. Moscow: Progress, 1988.

Alexopoulos, Golfo. "Soviet Citizenship, More or Less: Rights, Emotions, and States of Civic Belonging." *Kritika: Explorations in Russian and Eurasian History* 7, 3 (summer 2006): 487–528.

Anderson, Kirill M., et al., eds. *"Zimniaia voina": rabota nad oshibkami (aprel-mai 1940 g.): Materialy komissii Glavnogo voennogo soveta Krasnoi Armii po obobshcheniiu opyta finskoi kampanii*. Moscow: Letnyi sad, 2004.

Antonenko, S. V., and V. Rusanov, eds. *Velikaia Otechestvennaia. Komandarmy. Voennyi biograficheskii slovar'*. Moscow: Institut voennoi istorii, 2005.

Anvaer, Sofia. *Krovotochit moia pamiat'. Iz zapisok studentki-medichki*. Moscow: Rosspen, 2005.

Aptekar', Pavel A. "Opravdanny li zhertvy? O poteriakh v sovetsko-finliandskoi voine." *Voenno-istoricheskii zhurnal* 3 (1992): 43–45.

Balashov, Evgenii. *Prinimai nas, suomi-krasavitsa! "Osvoboditel'nyi" pokhod v Finliandiiu 1939–1940 gg. Part II*. St. Petersburg, Russia: Galeia Print, 2000.

Barber, John. "Popular Reactions in Moscow to the German Invasion of June 22, 1941." In *Operation Barbarossa: The German Attack on the Soviet Union, June 22, 1941*, ed. Joseph L. Wieczynski, 1–12. Salt Lake City: Charles Schlacks, 1993.

Barber, John, and Mark Harrison. *The Soviet Home Front 1941–1945: A Social and Economic History of the USSR in World War II*. London: Longman, 1991.

Barnes, Steven. "All for the Front, All for Victory! The Mobilization of Forced Labor in the Soviet Union during World War Two." *International Labor and Working-Class History* 58 (fall 2000): 239–260.

Basov, Aleksei V. *Krym v Velikoi Otechestvennoi voine 1941–1945*. Moscow: Nauka, 1987.

Bazarova, Roza A. *Sovetskii Turkmenistan-frontu*. Askhabad: Ylym, 1978.

Bessonov, Evgeni. *Tank Rider: Into the Reich with the Red Army*. Trans. Bair Irincheev. London: Greenhill, 2003.

Bidlack, Richard. "The Political Mood in Leningrad during the First Year of the Soviet-German War." *Russian Review* 59, 1 (January 2000): 96–113.

———. "Workers at War: Factory Workers and Labor Policy in the Siege of Leningrad." *Carl Beck Papers in Russian and East European Studies* no. 902. Pittsburgh: University of Pittsburgh, 1991.

Bilenko, Semen V. *Istrebitel'nye batal'ony v Velikoi Otechestvennoi voine*. Moscow: Voenizdat, 1969.

Bitva za Stolitsy: sbornik dokumentov: ot oborony k kontrnastupleniiu. Vol. 1. Moscow: Institut voennoi istorii Ministerstva oborony Rossiiskoi Federatsii, 1994.

Bobylev, P. N., ed. *Glavnyi voennyi sovet RKKA. 13 marta 1938–20 iiunia 1941 g. Dokumenty i materialy*. Moscow: Rosspen, 2004.

Bogdanov, V. L., ed. *Zhivaia Pamiat': Velikaia Otechestvennaia: pravda o voine.* Moscow: Sovet veteranov zhurnalistiki Rossii Soiuz zhurnalistov RF, 1995.

Borodkina, A. *Zapiski razvedchitsy.* Tula: Priokskoe knizhnoe izd-vo, 1967.

Braithwaite, Rodric. *Moscow 1941: A City and Its People at War.* London: Profile, 2006.

Brandenberger, David. "Soviet Social Mentalité and Russocentrism on the Eve of War, 1936–1941." *Jahrbücher für Geschichte Osteuropas* 48 (2000): 388–406.

Brody, Richard. "Ideology and Political Mobilization: The Soviet Home Front during World War II." *Carl Beck Papers in Russian and East European Studies* no. 1104. Pittsburgh: University of Pittsburgh, 1994.

Brooks, Jeffrey. *Thank You, Comrade Stalin! Soviet Public Culture from Revolution to Cold War.* Princeton, N.J.: Princeton University Press, 2000.

Buckley, Mary. *Mobilizing Soviet Peasants: Heroines and Heroes of Stalin's Fields.* Lanham, Md.: Lexington Books, 2006.

———. *Women and Ideology in the Soviet Union.* Ann Arbor: University of Michigan Press, 1989.

Bushnell, John. "Peasants in Uniform: The Tsarist Army as a Peasant Society." *Journal of Social History* 13, 4 (1980): 565–574.

"Byla voina . . .": Sbornik dokumentov i vospominanii o Rostove v period Velikoi Otechestvennoi voiny 1941–1945 godov. Rostov: Rostovskii kreml', 2001.

Campbell, D'Ann. "Women in Combat: The World War II Experience in the United States, Great Britain, Germany, and the Soviet Union." *Journal of Military History* 57, 2 (April 1993): 301–323.

Cardona, Euridice Charon, and Roger D. Markwick. "'Our Brigade Will Not Be Sent to the Front': Soviet Women under Arms in the Great Fatherland War, 1941–45," *Russian Review* 68, 2 (2009): 240–262.

Chatterjee, Choi. "Soviet Heroines and Public Identity, 1930–1939." *Carl Beck Papers in Russian and East European Studies* no. 1402. Pittsburgh: University of Pittsburgh, 1999.

Cheremnykh, V., and N. Petrova, eds. *Zimniaia voina 1939–1940.* Book 1, *Politicheskaia istoriia.* Moscow: Nauka, 1999.

Cottam, Kazimiera J. "Soviet Women in Combat in World War II: The Ground Forces and the Navy." *International Journal of Women's Studies* 3 (July–August 1980): 345–357.

———. "Soviet Women in Combat in World War II: The Rear Services, Resistance behind Enemy Lines and Military Political Workers." *International Journal of Women's Studies* 5, 4 (September–October 1982): 363–378.

————. *Women in Air War: The Eastern Front of World War II.* Nepean, Ontario: New Military Pub., 1997.

————. *Women in War and Resistance: Selected Biographies of Soviet Women Soldiers.* Nepean, Ontario: New Military Pub., 1998.

Danilov, A., and A. Pyshikov. *Rozhdenie sverkhderzhavy. SSSR v pervye poslevoennye gody.* Moscow: Rosspen, 2001.

Davies, Sarah. *Popular Opinion in Stalin's Russia: Terror, Propaganda and Dissent, 1934–1941.* Cambridge: Cambridge University Press, 1997.

Dokuchaev, G., ed. *Sibiriaki—frontu. Materialy nauch. konferentsii.* Novosibirsk: Nauka, Sibirskoe otd-nie, 1971.

Dollard, John. *Fear in Battle.* 1944. Reprint, Westport, Conn.: Greenwood, 1977.

Edele, Mark. "Paper Soldiers": The World of the Soldier Hero according to Soviet Wartime Posters." *Jahrbücher für Geschichte Osteuropas* 47 (1999): 89–108.

————. "Soviet Veterans as an Entitlement Group 1945–1955." *Slavic Review* 65, 1 (spring 2006): 111–137.

Ehrenberg, Ilya, and Konstantin Simonov. *In One Newspaper: A Chronicle of Unforgettable Years.* Trans. Anatol Kagan. New York: Sphinx Press, 1985.

Engel, Barbara A., and Anastasia Posadskaya-Vanderbeck, eds. *A Revolution of Their Own: Voices of Women in Soviet History.* Trans. Sona Hoisington. Boulder, Colo.: Westview Press, 1998.

Eremenko, A. I. *V nachale voiny.* Moscow: Nauka, 1964.

Erickson, John. "Red Army Battlefield Performance, 1941–1945: The System and the Soldier." In *Time to Kill: The Soldier's Experience of War in the West 1939–1945,* ed. Paul Addison and Angus Calder, 233–248. London: Pimlico, 1997.

————. *The Road to Berlin.* Boulder, Colo.: Westview Press, 1983.

————. *The Road to Stalingrad: Stalin's War with Germany.* New York: Harper and Row, 1975.

————. "Soviet Women at War." In *World War 2 and the Soviet People: Selected Papers from the Fourth World Congress for Soviet and East European Studies, Harrogate, 1990,* ed. John Garrard and Carol Garrard, 50–76. New York: St. Martin's Press, 1993.

Evdokimov, R. B., ed. *Liudskie poteri SSSR v Velikoi Otechestvennoi voine. Sbornik statei.* St. Petersburg, Russia: Blitz, 1995.

Figes, Orlando. *The Whisperers: Private Life in Stalin's Russia.* London: Penguin, 2007.

Fischer, George. *Soviet Opposition to Stalin: A Case Study in World War II.* Cambridge, Mass.: Harvard University Press, 1952.

Fischer, Louis, ed. *Thirteen Who Fled.* New York: Harper and Brothers, 1949.

Fitzpatrick, Sheila M. *Everyday Stalinism: Ordinary Life in Extraordinary Times: Soviet Russia in the 1930s.* Oxford: Oxford University Press, 1999.

Flynn, George Q. *Conscription and Democracy: The Draft in France, Great Britain, and the United States.* Westport, Conn.: Greenwood, 2002.

Fritz, Stephen G. *Frontsoldaten: The German Soldier in World War II.* Lexington: University Press of Kentucky, 1995.

Galagan, Valentina Ia. *Ratnyi podvig zhenshchin v gody Velikoi Otechestvennoi voiny.* Kiev: Vyshche Shkola, 1986.

Gallagher, Matthew P. *The Soviet History of World War II: Myths, Memories, and Realities.* Westport, Conn.: Greenwood, 1963.

Garrard, John, and Carol Garrard, eds. *World War 2 and the Soviet People: Selected Papers from the Fourth World Congress for Soviet and East European Studies, Harrogate, 1990.* New York: St. Martin's Press, 1993.

Gatrell, Peter. *Russia's First World War: A Social and Economic History.* Harlow, England: Pearson Education, 2005.

Gavrilov, Boris I. *Cherez "Dolinu smerti" podvig i tragediia voinov Volkhovskogo fronta Ianvar'–iiun' 1942 g.* Vol. 1, *Vospominaniia i materialy.* Moscow: RAN, 2002.

———. *Cherez "Dolinu smerti" podvig i tragediia voinov Volkhovskogo fronta Ianvar–iiun 1942 g.* Vol. 2, *Vospominaniia, dokumenty i materialy.* Moscow: RAN, 2004.

George, Alexander L. "Primary Groups, Organization, and Military Performance." In *Handbook of Military Institutions,* ed. Roger W. Little, 293–318. Beverly Hills, Calif.: Sage, 1971.

Glantz, David. *Forgotten Battles of the Soviet-German War.* Vol. 4, *The Winter Campaign 19 November 1942–21 March 1943.* London: Routledge, 2007.

———. "Women in War: The Red Army's Experience." *Journal of Slavic Military Studies* 12, 1 (1999): 208–212.

Glantz, David M., and Jonathan House. *When Titans Clashed: How the Red Army Stopped Hitler.* Lawrence: University Press of Kansas, 1995.

Goldman, Nancy L., ed. *Female Soldiers—Combatants or Noncombatants? Historical and Contemporary Perspectives.* Westport Conn.: Greenwood, 1982.

Gor'kov, Iurii. *Kreml', Stavka, Genshtab.* Tver: Rif, 1995.

Goscilo, Helena, and Andrea Lanoux. *Gender and National Identity in Twentieth-Century Russian Culture.* De Kalb: Northern Illinois University Press, 2006.

Grossman, Vasily. *A Writer at War: Vasily Grossman with the Red Army 1941–1945,* ed. and trans. Antony Beevor and Luba Vinogradova. London: Harvill Press, 2005.

Halfin, Igal, and Jochen Hellbeck, "Rethinking the Stalinist Subject: Stephen Kotkin's 'Magnetic Mountain' and the State of Soviet Historical Studies." *Jahrbücher für Geschichte Osteuropas* 44 (1996): 456–463.

Henriksen, Rune. "Warriors in Combat—What Makes People Actively Fight in Combat?" *Journal of Strategic Studies* 30, 2 (April 2007): 187–223.

Hill, Alexander. *The Great Patriotic War of the Soviet Union, 1941–45.* London: Routledge, 2007.

Hodgson, Katharine. "The Other Veterans: Soviet Women's Poetry of World War 2." In *World War 2 and the Soviet People: Selected Papers from the Fourth World Congress for Soviet and East European Studies, Harrogate, 1990,* ed. John Garrard and Carol Garrard, 77–97. New York: St. Martin's Press, 1993.

———. *Written with the Bayonet: Soviet Russian Poetry of World War Two.* Liverpool: Liverpool University Press, 1996.

Iampol'skii, V. P., ed. *Organy gosudarstvennoi bezopasnosti SSSR v Velikoi Otechestvennoi voine.* Moscow: Kniga i biznes, 1995.

———. *Organy gosudarstvennoi bezopasnosti SSSR v Velikoi Otechestvennoi voine: Sbornik dokumentov.* Vol. 2, book 1, *Nachalo, 22 iiunia–31 avgusta 1941 goda.* Moscow: Rus', 2000.

———. *Organy gosudarstvennoi bezopasnosti SSSR v Velikoi Otechestvennoi voine: Sbornik dokumentov.* Vol. 2, book 2, *Nachalo, 1 sentiabria–31 dekabria 1941 goda.* Moscow: Rus', 2000.

Irgalin, G., ed. *Bashkiriia v gody Velikoi Otechestvennoi voiny 1941–1945.* Ufa: Kitap, 1995.

Irinarkhov, Ruslan S. *Kievskii osobyi.* Minsk and Moscow: AST/Kharvest, 2006.

Isupov, V. A., ed. *Zapadnaia Sibir' v Velikoi Otechestvennoi voine (1941–1945 gg.).* Novosibirsk: Nauka, 2004.

Iudin, Ivan N. "Finskii pokhod glazami ochevidtsa: Vospominaniia I. N. Iudina." *Russkoe proshloe* 9 (2001): 152–165.

Ivanov, V. V., ed. *Saratovskaia oblast' v gody Velikoi Otechestvennoi voiny (1941–1945 gg.): arkhivnye dokumenty.* Saratov: Izdatel'stvo gubernoskoi torgovo-promyshlennoi palaty, 2005.

Ivashov, L. G. "Ne predstavliali sebe . . . vsekh trudnostei sviazannykh s etoi voinoi." *Voenno-istoricheskii zhurnal* 4 (1993): 7–12.

Jahn, Hubertus F. *Patriotic Culture in Russia during World War I.* Ithaca, N.Y.: Cornell University Press, 1995.

Jelleck, Jochen. "Fashioning the Stalinist Soul: The Diary of Stepan Podlubnyi (1931–1939)." *Jahrbücher für Geschichte Osteuropas* 44 (1996): 344–373.

Kalashnikov, Mikhail, with Elena Joly. *The Gun that Changed the World.* Trans. Andrew Brown. Cambridge: Polity Press, 2006.

Kamp, Marianne R. "Three Lives of Saodat: Communist, Uzbek, Survivor." *Oral History Review* 28, 2 (September 2001): 21–58.

Kariaev, T. F., ed. *Partiino-Politicheskaia rabota v Krasnoi Armii. Dokumenty, iiul' 1929g.–mai 1941g.* Moscow: Voenizdat, 1985.

Kazakhstan v period Velikoi Otechestvennoi voiny Sovetskogo Soiuza 1941–1945: sbornik dokumentov i materialov. Alma-Ata: Nauka, 1964.

Kellet, Anthony. *Combat Motivation: The Behavior of Soldiers in Battle.* Boston: Kluwer, 1982.

Khaustov, V. N., ed. *Lubianka. Stalin i NKVD-NKGB-GUKR "Smersh" 1939–mart 1946. Arkhiv Stalina. Dokumenty vysshikh organov partiinoi i gosudarstvennoi vlast.* Moscow: Materik, 2006.

Kirsanov, Nikolai A. "Natsional'nye formirovaniia Krasnoi armii v Velikoi Otechestvennoi voine 1941–1945 godov." *Otechestvennaia istoriia* 4 (1995): 116–126.

Kirschenbaum, Lisa A. *The Legacy of the Siege of Leningrad, 1941–1995: Myth, Memories, and Monuments.* Cambridge: Cambridge University Press, 2006.

Kirtoraga, T. G. "Narodnoe opolchenie Moskvy 1941 g.: Istoriia sozdaniia." *Vestnik Moskovskogo Universiteta* 8, 5 (2005): 36–53.

Klochkov, V. F. *Krasnaia Armiia—shkola kommunisticheskogo vospitaniia sovetskikh voinov 1918–1941.* Moscow: Nauka, 1984.

Knishevskii, P. N., et al. *Skrytaia pravda voiny: 1941 god. Neizvestny dokumenty.* Moscow: Russkaia kniga, 1992.

Kolesnik, A. D. *Opolchenskie formirovaniia Rossiiskoi Federatsii v gody Velikoi Otechestvennoi voiny.* Moscow: Nauka, 1988.

Kolesnikov, I. "O prichinakh, porozhdaiushchikh paniku v voiskakh, i merakh ee predotvrashcheniia." *Voenno-istoricheskii zhurnal* 1 (1963): 46–59.

Komsomol Belorussii v Velikoi Otechestvennoi voine: Dokumenty i materialy. Minsk: Belarus', 1988.

Kostin, V. *Margelev.* Moscow: Moldaia Gvardiia, 2005.

Krivosheev, Grigorii F., et al. *Grif sekretnosti sniat: Poteri Vooruzhennykh Sil SSSR v voinakh, boevykh deistviiakh i voennykh konfliktakh: Statisticheskoi issledovanie.* Moscow: Voenizdat, 1993.

————. *Velikaia Otechestvennaia bez grifa sekretnosti. Kniga poter'. Noveishee spravochnoe izdanie.* Moscow: Veche, 2010.

Krutovertsev, Tim I. *Vospominaniia veterana.* Moscow: Novyi svet, 2000.

Krylova, Anna. *Soviet Women in Combat: A History of Violence on the Eastern Front.* Cambridge: Cambridge University Press, 2010.

————. "Stalinist Identity from the Viewpoint of Gender: Rearing a Generation of Professionally Violent Women-Fighters in 1930s Stalinist Russia." *Gender and History* 16, 3 (November 2004): 626–653.

Kul'kov, E. N., ed. *Zimniaia voina 1939–1940. Kn. 2. I. V. Stalin i finskaia kampaniia. Stenogramma soveshcheniia pri TsK VKP(b).* Moscow: Nauka, 1999.

Kumanev, G. A. *Problemy voennoi istorii otechestva (1938–1945 gg.).* Moscow: Sobranie, 2007.

Linderman, Gerald F. *The World within War: The American Combat Experience in World War II.* New York: Free Press, 1997.

Livshin, A., and I. B. Orlov. *Sovetskaia propaganda v gody Velikoi Otechestvennoi voiny: "Kommunikatsiia ubezhdenia" i mobilizatsionnye mekhanizmy.* Moscow: Rosspen, 2007.

Lomagin, Nikita. "Soldiers at War: German Propaganda and Soviet Army Morale during the Battle of Leningrad, 1941–44." *Carl Beck Papers in Russian and East European Studies* no. 1306. Pittsburgh: University of Pittsburgh, 1998.

Lynn, John A. *Bayonets of the Republic: Motivation and Tactics in the Army of Revolutionary France, 1791–1794.* Urbana: University of Illinois Press, 1984.

Lyons, Graham, ed. *The Russian Version of the Second World War: The History of the War as Taught to Soviet Schoolchildren.* New York: Facts on File, 1976.

Makarenko, Iakov. *Vysokaia dolzhnost'.* Moscow: Pravda, 1963.

Makarov, V. I. *V general'nom shtabe nakanune griadyshchikh peremen. Avtobiograficheskie zapiski ofitsera General'nogo shtaba.* Moscow: Kuchkovo pole, 2004.

Martirosian, Arsen B. *100 Mifov o Berii: Ot slavy k prokliatiiam. 1941–1953 gg.* Moscow: Veche, 2010.

Matrosov, K. *Na Berlin!* Moscow: Eksmo/IAuza, 2005.

Matrosov, V. A., ed. *Pogranichnye voiska SSSR v Velikoi Otechestvennoi voine 1941: Sbornik dokumentov i materialov.* Moscow: Nauka, 1976.

Matveeva, Maria. *Ia byla na voine: dokumental'naia povest'.* 2nd ed. Moscow: Sovetskaia Rossiia, 1990.

Megargee, Geoffrey. *War of Annihilation: Combat and Genocide on the Eastern Front, 1941.* Lanham, Md.: Rowman and Littlefield, 2005.

Meissner, Boris. *The Communist Party of the Soviet Union: Party Leadership, Organization, and Ideology*. Westport, Conn.: Greenwood, 1975.

Meretskov, Kirill A. *Serving the People*. Moscow: Progress, 1971.

Merridale, Catherine. "The Collective Mind: Trauma and Shell-Shock in Twentieth-Century Russia." *Journal of Contemporary History* 35, 1 (January 2000): 39–55.

———. "Culture, Ideology and Combat in the Red Army, 1939–1945." *Journal of Contemporary History* 41, 2 (April 2006): 305–324.

———. *Ivan's War: Life and Death in the Red Army, 1939–1945*. New York: Metropolitan, 2006.

———. *Night of Stone: Death and Memory in Twentieth-Century Russia*. New York: Viking, 2000.

Mizin, V. M. *Snaiper Petrova*. Leningrad: Lenizdat, 1988.

Moniushko, Evgenii D. *From Leningrad to Hungary: Notes of a Red Army Soldier, 1941–1946*. London and New York: Frank Cass, 2004.

Moran, Charles McMoran Wilson, Lord. *The Anatomy of Courage: The Classic WW I Account of the Psychological Effects of War*. 1947. Reprint, London: Constable and Robinson, 2007.

Mukhin, Iuri. *Po povestke i po prizyvu. Nekadrovye soldaty Velikoi Otechestvennoi Voine*. Moscow: Iauza/Eksmo, 2005.

Mulligan, Timothy P. "Escape from Stalingrad: Soviet Nationals with the German Sixth Army." *Journal of Slavic Military Studies* 20, 4 (2007): 739–748.

Murmantseva, Vera. *Sovetskii zhenshchiny v Velikoi Otechestvennoi voine*. Moscow: Mysl', 1974.

———. *Zhenshcheny v soldatskikh shineliakh*. Moscow: Mysl', 1979.

Narody Dagestana v gody Velikoi Otechestvennoi voiny (1941–1945 gg.) (Dokumenty i materialy). Makhachkala: Tipografiia DNTs RAN, 2005.

Nazi Conspiracy and Aggression. Vol. 6. Washington, D.C.: U.S. Government Printing Office, 1946.

Newsome, Bruce. "The Myth of Intrinsic Combat Motivation." *Journal of Strategic Studies* 26, 4 (December 2003): 24–46.

Noggle, Anne. *A Dance with Death: Soviet Airwomen in World War II*. College Station: Texas A&M University Press, 1994.

Norris, Stephen M. *A War of Images: Russian Popular Prints, Wartime Culture, and National Identity*. De Kalb: Northern Illinois University Press, 2006.

Novikova, Irina. "Representations of Women in Russian Culture and the New Woman in Soviet Gender Ideology: Literary-Ideological Discourse of the

1920–30s." In *Der weibliche multikulturelle Blick: Ergenbnisse eines symposiums 1995*, 208–218. Berlin: Trafo Verlag, 1995.

Oja, Matt. "From Krestianka to Udarnitsa: Rural Women and the Vydvizhenie Campaign, 1933–1941." *Carl Beck Papers in Russian and East European Studies* no. 1203. Pittsburgh: University of Pittsburgh, 1996.

Oni srazhalis' za Rodinu. Predstaviteli repressirovannykh narodov na frontakh Velikoi Otechestvennoi voiny. Kniga-khronika. Moscow: Novyi khronograf, 2005.

Pak, Nikolai. *Sovety Tadzhikistana v gody Velikoi Otechestvennoi voiny*. Dushanbe: Donish, 1985.

Pakhomov, V. P. *Velikaia Otechestvennaia v dokumentakh i svidetel'stvakh sovremennikov*. Samara: Izd-vo Samarskogo in-ta povysheniia kvalifikatsii i perepodgotovki rabotnikov obrazovaniia, 1995.

Panin, Anatolii, and Tamara Butenko, eds. *Bylo u voiny i zhenskoe litso: Zhenshchiny na voine: ocherki, zarisovki, vospominania, fotografii*. Khar'kov: MTK-kniga, 2005.

Paperno, Irina. "Personal Accounts of the Soviet Experience." *Kritika: Explorations in Russian and Eurasian History* 3, 4 (fall 2002): 577–610.

Pennington, Reina. "Offensive Women: Women in Combat in the Red Army in the Second World War." *Journal of Military History* 74, 3 (July 2010): 775–820.

———. *Wings, Women, and War: Soviet Airwomen in World War II Combat*. Lawrence: University Press of Kansas, 2001.

Perezhogin, Vitalii. "Iz okruzheniia i plena—v partizany." *Otechestvennaia istoriia* 3 (2000): 25–33.

Pohl, J. Otto. *The Stalinist Penal System: A Statistical History of Soviet Repression and Terror, 1930–1953*. Jefferson, N.C.: McFarland, 1997.

Poslednie pis'ma s fronta. 5 vols., 1941–1945. Moscow: Voenizdat, 1990–1992.

Puskharaev, Lev N. "Slovesnye istochniki dlia izucheniia mental'nosti sovetskogo naroda v gody Velikoi Otechestvennoi voiny." *Voprosy istorii* 4 (2001): 127–134.

Roberts, Geoffrey. *Stalin's Wars: From World War to Cold War, 1939–1953*. New Haven, Conn.: Yale University Press, 2007.

Robinson, Neil. *Ideology and the Collapse of the Soviet System: A Critical History of Soviet Ideological Discourse*. Aldershot, England: Edward Elgar, 1995.

Rose, Arnold M. "Bases of American Military Morale in World War II." *Public Opinion Quarterly* 9, 4 (winter 1945–1946): 411–417.

———. "Conscious Reactions Associated with Neuropsychiatric Breakdown in Combat." *Psychiatry* 19 (February 1956): 87–94.

―――. "Neuropsychiatric Breakdown in the Garrison Army and in Combat." *American Sociological Review* 21, 4 (August 1956): 480–488.

―――. "Social Psychological Effects of Physical Deprivation." *Journal of Health and Human Behavior* 1, 4 (winter 1960): 285–289.

―――. "The Social Psychology of Desertion from Combat." *American Sociological Review* 16, 5 (October 1951): 614–629.

―――. "The Social Structure of the Army." *American Journal of Sociology* 15, 5 (March 1946): 361–364.

Rush, Robert S. "A Different Perspective: Cohesion, Morale, and Operational Effectiveness in the German Army, Fall 1944." *Armed Forces and Society* 25, 3 (spring 1999): 477–508.

Samsonov, Aleksandr M. *Krakh fashistskoi agressii 1939–1945: Istoricheskii ocherk.* Moscow: Nauka, 1980.

Sanborn, Josh. "The Mobilization of 1914 and the Question of the Russian Nation: A Reexamination." *Slavic Review* 59, 2 (summer 2000): 267–289.

Saratovskaia oblast' v gody Velikoi Otechestvennoi voiny (1941–1945 gg.): Arkhivnye Dokumenty. Saratov: Izdatel'stvo gubernskoi torgovo-promyshlennoi palaty, 2005.

Sarkesian, Sam C., ed. *Combat Effectiveness: Cohesion, Stress, and the Volunteer Military.* Beverly Hills, Calif.: Sage Publications, 1980.

Sartorti, Rosalinde. "On the Making of Heroes, Heroines, and Saints." In *Culture and Entertainment in Wartime Russia*, ed. Richard Stites, 176–193. Bloomington: Indiana University Press, 1996.

Schull, J. "What Is Ideology—Theoretical Problems and Lessons from Soviet-Type Societies." *Political Studies* 40, 4 (1992): 728.

Schuster, Alice. "Women's Role in the Soviet Union: Ideology and Reality." *Russian Review* 30, 3 (July 1971): 260–267.

Semiryaga, Mikhail. *The Winter War: Looking Back after Fifty Years.* Moscow: Novosti, 1990.

Seniavskaia, Elena S. "Chelovek na voine: opyt istoriko-psikhologicheskoi kharakteristiki rossiiskogo kombatanta." *Otechestvennaia istoriia* 1 (1995): 7–16.

―――. *Frontovoe Pokolenie, 1941–1945.* Moscow: Institut Rossiiskoi Istorii-RAN, 1995.

―――. "Obraz germanii i nemtsev v gody vtoroi mirovoi voiny glazami sovetskikh soldat i ofitserov." *Voenno-istoricheskii arkhiv* 13 (2000): 11–54.

―――. "Psikhologiia voennogo byta kak istoricheskaia problema." *Voenno-istoricheskii arkhiv* 8 (1999): 203–231.

Serdiukov, V. P. *Kniga pamiati: Sovetsko-finliandskaia voina 1939–1940.* St. Petersburg, Russia: Vesti, 2004.

Sevost'ianov, G., ed. *Voina i obshchestvo 1941–1945.* Moscow: Nauka, 2004.

Shestakova, A. V., ed. *Zhenshchina i voina. 1941–1945. Rossiia i Germaniia: Materialy Mezhdunarodnoi nauchnoi konferentsii g. Volgograd, 12–13 maia 2005 g.* Volgograd, 2006.

Shevelov, S. I., et al., comps. *Vse dlia fronta!: Sverdlovskaia oblastnaia organizatsiia KPSS v gody Velikoi Otechestvennoi voiny (1941–1945): Dokumenty i materialy.* Sverdlovsk: Sredne-Ural'skoe knizhnoe izdat, 1985.

Shils, Edward A., and Morris Janowitz. "Cohesion and Disintegration in the Wehrmacht." *Public Opinion Quarterly* 12 (1948): 280–315.

Sinani, Igor B. *V poiskakh mira. Povestvovanie po sledam pisem. Vospominaniia.* Moscow: Rosspen, 2005.

Somov, Vladimir A. "Pis'ma uchastnikov Velikoi Otechestvennoi voiny 1941–1945 gg." *Voprosy istorii* 8 (2007): 131–135.

Stalin, Joseph V. *The Great Patriotic War of the Soviet Union.* New York: International Publishers, 1945.

Statiev, Alexander. "The Nature of Anti-Soviet Armed Resistance, 1942–44: The North Caucasus, the Kalmyk Autonomous Republic, and Crimea." *Kritika: Explorations in Russian and Eurasian History* 6, 2 (spring 2005): 285–318.

Stephan, Robert. "Smersh: Soviet Military Counter-Intelligence during the Second World War." *Journal of Contemporary History* 22, 4 (October 1987): 585–613.

Stezhenskii V. I. *Soldatskii dnevnik: Voennye stranitsy.* Moscow: Agraf, 2005.

Stishova, L. I., ed. *V tylu i na fronte. Zhenshchiny-kommunistiki v gody Velikoi Otechestvennoi voiny.* Moscow: Izd-vo polit. lit-ry, 1985.

Stites, Richard, ed. *Culture and Entertainment in Wartime Russia.* Bloomington: Indiana University Press, 1995.

———. *The Women's Liberation Movement in Russia.* Princeton, N.J.: Princeton University Press, 1978.

Stockdale, Melissa K. "'My Death for the Motherland Is Happiness': Women, Patriotism, and Soldiering in Russia's Great War, 1914–1917." *American Historical Review* 109, 1 (2004): 78–116.

———. "United in Gratitude: Honoring Soldiers and Defining the Nation in Russia's Great War." *Kritika: Explorations in Russian and Eurasian History* 7, 3 (summer 2006): 459–485.

Stoff, Laurie. *They Fought for the Motherland: Russia's Women Soldiers in World War I and the Revolution.* Lawrence: University Press of Kansas, 2006.

Strachan, Hew. "Training, Morale and Modern War." *Journal of Contemporary History* 4, 2 (2006): 211–227.

Strelkov, A. T., ed. *Surovaia pravda voiny. 1941 god na Kurskoi zemle v dokumentakh arkhivov.* Vol. 1. Kursk: Gos. arkhiv kurskoi oblasti, 2002.

Sudakov, Valerii. *Kniga Pamiati Vologodskoi oblasti: Sovetsko-Finliandskaia Voina 1939–1940 gg.* Vologda: Izd-vo VIPK i PPK, 1995.

Temkin, Gabriel. *My Just War: The Memoir of a Jewish Red Army Soldier in World War II.* Novato, Calif.: Presidio Press, 1998.

Thompson, Ewa M. "Nationalist Propaganda in the Soviet Russian Press, 1939–1941." *Slavic Review* 50, 2 (summer 1991): 385–399.

Thurston, Robert W., and Bernd Bonwetsch, eds. *The People's War: Responses to World War II in the Soviet Union.* Chicago: University of Illinois Press, 2000.

Tumarkin, Nina. *The Living and the Dead: The Rise and Fall of the Cult of World War II in Russia.* New York: Basic Books, 1994.

V gody voiny. Stat'i i ocherki. Moscow: Nauka, 1985.

Vasilevsky, Alexander M. *A Lifelong Cause.* Moscow: Progress, 1981.

Velikaia Otechestvennaia voina: Voprosy i otvety. Moscow: Izdatel'stvo politicheskoi literatury, 1984.

Verevkin, S. *Vtoraia mirovaia voina: vyrvannye stranitsy.* Moscow: Iauza, 2006.

Vinogradov, V. K., ed. *Lubianka v dni bitvy za Moskvu: Materialy organov gosbezopasnosti SSSR iz Tsentralnogo arkhiva FSB Rossii.* Moscow: Evonnitsa-MG, 2002.

Von Hagen, Mark. "Soviet Soldiers and Officers on the Eve of the German Invasion: Towards a Description of Social Psychology and Political Attitudes." *Soviet Union/Union Soviétique* 18, nos. 1–3 (1991): 79–101.

Voroshilov, Kliment E. *Doklad (Voroshilova) o sovetsko-finliandskoi voine 1939–1940 gg. s prilozheniem istoricheskoi spravki o bor'be za Finskii zaliv i Finliandiiu.* Minneapolis: East View, 1993.

Vtoraia Mirovaia Voina: Kratkaia istoriia. Moscow: Nauka, 1985.

Wanke, Paul. *Russian/Soviet Military Psychiatry 1904–1945.* London: Routledge/Frank Cass, 2005.

Wegner, Bernd, ed. *From Peace to War: Germany, Soviet Russia and the World, 1939–1941.* Providence, R.I.: Berghahn Books, 1997.

Weiner, Amir. "The Making of a Dominant Myth: The Second World War and the Construction of Political Identities within the Soviet Polity." *Russian Review* 55, 4 (1996): 638–660.

Werth, Alexander. *Russia at War, 1941–1945.* 1964. Reprint, New York: Carroll and Graf, 1984.

Wertsch, James V. *Voices of Collective Remembering.* Cambridge: Cambridge University Press, 2002.

Wingfield, Nancy M., and Maria Bucur, eds. *Gender and War in Twentieth-Century Eastern Europe.* Bloomington: Indiana University Press, 2006.

Winter, Jay. *Remembering War: The Great War between Memory and History in the 20th Century.* New Haven, Conn.: Yale University Press, 2006.

Wood, Elizabeth A. *The Baba and the Comrade: Gender and Politics in Revolutionary Russia.* Bloomington: Indiana University Press, 1997.

Yekelchyk, Serhy. "Stalinist Patriotism as Imperial Discourse: Reconciling the Ukrainian and Russian 'Heroic Pasts,' 1939–1945." *Kritika: Explorations in Russian and Eurasian History* 3, 1 (winter 2002): 51–80.

Zapadnaia Sibir' v Velikoi Otechestvennoi voine (1941–1945 gg). Novosibirsk: Nauka-Tsentr, 2004.

Zhilin, V. A., ed. *Stalingradskaia bitva: Khronika, fakty, liudi.* Moscow: OLMA, 2002.

Zolotarev, Vladimir A., ed. *Russkii arkhiv: Velikaia Otechestvennaia: Nakanune Voiny: Materialy soveshchaniia vyshego rukovodiashchego sostava RKKA 23–31 dekabria 1940 g.* Vol. 1. Moscow: Terra, 1993.

———. *Russkii arkhiv: Velikaia Otechestvennaia: Prikazy Narodnogo komissara Oborony SSSR (1943–1945 gg.).* Vol. 13 (2-3). Moscow: Terra, 1997.

———. *Russkii arkhiv: Velikaia Otechestvennaia: Bitva za Berlin (Krasnaia Armiia v poverzhennoi Germanii).* Vol. 15 (4-5). Moscow: TERRA, 1995.

———. *Russkii arkhiv: Velikaia Otechestvennaia. Stavka VGK: Dokumenty i materialy 1942 god.* Vol. 16 (5-2). Moscow: Terra, 1996.

———. *Russkii arkhiv: Velikaia Otechestvennaia. Glavnye politicheskie organy vooruzhennykh sil SSSR v Velikoi Otechestvennoi voine 1941–1945 gg.: Dokumenty i materialy.* Vol. 17 (6). Moscow: Terra, 1996.

———. *Russkii arkhiv: Velikaia Otechestvennaia. General'nyi shtab v gody Velikoi Otechestvennoi voiny: Dokumenty i materialy. 1941 god.* Vol. 23 (12-1). Moscow: Terra, 1998.

———. *Russkii arkhiv: Velikaia Otechestvennaia. Tyl Krasnoi Armii v Velikoi Otechestvennoi voine 1941–1945 gg.: Dokumenty i materialy.* Vol. 25 (14). Moscow: Terra, 1998.

Zubarev, Stepan P. *Materialy k istorii Udmurtii v gody Velikoi Otechestvennoi voiny: sbornik statei.* Izhevsk: Udmurtski' nauchno-issledovatel'skii institut istorii, ekonomiki, literatury i iazyka, 1982.

Index